Professor Emeritus Brian Roberts has lived half his life in South Africa and half in Australia. An agricultural ecologist by profession, he has a passion for sustainable land use while his highly developed social conscience has led to decades of research into tribal peoples rights and responsibilities. Recognised as 'The Father of Landcare' he was awarded the Order of Australia in 1998, having earlier won the South African Community Service Medal for his work in rural soil conservation. He was the founding president of the Soil and Water Conservation Association of Australia, Organising Chairman of the Ninth International Rangeland Congress and has held professorships at three universities. Prof. Roberts chaired the Lower Balonne Advisory Committee on water sharing, the Queensland Rural Fires Council, the Queensland Freshwater MAC and the Nathan Dam Community Committee on Dawson River Water Supplies. As a senior member of the Cape York Peninsula Land Use Strategy and convenor of CSIRO's Water Quality Joint Venture team in North Queensland as Adjunct in Environmental Studies at James Cook University, he contributed to mainstream and Indigenous community conservation projects. He was a member of the National Soil Conservation Advisory Committee and The Queensland Sheep and Wool Research Committee. Much of his recent writing has been published in Quadrant Online. He is the author of 13 books, many book chapters and numerous journal articles since 1956. As a member of ANU's Fundamental Questions program he produced the seminal paper 'Land Ethics: A necessary addition to Australian Values' (1984).

Other titles by Dr Brian Roberts

*Professional Titles*
Birth of Landcare
Call of the Country
Common Grasses of Orange Free State
Grasses of the Northern Cape, RSA
Ground Rules
Landcare Manual
Sustainable Agriculture and Land Use
Western Grasses, Queensland
Wildlife Management on Farms

*Private Titles*
Essays on Aboriginalism
Whitefella Dreaming
Jean's Story
Lot 22: The Story of a Daintree Block
Son of the Veld
South Africa Revisited
Veld: Collected Papers 1956-1975
Where Angels Fear to Tread

"I read Whitefella Dreaming with great interest, finding it exceptionally clear-minded and full of suggestive ideas and parallels. I fear the times are not welcoming towards free thought, and many of the notions Dr Roberts has advanced that seem most worthwhile to me, are in the category of present day Australian heresy. I am struck by the way that modern experts tend not to recognise the ways in which they re-enact colonial patterns of engagement."

*Nicolas Rothwell, award-winning author and journalist*

"Dr Roberts' views are very broadly balanced because he cares both professionally and personally. His concern for the realism of management of culture in the future to continue to be authentic is genuine; for people of all cultures to manage their issues and cultural knowledge in the way their profound learnings have taught them. True culture brings balance in a way that our children of the future can feel free, affected by their cultural learning in a positive way, with great pride and dignity, that will always have a 'genuine fit within our changing world' because as Australians we are one and, we are many. Thank you always for your genuine caring through the important and clear messages within your big picture presentations. It would be sad if Indigenous students and staff did not study your positive, balanced Indigenous texts."

*Jeannie Aileen Little, "Gaarkamunda" OAM*

"Brian has done us a great favour with his observations of Aboriginal affairs. It is refreshing to read writing straight from the heart, without any axe to grind or agenda to push. He not only gets you thinking, but thinking in new ways. And new ways of thinking on Aboriginal affairs is precisely what we need."

*Dr Anthony Dillon, Australian Catholic University*

"Dr Roberts has an extraordinary capacity to grasp and hold onto the big picture while conducting a forensic examination of every facet of the Aboriginal debate. He writes with empathy to distinguish between the urban Aborigines and those who remain isolated and basically culturally unchanged, while highlighting the difficulties the Aboriginal cause has in speaking with one voice for constitutional change, recognition, equity and advancement."

*Alec Lucke, Road to Exploitation: Political Capture by Mining in Queensland*

# OVERCOMING DISADVANTAGE

## PAST LESSONS FOR INDIGENOUS FUTURES

DR BRIAN ROBERTS

First published 2019 by Dr Brian Ross Roberts
Cairns, Australia

ISBN 978-0-9953824-6-6
eISBN 978-0-9953824-7-3

Copyright © Dr Brian Ross Roberts 2019
brianroberts.am@gmail.com

Edited by Erica Blythe

Interior design by The Booktress
www.thebooktress.com
Cover Design Jodi Cleghorn

The right for Dr Brian Ross Roberts to be identified as the author of this work has been asserted by him in accordance with Part IX of the Copyright Act 1968

All rights reserved.

No part of this publication may be reproduced, stored in or introduced into a retrieval system, or transmitted, in any form, or by any means (electronic, mechanical, photocopying, recording or otherwise) without written permission of the author.
Any person who does any unauthorised act in relation to this publication may be liable for criminal prosecution and civil claims for damages.

Dedicated to my late father Wilfred Ross Roberts whose integrity and tolerance made him a role model to us all.

# TABLE OF CONTENTS

| | |
|---|---:|
| **PREFACE** | 1 |
| | |
| **SECTION ONE: The Indigenous Story** | 3 |
| Extracts from Past, Present and Future | 5 |
| **The Past** | 9 |
| Stonehenge: When Blackfellas Became Whitefellas | 9 |
| Links To Land | 10 |
| Race and Place | 12 |
| Culture and Religion | 14 |
| Missionaries – Heroes or Villains? | 16 |
| Case of Queensland Anglican Missions | 18 |
| The Rabbit Proof Case | 23 |
| Attack and Defence | 25 |
| Anthropologists – A Breed Apart | 25 |
| Settlers, Missionaries and Aborigines | 32 |
| Luggers' Influence | 33 |
| Establishment of Reserves – Then and Now | 35 |
| Women, Violence and Rage | 36 |
| White Supremacy – Imperial Driver | 38 |
| War and Loyalty | 40 |
| The Channel Country Settlement: Women's View of the Frontier Legend | 41 |
| Historic Land Rights | 48 |
| Victoria River Walk-Off: Hinge of History | 51 |
| Black Cheers and Three Arm Bands: Using History to Proclaim Morality | 52 |
| **The Present: Aboriginal Identity** | 53 |
| Paternalism as a Response to Vulnerable Tradition | 56 |
| Forced Separation or Forced Integration: Lose – Lose | 58 |
| Unbeing: The Flip-Side of Being a Changed Individual | 61 |

| | |
|---|---:|
| What is it that Threatens Aboriginal Culture? | 63 |
| Caring/Sharing and Respect for Nature | 64 |
| The Knowledge – What's it Worth? | 66 |
| Lessons From Wik Families | 70 |
| Seeking an Agreement | 73 |
| **The Future** | **87** |
| Pearson's Powerful Prose | 87 |
| Sutton's Subtle Suggestions | 97 |
| Significant Extracts From Sutton | 104 |
| Martin's Moral Magic | 124 |
| Isn't the Problem Obvious? | 129 |
| Australian Apathy – No Worries | 131 |
| Mainstream, Sidestream and Slipstream | 133 |
| Integration – The European Wogboy's Experience | 134 |
| The Essential Choice | 136 |
| Mining: Tapping into the Mother Lode | 138 |
| Indigenous Aspirations | 144 |
| Objectives and Policy Settings | 146 |
| | |
| **SECTION TWO: Roots and Wings** | 151 |
| Preface | 153 |
| **A Reconsideration of Indigenous Identity and Well-Being** | **155** |
| Indigenous Identity – Just What is It? | 155 |
| Future Indigenous Religion | 159 |
| Self-Governing Homelands – Be Careful What you Wish For | 162 |
| What Can We Learn From Apartheid – Apart From What Not to Do | 165 |
| Can Homelands Really Work? | 167 |
| Indigenous Democracy – What's The Place of the Family | 169 |
| Whitefella Cultural Identity | 170 |
| Community Norms – What Can Whitefellas Offer? | 171 |
| Margaret Turner's Story | 173 |
| DNA and Modernity – Give Credit to Your 'New' Genes | 175 |
| Pride in What We Haven't Achieved | 178 |
| The Image of Primitivism: Can it Contribute to Respect and Admiration | 179 |

| | |
|---|---|
| Colonial Thanksgiving Day | 180 |
| Community Triage as a Priority-Setter | 183 |
| **A Declaration of Indigenous Rights: Response To Thirty Concepts** | **185** |
| Proposed Declaration of Indigenous Responsibilities related to Rights | 205 |
| The Essence of Issues and Recommendations on Indigenous Futures | 212 |
| Seeking Answers | 214 |
| | |
| **SECTION THREE: Convenient Half-Truths** | **225** |
| Introduction | 227 |
| **Messages From Contemporary Case Studies** | **229** |
| Background | 229 |
| World's Oldest: The Hadza of Tanzania | 230 |
| Evolutionary Succession | 233 |
| Racism: The Irish Barbarians | 235 |
| The Anglo-Celtic Identity in Australia: A Mainstream Myth Diminishing the Irish | 236 |
| Christian Children and Ancestral Country | 238 |
| Cultural Continua in Aboriginal and Muslim Australians | 240 |
| Diversity is Not the Problem, Integration Is | 245 |
| Islam – Where Did it Come From, How Did it Originate and Does it Relate to Aboriginal Policy | 246 |
| I was Indoctrinated | 247 |
| Tolerance – The Crux | 249 |
| What Does the Koran Teach Which May Match Aboriginal Aspirations | 250 |
| Genesis and Dreamtime | 254 |
| Civilisation is Only One Generation Deep | 258 |
| What Does Western Culture Value from its Hunter-Gatherer Ancestry | 260 |
| Indigenous Lifestyle Choices: How Essential is On-Country Life | 262 |
| One More Time: What Values Do We Stand For? | 266 |
| Meantime in the Dreamtime | 269 |
| The Aboriginal Gift: Spirituality for a Nation | 272 |
| Downunder Doctrine | 274 |
| And if the Salt Shall Lose its Savour, Wherewith Will it be Salted? | 278 |
| Racial Vilification: Andrew Bolt's Case | 279 |

| | |
|---|---|
| "Government Bans Grog, Tobacco and Pokies": An Unlikely Heading | 282 |
| Parental Example and Heroic Dads | 283 |
| Lionel Rose: So What's the Big Deal? | 284 |
| You Know Goodness When You See It: Harnessing the J Factor | 286 |
| Cultural Adaptation | 288 |
| The Inflexibility of Remote Infrastructure Investment | 291 |
| Whiteman Dreaming, Blackman Screaming – A Consideration of Gary Johns' 'Aboriginal Self-Determination' | 293 |
| Outback Refugees | 297 |
| Some Families Went to Town – So What's New? | 300 |
| Bess Sets the Record Straight on Culture | 302 |
| The National Aboriginal Congress | 304 |
| Political Traps for Indigenous Players | 307 |
| The Indigenous Press – Stephen Hagan's Editorial Effort | 309 |
| Let's Be Honest: Guilt has Driven Indigenous Policy | 312 |
| Indigenous Planners Ignore Noel Pearson at Their Peril | 313 |
| The Pearson/Sarra Spat | 324 |
| Wild Rivers – A Case Study in Values | 329 |
| **Funding Carbon Reduction on Indigenous Lands** | **331** |
| Background | 331 |
| Sceptics and Believers | 332 |
| Lomborg's Case and Aboriginal Burning | 334 |
| Beyond Copenhagen – Let's Get Real | 341 |
| All Aboard the Carbon (Gravy) Train | 344 |
| Copenhagen Consensus Outcomes – Data for Aboriginal Negotiators | 346 |
| | |
| **REFERENCES** | 351 |
| **APPENDIX 1** | |
| Customs Officer Searcy – Empire Personified in Blackfella Country | 364 |
| **APPENDIX 2** | |
| What Constitutes a Fair Go for Aborigines? | 371 |
| **APPENDIX 3** | |
| 'Spoilers' | 401 |
| **INDEX** | **402** |

# PREFACE

These writings are the product of over 20 years study of Indigenous policy and progress. Originally, the author started with one central question, 'What Constitutes a Fair Go for Aborigines?', which was the title of the first paper in 1998. A decade and a half later, the answer remains elusive, due primarily to a failure to agree on goals of Indigenous development.

In the first section, it seemed logical to examine the lessons of history first, as a background to understanding the present views of both Blacks and Whites in Australia. The historic review could only capture a limited number of case studies, but hopefully enough to allow for an assessment of the carry-over influence of the colonial missionary era as a major driver of contemporary action.

The author draws largely on the most credible of Indigenous observers to seek goals and directions, before suggesting policy objectives which aim to combine the most appropriate actions for improving Indigenous well-being.

The second section concentrates on the rights and responsibilities of Indigenous people and how their central issues may be clarified as essential actions which are introduced as 'In Essence' in a bid to suggest to the wider public and the Indigenous communities themselves, where the most appropriate values and behaviours lie, if their grandchildren's future is the prime concern.

In this second section, the role of culture and identity features centrally in the suggested nuances of tradition and well-being, as the amalgam of personal choices likely to produce appropriate futures for Indigenous people. The virtues or otherwise of separatism and exclusiveness feature strongly in the case which is made for joining the Open Society in what has previously been termed Mainstreaming. [Since the political era dealt with in this book, two more recent books by the author can be refered to for updating the more contemporary debate i.e. Essays on Aboriginalism and Whitefella Dreaming available on booktopia.com.]

The third section is a loosely-structured series of case studies which highlights a wide range of factors currently bearing down on Aboriginal people, both rural and urban. With mixed success, the author has attempted to extract what he hoped would be a useful 'message' from each case. These case studies were not selected at random but consciously, as a means of illustrating what the author's wide study of the issues appears to identify as building blocks of substance which, in combination, offer a framework for future policy. Such a policy will be built on values appropriate to future Aborigines, not those past traditions best left in the past.

The author makes no pretence at unbiased objectivity in his proposals. As a political refugee from Apartheid, he is consciously influenced by his family's experiences and he follows not cold logic and rationalism, but rather what that quiet inner voice convinces him, is right and good. This is not to deny that he uses rational thinking as his central process, but rather to admit to intuition and generations of frontier family history to seek appropriate means when sorting the substance from contemporary political silliness and expediency.

If the concepts promoted in this work can be judged not on their source but on their merit, the years spent on the studies will have been worthwhile.

This review does not list the detailed references of each source quoted but readers wanting to make contact with any Indigenous person or organisation referred to in these studies can find them on Paul Newman's Black Pages at www.blackpages.com.au. This comprehensive site lists virtually every Indigenous business, organisation and department in Australia. [Since the political era dealt with in this book, two more recent books by the author can be refered to for updating the more contemporary debate i.e. Essays on Aboriginalism and Whitefella Dreaming available on booktopia.com.]

The author's sincere thanks go to Erica Blythe for producing the typed manuscript, to Lynne Blythe for indexing, proofreading and making additions and to Christopher Roberts and Lesley Moseley for further proofreading. Special thanks to Sheik Waseem Jappie for checking translations of the Koran.

Brian Roberts, Cairns, 2019

# SECTION ONE
# THE INDIGENOUS STORY

# EXTRACTS FROM PAST, PRESENT AND FUTURE

The objective of this overview of progress of Aboriginal affairs in Australia is to assist in clarifying the factual situation in Aboriginal well-being, to identify the effects of myths and selective information in setting priorities to date and to seek informed opinion on future policy and process. This is done against the backdrop of history and its effects on current thinking.

In this process the author draws on his own experience but relies on recognised commentators and experienced field workers for research into primary sources. This methodology leads to the evaluation of opinions of well-known writers and the use of their literature sources as recorded evidence for their statements.

The narrative is simply arranged in past, present and future and employs selected geographical examples as a framework for examining each of the major issues affecting Aboriginal welfare. In taking this approach, the author is aware of its liability to bias and the associated criticism which comes with such a selective method. However, the reader will be hard put to establish whether the author is sympathetic or antithetic toward a particular Indigenous cause. Support for, or evidence against accepted values and policy, is not the basis of this book, rather it is a serious attempt to sort the grain from the chaff in a complex and artificially sensitised sphere of Australian social policy. When using such an approach, the question immediately arises as to who is qualified to identify the chaff? Such qualification appears to have changed from early anthropologists to informed bureaucrats, to ambitious politicians, to Aboriginal spokespersons to public academics and finally to concerned citizens. Currently all the above are engaging in the somewhat unbecoming culture wars in which everyone is an expert with self-recognised credentials.

What has happened in Aboriginal affairs is an unusually complex mixture of racism, ignorance, personal bias, guilt, anger and egotism. This makes it difficult for objective voices seeking rational debate, to be taken seriously. In this situation and against this emotive background, it is unlikely that politically neutral policy proposals will be accepted as valuable rational proposals, and thus as a basis for future policy.

In this overview, a central issue is the extent to which separate development could or should be promoted, or whether Aboriginals and the Australian community in general, will be better served by re-jigging policy to base government support on disadvantage rather than on race. In asking this question the author makes a serious case for a fundamental change in the way group identity is catered for in policy-making, and thus a case for urgent change in separatist policy.

It will be noted that some sections of this narrative appear either fragmented or repetitive. The non-sequiturs in some sections arise from the narrator's attempt to inject significant concepts at particular positions in the logic of policy background. The repetition of examples has been used to consider some basic concepts in more than one context e.g.: customary practice repeatedly returned to in the contexts of education, violence, health, employment or housing. There is no single best sequence for considering the building-blocks of ethnic policy but using past, present and future as periods of progression allows simultaneous evaluation of all factors affecting one population group in comparative temporal sequence.

What's required now is bi-partisan consultative agreement on basic goals of Indigenous policy, first to overcome the past problems in which disagreement on processes ran ahead of agreed objectives, and then to accept the reality of what is required for the welfare of future generations.

"Governmentality" is a term coined by Michael Foucault in 1991 to describe the congenital failure of policy. When this concept is applied to Indigenous welfare, we need to recognise that there has been a historic tendency to blame either government or Aboriginals for their present worsening condition. This overview attempts to show that such simplistic blame-shifting paints a false picture.

Foucault's governmentality concept includes both official optimism in improvement policy and repeated failure to gain planned results. What today are referred to as 'unplanned outcomes', can be almost guaranteed to appear some time after Indigenous program launches. Why is this? First, it is because too often government produces policy as a public response to criticism of embarrassing media exposés of squalor in remote communities. This leads to policy big on empathy but light on serious consideration of acceptance and sequential reactions. Second, too often remedial policy programs are based on structural/institutional changes which advertise the short-term 'fix it' image of the initiative (more correctly, knee-jerk reaction). Unfortunately, many of the issues turn out not to be structural problems but rather process and managerial shortcomings. Third, government too often misjudges community acceptance of what the bureaucrats assume to be obvious benefits. So between political gloss, reliance on structure and cultural misunderstanding, the mentality of government seems unable under current political pressures to take the long view, value culture appropriately and recognise the need for accountable management as the key to program implementation.

While the early demise of Indigenous people was seen to be caused by the impacts of settlement policy and police implementation of dispersing the Blacks, the response of Indigenous people to genuine efforts to improve education and health, has often been less than helpful. The failure of the men to control alcohol use is currently a major reason for stagnation and retrogression. Decades of playing the Blame Game has not contributed to the betterment of remote communities' well-being.

# THE PAST

## STONEHENGE: WHEN BLACKFELLAS BECAME WHITEFELLAS

When the present author's ancestors held their corroboree at Stonehenge (which they'd worked on for 1,000yrs) in southern Angloland, they worshipped the sun as it rose between the mighty rock pillars. They had no wheels (they came in 3500BC), no iron, no gunpowder, no written language, no textiles and no paper. They did have fur clothes, leather shoes, flint spearheads, transported fire, stone tools, grinding stones and wooden levers.

This was 3600BC when they were hunters and fishermen trading axes and keeping tamed sheep and musk oxen. They had migrated from Europe where their earliest ancestors lived in the present Germany about 500,000 years ago. Their forebears in turn went back to primeval man as far back as 1.75 M years ago. Their oldest British ancestor was found in the Thames Valley and was dated 250,000 years BP.

In 2000 Dr Johan Mokan of the University of Oslo published evidence that my European ancestors were dark skinned up to about 5,500 years ago, when their diet of new agricultural crops, mostly grain, caused them to develop a light skin as a result of vitamin C deficiency in their food. So while they were genetically similar, the Blackfellas became Whitefellas, while non-agricultural nomads elsewhere continued on their foraging ways, spreading out across the globe. Back at Stonehenge, my ancestors harvested seed-grass with flint sickles, hunted with flint-head arrows and cooked in crude ceramic pots – fired but not glazed. They paddled dugout canoes, as those before them had paddled from Europe.

At about 1800BC bronze was brought across the channel, followed by iron brought by the Celts in about 500BC. Their iron plough drawn by two oxen allowed food production to expand far beyond the food available to the other branches of the family who were finding new lands but still hunting and gathering. When the Romans arrived in 52AD my tribe benefitted from their advanced technology and writing.

On the other side of the world, the Asians had developed agriculture, pastoralism and stone-built cities from about 8500BC and bypassed the hunter-gathers who kept going with their nature-based societies. So in the late 1600s when European mariners arrived on the coast of the Great Southland, they were more than a little surprised to find wild people with no metals, no wheels, no finer textiles, no firearms, no writing, no cultivated crops, no domestic animals (except the dingo) and unbelievably, no buildings. This natural society contrasted starkly with what the mariners had seen in nearby Asian countries where relatively advanced settled societies had welcomed them, notably in Java in 1595. We shall deal later with claims of intensified food harvest and trapping.

# LINKS TO LAND

It took European observers a long time to appreciate the depth and strength of the bond between Aboriginals and their land. This issue has become a major consideration in current planning and policy development. In his "Fair Go" paper of 1997 the current author poses the question of whether the frequent exercise of "living on country" could or should remain a necessary element of modern practice of culture. (See Section 1 Appendix II).

Much has been written about the significance of The Dreamtime stories in which great mythical creatures such as the Rainbow Serpent formed the beginnings of human's relations to the earth. The spiritual importance of Aboriginal land links has been undervalued by governments over the years. In essence, Australia has to deal with the implications of land-based religion which is the faith of the majority of the population in Northern Australia. Whether it is possible to meet the requirements of religious freedom as a constitutional right, becomes problematic under modern land use conditions.

Originally, Indigenous individual's personal identity was essentially dependent on their lifelong bond to their country – not any country but their clan's millennia-old habitat. Deborah Bird Rose puts it well when she says "country" to Aborigines is not a common noun but a proper noun – a special entity worthy of status and respect. Europeans might spend a day in the country or visit the country but Indigenous people will tell you that the country is alive – it hears, it smells, it takes notice, it is clean or dirty, happy or sad, according to Rose.

Country, to its people, may be sea country or even sky country and it consists of the earth, the biota and the humans. Importantly individuals' clan country includes their totems and the spirits of their ancestors who may be in the land itself or in the trees or animals.

This internalised view of land is often lost in land claims prepared by anthropologists versed only in formal land valuation procedures. Pat Dodson maintains that neither the law nor the language used in title claims is adequate to reflect the real value of land to his people: "I belong to the land". Ronald Berndt says Aborigines see themselves as part of the land, "They also believed that they shared the same life essence with all the natural species and elements within that environment. Their social world was expanded to include the natural world. In other words the natural world was humanised, and this was true for the land as such."

Within this overall reverence for nature were clearly delineated boundaries. The importance of clan country boundaries is described by Williams as follows; "The violation of a clan boundary would be tantamount to depriving the patrilineal custodians of the violated estate of their identity. A person's being and therefore their identity, is in their patrilineal estate from whence their spirit was conceived and shall return upon the death of a person."

The present author's reading of the regional literature leads him to believe that clan boundaries were not as shown in the form of circles or ovals in Tindale's maps, but rather ran along rivers and ridges where communal tracks were generally found – and used by explorers and prospectors.

This review will return to family relations and land values when drawing on the Western Queensland case studies. It is this bond to country which caused the tendency to "walkabout" and leave the missions for weeks, which frustrated those who saw a sedentary existence as a necessary requirement for civilisation of their nomadic potential converts.

# RACE AND PLACE

Christine Choo, in her book "Mission Girls" gives insight into race relations rarely analysed by Australian writers. Choo quotes Jackie Huggins: "Aboriginal women are not prepared to engage in discussions with White women until meaningful and anti-racist discourses are constructed which transcend the barriers which separate us. At present (1994) Aboriginal women's experiences with White feminists prevent them from seeing dialogue as anything but a naïve and tokenistic beginning, as race is finally surfacing on the agenda but still yet to be understood."

If this view reflects the position of the wider Indigenous community, it partially answers the author's (Roberts 1998) question in "What constitutes a fair go" as to why the feminist movement has not openly and vigorously supported action to prevent violence against Indigenous women. Because Choo writes as a feminist and champion of women's rights, her book "Mission Girls" has a heavy overlay of empathy for the females in the mission narrative. At the same time her approach gives new insights into the role and influence of human sexuality, gender relations and the prime role of women in the survival of the Aboriginal people and their culture.

Any review of Aboriginal Policy must recognise the place of racism in the development of policy. Choo reminds us of Essed's (1996) definition of such prejudice: "Racial-ethnic prejudice is an attitude, an element of common sense, based on false generalisations of negatively valued properties attributed to racial-ethnic groups other than one's own. Common sense should not be understood as a product of deliberate, systematic and deliberate thought. It is derived from, and designed to cope with, the routine activities of everyday life. Racism is transmitted through acts generated from a social attitude that takes the legitimacy of the racial-ethnic social order for granted. These acts [are] defined as discrimination…"

It is within this racial framework that Choo explores the effects of colonisation and missions on the people of the Kimberley. Choo explains much of the docile acceptance of White values by drawing on Dodson's view of Aboriginality relative to European typology: "Our constructed identities have served a broader purpose of reflecting back to the colonising culture, what it wanted or needed to see in itself.... Whether Indigenous peoples have been portrayed as noble or ignoble, heroic or wretched had depended on what the colonising culture had wanted to say about itself...the destruction or assimilation of the Indigenous cultures has become a necessary, and even morally correct, part of the battle to overcome "the primitive", and thereby to save both Indigenous peoples and colonists from a life that is 'nasty, brutish and short'. By our lack we provide proof of their abundance and the achievements of 'progress'. By our inferiority, we proved their superiority; by our moral and intellectual honesty, we proved that they were indeed the paragons of humanity, products of millennia of development."

This review will return to this matter of identity, but it should be noted that this element of racism was applied in colonial times on an informal sliding-scale to Japanese, Chinese, Malays, Indians, Kanakas and Timorese and mixtures of these, collectively referred to as coloureds.

Superimposed on the inbred racism of the European patriarchy of the settlement era, was the viewing of Aboriginal women as dangerously sexual and thus a serious threat to the maintenance of wholesome White Australia (Choo 2001). When social Darwinism became fashionable in the mid 1800's, its values became responsible for the justification of destruction of Aboriginal society. Compared to Africa and America, the relative primitiveness of Indigenous Australians led to extreme comparisons of the world's highest ranked society (Europeans) and the lowest (Aboriginals). This record distance between societal values led Isobel White to suggest: "Some European Australians believed that the Australian Aboriginal didn't deserve to survive".

There are so many references in the historic literature to "smoothing the pillow of the disappearing race" (or words to that effect) that the driving fear of dilution of white purity via half-bred children is somewhat disguised by the façade of easing the pain of a race becoming extinct. Rather than requiring restraint from White males, the sexuality of Black females was seen by authority to require legal control. This was done through Section 40 and 43 of the Aboriginal Act 1905 and then by Sections 45 and 46 of the Native Administration Act 1905-1936. These Acts made cohabitation between these races a punishable offence. In explaining this legal background, Choo points out that Indigenous women, being at the lowest rung of society due to their colour, gender and class could not exploit any other group. At the same time they can be credited with the survival of their race and culture. So the historical reviewer is left with a record in which Aboriginal women are essentially invisible at least as far as written views and recorded opinions are concerned. Only in recent years has the robust oral tradition of these women become a major reservoir of tribal tradition.

## CULTURE AND RELIGION

The historian faced with sorting the factors which affected the social and personal development of the Aborigines has to deal with an unusual mix of values – values derived from cultures which conflicted at the religious, social, technical, economic and development levels. Neil Gunson in 1988 credited the Missionaries with developing a higher proportion of Christians among the Aborigines than among the rest of the Australian population. The manner in which these primitive people with their ancient and strong spiritual beliefs were torn between local and imported belief systems is probably known but not understood by most Australians. As referred to elsewhere, with few exceptions, the Missions attempted to obliterate the culture and traditional practices of those in their care. In this "civilising" effort, the Missions were in partnership with government, who also saw as their calling, the "uplifting of the primitives" from their short brutal existence, to the God-given conversion to European Christian civility.

Some would claim that the enculturation of the Aborigines has had an overall beneficial influence, allowing otherwise 'lost souls' to become productive sociable Christian citizens. However, many experienced sociologists and psychiatrists bring evidence of the destabilising effects of youthful trauma on the normal functioning of affected adults. Why is this important? Because there is a general assumption among policy-makers and bureaucrats that all that is needed is financial assistance and "capacity-building" through training, for adult Aborigines to become functional contributors to the mainstream economy. The truth is that many of today's adults lack the health, self-confidence, literacy, interpersonal skills, motivation and supportive social networks to rise to the occasion.

Choo reflects on the effects of patronising rather than of trauma: "The institutionalised mission children grew up to be adults who were protected and patronised by the missionaries, who treated them like children. This infantilisation of Aboriginal people has been a subtle controlling influence from which it has been extremely difficult for former mission inmates to free themselves. Because the control has been internalised by mission Aborigines, it has negatively influenced the self-perception of many older people…". Slowly but surely the missionaries appear to have diluted, then totally removed, the cultural mores which underpinned Aboriginal identity and pride. This influence explains the greater level of self-confidence and independence of those born after about 1945 when missions were in decline. So we are left with a generation of seniors who today reflect the scars of this battle for their souls between their clan and the church. The fact that Aboriginal culture not only survived but enjoyed a re-birth after the 1970's is a minor miracle in itself and attests to the inherent ancient strength of the culture – the product of at least 40,000 years of survival in an often harsh environment. We shall return to consideration of the impact of the missions.

Today the hindsight view of the benefit or otherwise of the earlier attempts to assimilate Blacks into White culture offers two rather polarised evaluations: on the one hand complete and successful assimilation was expected to save the disappearing primitives, on the other hand the destruction of one of the world's oldest living cultures was seen as a crime against humanity.

This polarity of views remains at the heart of valuing present policy, and most aspects of Indigenous policy depend centrally on its resolution. The author may have been wrong in his "Fair Go" paper when he suggested that respect for a culture needs to be deserved, not assumed to be automatic as a result of the antiquity of the culture. The problem with 'deserving' as a concept, is that it requires agreement on the attributes by which the culture is judged.

As soon as Western Christian standards are used as the measure of a respected set of norms and practices, the intrinsic value or correctness of those standards becomes open to question – the kind of question the author shows Christianity to fail in his book "Where Angels Fear to Tread". Cultural comparisons invariably lead to value-judgements on social mores such as marriage arrangements, women's rights, female education, division of labour and other relations between the genders. In addition, religious beliefs and practices feature prominently as identifiers of cultures. While all religions have difficulty in presenting credible evidence for the actual existence of their deity or spirit (God, Allah, Rainbow Serpent), this does not deter cultural adherents from claiming, and living by, the guiding hand of their particular sky-god or earth-god.

It was particularly unfortunate that the invasion of Aboriginal country took place at a time when the European Christianity was at an Imperial Empire-building stage in which it not only knew what was good for 'lesser mortals' who hadn't yet seen the Light, but insisted that it had a moral duty before God to save these dark souls and uplift them to the enlightened society of Christians.

# MISSIONARIES – HEROES OR VILLAINS

Christian missionaries were active in all states during the 1800's. It is assumed that missionaries of other faiths were disallowed by the authorities. This review examines the Catholic missions in Western Australia and the Anglican missions in Queensland. This selection does not devalue the significant effort of the Lutherans, Presbyterians and Methodists and is based only on availability of records which contribute directly to the central narrative here.

Amongst the Catholics were groups such as the French Trappists, who tended toward contemplative seclusion from the world, and the German Pallottines who were tough practical men who taught a range of trades and worked "in the world". The Trappists had established their mission on the Kimberley coast at Beagle Bay in 1890. They found the region "spiritually arid" and moved off in 1901 when the Pallottines took over. While saving souls remained an uphill battle in the Kimberley, the aim of the Pallottines to educate and train the locals in trades for boys and domestics for girls, seemed appropriate objectives for transition to the modern world.

Choo's evaluation of the Pallottines' approach to evangalisation states: "They attributed the particular difficulty in the Kimberley mission effort not to the Aborigines' lack of intelligence but to their nomadic nature and lifestyle, and their preference to remain within their own territory." While it soon became clear that the drawcards of the mission were the food and tobacco rather than the word of the Monks, the evidence is that many young people would thank the mission for the opportunity to join the paid workforce – however underpaid."

Whereas many missions have been criticised for punishing children for using their language or practising their culture, the words of the Pallottines' Father Walter reflect an unusual acceptance of Aboriginality: "For Aborigines, correct mission method is to let them get used to a settled lifestyle and regular work without using force or restricting their freedom....As soon as possible, children can be removed from the adult camp and the nomadic ways of their parents, and be housed in dormitories on mission premises to be educated at school and in the trades. It is not the duty of a missionary to repress a child's Aboriginal nature and for this reason the children are given as much freedom as possible to follow their customs and practices. From time to time all children are allowed to attend corroborrees and to hold their own corroborrees. Outings are utilised to make them sufficiently familiar with bushcraft to survive." This Pallottine way of dealing with hunter-gatherers in transition became the basis for policy in Western Australia for several decades. The way in which this mission dealt with half-caste children was used as a model for others.

The "good guys/bad guys" reports of the effects of missionary effort leave the reviewer with a mosaic of saints and sinners forming a continuum from the saintly Mary McKillop to the sadistic sisters whose treatment of the innocents hardly reflected the caring expected from "the Brides of Christ". Their vows of "chastity, poverty and obedience" stopped short of the golden rule of 'doing unto others'. A similar range of hero/villain behaviour amongst Monks and Priests is reflected in historical records of mission life. It is unclear what the proportion of Good Samaritans is among missionary ranks, as is the judgement on whether well-meant discipline and routine should be valued as positive or negative.

Within the missionary activity described by Choo, was the complicating influence of female mission workers such as the Sisters of St. John of God who arrived at Beagle Bay on 6 June 1906. Their first job was to "take charge of the native children". In 1928 Father Walter wrote of these Christ brides, "Their active contribution and prayerful lives helped mould the mission. With maternal care they devoted themselves to the children and nursed the old and the sick". Apart from the 90 girls and boys at the school, these sisters were later asked to also care for leprosy sufferers near the Beagle Bay mission.

Reviewers are left wondering where, despite all this devout effort, it all went wrong – wrong in the sense that the proportion of genuine converts was very low, and wrong in the sense that much of the negative sentiment associated with the Stolen Generation was sheeted home to these devoted believers who gave their own lives for the noble cause of uplifting the heathen. By 1904 the pastoralists' treatment of the Aborigines, and the effects of the missionaries on their society, became the subject of a Royal Commission chaired by the famous anthropologist Walter Roth. The Roth Inquiry led to the passing of the Aborigines Act 1905, aimed at curbing at least the worst of the crimes against the natives, notably rape, floggings, child stealing, chaining up and slavery.

# CASE OF QUEENSLAND ANGLICAN MISSIONS

The most comprehensive case study of Missions in Queensland is that of Noel Loos, (a James Cook University researcher, very active in the church), titled "White Christ, Black Cross: The emergence of a Black Church". Loos together with Henry Reynolds must be given credit for encouraging and helping Eddie Mabo, then a gardener at James Cook University, to initiate and win Australia's first Native Title Claim.

Unsurprisingly with his evangelical background, Loos gives an unusually positive overview of the outcomes of the missionary effort in Queensland. He makes a stronger case than other writers, to show how Aboriginal spirituality could be (had been) reconciled with the Christian religion, particularly as practiced by the Anglican Church. On meeting an old woman at Kowanyama who believed the Aboriginal stories just as strongly as she believed the Bible stories, Loos gives a simple explanation: "In effect I discovered there was really no mystery. Aboriginal people took the new into their old intellectual universe. They were not empty wine skins waiting to be filled, but wine skins holding good old wine. The new wine blended with the old and produced a wine that is *nearer to Christianity* in many ways, than that which the White missionaries took with them" (my emphasis).

Loos points out that the Western missionaries had forgotten that the nature-based spiritual process was the same as that which Christianity had practiced for its first 500 years. The Aboriginal dreamtime stories were seen by many of them as their Old Testament, and they regarded the Bible stories as their New Testament. Thus the Christian beliefs were accepted as completing their old story rather than competing with it. Loos maintains: "The missionaries had tried to force a complete replacement [of the stories]. Increasingly I discovered they had failed and many Aboriginal people retained those aspects of their old religion which they still found relevant and acceptable to their new understanding". Loos watched the Lutheran pastor at Hope Vale discussing with local Christians how Christian values might be found in Aboriginal creation myths. Monty Prior, an Aboriginal Catholic deacon told Loos, "You know, we had years of Jesus before you Whitefellows came". He apparently meant that his people had the word of God but not as the Jesus story.

The author quotes Loos at some length here because the author has always maintained that early in its existence, Christianity was closely tied to the earth and only later did the translators in the Church maintain that humans were set above, and separate from, Nature. In the author's book "Where Angels fear to Tread (2009)", he includes a long subsection titled "The Greening of the Church" in which he maintains that the historic separation from Nature was Christianity's biggest mistake. This separation based on Biblical instruction to "have dominion over the earth and its creatures", was, in the author's view, not only the greatest difference between Christian and Aboriginal beliefs, but a major reason for Christianity losing credence in a world environmentally threatened by human arrogance in raping the earth.

This conflict of values is of central importance in Aboriginal identity and, as such, moved the author to coin the phrase "Indigenocentric" in a triangle of values in which the well known "Eurocentric" and "Envirocentric" represented the other positions. This approach was first used in a paper to the Ecojustice Conference in Adelaide (Roberts 1997) in which the author attempted to explain that the environmental threat came not only from the Euro/Enviro conflict but from the absence of a moral conscience about the earth on the part of the European religion and thus from that dominant society's value system.

## OVERCOMING DISADVANTAGE

Returning to the mission field in Queensland, the churches would like to take credit for the life's work of men like Earnest Gribble at Yarrabah, Nicholas Hey at Mapoon (Weipa) and Pastor Schwartz at Hope Valley (Hope Vale). Loos points out that they were allowed to minister by the grace and favour of governments and settler lobbies intent on destroying Aboriginal culture. In later years the academics Elkin and Capell were strong advocates of assimilation. They were ordained priests at Sydney University who were widely consulted by the Australian Board of Missions, the peak Anglican body.

By 1946, to Elkin's credit, he recognised the essential failure of the overall mission effort: "Our church services and bell-ringing are all of a piece of the general routine we have introduced. The compound is a boarding school from which only death, or perhaps old age, will release its inhabitants", as recorded in Elkin's report to the Board of the Forrest River Mission in November 1946.

This damning opinion by one with an insider's view of the outcomes of the mission effort is of special significance as it carries a knowledge and authority of one with no intent to protect for the church, government or Indigenous interests. Elkin's final conclusion is worthy of serious reflection here: "The young men of 1928 are still lining up daily to be allotted their tasks, having become specialists in nothing, having so sense of independence, having no money or other exchange economy (meaning saleable goods or skills) through which to express themselves in satisfying physical and mental needs. And all they can look forward to is a parasitic old age, probably out in the camp, when they should be in their prime as leaders of social groups, they are leading an aimless existence; unpaid workers on a Mission which, outwardly at best, gets nowhere". In essence Elkin suggested: "We are the cause of the apathy and penury of the people, and we ought to do something about it".

Why is this somewhat dated evaluation of mission work of importance to current policy? Because "the self-perpetuating apathy of these closed institutions" (Loos's words) formed the very low base from which today's constraints of "culturally-appropriate" options for the Indigenous economy carry the same moral warmth of the current European "ethical investments" in non-nuclear projects.

Modern observers might question the relevance of past mission practices to today's policy settings but this is to underestimate the wounds burned deeply into the psyche of living Elders subjected to a civilising process dominated by a guard/inmate relationship which relied on harsh discipline, beatings and chaining as means of denigrating Aboriginal spirituality and customs. As Reverend R.B. Cranswick reported in 1947, "This prison-like discipline seemed to be enforced for its own sake and for little apparent reason". In this way Christianity became synonymous with punishment, imprisonment and public humiliation – not a good look for an enlightening and uplifting organisation.

Added to this depravation of culture and the loss of self-respect associated with it, was the simultaneous lack of understanding by the Missions and the government of the bonds to clan country so vital to Aboriginal identity. This sense of place, as referred to earlier in this section, was totally over-ridden by the authorities (church and state) in places like Mapoon (Weipa) where people were forcibly shifted from the bauxite leases of Comalco, and the removal of many of the Lockhart River people from Iron Range to Bamaga 300 kilometres away, and given the new name of Umagico. By 1957 many of the Queensland missions had collapsed due to financial pressure and in May 1967 the State Government took over Lockhart River, Mitchell River and Edward River missions. The burning down of the Mapoon (Presbyterian) mission church and people's houses as a means of expediting the removal of that community to the new Mapoon outside the mining lease, is still held up as one of the glaring examples of government and industry's disdain for Indigenous people's welfare. The government had taken over the Mapoon mission in 1963 and moved the people to Bamaga. In 1966 a large portion of the Aboriginal reserve at Weipa was "cancelled" so that the aluminium company could start work.

Archdeacon Frank Coaldrake in 1962 recognised that all the negotiations between the missions, government and mining companies were underpinned by the goal of assimilation, "sometimes expressed with such frankness that it seemed to be assimilation gone mad" according to Loos. Coaldrake observed that: "the training of Aborigines in the development of skills which will enable them to take their place in the general community is the avowed aim of government programmes". He predicted that this would mean "the eventual movement of Aboriginals from Cape York to southern townships and rural areas". We shall return to the value of such migration.

While the insight of hindsight makes it easy to criticise the heavy-handed application of assimilation policy, it is clear that voluntary assimilation could have had a major beneficial effect on Aboriginal well-being. In essence the movement of communities was driven by the benefits to industry rather than to Aborigines – the economic bonanza of mineral royalties for government from bauxite and silica sand on the Cape over-rode Indigenous needs.

While all this remote migration was taking place, the urban end of the Indigenous lifestyle continuum was expanding. By 1974 there were about 8000 Aborigines at Redfern and another 2000 at Mt. Druitt in Sydney. Only a very small proportion of these were apparently church-goers, suggesting that whatever the missionaries had achieved by way of conversions in remote areas (they always recorded the number of christenings as their measure of success) they had made minimal impact on the city cousins. This review will return to the concept of urban Aboriginal culture and religion in a community in which living memory of personal country has been overtaken by urban disadvantage.

It is perhaps appropriate to conclude this consideration of missionary influence with a reference to the current "history wars", an academic conflict of views on what the historian Geoffrey Blainey called the "three cheers and black armband" views of history. At the heart of this war is the claim by Keith Windshuttle that Henry Reynolds had exaggerated, even fabricated, the extent of violence and number of deaths during the period of dispossession. This is not the place to repeat or judge the details of the conflicting claims, suffice to say that the position taken by each of the protagonists is almost always related to the left/right leanings as perceived by the commentators in the popular press.

Unsurprisingly, reporters commonly link the academics to political philosophies, as when Bain Attwood in his "Telling the Truth about Aboriginal History" refers to Windshuttle and other Howard (right) intellectuals. How seriously this egocentric debate reflects on the reality of current Aboriginal well-being, is a parallel debate. The reason why the writings of the above protagonists, plus others like Manne, Macintyre and Dawson, have caused such a flood of Letters to the Editor, is because Australians are affected, whether they admit it or not, by what Tim Fischer, Howard's Deputy, referred to as the "guilt industry". Ernest Gribble, the missionary at remote Yarrabah would be proud to know that not only was he the instigator of the only Royal Commission into an Aboriginal massacre but is credited by Windshuttle with igniting the greatest controversy in Australian history.

THE PAST: THE RABBIT PROOF CASE

It is fitting to close this section with a reference to the seminal report "Bringing Them Home" on the Stolen Generation which not only called for correctional action but called on the religious organisations to improve the weak response of the church. I give Loos the last word: "In the western world, except in the United States, Christianity seems to be in full flight to the fringes of a society whose faith is secular humanism or consumerism. At present I suspect that the Aboriginal Christians I have met would consider the possibility of the demise of Christianity as just another example of Western rationalism and an effete denial of the spiritual dimension. They would see it (the demise) as a statement of unfaith". We shall take this further in considering contemporary Aboriginal identity.

# THE RABBIT PROOF CASE

In recent years the mission era has once again been brought into sharp relief, first by Doris Pilkington's "Rabbit Proof Fence", then by the official report on the Stolen Generation titled "Bringing Them Home". Phillip Noyce's film of Pilkington's story of the same name, touches the heart of many because of the way it portrays the strength of family love that drives three little girls, Molly, Gracie and Daisy, to escape from the Moore River Mission near Perth and follow the rabbit-proof fence for 1600 kilometres to their mothers' settlement at Jigalong in the country of the Mardudjara people.

This epic story starts with the rejection of half-caste (muda-muda) babies by their grandmother although they are precious to their mother. Their biological father turns out to be the boss of the European gang working on the construction of the fence. His name is Thomas Craig but he disappears from the narrative and, in real life, buys a farm in the Lake Grace area far to the south.

Jigalong was established as a depot in 1907, one of the many along the 1834km of fence, patrolled in 240km sections by pairs of maintenance men whose only company was Blackfellows. What makes this story so compelling is the way it portrays the Imperial Empire-builders with their self-proclaimed superiority and confidence, in juxtaposition to the primitive desert people of the Kimberley, exaggerating the cultural differences and forcing the reader to experience the dilemma of the clash of values between two peoples at the extremes of the continuum of civilisation. This clash is magnified by the fact that this meeting occurs in the early 1930's when the British Empire was near its zenith and its adventurous patriots were not only spread over the globe acquiring resources for the Mother Country, but instinctively knew what was good for the savages who inhabited their new colonies.

From a historic point of view, Pilkington does justice to the tribulations of the first White explorers and settlers, giving them credit for their courage and resilience against the odds; Captain Fremantle and his small band of 1829 settlers on the Swan River. The present author notes close similarities between the reactions of these settlers and those of his own ancestors dumped on the South African veldt in 1820, who only on arrival found that they were to form a human barrier against the marauding Black tribes attacking the Cape frontier of South Africa. [These tribes were in fact defending their 'new' lands.]

The Rabbit-Proof Fence story centres on the "degrading and inhumane" conditions at the Mission where forcibly-removed half-caste girls and boys would be taught civilised living, and through schooling and vocational training would be a source of station labour and domestic servants for the emerging pastoral society of the West. The way their language and customs were beaten out of them, because these were the Devil's ways, led them to despise the European Christian ways forced upon them. Pilkington does a fair job of explaining that the authorities were driven by the best of sincere intentions of betterment for this heathen race. She brings the Canning Stock Route into the story, not only because it was in fact part of the escape journey, but because like the fence, the stock route represents another big Whitefella construction that disturbs tribal life and walkabout patterns.

While the personal evidence chronicled in the "Bringing Them Home" report easily brings tears to the eyes of empathising readers, "Rabbit Proof Fence", especially in the film version, encapsulates many, perhaps most, of the powerful human emotions of love, hate, courage, ambition, hope, survival, lust, cruelty, religious intolerance, fear and arrogance. In fact, this simple true narrative can be used as a framework for evaluating early Indigenous policy in a very meaningful way by study groups wishing to contribute to Aboriginal futures.

THE PAST: ANTHROPOLOGISTS – A BREED APART

# ATTACK AND DEFENCE

While the literature is full of references to attack on settlers by Aborigines, invariably caused by violation of the latter's hunting grounds or women, little is written of attack on mission stations. A case in point is the Benedictine Fathers of New Norcia (a present day tourist attraction north of Perth) who agreed to set up a mission on the Drysdale River in the remote Kimberley in 1905: "It was on the Barton River nearby, that Father Leandro came close to being speared" by the people of that region whom Choo quotes as "actively resisting the invasion by the Benedictines of their country". The Benedictines in turn interpreted this attack as "treacherous behaviour which served to prove the malice of the savage tribes" (Perez 1958).

Much more frequent in the literature is reference to Aborigines fleeing to the missions from pastoralists who persecuted them (many being shot on sight) or from other tribes seeking retribution. While all this was going on, the officially appointed Protectors of Aborigines were "zealously engaged in removing half-caste children from their Aboriginal families and sending them to the Missions" (Choo 2001).

Perez makes the significant observation that the promising of very young girls to older men in marriage was responsible for the very low rate of 'rapine and barter' of women in Aboriginal society. The practical effect of this arrangement was that virtually all young women were fiercely protected by their future husbands and their clans, leading to the oft-reported attacks on White men interfering with their promised wives. One seeks in vain for any admissions in the Missionary reports of sexual relations between the Mission staff and the locals – a far cry from the revelations of recent years, notably in supposedly chaste Catholic establishments.

# ANTHROPOLOGISTS – A BREED APART

No account of Aboriginal history is complete without reference to the role of the scientists who studied and recorded the lives and customs of Indigenous people in their natural habitat.

## OVERCOMING DISADVANTAGE

The present author had grown up in the frontier region of the Eastern Cape of South Africa where missionaries and their societal goals were at odds with those of the settlers, police and merchants of their day. This 'missionary zeal' is dealt with here in Part 1, but the anthropologist's role in colonial Australia was being played out simultaneously with very different goals. Predictably the sympathetic approach of the anthropologists was to clash with the more utilitarian approach of the settlers seeking labour and protecting their stock. However, this sectoral clash of values was apparently not as serious as the conflict between settlers and missionaries, or, not so predictably, between the different schools of anthropologists. In McKnight's words "Australian anthropology from the very beginning has been marred by quite exceptional ill will, bitterness and personal vendettas". So why should those wanting to contribute to positive Aboriginal futures be concerned with collegial competition between past scientists?

The inter-tribal skirmishes between groups of university-based anthropologists would be comical if they weren't such a serious reflection on ego-driven individuals spending public money. Early in the piece, the jealousies and back-stabbing was set off by the decision on where the first Chair in Anthropology would be located. This was followed by cloak-and-dagger manoeuvring for the right to exclusive use of identified study sites or groups of Aborigines.

The present author had not been aware of the early importance of Papua New Guinea as an anthropological focus for Australian experts. Geoffrey Gray's book "A Cautious Silence: The Politics of Australian Anthropology" is an unusual overview which brings unusual reviewer's comments such as "I expect that this book will generate considerable debate" (!). It seems that anthropologists were co-accused with missionaries and administrators, in covering-up the appalling state of Aboriginal living conditions in remote areas. The basic problem seemed to arise from anthropologists' fascination with 'the noble savage' whom they seemed to want to preserve in a sort of living zoo. Gray says that they saw themselves "not as advocates of change, but as practitioners of neutral value-free science above and beyond politics." They were not supposed to offer solutions or define policy but to diagnose and predict (in this case, survival chances).

These Human Scientists did not describe the social and political realities of the bush people. Rather, they were concerned with the immediate capture and recording of disappearing primitive people. Their objectives clashed with those of the missionaries who were committed to "progressing from primitive to Christian citizens". This goal required erasing Indigenous culture and social life. Anthropologists however, were divided as to whether their recording of customs (including sorcery, child brides and polygamy) represented a benefit or a threat to the people concerned. So-called "applied anthropology" was meant to offer a factual basis for betterment of the people concerned, even if the original intent was on documenting the 'pristine primitive' or the 'savage savage'. Gray's title "Cautious Silence" refers to the 'peculiar historical response of Australian anthropologists', by which he means the unholy personal conflicts never revealed to outsiders but obviously a major factor in limiting positive co-operative scientific endeavour.

Over the years, notably between 1900 and 1960, governments often called on anthropologists to advise on 'native questions'. One such example is Donald Thompson who recommended that "until better policies were formulated the people of Arnhem Land should be protected through a *complete and rigorous segregation*, thus ensuring their future" (my emphasis). Another example is A.P. Elkin who advised John McEwen, then Minister for the Interior in 1962. Elkin was one of the few anthropologists who understood the humanitarian and welfare needs of the people he studied and when he made a strong case for vocational training so that Aborigines could participate in the broader economy, his purest fellow-scientists saw this as social engineering not becoming of the real anthropologist.

Gray follows the appointments, projects and promotions of figures who became giants on the local anthropological scene. He describes how Elkin and Chinnery oversaw the early pastoral industry survey by the young Ronald and Catherine Berndt who would later dominate this science in Australia. Over the decades anthropologists had a continuous battle convincing government of their worth – not only as effective users of grant funds but also as advisors on racial matters. Not unexpectedly, government could be depended on to support and ask advice from scientists whom government knew held similar values to those of the government in power. This unspoken selling of their souls for financial gain and official recognition, seems to have been a sore point within the academy of purists who had some difficulty in disguising their jealousy.

Just when one thought all possible conflicts among anthropologists had been dealt with, some young female scientist is accused of "trying to induce the natives to stage one of their devil-devil corroborees for her, undoing all the work of those who befriend the natives". The extent to which this upset the Missionaries was apparently of biblical proportions, seen as revitalizing the satanic traits they'd been beating out of the same people. So here we had customs which were the antithesis of Christianity being recognized by competing scientists as valuable cultural knowledge to be appreciated, recorded and published. In one case the natives were recorded drinking blood – horror of horrors. When young researcher Phyllis Kaberry reported that "station Blacks were in better condition physically than mission Blacks" as well as noting that "the station Blacks were more sophisticated" the reaction from the Men of the Book can only be imagined.

Gray sums up these early lessons in political correctness when he refers to young Ralph Piddington: "But as Piddington learnt, and it served as instruction to others, a career in anthropology in Australia required a cautious silence about what was often written, said or heard" – a theme that is examined in Gray's following chapters which he proceeds to illustrate with seemingly unending real life examples.

The activities of anthropologists on Cape York is of particular interest to the present author who lead the Cape York Pastoral Industry Study in 1993 and whose son has devoted two decades to the Cape people. The first anthropologist to work in the Cape was Ursula McConnel of the University of Queensland in 1918. Her interest was in the origin and meaning of 'dream symbols', which was the subject of her thesis at the University of London. Gray maintains that this young woman "was malleable in the face of theories promoted by her male mentors" and shifted her study toward "a related broader but much older debate on the origins of religion." (The present author reviews this topic in his recent book "Where Angels Fear to Tread", Roberts 2009).

One of the publications of McConnel was "A Moon Legend from Bloomfield River, North Queensland" which produced information on sexual life among the Bloomfield tribes. This was at a time when "fundamentalist anthropology" was emerging to challenge fundamentalist religion and McConnel wanted to reserve the Weipa-Aurukun tribal areas as her research territory, making it clear that other researchers were welcome to study Cape tribes elsewhere. Thus started the territorial competition between anthropologists in the Cape. Soon Donald Thompson was revelling in the fact that Mc Connell had actually been excluded from the Aurukun mission area. She found Mr. McKenzie who managed the Presbyterian Mission there, "frightfully dominating". He was making his own study of the Wikmunkun languages and customs. So here we have the first example of professional jealousy based on what today is called 'my turf'. McConnell accused the McKenzies of studying an artificial population but "they had no idea of kinship systems or what a moiety or clan was".

The Mission practice was to bring in all the young girls and send the young men to work on the pearling luggers. They told the married men that they shouldn't have more than one wife and that all single women should be at the Mission and learning to be useful domestic servants. The girls' fathers responded "by giving their daughters away to prevent them from going to the Mission". Soon McConnell was described by the local Protector as 'objectionable', having read her 'vehement condemnation of the cruel practices of the superintendent' (Gray 2007). Kidd (1997) tells us that 'her professionalism was impinged' and she was described by John Bleakley, Chief Protector, as 'eccentric and somewhat hysterical'. The outcome of this clash of personalities was the declaration by the Presbyterian Church that 'it would not give permission for any other anthropologist to work on its Missions in Queensland'.

So why is this little historic spat of any importance to those considering Aboriginal futures? Because here we have a real-life example of three attributes of the Victorian White man which affected the Indigenous people at their very heart:

- Both Anthropologists and Missionaries took unto themselves the authority to investigate and judge the Aborigines' culture according to both Darwinian and Christian beliefs.
- Both White organizations somehow instinctively knew not only what was best for Aborigines but felt obliged to advise government on active policy to guide their future.
- Both showed neither respect nor appreciation of the ancient religious attachment of these people to their land and denigrated their

ecological knowledge as not only primitive but also satanic.

This is the present author's reading of the situation and will no doubt be challenged by the organizations concerned. Their answers to the question of why they couldn't just leave these people alone, only serve to support the author's opinion. Where the self-appointed authority to segregate and protect these capable ancient survivors arose is not clear but it can be found all over the British Empire.

To return to the McConnel example, one gets the impression that author Gray had remarkably open access to internal correspondence, such as Kidd had to Queensland government files. It turns out that McConnel was the sister-in-law of the Yale anthropologist Dr. Mayo. She was funded by the Rockefeller Foundation for over a decade from 1927 and wasn't inclined to be put off by either the Head of Missions or the Protector of Aboriginals. Gray digs up references from experts describing her field work as "able and careful" or that she is "incompetent and has no right to be doing anthropology". She carried on and produced her book "Myths of the Munkun" in 1957, the year she died.

McConnel was followed by Donald Thompson a Melbourne anthropologist, who took advantage of McConnel's exclusion from Aurukun although his work was not assisted by the suicide of Henry Chapman, honorary treasurer of the national research body (ANRC) from which he had embezzled $15,000 including Rockefeller's anthropology fund. Thompson's work would have been unremarkable if he had not sought an audience with the Presbyterian Church in Melbourne to outline what he had witnessed on the flogging and chaining of Aboriginals by McKenzie's staff at Aurukun before their removal to Palm Island. Nothing had been done about McConnel's allegations against McKenzie and in December 1946, Thompson went public with a series of articles in the Melbourne Herald titled "Justice for Aboriginals." His iconographic photograph of chained Aboriginals with police on horseback starting their long journey to Palm Island, apparently had the same effect on politicians as modern day images of the pain of innocents.

The Cape was then to receive the attentions of the young American anthropologist Lauriston Sharp, a Wisconsin PhD student who started at Mitchell River, where he studied Aboriginal mythology and belief from about 1935. Incredibly, there seems to be no record of co-operative research between

## THE PAST: ANTHROPOLOGISTS – A BREED APART

McConnel, Thompson or Sharp. This didn't prevent Sharp from completing his PhD at Harvard in 1937 titled "Social Anthropology of a Totemic System in Queensland". Somehow he'd caused no problems with Missions or Government and this positive relationship caused Elkin to recommend Carolyn Tennant Kelly as the researcher at Cherbourg in 1934. She would investigate scientifically, the social anthropology of the Aborigines. Apparently her well developed social conscience led her to expose the Queensland Governments' exploitation of Aboriginal earnings. It is likely that this discovery by Kidd led to the latter's comprehensive examination of the "stolen wages" issue in later years. Chief Protector Bleakley observed that the Queensland department's experience with female anthropologists "had not been a very satisfactory or harmonious one". Despite his advising the New South Wales Protection Board against employing Tennant because her familiarity with the natives was subversive to discipline, Kelly and Elkin went on to get the New South Wales Government to change their Boards' name from 'Protection' to 'Welfare' and to appoint an anthropologist and an Aboriginal to the Board.

Queensland apparently remained anthropologist-free until Jeremy Beckett worked in the Torres Strait a decade later in the early 1960's. Beckett maintained that there had never been an Australian school or even style of anthropology. This upset those local experts who'd imagined that they had in fact developed just such a local brand. He completed his doctoral studies on Saibai Island on a topic which remains hard to find in the literature.

If Gray set out to explain the politics of Australian anthropology, he has failed to convince the reader that taxpayers should have to put up with the childish, egotistic and unaccountable behaviour of well-educated professionals. This unusual catalogue of who got which grant, who was appointed to university posts, who didn't co-operate with whom, and even what referees wrote about who, is in the present author's long experience in science literature reviews, without parallel. As such, it must have a serious message for both professional bodies and for funding bodies. What that message is, is not clear, except that Aboriginal people seeking guidance should not have to put up with this disgraceful conduct by so-called scientists.

## SETTLERS, MISSIONARIES AND ABORIGINES

While the missionaries were busy "uplifting" the natives, the pastoralists had a very different view of the place of these locals in the emerging frontier society. This view arose from the illegal assumption that as holders of pastoral leases pastoralists had total right of access over their stations, and the right to meet their need for cheap labour to run their businesses.

Several of the writings of Henry Reynolds present clear evidence that the squatters' only legal right was to "de-pasture stock" and establish a homestead and yards on their lease. There is an abundance of reports to government, many written by missionaries, which repeat the causes of conflict as the original decimation of the food sources of the Aborigines (notably kangaroos), the pollution of their waterholes by cattle and sheep and the predictable use of domestic stock as a replacement food source by Aborigines deprived of their natural hunting grounds.

Many writers have chronicled the way in which the "dispersal" (commonly used term by squatters' and Native Police in reports on death of Aboriginals) of local natives, led to their seeking refuge from the cruelties of the frontier. All the evidence points to the need for protection rather than for an enlightening gospel, as the drawcard of the missions. This in turn led to the accusation by settlers against the missionaries, as being the source of indolent natives unwilling to provide much-needed labour to the settlers. There was nothing new in this, as the same pattern of conflict was recorded in Africa and America.

What is the significance of this unholy triangular conflict which many now regard as ancient history from which we should move on? The answer to this question is that the hangover of these hostilities is still alive and well as evidenced from the rural communities response to Native Title claims – not so much to the Mabo case which was island land far removed from working properties, but very much so in the Wik case on the best pastoral country on Cape York. News clippings from that time (especially from Queensland Country Life) give the impression that the present generation of landholders had no idea of the illegality of their forefather's actions against Blacks. Reynolds brings repeated strong evidence of how the political strength of the squattocracy influenced the administration of justice in what today may well be termed genocide.

Apart from the fact that the Native Title claims have become a "lawyers' picnic" and have taken an average of 9 years to complete, the original acceptance by the judicial system that "continuous connection" to the claimed land as a prime criterion of ownership, is beyond comprehension, given the recorded devastation of many of these populations. After decades of inhuman treatment of the rightful owners of the land, a tearful nation was able to gain their first collective recognition of what had happened, when they studied the televised faces of old Aborigines as Prime Minister Rudd finally said "Sorry" in 2008. This review will return to the importance of colonial history to present and future policy.

# LUGGERS' INFLUENCE

The earliest outside contact made by the Aborigines of northern Australia, was with the Asian trepang (sea cucumber) collectors who dealt with the locals from about 200 years before Captain Cook arrived. These Indonesians, Macassans and Malays were followed in the late 1800s by the pearlers from Japan and elsewhere in Asia. These mariners recognised the Aboriginal local knowledge of the tides, weather and marine life, and used the men for diving and the women for food collection and sexual services.

The later years of this inter-racial industry are well recorded in a remarkable (facsimile printed) book "In Australian Tropics" by Alfred Searcy in 1909 – Collector of Customs at Port Darwin in the late 1800s. (See Section 1 Appendix I.) It appears that the Aborigines found themselves at the bottom of the pecking order among Koepangers (West Timor), Filipinos, Chinese, Malays, Manillamen and even some Indians. At the top of the order were the Japanese who, during the lay-up of the luggers apparently maintained greater respect than the other races in the way they conducted themselves and treated their employees, during a period when the procurement of Aboriginal female partners was an integral part of the lugger crews' lifestyle.

These coastal fleets of luggers spread their influence from Broome on the Kimberley coast, through the Gulf of Carpentaria and down the East Coast of

## OVERCOMING DISADVANTAGE

Cape York at least as far as Iron Range and the Pascoe River where even today Aboriginal Elders can be heard using Japanese terms learned in their youthful pearling days. Because most of the missions had been established near food-rich estuaries supporting large Aboriginal populations, the missionaries soon came into conflict with the lugger crews who sought food, water, firewood and women from the same fertile coves. Because the native women had few qualms about sexual favours in exchange for tobacco, alcohol, food and trinkets, the missionaries recognised early in their soul-saving program, that far from dealing with innocent, childlike heathens, they had to contend with one of the world's greatest mixing bowls along a vast coastline where natural instincts rather than the law ruled. Perhaps this was the original Australian multiculturalism, the results of which can be seen today by simply visiting the Sunset Markets on Darwin beach or inspecting the remarkably diverse gravestones in northern coastal cemeteries.

What the author refers to as the "luggers' influence" is thus not simply a minor perturbation of the Black/White relationship, but a significant factor affecting the gene pool of the whole of northern Australia where the great majority of Aborigines still live today. When the emerging 'science' of eugenics developed out of social Darwinism in the late 1800s, the measuring of skulls and body dimensions became a fascination of the upper class in Europe who wrote at length about the differences between full-bloods, half-castes, quadroons, octoroons, etc as a means of classifying the relatives of these newly-discovered 'living fossils'. This was followed by attempts in the early 1900s to preserve as a sort of "human zoo" the last of the Myalls in the Tanami desert. This in turn was followed by Nugget Coombes formal policy of cultural preservation (the opposite of integration) right up to the 1970s. These racial purity issues are mentioned here because of the complication and confusion they caused in the development of agreed goals and worthy outcomes for Aboriginal policy. Not surprisingly, any attempt to classify individuals for eligibility on government benefits, led to the same irrational classification of "coloureds" in Apartheid-ridden South Africa after 1948.

The whole question of eugenics and 'breeding out of colour' is well reviewed in Henry Reynolds' book 'Nowhere People' (2008) which draws on his earlier research on colonial marriage policy and mixing of Australian races. Christine Doran's 'Separatism in Townsville' (JCU, 1981) gives a good example of local application of social policy from 1884 to 1894.

# ESTABLISHMENT OF RESERVES – THEN AND NOW

Once the early pastoralists had taken it upon themselves to 'disperse' any Blacks found on their land it soon became clear to the authorities that these landless people needed somewhere to go. Had the reserves been significantly larger, this Homeland concept may have had a better chance of working – as with the South African reserves under Apartheid. In both cases, the reserve system could be argued to preserve native culture, in fact Archibald Meston, the Queensland Protector of Aborigines, wrote in unusually humanitarian terms in his 1896 Annual Report: "Specially entitled to practical sympathy are the Aborigines scattered among the settled districts and wandering about the towns. They have lost their old habits and customs, abandoned their old hunting life, and descended gradually through various stages of degradation to a condition which is a reproach to our common humanity. They require collection on suitable reserves, complete isolation from contact with the civilised race to save them from that small section of Whites more degraded than any savage; kept from drink and demise, the young people and the able-bodied taught industrious habits, and to raise their own food supplies; the old being decently cared for and receiving the modest amount of comfort they require.....Even acceptance of the 'doomed race' can in no way absolve a humane and Christian nation from the obligations they owe to this helpless people, or our solemn duty to guide them kindly across the period which spans the abyss between the present and the unknown point of final departure". The wisdom of hindsight allows contemporary observers to attack Meston, who personified the belated empathy mouthed by the dominant culture of that era, with a choice of words which disguises the cruel annihilation of the original landowners.

Note how Meston suggests that the Aboriginals lost their customs, abandoned their hunting and descended through degradation – and how they'd be saved from the small section of Whites. Meston would have been well aware that they were beaten, shot and poisoned off their land, that they'd had their land, children and women forcibly stolen, and that that small section of Whites included virtually all classes of Whites. Repeated suggestions that it was only ex-convicts and course labourers who used Aboriginal women and alcoholic inducements are untrue, for it is widely recorded that educated squatters and merchants were as active as any in the degradation and murder taking place. It was also well known that it was some missions that were at the forefront of the "lost customs", beating both language and tribal behaviour out of stolen generations. Note also how the Protector reflected no intention of protecting Aboriginals against their "final departure". Significantly, Meston makes no mention of the convenience of the reserves as sources of virtually free labour for nearby property holders. We refer elsewhere to the writings of Watson who gives special mention to those property holders who went out of their way to help the Aborigines on their leases.

It is interesting to note that the first writer to use the 'pillow' metaphor for the disappearing race was Bishop Frodsham in 1906: "The Aborigines are disappearing. In the course of a generation or two at the most, the last Australian Blackfellow will have turned his face to warm mother earth and given back his soul to God…..Missionary work then may be only smoothing the pillow of a dying race….."

Why is the repeated use of this quotation in the contemporary press important? Because it reflects not only the early colonial lack of concern for Aboriginals' future, but seems to linger in the mindset of those scribes who still seem to doubt the worthwhileness of a strong Indigenous group identity in Australia's future. This sentiment is central to the serious effort which this nation may or may not make, going forward, to help plan and implement the formation and consolidation of a proud First Nation within this broader nation. The implications of this mindset for future integration, assimilation, Apartheid or parallel development are discussed elsewhere.

# WOMEN, VIOLENCE AND RAGE

Allied to Choo's feminist writings are the recent unexpected writings of that well-known contrarian Germaine Greer in a small book entitled "On Rage" in 2008. She attempts, successfully in the author's view, to explain the origin of Aboriginal male rage causing widespread domestic violence. Predictably, Greer was at the receiving end of serious criticism from Aboriginal leaders, despite her attempt to credit (and fully reference) the positive contributions of several of these same leaders. The Greer incident is an important example of the "don't patronise us" response, so common from Aboriginal organisations in recent times.

This response stems from reaction to the White originator rather than to the inherent value of the opinion. So, just as the stating of the benefits of "mainstreaming" (economic independence) had to come from a leader such as Noel Pearson before it gained credence, so the rational explanation of male rage and violence may have to wait for a Black explanation. It should be added that Greer's history of pretence at support for other emotive causes, has tainted her with an image of feigned outrage as an attention-seeking ploy, too often repeated to be overlooked by the warriors of Australia's cultural wars. Greer's uncanny knack of combining strong personal views on blurred emotive issues, with a toxic challenge to purists, can be guaranteed to get Greer-haters to rise to the bait. This personal example of dalliance would not be important if it didn't exemplify a serious negative response from Indigenous leaders to perfectly logical and factually correct statements and proposals by non-Indigenous well-wishers. A case in point is the way Greer deals, rather insensitively, with the disbenefits or otherwise of the Stolen Generation. Far from being torn from their mother's arms by unscrupulous officials, some such as the great Lowitja O'Donoghue and her five siblings, were allegedly delivered to an institution by their father, in this case an Irish White man.

While such revelations are embarrassing because they don't fit the narrative of demonising the institutions' policy, they serve to remind us all that, in their effort to expound the concept of victimisation, serious exaggeration and selective use of the evidence, has led to a popular but simplistic image of the complex realities of Aboriginal history in which shades of grey are dispensed with and clear-cut stereotypes loom large. Greer suggests that McKnight's observation on Mornington Island that "many young women favoured Whites because they treated them better" can be seen all over Australia. With Greer's strong feminist reputation (starting with her bestselling Female Eunuch 1970) it is not surprising that she points out that the 1996 census showed that Aboriginal women are almost as likely to be married to or cohabiting with a non–Aboriginal man. By 2001, Marcia Langton, that indomitable crusader for Indigenous rights, reminded Australia that the Aboriginal population was increasing at twice the rate of the general Australia population i.e. at a growth rate of approximately 2.3%.

Greer is probably correct when she maintains that the male Aboriginal's rage is caused by the frustration of having no other way to meet their rejection, most recently by their own kinfolk. This rejection has escalated in recent years when the clans' women, by default, took a stand on sly-grogging in outback settlements. Rosemary Neill has pointed out that today's male rage needs understanding: "Without this understanding it is too easy to resort to racist stereotypes suggesting that Indigenous men are inherently violent or alcoholic, or that rape and assault of women went unpunished in traditional society". A common alternative to rage is suicide, as explained by the present author's undergraduate associate from South Africa, Colin Tatz.

Tatz maintains that suicide was unknown to Aboriginal communities until about 1970 but has become an act of terminal rage (Greer's term) which turns violence from others to self. If John Taylor, the demographer, is right and there will soon be one million Australians claiming to be Indigenous, this issue could become critical politically.

# WHITE SUPREMACY – IMPERIAL DRIVER

Many writers on colonisation, slavery and Empire-building have referred to the Europeans sense of superiority as the driver of their domination of Indigenous peoples, notably in Africa, America and Asia, including Australia. Of particular interest to this author is George Fredrickson's book "White Supremacy – a comparative study in American and South African History". It is the unquestioning assumption of supremacy, which explains virtually all the policies and practices accepted as appropriate to handling the Indigenous population of colonised countries. This is no less so for Australia and, in this author's experience, very much the case in Southern Africa – in fact the names of the same British administrators repeatedly appear in the history of both countries.

Frederickson maintains that the self-image of superiority (the German *Ubermensch*) arose from the way in which "civilised" societies regarded savages and the savagery of their tribes. Many writers allude to the way in which superior nations repeatedly drew the comparison of their standards with those of the savages, specifically to validate the superiority of their society and its norms. Thus it is easy to find statements from the mid 1800s which include words to the effect that "Whereas these primitive people are dirty, lazy, ignorant, violent and crude, our advanced society is……." .

It may be claimed that these views are historic only, and have long since been superseded by enlightened, tolerant, multi-cultural views. While such progress may be true, it is this author's view that these old stereotypes still influence current views and reflect an unspoken discrimination. Thus, Europeans have since the Renaissance and the Reformation, divided humanity on the basis of two crucial attributes – Christianity and Civilisation. So people were regarded as civil or savage and Christian or heathen. This classification of some, usually Black, peoples as savage was sufficient to treat them as *Untermensch* and thus to enslave them and disregard any human rights – subhumans did not have rights and could be treated as animals. This image was widely promulgated in Michel Montaigne's famous 1580 essay "Of Cannibals".

This was followed by an opposing trend which humanists of the late sixteenth century used to "idealise the primitive state as a way of criticising their own civilisation" according to Frederickson. However this appreciation of the "noble savage" soon gave way to the general acceptance of European superiority which extended to the colonisation of Ireland by the English because, as Canny (1973) puts it, "The Celtic Irish were savages, so wild and rebellious that they could only be controlled by a constant and ruthless exercise of brute force".

In this case the colonial government disregarded the fact that these savages were both White and Christian, which made them a different type of savage from the Hottentots, Indians and Aboriginals. (Interestingly the savage Irish who lived outside the Dublin region known as The Pale were regarded as "beyond the Pale".) The emotive parallel between the modern Irish Riverdance and the re-emergence of Aboriginal dance to the sounds of the didgeridoo is not lost on ethnic audiences who recognise the phoenix-like revival of "primitive" cultures, so long subjugated by the colonising powers.

OVERCOMING DISADVANTAGE

# WAR AND LOYALTY

The literature on the role of Aboriginals during World War II (1939-1945) is fragmented and difficult to find. In essence, what record does exist indicates that the possibility of Japanese invasion at the time of the bombing of Darwin, led to an increasing fear of disloyalty by the Aborigines. Choo maintains that local folklore suggests that, "the army was prepared to kill Aborigines to prevent their collaboration with the enemy". Written evidence of this arrangement is understandably not available so it is not surprising that Robert Hall in his military history only quotes oral sources. In his Chapter 6 of "The Black Diggers", Hall uses a telling subheading "Treat a man like a dog: Aborigines as a security risk".

The Australian military had orders to clear all Aborigines from the coast, to intern local Japanese and Germans and to maintain a watch on the Jehovah's Witnesses. However, when 20 Japanese bombers and over 20 Zero fighters mistook the Kalumburu Mission for an RAAF base on 27 September 1943, and demolished the whole settlement, the Aborigines were left with more confused loyalties. Meanwhile it should be noted that elsewhere in Australia and overseas, many Aboriginals not only signed up early in the war but served with distinction only to find they were snubbed by their nation on their return.

Toward the end of the war the Aborigines in the Kimberley were in an especially poor way. In 1945 Constable R. Carr, the first and only White man to walk from Drysdale Mission to Kunmunya (Forrest River) Mission, reported on the condition of the 1400 Aborigines he came across: "The bush natives are in a shocking state…dying in large numbers from malnutrition….will not exist very much longer….only two looked at all healthy". Carr reported that almost half of the elderly were blind and that there were no young ones to hunt for them. At about the same time the Reverend Best of Forrest River Mission reported on the scarcity of young children in the bush: "They do not even seem to be propagating at all….". The same trend was reported by the Benedictines at Kalumburu, according to Choo. This mission recognised that apart from Christianisation, the race could be preserved from death and disease simply by providing survival rations.

THE PAST: WOMEN'S VIEW OF THE FRONTIER LEGEND

# THE CHANNEL COUNTRY SETTLEMENT: WOMEN'S VIEW OF THE FRONTIER LEGEND

When the present author first arrived in Western Queensland in 1972, the first books he read were Mary Durack's "Kings in Grass Castles" (1959) and Alice Duncan-Kemp's "Where Strange Paths Go Down" (1964). In his work as botanical surveyor for the Department of Primary Industries (DPI) stationed in Charleville, he was soon to experience the wonderful recovery of the Channel Country pastures after floods on Cooper Creek and to meet with local Windorah graziers like Bob Morrish and Sandy Kidd. He had met the folks at Thylungra Station where the Durack's had originally settled this amazing sandhill country in the mid 1800's, and worked with the descendents of the Tully's and Costello's, also pioneer settlers of this unforgiving country. The author's surveys covered a range of vegetation types and along the creeks he noticed Aboriginal artifacts such as grinding stones. Because he never got to know any historic accounts beside those of his White acquaintances he accepted the graziers' pioneer legends of how this region was settled.

This view of local history lasted until 1998 when Pamela Lukin Watson published her "Frontier Lands and Pioneer Legends". By any measure, this personal investigation by a descendent of a community leader who was one of the first to call for justice on the western frontier, is an unusually original historic interpretation. Instead of doing what most of us have done in accepting the White writers' view of western settlement, Watson goes back to original sources and examines the recorded lives of pioneers like John Costello, Robert Collins and Oscar de Satge – all recognised heroes of the pastoralists' emerging society in the West. She then goes on to get the women's point of view from Mary Durack and Alice Duncan-Kemp; followed by recorded actions and statements of the local tribe of Aboriginals. She subtitles this work "How pastoralists gained Karuwali land".

The country in question is north of Birdsville and Windorah and covers the catchments of the Mulligan, Georgina, Diamantina, Barcoo and other tributaries of the Cooper. Watson establishes the location of the home country of 24 language groups as they were when the pastoralists arrived, and then concentrates on the lands of the Karuwali centred on Farrar's Creek north of Betoota.

An earlier anthropologist named Tindale had estimated the size of this language group's land at over 33,000 square kilometres. Over time, this land 'came into the hands of the pastoralists', but the truth of how this change of occupation occurred was not exposed in the respected memoirs of each of the three landed gentry who Watson examined.

The three heroes of the frontier legend who Watson selected were all political heavyweights, being Members of the Legislative Council and relatives of British high society. She builds on the 1992 "Images of Australia" by J.B. Hirst who analysed the legend of the pioneers, which is portrayed as the heroic central experience of European settlement in taming the wild environment for use by civilised humans.

This legend of Hirst's pioneers has a number of essential features which Watson maintains play a lasting role in how European Australians see themselves – as successors to this heroic endeavour. The pioneer legend portrays early settlement as essentially a struggle for power and control over nature – a personal contest between pastoralists and drought, flood, fire and Aborigines. It is portrayed largely as a struggle without violence (except for the odd "dispersal" of Blacks) and is a narrative in which little or no blood is spilt – no Zulu or Aztec-type battles. The legend shows how hardships are overcome by resourceful individuals without outside help or even cooperation from others. The pioneers are portrayed as succeeding because of their courage, endurance and moral strength. They are held up as individuals who strove, so that others might benefit and whose enterprise created a great national estate. Watson maintains that Hirst's legend shows respect and reverence toward the pioneers as an integral part of the legend. In addition, anything but unswerving acceptance of the values and tenets of the pioneer legend, is seen as unpatriotic and letting the team down in a moral sense. This accusation comes about because, in an essentially conservative value-system, when historic events are glorified, the cultural investment in them becomes difficult to challenge or refute. Says Hirst, "Once there is a valued past, the future is more confined". This may be more significant than is generally accepted, for the White Australian self-image. Hirst adds that in emphasising the struggle between pioneers and nature, the Black/White struggle virtually disappears from the narrative. This omission is seen as adding greatly to the legend's impact, i.e. as a ripping yarn of the good guys who did no harm to others but deserve sympathy for their gallant struggle to carve a place for civilisation out of the wild bush.

Perhaps both Hirst and Watson read too much into the pioneer legend as a falsification of the reality on the frontier. They maintain that the pioneer legend was deliberately constructed during the rise of Australian nationalism in the 1880's and 1890's. The new nation apparently required suitable symbols, icons and visions to pull the national psyche out of the previous degrading actuality of the convict era. Hirst suggests that journalists and poets found positive values in the bush, beyond the miserable economic situation in Sydney and Melbourne. Thus the bushy writings of Banjo Patterson and Henry Lawson, somehow became integral to how the citizens of the new nation saw themselves. Watson recognises two separate legends – one which ennobled the bush workers like shearers, drovers and stockmen; the other which glorified the pioneer pastoralists. These stories emphasise the virtues of egalitarianism, practicality and anti-authoritarianism. To this day Patterson's poems are used in schools reflecting what is advertised as 'the spirit of Australia'.

The government had established the small penal colony at Brisbane in 1840 (20 years after the present author's ancestors arrived as the first settlers in South Africa's Border region) and the squatters moved west from Moreton Bay to take up pastoral leases at very low cost. This land was seized from the western tribes, without any treaties or annexations being necessary in *terra nullius*.

Characteristic of the squattocracy's unilateral take-over, was the inability of government to keep up and maintain law and order. It was this legal vacuum which allowed the pastoralists to become a law unto themselves. Their strong political connections in government aided and abetted this wild frontier behaviour which included the shooting of "trespassing" Blacks in the same manner as vermin damaging their stock. From 1870 onwards John Costello registered his claim to 34,000 square kilometres of land in the Cooper Creek region despite the presence of what his memoirs describe as "numerous and treacherous, wild and hostile Blacks in their hundreds". He went on to acquire a similar-sized run on the Roper River in the Northern Territory.

Robert Collins' memoirs state, "We will have no unnecessary bloodshed" on his Dawson River properties although his staff warned him that neighbouring pastoralists didn't hesitate to shoot Blacks and unless he did likewise White lives would be at risk. Collins was honest enough to write to his family that, "I am fully convinced that there has been any amount of perjury resorted to in obtaining country and in order to get renewal of licenses…..some men throw all consideration of truth and honour to the winds….fraud took several forms."

Oscar de Satge took a different approach. He took over huge areas, stocked them heavily for some years then sold them off. He was a young Englishman, second son of an aristocratic European dynasty. Fresh from the playing fields of Rugby he arrived in 1853, worked as a stockman and drover in the Darling Downs and Dawson areas, then moved to the Channel Country. De Satge quickly expelled all the Blacks from his acquired land, having vowed "never to let Aboriginal people remain on any pastoral station I controlled." Judith Wright, in her "The Cry for the Dead" describing her family's involvement in this region, records de Satge's income being "greater than most European princes". Here we have a man who ruthlessly cleared out all the traditional owners, recording how he also served three terms in the Queensland Legislative Assembly (1869-1888) and summing up his pioneering pastoral peers as "men of education and refinement who brought to that favourite portion of Queensland, the habits and ways of gentlemen".

It is this selective recognition of virtues which Hirst seizes on in his re-evaluation of the pioneer legend. Examining the memoirs of Costello, Collins and de Satge, Watson finds that they reflect every major human attribute which Hirst refers to in his legend analysis – courage, enterprise, moral value, power and control. Their stories all relate a bloodless struggle against the remorseless environment. Collins and Costello repeatedly record how they "treated the Blacks fairly and kindly" says Watson.

Watson then moves on to show how this initial brutal incursion by the Costello's was followed 21 years later on the same Karuwali tribal country, by the very different management style of William Duncan and his family. Costello and Duncan were both second generation Channel Country Whites but their backgrounds and human values produced almost opposing views on the Aboriginals and their treatment.

Duncan was a well-educated Scot who had an appreciation of comparative religions. He would listen with genuine interest and respect, according to daughter Alice, to the Karuwali Elders explaining their tribal law and their personal connection to their country. There is no record in any of Alice Duncan-Kemp's books of their family attempting to convert the Karuwali to Christianity. Whereas the Durack's and others kidnapped young Black boys to work on their stations and hunted them down if they escaped (Watson, 1998, p.28), the Duncans studied and respected the Aboriginal culture and land ownership.

William Duncan had come to Mooraberrie in 1891 and with his daughter Alice (born 1901) encouraged understanding of local customs and values. This led to later contact with Dr. Winterbottom and Dr. Elkin the anthropologists, encouraging proper scientific study of the Karuwali.

In reality these tribal people were now living double lives – as stockman and domestics for the Duncans, and as respected Elders and ritual leaders for their own people. Mary Durack, questioning the wiping out of tribal people following the provoked spearing of young Johnny Durack, asks whether the pastoralist's labour system was a form of slavery. So here we have two female writers challenging the pioneer legend from their own first-hand experience. Both Mary and Alice construct their pioneer stories as an inter-dependent co-habitation relying on mutual support in a harsh environment.

By constructing a woman's view of the settlement of the frontier, Watson has given a more detailed account of sexual relations between White men and Black women in Western Queensland. Her take on the situation in the late 1800's warrants quoting in full:

"Popular understanding of Australian history implies that early pioneers led asexual lives. There is no tradition of White prostitutes relieving the pressures of unwanted celibacy and nothing resembling the stories of American cowboys whooping it up in the saloons (of the Wild West). But many early settlers were in fact far from abstinent, obtaining sex from Indigenous women and sometimes children". Watson quotes Mary Durack in her book "Sons in the Saddle" as referring to a White stockman's comment that the men considered brief sexual contacts with tribal woman as a physical necessity. Says Durack, "It was rarely discussed, silently condoned and understood." Any emotional involvement was viewed negatively and co-habitation ruined men's reputations. Resulting children were usually ignored by the White fathers.

Watson suggests that tribal women were occasionally willing sexual partners, often driven by the promise of food. She notes that it was common practice for squatters to use access to Black women as a drawcard in recruiting White labour. Watson also refers to official police correspondence in 1898 which reports that "Many stations in the Kuluawari territory kept 'stud gins'." She relates how scrub-cutters, offered work at Ardoch Station, "were horrified to find eight or nine Aboriginal women fenced in with rabbit-proof netting adjoining the house." This was a property which was regularly inspected by the Queensland National Bank (as creditors) who apparently turned a blind eye to this sex-slave activity, but in 1900, a shearing contractor, H. Fisher, working on Durham Downs wrote directly to Archibald Meston, the well-known Protector of Aborigines. Fisher stated that the Black women were graded into three classes: the stud gins reserved for the sole use of the boss, the second class of gins for use of colonial experience men and the third class for general use by labourers. At the end of the shearing season the gins were turned away until they needed to be rounded up again.

The present author met personally with Mary Durack at her Perth home many years later, specifically to discuss this matter of the Durack's record of labour management. Mary recognised that Alice's three books, "Our Channel Country" (1962), "Where Strange Paths Go Down" (1964) and "Where Strange Gods Call" (1968) had done much more for reconciliation than her own "Kings in Grass Castles" (1959) had.

Mary knew that William Duncan had regarded it as an uncontestable fact that Aboriginals were the rightful owners of the land on which the squatters ran their stock. He would refer to the Elders as 'landlords' and he epitomised what Earl Grey of the Colonial Office had instructed the Queensland government to do, namely to respect the hunting and living rights of the Blacks on pastoral leases. Those who drove the Karuwali off, Duncan referred to as 'usurpers and trespassers'. He even accepted the Elders' decision on where the Moonaberrie homestead should be located. In addition, the Duncans respected the Elder's wishes that Whites stay away from certain secret ceremony sites. This mutual respect allowed the Duncans to benefit from the Aboriginals' weather forecasting, advanced warning of floods and drought – based on animal,

## THE PAST: WOMEN'S VIEW OF THE FRONTIER LEGEND

plant and insect indicators. They advised accurately on the reliability of each waterhole and guided the stockmen through the almost impenetrable Lignum swamps of the Cooper. Their advice on the longevity of ephemeral grasses and herbs was of inestimable value to decisions on stock movement. No wonder the Duncans killed two beasts every month for their labourers and teachers.

Alice Duncan-Kemp was apparently given to visionary experiences – an inner voice telling her to go amongst these people and record their knowledge before it was too late. She was also able to gain greater insight into Aboriginal customs, beliefs and worldview through Moses, a local Black who was sent to boarding school in Adelaide, and returned with the ability to bridge the cultural divide in the most unusual way. Moses with his new-found settler education succeeded in his dual culture, unlike other educated Blacks who were not socially accepted by the White pastoralists of the Cooper area, and also "alienated from Black life" in Watson's words. Moses became initiated and traditionally educated as a Karuwali male and became an important tribal spokesperson. He married Maggie, a skilled stockwoman, but he was alienated from the more anti-pastoralist tribes in the area. Moses was important to Alice as a writer, in the manner in which he was able to challenge settler values and his unique ability to give her an appreciation of the value of his culture. After some years of learning from the discomfort of the sort of "dual citizenship" which the Duncans began to be known for, they were seen as the most unusual example of enlightened cross-cultural understanding.

Alice Duncan-Kemp's writing was able to construct the Aboriginal people as "intelligent members of a culture that is both complex and alien (to Whites)". As Watson puts it, she graphically conveys "the anxiety and bewilderment felt by isolated White individuals attempting to negotiate their way in this totally unfamiliar situation…..In putting tribal people back into this picture, she created one of the few interesting sagas about pioneering in Australia".

So why is this Channel Country saga of importance to anyone but social anthropologists today? Firstly it explores the duplicity of the 'refined' squattocracy. Secondly it explains the faulty basis of the heroic frontier myth. Thirdly it demonstrates how, with a little education on cultural sensitivities, arrogant domineering Whites driven by their superiority, can begin to appreciate alternative worldviews. Fourthly it gives more evidence that the insight of a feminine view can successfully challenge the prevailing male stance on race relations. Fifthly it again shows how useful Aboriginal ecological knowledge was to Whites in a strange land. Lastly it confirms the power of the human spirit, driven by conscience, in initiating changed opinion even in narrow conservative societies.

These new insights are so different from those of individuals such as de Satge who produced his autobiography several years before the others and actually denied that an Indigenous population even existed in far west Queensland. He would have been surprised to find that over 100 Aboriginals had established themselves around the Lutheran Mission on the lower reaches of Cooper Creek.

Where early explorers had reported the western tribes to be no more than nomadic aimless individuals, Duncan-Kemp established for the first time that they were in fact an "integrated society governed by laws, strengthened by relevant education systems and endorsed by spiritual beliefs" as quoted by Watson. Moreover, Duncan-Kemp recorded the Aboriginals' unusually rich diversity of ways of living off the land, as well as in their philosophy and individual character.

# HISTORIC LAND RIGHTS

The response of the popular press to the successful Wik Native Title claim was very different from the response to the Mabo victory. This difference is due, according to Henry Reynolds, to the fact that in the Wik case the future of pastoral leases was at stake. Since the late 1800s, what W.E.H. Stanner referred to as The Great Australian Silence in his book "After the Dreaming" in 1968, was a major factor in distorting history and it was this silence on Indigenous rights which Reynolds blames for the degradation of the race. Stanner, in attempting to explain the loss of national memory says it was on a scale too large for simple absentmindedness. He explains it as "a view from a window which has been carefully placed to exclude a whole quadrant of the landscape (land theft and homicide). What may well have begun as a simple forgetting of other possible views, turned under habit and over time, into something like a cult of forgetfulness practiced on a national scale". Reynolds

## THE PAST: HISTORIC LAND RIGHTS

asks whether this is forgetfulness or whether generations never actually knew, especially about Land Rights.

The central case in point in Reynold's "Why Weren't We Told" (1999) is the "forgetting" by the authorities of what the British colonial government laid down regarding pastoral leaseholders rights being limited to grazing rights. In December 1996 when the High Court handed down a 4-3 majority ruling on the existence of the Wik and Thyorre peoples' Land Rights, it reflected the correct interpretation of Earl Grey's unambiguous intent in offering leasehold to pastoralists in 1848. As Secretary of State, Grey sent the following dispatch to Sydney:.. "I think it is essential that it should be generally understood that leases granted (for pastoral occupation) give the grantees only an exclusive right of pasturage…. But that the leases are not intended to deprive the natives of their former rights to these Districts, or to wander over them in search of subsistence, in the manner to which they have been heretofore accustomed…." Grey reiterated this native right in 1849, writing: "The British government did not intend and *had no power* (my emphasis) to exclude the natives from the use they had been accustomed to make of these unimproved lands". This is what colonial governments and settler organisations had "forgotten", i.e. that the Colonial Office created pastoral leases on the clear understanding that they were available for mutual use by pastoralists and the original owners. This clearly meant that pastoralists had no authority to deny access to the owners.

Sometime later the Colonial Office actually included a written clause in each lease which protected the Aboriginals' rights and "such free access to the said Run or Parcel of land….and to the trees and water thereon as will enable them to procure the animals, birds, fish and other food on which to subsist." Such clauses started in New South Wales, then Queensland and finally in Western Australia and South Australia. Each state had different wording but all meant precisely the same.

Reynolds comments on the "forgetting" of these legal clauses as follows: "The honour of both Britain and Australia was at stake – but the Aboriginal right of residence and use, was usually over-ridden by both settlers and colonial governments, and has largely been ignored in retrospect by the historians of land settlement." Reynolds points out that under the law, those leaseholders who kept the Blacks out and maintained that Blacks and cattle don't mix, were in clear contravention of their lease conditions and should by law have forfeited their leases for non-compliance of the conditions that they signed up to. Even the official statement by Walter Roth, Protector of Aborigines in North Queensland didn't stop pastoralists from "dispersing" (accepted term for shooting) the Blacks on their leases: "The principle must be rightly instilled (in pastoralists) that the Aboriginal has as much right to exist as the European, and certainly a greater right, not only to collect native fruits, but also to hunt and dispose of the game upon which they vitally depended from time immemorial."

Any student concerned with the effect of history on contemporary justice requires an answer to the question of how the colonial governments were able to get away with ignoring the Colonial Office instructions. Reynolds' research finds that Queensland began offering leases without any Aboriginal rights clause, "sometime early in the twentieth century, in circumstances which are still unknown." Whether this was an internal unrecorded decision by the Lands Department is not clear. Reynolds finds no reference in the Government Gazette or Parliamentary Debates or in Legislation passed in that era. In practice, pastoralists and their legal advisors assumed that the absence of the Aboriginal rights clause, gave them the legal right to keep the Blacks out, i.e. to ignore Native Title. [The present author's search of the Queensland archives shows no leases with the Aboriginal Rights clause, at least not after 1878.]

It was thus a shock to rural Queensland and its government when the High Court saw things differently. The judges ruled 4 to 3 that if the Aboriginal right (Native Title) had been extinguished, government would have recorded this in formal lease condition regulations. In addition, the Court found that the pastoral lease documents did not preclude Native Title and had clearly-worded limits to the uses to which lessees could put such land. Finally, the High Court judges determined that the rights of Aboriginals had not been created by the court but that Native Title was an ancient title which had only now (1996) been re-discovered as the oldest continuing land tenure system on the planet.

Why is this historic ruling of importance to contemporary Queensland? In essence, because pastoralists, who for generations had acted as though they owned the land, were publicly reminded that land use rights on leasehold properties were not only limited, but the ruling demonstrated to the nation that pastoralists had been acting illegally for a century. As a seminal truth, this recognition is the single most far-reaching development in Aboriginal Land Rights progress.

For policy students still unconvinced of the size and duration of the Lawyers' Picnic which is Native Title claims, look no further than Simon Young's book 'The Trouble with Tradition' (2008). The reader is left wondering whose responsibility it is to curb the appetite of this un-satiated legal beast which just keeps devouring valuable dollars and time, taking nine years on average to settle each case. Why it took a quarter of a century to drop the obviously fraught 'continuous possession' requirement is beyond belief.

# VICTORIA RIVER WALK-OFF: HINGE OF HISTORY

The present author was privileged to have met the Dagura people in 1972 at Wattie Creek where they had gathered after walking off Vestey's Stations in the Victoria River District that year. In detailing the significance of this protest, Doolan (1977) rates it as "a period during which Aboriginal people of the area have probably done more through their own efforts to secure for themselves a better way of life, as they see it, than during any other period since occupation by Whites in the early 1800's". In March 1972 the Gurindji had walked off the VRD outstations Moolooloo, Pigeon Hole and Mount Sanford and headed for Wattie Creek (Dagararu) where an earlier walk-off from VRD in 1966 had created this camp. They insisted that they would not return until they were given certain tribal lands back, although the reasons for the walk-off were wages, housing, social service cheques and interference with their women.

When the present author visited Wattie Creek he was met by a White woman who spoke on behalf of the people. Doolan notes that other Europeans in the area had encouraged the Gurindji to walk-off in protest. Vincent Lingiari was the active leader of the protestors but he was advised by Charcoal 'the manager' and Big Mick 'the lawyer' representing at least six clans from the Victoria and Humbert Rivers. What this protest group wanted was a place of their own where they could run their own cattle and hold their own ceremonies. Interestingly, they made it clear that they "wished to have as little contact as possible with Europeans in the future", according to Doolan.

# BLACK CHEERS AND THREE ARM BANDS: USING HISTORY TO PROCLAIM MORALITY

When launching Tom Keneally's book "Australians: Origins to Eureka", Prime Minister Rudd was on a hiding to nothing when he ventured into his homemade view of the "history wars" (a subset of the culture wars). Having tired of the 'arid intellectual debates of the history wars' he wanted to move ahead. Rudd invited the nation to move beyond the conflicting Three Cheers view and the Black Armband view. He wanted Australia to celebrate the good and explore the bad. Most observers may have thought this a reasonable and widely acceptable sentiment, but professionals like Greg Melleuish, historian at Wollongong University, reminded us that history is not about moral judgments; it's about correctly interpreting the evidence.

What has this event got to do with Aboriginal disadvantage? It reflects the way in which stereotypical identities have come to dominate the Australian psyche on the good guys and the bad guys, the superior and inferior self-image of White and Black Australians which is reflected in reconciliation, voting, policy formulation and funding. Says Melleuish: "Unfortunately, Rudd's speech does nothing to assist Australia's history wars to move from an unhealthy obsession with cheering and booing the past, to one in which there is informed intellectual debate. If anything, his speech encourages the unhelpful idea that the real purpose of history is to serve moral and political concerns."

# THE PRESENT

## ABORIGINAL IDENTITY

In 1977 the Australian Institute of Aboriginal Studies in Canberra collated a number of papers on Indigenous identity as a subset of a broader consideration of "Aboriginals and Change".

In placing this concept within the narrative of this review, the present author could justifiably place it in past, present and future sections. Equally one could argue that Aboriginal identity is no business of non-Aboriginals and can only meaningfully be fully discussed and evaluated by the subject people themselves. The present author rejects that view for two reasons:

1. The Indigenous people's own failure to define their identity (and values) to date, has been unhelpful, indicating that they could benefit from outside help;
2. Numerous outsiders have wide experience with Indigenous peoples in various countries and can recommend from experience, the strengths and weaknesses of cultural Imperialism as applied at various levels elsewhere.

Identity however can, and often has, become a somewhat nebulous concept susceptible to seemingly endless abstract debate. For instance, the idea of social identity seems to be understood as the 'role pattern' in terms of reciprocal rights and duties, held by a group of persons within a given cultural framework. It is a behaviour regulator which is to some extent both measurable and predictable according to Kolig (in Berndt 1977).

The present author has attempted to cut to the chase in his "Fair Go" paper, by suggesting that group identity can most meaningfully be defined in terms of the values which that group holds dear; e.g. The Ten Commandments or the Sermon on the Mount. However, there is a very long list of anthropologists and sociologists whose extensive writings easily convince one that this approach is simplistic and inadequate.

In "Fair Go" the author suggests that European Australians in a general kind of way know what they stand for, what's right or wrong, and they believe their culture deserves the respect which they keep demanding. This in turn leads to a further question which asks whether simply being ancient is sufficient grounds for respect in this day and age.

So why is identity important in considering Aboriginal futures? Because it defines, drives and limits the goals and progress of the society concerned. In practice, it is the lack of agreement on "who we are and what we want" which is at the root of the stagnation of Indigenous progress. At stake is the appropriate cultural intensity which, at the extremes, promotes or prevents group well-being through culture's potential effect on education, health and wealth-generation.

It is unlikely that we shall find early agreement on the details of Aboriginal identity, for *Homo sociologicus* has contrasted with other forms of human identity ever since Kant's moral man was agreed to be incompatible with Hegel's social man. This is not the place to re-examine the differing views of self in the Freudian sense, but simply to acknowledge both the difference and authenticity of the anthropological and social concepts of this elusive concept of personal identity. So perhaps we should simply agree that social man should be able to recognise the identity which binds him to others rather than separates him as a unique individual. In addition we might assume that the finding of meaning in life is difficult in the absence of relations to others, although creative loners tend to disprove such an assumption. Kolig suggests that "The emergent Aboriginal identity (late 1970s) is one of socio-political contrast vis-à-vis the unwanted dominance by racial aliens". In one sense the creation of an Aboriginal identity is a very un-Aboriginal process, for which there is no historical substructure. Perhaps dark-skinned oppressed Indigenous populations all over the world have developed a belated identity as "First Nation" through which racial solidarity can be nurtured.

Von Sturmer, after studying the way in which Aboriginal identity in Cape York had changed with time (1973), is rather blunt in his assessment, saying "Aboriginality is a fiction which takes on meaning only in terms of

## THE PRESENT: ABORIGINAL IDENTITY

White ethnocentrism". Regarding the culturally sensitive concept of identity as a myth, causes those who have tired of the culture wars, to suggest that Aboriginals "get over it and get on with it." One reading of Tugby's book "Aboriginal Identity in Contemporary Australia" (1973) on this subject easily convinces the reader that chasing cultural rainbows can only lead to frustration.

The White ethnocentrism which Von Sturmer refers to, seems to have had two sides to it. As shown by Tonkinson, who studied the locals' reaction to the Apostolic Mission at Jigalong in Western Australia, these "Christians" (Missionaries) were regarded differently from the "Whitefella" outside the missions. Studies showed that the churchmen were regarded as anti-Aboriginal (in language, custom and law), tight-fisted, joyless and unfriendly. Whitefellas on the other hand were "judged individually, as good or bad or a bit of both depending on their treatment of Aboriginals" (Tonkinson 1977). This opinion is at odds with many other authors who record the "mission as refuge" phenomenon in cruel settler country.

Kolig may be correct when he suggests that tribal identities, so essential to the Elders, have largely become devoid of meaning for Aborigines under twenty-five years of age. It seems self-evident that societal identity needs to reflect two attributes if it is to survive (remain 'sustainable' in modern parlance):

1. It must distinguish between the needs/values of the elder generation and those of the up-and-coming generation, and
2. It must continuously adapt and modify if it is to be useful to its practitioners.

Both these requirements are essential if Aboriginal culture and its associated personal identity are to serve the well-being of its members well into the future. Berndt (1971) believes that people of Aboriginal descent, especially in southern States "are for all practical purposes Australian-Europeans, their knowledge of traditional Aboriginal heritage is not at first hand and indeed for most of them it is far removed". Berndt suggests that despite this distance from their Aboriginal past, they still seek common identity in that era. However, they want only the idea of it, because anything closer to traditional actuality (lifestyle) "would find them completely at sea".

It may be simplistic to compartmentalise Aboriginal development into three obvious time zones but if the health / education / housing framework and the identity/autonomy/Homelands issues are to be dealt with in a meaningful way, integrated time zones form the best basis for proper analysis.

The past has been dealt with here in the form of a historic narrative of how Aboriginals originally lived and what the effects of White incursion were on their lifestyle and values. The present can be dealt with as a period starting from 2000 as an arbitrary date and dealing with the events and changes during the decade starting at about that date. The alternative mark often used in tracing Indigenous progress is to recognise particular events, such as Mabo or Wik Native Title decisions and refer to pre-and-post periods such as the Whitlam era or the Howard era. Most researchers recognise that the fortunes of the Aboriginal people were centrally influenced by the ruling philosophy of the day and its effect through policy on the fortunes of Indigenous communities. Yet another appropriate alternative basis for Aboriginal study is the geographical division of Remote, Regional Town and City community distinction.

The present author recognises Noel Pearson as one of several Aboriginal voices which have made an impact on public opinion since the 1980's. In fact one of the problems with getting a clear view of Indigenous opinion, has been the tendency for the public and the government to assess the value of Indigenous spokespersons' utterances and the values they portray, by the person rather than by the intrinsic value of the concepts espoused. Thus by prefacing any policy statement with "according to Noel Pearson, Mick Dodson, Marcia Langton, Michael Mansell or Warren Mundine" the objective consideration of what follows is often compromised.

# PATERNALISM AS A RESPONSE TO VULNERABLE TRADITION

Catherine Berndt in 1977 gave some valuable insights into Whites' views of Aboriginal culture and its worth. As an experienced field anthropologist, Berndt was among the first few Whites able to understand Black aspirations: "Many [White] people disparaged Aboriginal culture. Even the few who did

## THE PRESENT: PATERNALISM...RESPONSE TO VULNERABLE TRADITION

not, could see no place for any of it in the new style of life they anticipated for Aborigines. As a rule they do not say so publicly .... but for the majority of other Australians, Aborigines are outside the range of ordinary living – irrelevant to it, or regarded as if they ought to be."

Berndt reminds us that, when anthropologists in the 1930's to 1950's pressed for the safeguarding of Aboriginal Reserves, they were accused of supporting a policy of Apartheid. They were alleged to be interested in research, not welfare or at the expense of welfare. In defence of anthropologists, Berndt says, "The main aim was to provide at least some Aborigines with a spatial buffer against the kind of fate that was overtaking so many others and to increase Aborigines' chance of being able to decide for themselves what their relations to other Australians might be". The Berndts' plea in 1954 regarding the Gove Peninsula was that "Arnhem Land must remain a country for the Arnhemlanders alone". This was in response to persistent calls since the 1940's to set up a tourist village at each Mission Station and to open the land to crocodile hunters. Looking back, the Berndts must be credited with being first in articulating pride in Aboriginality among the White community. Apart from the White's settlement schemes for Blacks, there was a "threat from within their own society – the Trojan Horse of the young people who were enticed by the prospect of brighter lights and greener pastures. Aboriginal children who go to country towns and cities for schooling and employment or training are no more likely than other outback children to return permanently to what they came to see as isolated areas – not if they can avoid it". In this view Berndt is repeating the sentiment that a good home should develop both roots and wings in children.

It seems that the Aboriginals have always been realistic about the inter-generational inheritance of their culture. They didn't expect culture and knowledge to be transmitted genetically or mystically as in their genes. For this reason they worked constantly at actively teaching the coming generations, but White interference interrupted and destroyed this learning process to a point where most young Aboriginals reportedly reflect little knowledge of, or interest in, the customs and values of their Elders. This was the Berndts' finding in many districts of Northern Australia over a period of decades.

Catherine Berndt notes that even when the population decline had been reversed, the culture still seemed to be doomed: "That trend has been checked too, but the rate of the cultural revival has not kept pace with the public interest in it (as at 1977) – or rather in sentimental ideas about it or in congenial bits of it; art and dance for example, and 'closeness to nature'. Traditionally-oriented Aborigines have achieved a 'good' image. So has their culture, seen as a simple but appealing and ulcer-free type of adaptation to the natural and social environment".

This acceptance of Aboriginal culture as simple and appealing, remains the source of political conflict 40 years later. There is however a dilemma regarding the selection or retention of some traits and customs which form a consciously constructed and recognised culture as compared to actually living a real culture as a way of life. From this dilemma arises the artificiality of generalising cultural images, habits and icons as if regional differences can be blended into a generic representation of Aboriginality.

# FORCED SEPARATION OR FORCED INTEGRATION: LOSE – LOSE

Any attempt to suggest "a most appropriate" social policy for the Aboriginal future, must recognise the dangers of a single choice, especially if that choice is imposed by another social group.

Tatz (1977) and others with a personal knowledge of Apartheid including the present author (Roberts 2008), have examined the problems of eliminating choice on the part of individuals, in the determination of racial policy by governments. Tatz maintains that these basic problems cannot be overcome by changes in political philosophy, abolition of discriminatory legislation, new human rights bills, revamped institutional structures or the infusion of funds:

1. The first problem is the way Whites talk about Blacks rather than with them so that the Blacks can act of their own behalf.
2. The second problem is "the cultural impossibility, for most Whites, of evincing empathy rather than sympathy" for Black viewpoints on their consciousness, identity, alienation and deprivation, and the frustration arising from this combination of emotions.
3. The third problem is the improbability of Whites ever comprehending,

> let alone conceding, that a major avenue for Black survival (as a people) and progress, is their rejection of White society and its values, together with the programmes which Whites develop for Blacks' benefit.

Tatz, a long time advocate for the underdog, is critical of the way that all the Indigenous policy conferences at national level have been White-centered operations – 1937, 1951, 1961, 1963, 1965 and the Woodward Commission of 1974 all emphasised the White view of what the Aborigines needed. He suggests that group cohesion and identity is strengthened by persecution, massacre and violent clash as elements of a common past. Tatz says that these experiences "are often the social cement that holds an identity together." (as Tatz knows from personal experience as a former member of a South African minority)

Two South African writers regard Black consciousness as a revival of what is termed 'negritude' – Nardine Gordimer and Alan Paton, liberal thinkers who could later take considerable credit for the rise of Mandela two decades later. Gordimer maintains that rejection of Whites is a sign of a 'healthy negritude.' Paton suggests that Black leaders can only be satisfied for a limited period with "a mush" of culture, mysticism and lyricism, before they realise that real power means having much more than vague philosophies. By 1970 Rowley was able to record that: "The Aboriginal voice is now continuous and this in itself is indicative of a growing confidence and a potential for leadership". By the 1972 Federal election, Labour's call was that they would solve the Aboriginal problem and "we will *grant Land Rights*" (my emphasis).

There has always been a problem with how to cater for urban Aborigines – the Redfern Mob is often used as a case study in this matter. Anthropologists seem to have dominated the futures debate on remote communities while sociologists seem to have led the debate on urban futures. So? So Australia is left with a confused view of whether the concept of Aboriginality indeed needs to be treated differently when the people are distanced from the land, customs and language which constitute the heart of their Aboriginality. This divide is likely to change in the future as a result of the rising urban population relative to the Aboriginal population overall.

Makin, in a PhD study of urbanised Aboriginals in Perth in 1970, illustrated the complexities and value shifts which occur when bush people move to town and generational watering-down of 'links to country' changes the aspirations of the emerging society. This complexity had been taken a step further by Eckermann back in 1933 in a study of Aboriginal societies in industrial and town situations. Eckermann makes an interesting comparison with other working class people, suggesting that only their ethnic origin and colour is what differentiates Aboriginals from the others in south-east Queensland. Eckermann notes that all these 'battlers' share many negative attributes not related to race, i.e. low education levels, financial insecurity, low occupational status and use of alcohol. Working-class people strive to be equal but have feelings of inadequacy and thus rejection of achievement-oriented values, but Aborigines are affected not only by the these sentiments but also by Whites' paternalism, discrimination, distrust and even hostility. This makes them not simply poor, as in poor Whites, but somehow allows them to see their Aboriginality as something positive – some quality which no Whites can claim – pride in 'colour' and all its traditional ethnic origins.

This early tendency to regard colour as an asset rather than a social negative, is the basis of how Aboriginality has increasingly become a badge of honour in recent years. This is a far cry from what Lickiss found when studying the lack of pride amongst urban (Sydney) Aboriginal children several decades ago. Robert McKeich took this complexity and identity confusion a step further in a 1971 study of education of children of mixed parentage. He points out not only that these people have a problem but are regarded as being a problem because their values and ways are not the ways of the mainstream. McKeich produces an impressive literature review of research into racial intelligence and motivation and maintains that part-Aboriginals have unconsciously constructed their own worldview. Their world and values arise from this construction.

This research showed that the part-Aboriginal subset of Australian society held views that were much the same as those of the population at large with its Western Christian morals. Positive traits of the 'ideal person' were listed by this subset as those who have a job, are polite and well-mannered, are tidy, clean, neat, kind, hard-working, sociable and show character and personality. In addition their ideal person was, as they were, part-Aboriginal, although shade of colour was unimportant. Unsurprisingly they regarded as negative, those who drank, smoked, fought, were lazy, grumbled and used bad language. Also negative, were people who were dishonest, selfish or snobbish. Even larrikinism was frowned on.

This analysis and value-formation exercise is of particular personal interest. The present author asked in his 'Fair Go' paper, "What are the values of today's Aboriginals, what do they stand for by way of personal attributes?" The author suspected that at basic level, the fundamental values of global humanity would be reflected in Aboriginal values. In addition he didn't believe such generic goodness would reduce the significance of Indigenous culture as a set of traditional beliefs worthy of preservation. That is not to say that certain customs and behaviours related to the treatment of women and commitment to income generation did not need updating to meet modern Aboriginals' needs. On the contrary, this modernising and fine-tuning of cultural values allows today's communities to take the best from their past and build on it, as suggested in 'Fair Go'. This conscious selective approach to cultural inheritance has had positive outcomes for many cultures, including the dominant Anglo-Saxon tradition, which benefits from a latter-day admission that the Crusades for instance, reflected an intolerance and violence unbecoming of members of a sustainable global society.

The periodic re-appearance of traditional Luddites in the current 'culture wars' do their constituents no favours by insisting on maintaining, and in some cases artificially resurrecting, inappropriate practices and values simply because they are time-honoured. Examples of this drag on well-being include promised young brides, polygamy, exclusion of women from education opportunities, violence norms and work ethics, all of which appear to have customary backing.

# UNBEING: THE FLIP-SIDE OF BEING A CHANGED INDIVIDUAL

One informed commentator has noted that new identity and group loyalty develop as a result of two simultaneous processes: one is being someone new, the other is 'unbeing' what you were. Taking on the new identity is difficult for traditional people, but letting go of the old identity is even more difficult.

## OVERCOMING DISADVANTAGE

Why? Because most individuals unconsciously seek refuge in their cultural identity – it's where they belong, where they're comfortable, where they're safe.

This form of reducing personal risk by remaining within one's comfort zone is not only natural and predictable but is underestimated by many commentators, including the present author, as the prime factor constraining the transition of Aboriginal adults to mainstream values and lifestyles. It is for this reason that the social engineers in government must be dissuaded from pretending that all that needs to be done is to create the right environment and incentives to help Aboriginal adults join the mainstream. Unbeing is much, much more difficult than policy-makers presume. However, younger people, especially the very young, are much more able to take up different values and norms. (The Catholic Church has used this 'catch them young' idea for centuries.)

So what's the relevance of unbeing to policy? Clearly the point at which to break the poverty/ignorance cycle is in early childhood. With all the emphasis on 'capacity building' during the past decade, there has been a focus on skills, resources and infrastructure as the necessary basis for national and sectional progress. Nothing wrong with that, but the over-optimism on Aboriginal individual's ability to actually build personal capacity has too often resulted in grave disappointment.

Such apparent incapacity should not be misread as a racial weakness but rather it should help to concentrate attention on the young. The young carry no preconceived ideas of limited potential or debilitating victimhood and do not inherit historic disadvantage in their DNA. Given the chance, they can form their own worldview, invent their own challenges and form their own sense of values. But they need to be exposed to enlightened ways of thinking and doing, because new thinking is not *sui generis* (or self-made) – it needs exemplars, role models, demonstrations and collegial case studies. Indigenous sportspeople have shown how innate ability, given encouragement and coaching can make world-beaters – from Goolagong to Freeman, from Ella to Meninga, Indigenous sporting capacity was built to make them the pride of the nation. There is no reason why this can't also happen in the intellectual and professional field. While there may have been some historic 'Jacky-Jacky' element to the first Aboriginal appointments to senior University posts, the stage is set for a great influx of Indigenous thinkers in the coming years.

THE PRESENT: THREATS TO ABORIGINAL CULTURE

# WHAT IS IT THAT THREATENS ABORIGINAL CULTURE?

Originally the threats to culture were a combination of murderous pastoralists, ruthless miners, Native Police and, in a different way, the Missionaries. To the Missions credit, when the extent of murder and brutal treatment by the settler population and their police became overwhelming, the Missions and later the Reserves, became a last refuge for a people under siege. As an alternative to certain brutality and almost certain death, the Missionaries discipline, work programs and compulsory services were a strange but welcome relief.

This frontier situation was followed by the threat of apathy and disinterest from government in the housing, health and education of Aborigines, especially in remote areas. Under conditions in which tribal discipline and custom were difficult to maintain, when hunting and gathering were not possible and when alcohol became freely available, the threats to culture and language changed from earlier imposed violence to later domestic violence. Today the threats are largely in the hands of the Aboriginal people themselves.

A review of the laws, regulations and support systems suggest that there has been a significant effort during the past two decades at least, to offer government support to a beleaguered people. Politicians proudly quote the funds approved for infrastructure and services and repeatedly give the impression that progress and well-being are now up to the communities themselves.

So in present times, a few basic questions become relevant before the current threats to Aboriginal culture/identity can be considered. These should be answered by the Indigenous people themselves:

1. Why do we want to conserve and nurture the culture? What are the benefits to the nation overall, of rescuing and maintaining this culture? What are its values? How would these values enrich the nation? Who should decide these things?

2. If the benefits of cultural preservation are agreed to warrant effort, funds and time, how should this culture be defined? How should its values and morals be described, scoped and taught? And who should

decide, who should pay and who should advise?
3. Does cultural rescue and propagation require geographic anchoring, land-based practices and customs, and access to remote sacred sites? Does the cultural group need to own the land concerned? Does it need to be autonomous?

In summary, is it worth saving, what's it consist of, and where should it happen? All these questions relate to culture, but is it not more beneficial to the race concerned to approach their well-being, not from a cultural preservation objective, but by asking "What's best for this race, irrespective of culture"? The answer may have a greater or lesser (or no) cultural content and would value culture relative to other attributes of well-being.

The third approach beyond the cultural and well-being elements of the race concerned, is based on the agreement on national goals and the determination of how the race, as a population subset, could contribute to and benefit from nation-wide aims. Doug Cocks of CSIRO in his book "Use With Care" was the first to attempt a cataloguing of productive, environmental and social goals for Australia. One of his social goals is a prosperous future for the Aboriginals, together with a tolerant and co-operative multicultural national population. (See Section 1 Appendix II.)

# CARING/SHARING AND RESPECT FOR NATURE

We need to get The Knowledge into modern perspective. Demographers have long debated the extent to which Aboriginal natural harvest methods were successful as a survival strategy only as long as population pressure was below ecosystem productivity levels. The Knowledge, as passed down through the generations, applied to the subsistence of small numbers of people lacking the mechanical and chemical technology necessary to boost production and the capacity to damage ecosystems. The Knowledge on fire management was aimed at food production irrespective of 'detrimental' changes in tree/grass balance, fire-prone species of animals and preservation of threatened species. The jury is still out on the extent to which Aboriginal fire and hunting has

## THE PRESENT: CARING/SHARING AND RESPECT FOR NATURE

caused species extinction in the way large flightless birds were eliminated from Mauritius and New Zealand.

Many thousands of years ago the tool-making primate was able to gain advantage over other carnivores through the use of crude weapons and fire. While their capacity to forage and nurture their young was akin to other advanced animals, their ability to expand their population was, as with other species, dependent on food supply and immunity to disease. The survival knowledge which accumulated was based on superior hunting ability and, as a result of inability to control Nature, a respect for both the forces and the fruitfulness of the Earth.

It is argued by ecologists that many survival techniques can work while ever human population is low and technological damage is minimal. It is deduced from this, that as numbers of people and thus harvest intensity increase, so the need for population control becomes essential to survival. The concurrent advance in technology in hunting, plant production and harvest then becomes a parallel danger to the long term productivity of ecosystems. Eventually neither resource destruction nor pollution can be controlled without population control.

The Aboriginal knowledge never allowed their society to be subjected to the "Tragedy of the Commons" – the classical paradigm in which each family grazes more cattle on the communal grazinglands until they collapse. In Australian continental terms, the population pressure never reached critical levels. When Europeans arrived that all changed. Not because of people numbers but because of hard-hoofed domestic animals, ringbarking and the plough.

What has this to do with The Knowledge? First, it shows that returning to 'living in harmony with Nature' in the primitive way is not possible with present numbers and their associated demand for food. That is not to say that sustainable agriculture is not possible with considered population and immigration policy. What it does mean is that Aboriginal knowledge can contribute to both the philosophical and practical approach to resources. It can teach our dominating technical society that ultimately we are dependent on the environment for our future and for this reason alone, respect for Nature becomes the secret of long-term success. It can also teach that caring and sharing in a low consumption, low polluting global comminity is ultimately the only way out for a previously destructive society.

In this way the 'quaint myths of the savages' as they were regarded by early observers, do full circle and become the essence of future wisdom in a very different world. Recognising that Aboriginals have no monopoly over other ancient cultures in valuing 'the Golden Rule' of 'doing unto others', the example Indigenous people set in communal sharing must eventually be recognised as the key plank in society's survival platform.

Without wanting to devalue human achievement, viewed cosmically, *Homo sapiens* has no greater right or chance of survival in universal time, than other living species – but let's not spoil our 'God-given' story of being the chosen few. Instead let's use the knowledge to pursue our time-limited horizons. Let's now attempt to value this knowledge for future use.

# THE KNOWLEDGE – WHAT'S IT WORTH?

The antiquity and complexity of local Indigenous knowledge of nature and how ecosystems function, are almost without international peer. While every effort should be made to record and interpret this unique dataset, its continued application by modern Indigenous communities will require realism and acceptance of the need for future lifestyles which enhance modern well-being.

Apparently each language has developed over eons of survival within a particular eco-system or eco-region. In this context the clan language group has developed a unique code for interpreting their particular habitat. Such codes are apparently very different from the way scientists structure their ecological studies. The Knowledge must have originally had an essential survival value and have been passed down the generations without ever having been written down for use by outsiders or preservation for the clan. The way in which local knowledge was developed for the specific locality (tribal lands) did not allow for generalisation or the construction of generic principles. So while there may be knowledge similarities when clan language areas are compared, if Western understanding of traditional ecological knowledge (TEK) is to be gained, it will need to be studied and interpreted on at least a regional, and perhaps sub-regional scale.

## THE PRESENT: THE KNOWLEDGE – WHAT'S IT WORTH?

To some who highly value TEK for its own sake, the loss of continued widespread practice of Knowledge on country, is regarded as an unacceptable end to at least 40,000 years of unique tradition. For others, an immediate comprehensive recording and interpretation program in the regions will ensure both preservation of this huge volume of information and the opportunity for the coming generations to benefit from modern lifestyles, knowing that their ancient learning is safe.

In practice, the reality is that for some years now a significant proportion of the young men and women have reflected a waning interest in learning TEK from their Elders. Apparently in some regions the effect of outside influences has been so overwhelming that not only are knowledgeable Elders becoming scarce, but young ones have shown an increasing attraction to European ways – music, sport, clothes, food, drinks, transport, firearms, chainsaws, Toyotas (their generic term for 4WD vehicles) mobile phones, the world wide web and drugs.

There is however, another very important aspect of The Knowledge in its original form as a central vehicle connecting humans to the earth. The primeval link between knowledge and survival (use of fire, identifying edible plants, understanding animal behaviour) may have an eternal application for future humankind's survival on a dynamic planet. The old adage that man only begets wisdom when he has no option, may just have become a reality, thanks to global warming.

Within this link to land is a spiritual grounding in the earth which has always given the Aborigines both their identity and perhaps more psychologically important, their sense of belonging. Many observers have claimed that it was the breaking of this bond which is at the heart of Indigenous dysfunction. By inferring that stealing their land also stole their very being, as grounded people, this claim warrants serious consideration. At the centre of the idea of sacred sites or mother earth, is a learned respect for Nature. In this enculturation process, the youth have always been imbued with the understanding that they are not only dependent on, but are also an integral part of, the ecosystem.

The phrase 'mother earth' has been attributed to several ancient societies, including Chief Seattle's Indians, but the Australian tribes have been valuing and surviving on this dependency concept since long before the first Sumarian civilisation. Virtually all ecologists and environmentally-informed sociologists now refer to mother earth as their way of recognising and promoting the need for environmentally-friendly lifestyles. Before the great awakening of developed societies to the survival value of eco-living, modern economies discounted the impacts of production and consumption on mother earth. All of a sudden Herman Daly's Steady State Economy of the 1970's is trendy, as is the ingrained natural respect of the Indigenes for the Earth.

To date, White Australians have been interested almost solely in the utilitarian value of TEK, that is, the extent to which Indigenous knowledge could augment scientific knowledge to improve activities such as short term weather forecasting, fire management, pharmaceutical exploration, inshore marine management, new food sources, natural fibres, woodwind music, animated dance routines, diet and language codes.

However, there is also the intrinsic value of knowledge – its value in and of itself as a unique cultural artefact, irrespective of its usefulness to modern society. Such intrinsic value is responsible for all the world's museums, galleries, collections and exhibitions of art, history and culture. As one of the oldest living cultures on earth, Australian Aboriginality has perhaps one of the strongest cases of all, to be permanently preserved for appreciation by future generations. This does not imply that contemporary Aborigines need to be encouraged to live as hunter-gatherers. On the contrary, with funding, cooperation and appropriate recording and interpretation, today's urban descendants of the Myalls can lead the urgent campaign to capture The Knowledge forever. Time is of the essence, however.

When considering the cultural significance of loss of traditional knowledge, observers might well compare this loss with that of the changes in Anglo-Saxon tradition. Many who were brought up in the Christian-Shakespeare culture would regard the demise of these teachings (Whitefella knowledge?) in contemporary school curricula, as a serious loss of the richness of English tradition, which affects the very heart of their identity as a proud ethnic group. The reason for this, when one looks beyond the predictable personal emotion of who one is, can be found in the belief that English literature (including the King James Bible) at its best, offers the most useful guidelines for moral and respectable living – the English equivalent of other noble cultures in the East.

The comparison of Aboriginal and English cultural loss immediately

## THE PRESENT: THE KNOWLEDGE – WHAT'S IT WORTH?

brings up one major difference – the total dependence of Indigenous culture on the oral tradition, supplemented by visual art, as methods of inter-generational transfer. Without the Magna Carta, the Domesday Book, Westminster, Caxton's Press and The Bible Society, as cornerstones, the transmission of Aboriginality needed the invention of alternative cultural vehicles.

There will forever be the problem of cultural superiority as a worldview of those dependent on ethnic identity for their personal self-confidence. It should thus not come as a surprise that Europhiles could regard Aboriginal culture with some disdain. – "What is there to respect in a tribal tradition which has no written language, no literature, no religious texts?" they ask. Regarding illiterate 'savages' as being at the far end of the cultural spectrum comes naturally to those imbued with their own superiority.

Against this comparative background, the contemporary 'cultural relativism' offers a means by which different cultures can be appreciated using differentiated criteria, i.e. acceptance of the approach which considers cultures as richly different, rather than better or worse. Apples and oranges both appreciated. While such non-comparisons have their appeal, the tendency to regard 'primitive' cultures as quaint but hardly useful to modern society, persists. As the present author noted in his "Fair Go" paper, being first or oldest, doesn't seem sufficient an attribute to command respect from other cultures.

In practice, such an either/or choice of valuable cultures is not valid, nor is the assumption that cultures remain static, locked in time. Rather than being mutually exclusive and unchanging, Australian society could benefit from the diverse richness of its ever-evolving cultures. Beside Anglo and Aboriginal, at least 90 other Migrant cultures add to the flavours of this 'cultural soup' – all contributing in their unique way.

So what has this cultural relevance got to do with The Knowledge? In short, Aboriginal experience over the millennia brings appreciations of three types: survival knowledge, cultural knowledge and spiritual knowledge. Such appreciation should value the modern dynamics which develop some symbols beyond their historic use. So the critics of the commercial dot-paintings, white handprints and red dance pants should be careful not to discourage the growing pride and associated well-being which comes from expansion of the visual and performing arts.

## OVERCOMING DISADVANTAGE

It is interesting to compare the Aboriginal knowledge of plants with the earliest of the English Herbals – 16th century descriptions and drawings of an enormous range of medicinal herbs. Similarly a comparison can be made of The Dreamtime creation stories of the Rainbow Serpent and Fire Mountains, with the Genesis story and the Sermon on the Mount as cultural cornerstones. None of these stories need be true in their alleged origins, to be useful groundings for modern beings.

The bottom line is, as with threatened species, since we're unaware of the importance of what we're losing, there is an urgency to preserve, record and interpret those elements of knowledge which are on the brink of extinction. Just do it!

# LESSONS FROM WIK FAMILIES

Although Queensland has a population of over 13,000 Aboriginals in the Cape York region (north of Port Douglas), few Aboriginal writers have recorded their family's story in this far northern region. One exception is Fiona Doyle's (Oochunyung) account of her grandmother Jean George (Awunpun), who was a major player in the Wik Native Title Claim. Doyle's book titled "Whispers of this Wik Woman" (2004) is a good example of how former mission children not only led their people's future struggles for equality, but having the advantages of literacy allowed them to articulate the Aboriginal world view in the Whiteman's courts.

Because of her childhood at Weipa South (Napranum) and Aurukun on Cape York, Doyle is able to relate firsthand the way in which hunter-gathers, over a period of only a few generations, had to adapt to a whole new world. What comes through so strongly in Doyle's account of her Nana's tale, is how she repeatedly reflects on the extent to which the very strong sense of identity seemed to enable her to overcome what today is referred to as "post-traumatic stress disorder". Add to this the "inter-generational trauma" and Doyle's family history becomes a living breathing case study in how the human spirit can triumph against all odds.

An important issue raised by Doyle is the evidence of tribal claim to Indigenous land – not simply generic claim but claim at tribe, clan, language

## THE PRESENT: LESSONS FROM WIK FAMILIES

group and family level. The family relationships that make up the so-called "moiety" links between individuals are so complex that few if any Whites, anthropologists included, actually grasp the meaning of the network of relationships across families, generations and genders. In this way great-grand-mothers and fathers are referred to as sisters and brothers. In Nana we have a contemporary example of Elders who always address their ancestral spirits (the "Old People") when they enter sacred places in their clan country. She also continues to make the younger generation aware of the need to speak to her totemic spirits of the past, now embodied in birds, reptiles and mammals.

Since Doyle's own father is European, she has "no primary connection to the land", to which her mother, the well-known Annie Bandicootcha, has land connections through her own father Roy George, a locally-famous leader. These intertwined land relations have made claims very complex, especially where the bureaucrats regularly lump families into manageable tribes for legal claim purposes. There are apparently regional differences by which the cultural land identity is determined. In Cape York, Doyle maintains that an individual's totemic ancestry (such as crocodile and bandicoot in her family) is determined by both the country they are connected to and the "mob" they are descended from. Problems arise when individuals feel the need to return to their country three or four generations after "temporarily" leaving. Not unexpectedly, this causes resistance from current inhabitants of the country and this was certainly the case at Weipa when Jean George was sent back to represent her family at Moingam (Hey Point, Weipa).

Doyle makes special mention of how each family was given a plot of land at Weipa Mission, on which they grew potatoes, corn (maize), cucumbers, pineapples and watermelons. This supplemented the bushfoods which were becoming scarce near the Mission. These European vegetables are in fact often closely related to the food plants they had always subsisted on, as catalogued in the present author's book "Lot 22" which deals with food and fibre of the southern Cape York coast.

Nana and Doyle's mother spoke often about how good their time at the Weipa Mission was – established originally by Reverend Edwin Brown of the Presbyterian Church on the upper Embley River in 1898. In 1904 this church also established the Archer River Mission. By the mid-1950's when the bauxite mine at Weipa started operations, the all-pervasive effect of the

## OVERCOMING DISADVANTAGE

Whites' lifestyle, entertainment, sport and alcohol rapidly contributed to the disintegration of social cohesion among the Aborigines. A major effect was the increasing attraction of White ways to the younger generations, leading to a breakdown in the age-old passing down of "the knowledge of country" to the next generations by the Elders. Included in this cultural breakdown was the loss of language, the very heart of their identity as traditional people. Thus, although most Missions had prohibited the use of local lingo, the old people had kept language alive for nearly 100 years of occupation. Doyle gives credit to the McKenzie family who ran the Aurukun Mission for forty years up to 1965, for encouraging use of the Wik languages. The further that individuals were removed from their country and their language, the greater was their loss of personal identity. Added to that, when mixed-race like Doyle never knew their fathers (in her case an Austrian named Ferdinand Wirrer), their inability to answer the question "Who am I?" became destabilising and depressive in many cases. This decline in self-image caused Doyle to ask, as her Elders were asking, "What are our boys growing up into?" Their men's example to their children was becoming critical to survival of their culture.

The story of Doyle's Nana's and Doyle's own conversion to White ways is an important narrative which represents the mixed cultural development of thousands of Aboriginals caught between two cultures – one with rich bonds to country and ancestors, the other with the potential to give the coming generations a much-needed improvement in general well-being.

Nana as an example, had morphed from being a bush woman skilled in food gathering and child rearing, to become a police woman, a Justice of the Peace, a Councillor and an Elder of the Uniting Church. Doyle herself, while valuing her traditional heritage, went on to gain a degree in education and to become a leader in Aboriginal culture, especially in drama and dance.

The 1996 judgement by the High Court, that Native Title co-existed on Wik country because pastoral lease conditions did not confer rights of exclusive possession on lessees, was a seminal point in time for Aboriginal people. The television image of Doyle's Aunty Gladys Tybingoompa dancing with her clapsticks in front of the Canberra court remains fixed in the national psyche.

It should be noted however, that it took less than six months after this ruling (4/5/1996) for the Howard government to respond to this ruling with its "Ten Point Plan" – a defensive response to the Wik judgement by the Nationals in coalition, aimed at limiting further Native Title Claims.

## SEEKING AN AGREEMENT

Back in 1970 Rowley maintained that Aboriginal futures rest on the willingness of governments to negotiate. Negotiation is preferable to reconciliation, because reconciliation infers admission of past injustices. However, unless negotiation results in the emergence of a structure of authority within the Aboriginal community it will fail. In 1973 the National Aboriginal Consultative Committee was formed for this purpose.

The origins of the Land Rights debate go back a very long way – to the Magna Carta in fact. The debate has not only legal dimensions, but moral, social, political, economic, ethical and even religious dimensions. The voluminous literature on Australian Land Rights cannot be adequately even summarised in a review such as this, but an attempt needs to be made to at least identify the building blocks of the case for Aboriginal Land Rights, by whatever name. Legally the concepts of Land Rights, Sovereignty, Native Title, Treaty, Compensation, Self-determination and Autonomy can all be persuasively argued in favour of Indigenous people who were never conquered or signed up in any form of Treaty. It is now well known that the assumption of a 'vacant' land (*Terra Nullius*) was the basis of the original take-over of this continent – The Great Southland. The definition of 'vacant' was a European construction determined by the absence of infrastructure rather than people. Thus no houses, roads or fields indicated a vacancy – *nullius* meaning *no owner*.

The first balanced and informed treatise on this matter of Land Rights is that of Frank Brennan who chose for his 1991 book, the simple title "Sharing the Country". Aware of accusations of patronising, Brennan speaks for many Whites who want to see justice but are sensitive about intervening, when he introduces his search for reconciliation with these words: "I am not an Aborigine and I do not presume to speak for Aborigines. I write this book hoping that Aborigines might belong again throughout this land; and those of us who are not Aboriginal might belong for the first time without shame". He expands his preface by adding that he seeks "a reconciliation based on justice for all Australians, including the descendents and inheritors of those who dispossessed Aborigines and the most recently arrived Migrants and refugees who have done no wrong to Aborigines".

As a lawyer, Jesuit priest and advisor to the Catholic bishops on Aboriginal affairs, Brennan brings a rare set of skills and values to the Aboriginal futures debate. His stance is simple; an Agreement is not just achievable but essential if we are to become a just and mature nation. It was because of this background that the present author invited Brennan to address the fledgling 'Australians for a Just and Civil Society' (AJACS) in a packed Mayne Hall at the University of Queensland in the early 1990s.

With the clinical logic of a barrister, Brennan sets about his country-sharing analysis by asking three basic questions:

- What do Aboriginals want?
- Which of these claims are justified?
- Which justifiable claims are politically achievable?

He has a clear view that only Aborigines can answer the first question about wants. But he quotes Bill Stanner's "White Man Got No Dreaming" (1979) which refers to a state of mind among White Australians, "a feeling of irritation apparently based on a conviction that we are saddled with the responsibility for problems [which are] not really of our (present generation's) making, and by their nature probably insoluble....To argue that every new generation of White Australians must accept a liability to compensate every new generation of Aborigines is simply not an argument from the domain of the real world". Stanner then adds the question of whose reality is to be recognised, and distinguishes past wrongs from present wrongs – a distinction which changes our updated reality.

The legal fiction on which this nation was founded in 1788 is "still working injustices today" claims Brennan and it is these inequalities of the here and now that demand our focus. How these injustices are addressed becomes problematic in the absence of an agreed Aboriginal viewpoint, the absence of a national Aboriginal leader and the absence of a well-resourced Aboriginal coordinating agency. So the old "divide and rule" approach continues to dominate Black/White relations. In this way the earlier conflicting viewpoints of, say Michael Mansell and Charlie Perkins, could be played off against each

## THE PRESENT: SEEKING AN AGREEMENT

other. Mansell would not accept that Aborigines were Australian citizens – Australian Aborigines yes; Aboriginal Australians no. Perkins, who must be credited with galvanising Aboriginal identity through the media, stood for Aboriginals as a proud part of the Australian nation, getting involved in national issues far beyond Aboriginal affairs.

Returning to Brennan's other two questions about justifiable and achievable claims; he makes a strong case for all Australians to be involved in these vital decisions. The present author would go further on the first question of leaving the determination of wants solely to the Aborigines. The reason for this is that unless present leadership has the vision and objectivity of gauging "cultural appropriateness" correctly, value judgments on work ethics, employment, financial independence, social well-being and education, may well disadvantage future generations. In this way the distinction between wants and needs may elude Aboriginal leaders, as it has tended to do if judged on the performance of peak bodies such as ATSIC in the recent past. Given the personal traumas and limited educational exposure to enlightened social policy of past peak bodies, the extent of vision demonstrated is understandable almost to a point of being excusable – but not acceptable to the emerging class of Indigenous thinkers. In these circumstances the grace to consider non-Indigenous insight into wants/needs seems appropriate.

The whole idea of reconciliation is probably seen by most Australians as a good idea, understood to mean putting the past behind us (not forgetting it) and moving forward in a cooperative, friendly, respectful, multicultural way. There is some vague assumption that all this really requires is for Whites to give Blacks a fair go and for Blacks to get on with productive self-sufficiency. This easy comfortable view is countered by a more strident demanding view such as that of the 1988 Barunga Statement from the Northern Territory Aborigines demanding Land Rights, compensation and a binding treaty. When expressed in the words of Wenten Rubuntja, an Elder from the Centre, this proposal sounded reasoned and morally appropriate: "Today there are lots of people living in this country. People who come from all over the world….. This is their country too now. So, all of us have to live together. We have to look after each other. We have to share this country and this means respecting each others' laws and culture…….Hopefully that's what this treaty will mean".

With this 1988 statement being somewhat outdated after more than

## OVERCOMING DISADVANTAGE

30 years, it may be appropriate to ask why the Treaty concept has become something of a non-event in Australian politics. Not that it has not been revitalised by a number of individuals, but somehow it doesn't get traction – as with the push for an Australian republic. The Institute for Public Affairs went as far as providing a forum titled "A Treaty with Aborigines?" at which Prime Minister Hawke gave one of the clearest official responses to this long-standing question. John Howard responded to the Treaty idea with a dire warning of how this would lead to apartheid-type separatism.

The sovereignty concept had been tested in 1978 when an Aboriginal barrister named Paul Coe instituted proceedings in the High Count. He sought Aboriginal sovereignty from both the Australian and British governments based on the fact that the 1788 annexation without treaty or conquest was null and void. The case was dismissed by Justice Gibbs who claimed that the American Indian tribes quoted by Coe were recognised as "domestic nations" but that "there is no Aboriginal nation, if by that expression is meant a people organised as a separate State or exercising any degree of sovereignty". The American Indians form of sovereignty is termed 'Domestic Dependent Sovereignty'.

Brennan recognised that despite Coe's valiant failure, all was not lost and he proposed dropping the term 'sovereignty' and focusing on Aboriginal entitlements in the form of Land Rights and title. This approach was successfully applied to three Torres Strait islands when Eddie Mabo led his mob to the High Court in 1982. This case seemed clear-cut due to its continuous, exclusive occupation by the Islanders. However, in 1985 the Queensland Parliament passed the Queensland Coast Islands Declaratory Act which declared that the Queensland islands which had been annexed as part of Queensland in 1879 "were vested in the Crown in right of Queensland freed from all other rights, interests and claims of any kind whatsoever". This act also provided that "no compensation was or is payable" to any claim of alleged previous ownership. So this Act contributed nothing to removing injustice in land claims.

Eddie Mabo was not done yet; he and his Murray Islanders challenged this State Act in the High Court and won – Australia's first Native Title recognition. This was followed by further wins to the Aboriginals based on payment for mineral extraction on their land: Then the Wik case, south of

## THE PRESENT: SEEKING AN AGREEMENT

Weipa, granted large areas of good cattle country to the holders of Wik Native Title. In other cases, sacred sites complicated the legal process further, notably because the location of major sacred sites is, by tribal custom, kept secret from everyone except initiated members. Mining companies in turn declined to indicate the location of mineral lodes on the map; allegedly for commercial in-confidence reasons but suspecting that claimants "manufactured" sacred sites on proposed mine sites once these were revealed.

Consideration of State and Federal rights and rivalries, cause considerable delay in land claims and are an important reason for Native Title cases still (2009) taking an average of nine years to settle. Apart from land title, Indigenous communities have long sought some form of self-determination. Noel Pearson of Cape York has forcefully maintained that dependence on Whites through programs of "passive welfare" has been the prime cause of a lack of identity, pride and sobriety in the communities. Whether self-determination can act as the key to lifting people out of degradation remains to be seen, but as a goal, self-determination has been around since 1967 when "H.C. (Nugget) Coombs and Professor W.E.H. (Bill) Stanner called for a doctrine of "Four Aboriginal Freedoms":

- Freedom to decide for themselves to what degree they will identify with one (mainstream) Australian society.
- Freedom to decide for themselves the rate at which such identity would develop.
- Freedom to have the right to preserve their own culture.
- Freedom to develop (expand and nurture) their own culture.

These freedoms became Federal policy under Prime Minister McMahon in 1972 and represent a significant point in Indigenous development – it signalled the official jettisoning of the previous policy of assimilation. The significance of these freedoms as official objectives of policy were not (and probably are still not) appreciated by the Australian public. But policy architects such as Stanner recognised that in one sense this was the hinge of history and as a result he suggested that 1972 be remembered as "The Year of the Blackfellow" because it was predicted to be the beginning of Aboriginal Affairs becoming "irretrievably political".

Today we look back and often accuse Coombs for causing all the problems of remote communities through his separationist policy, because in this new era, mainstreaming has again taken over as the favoured policy. Not that the meaning of mainstreaming or integration or assimilation or self-determination or self-sufficiency are agreed on by protagonists of competing ideologies. The ideal of self-determination, although strongly held by most modern Aboriginal leaders, was never accepted by the Coalition government, either under Fraser or Howard. The term 'integration' had been in use in earlier years as a way of describing how Indigenous people meld with non-Indigenous people. As such, it was very different from self-determination which infers another layer of government in a country which already has too many layers. Back in 1960 the United Nations produced a "Declaration of the Granting of Independence to Colonial Countries and Peoples" (today termed Indigenous). This declaration, at highest global level, gave local Aboriginals hope that they too could gain "the right of all peoples to determine freely their political status and pursue freely their economic, social and cultural development" (UN Resolution 1514 of 1960).

In the real world, political parties saw to it that internal self-determination only allowed greater autonomy within the existing national political framework, i.e. not as a new independent people or breakaway nation. In defence of this constraining interpretation of self-determination, Government spokesmen repeatedly quoted the additional provision of the UN which states that "any attempt aimed at partial or total disruption of the national unity and the territorial integrity of a country (nation state) is incompatible with the purpose and principles of the Charter of the United Nations". This didn't stop Michael Mansell and Bob Weatherall from forming their Aboriginal Provisional Government centred on Alice Springs.

As one of the national and constructive voices in Aboriginal policy, Fred Chaney, as Leader of the Opposition in the Senate in 1989, echoed the sentiments of many, when he avoided the term 'self-determination' because it "can have political connotations which have nothing to do with the social advancement that we are concerned about". This stance was interpreted by 'radicals' like Mansell as patronising colonial mastery over the oppressed, but Chaney accurately forecast the social disaster awaiting unhealthy, uneducated, under-resourced remote communities, whose leaders mistakenly over-valued autonomy and under-valued co-operative future partnerships. Thus it was,

## THE PRESENT: SEEKING AN AGREEMENT

that by the early 1990's the terms 'self-determination and self-management' became the key phrases in the original ATSIC legislation promulgated by Gerry Hand of the Whitlam government. Note that the Act concerned does not use the term 'self-government', thus eliminating the notion of a separate nation.

It is interesting to note that despite the goals of self-government, by whatever name, the Hawke government saw fit for Senator Richardson to override any objections which the Yarrabah community might have had against World Heritage Listing of their land to be included in the Wet Tropics Rainforest global reserve in 1988. As a negotiating carrot Richardson asked the Yarrabah people to provide 'plans or details of future logging and possible expansion of sawmill operations' at the same time as he was offering the White millers at Ravenshoe nearby, several million dollars to close their already-failing timber enterprise. (Strong local rumours claim that through bureaucratic misunderstanding this significant payment was actually paid twice!)

This issue of self-sufficiency leads on to the matter of compensation – repayment for resources lost (stolen?) and for suffering endured over time. This matter becomes complicated when the claims of urban Aborigines are considered as claims for lost land – the very reason that they're urban dwellers.

The Northern Territory's Barunga Statement referred to earlier, called for compensation for lost land on the grounds that the original Native Title has never been extinguished. The Northern Territory's Chief Minister of the day (1990) Marshall Perron, in fact asked Prime Minister Hawke whether, as a means of money-raising, the government would levy a national Aboriginal compensation tax. Hawke, like all Prime Ministers before and after him, kept well away from committing to compensation – in this case by simply not responding. This never stopped local candidates who were seeking Aboriginal votes in Northern Australia, from hinting at compensation as a future option. It took an Aboriginal Labour member in the Northern Territory to point out that compensation need not be monetary in the cash hand-out sense, but could and should be in the form of land, infrastructure and services. Perhaps the best form of compensation for past injustices is the provision of funds allocated to purchases of land to be vested in dispossessed Aboriginal groups. The New South Wales Land Rights Act of 1983 in fact makes provision for a fixed percentage of State land tax to be expended on Aboriginal land purchases. Though the funds raised in this way may be seriously insufficient, the principle is much more attractive than suggestions based on compensating individuals financially – an administrative nightmare.

On the issue of Treaties, Brennan maintains that it is 200 years too late to introduce legally-binding arrangements which meet individual settlements based on race. He suggests that it is more appropriate to construct a charter which recognises group entitlements, allowing self-management and self-determination funded by society at large (taxpayers) "in pursuit of the common good". Brennan further recommends that Aboriginal leaders "abandon the rhetoric of sovereignty" and enter into negotiated agreements which enhance their contribution to the well-being of the nation. He warns that this can only be achieved after two conditions are met:

- Their land claims have been finalised.
- Their disadvantage in society has been rectified.

These conditions require long term programs funded by government and are not likely to be met any time soon. As a result, frustrated community leaders ask whether there's some way that progress with self-determination can commence while land and disadvantage are attended to. In one sense this has been tried before in one form or another. When the Fraser government set up the elected body called the National Aboriginal Council in 1979, it sought what it termed a Treaty of Commitment. This was the formal start of the Treaty debate.

At precisely the same time (April '79) the fourteen member Aboriginal Treaty Committee held its first meeting and ever since then, the Treaty issue has surfaced periodically, though not frequently, always to be postponed, delayed, re-constituted, further examined or otherwise put off. In essence two basic problems exist: the first is the reticence of governments to commit to a Treaty and the second is the inability of Aboriginal communities to agree on clan and family rights and inheritance. By 1987 those advising the Hawke government concluded that since the Aboriginals were not a sovereign entity under present law, they could not enter into a Treaty with the Commonwealth. And so the circular legal arguments continued, and still continue.

Since the early 1980's the increasing contact between Aboriginal leaders and Indigenous leaders in countries such as Canada has significantly increased the confidence of local leaders in their commitment to the need

## THE PRESENT: SEEKING AN AGREEMENT

for fundamental change to the rate at which Aboriginal disadvantage was being addressed. Leaders such as Marcia Langton met with the International Working Group on Indigenous Populations in the mid 1980's and on behalf of the Federation of (Australian) Land Councils, put the Aboriginals' case before the Working Group's subcommittee on Prevention of Discrimination and Protection of Minorities. As with the powerful oratory of Noel Pearson on Passive Welfare's effects, Langton's tough demanding style had its effect on a somewhat disinterested Australian voting public.

By 1986 the Land Rights issue was both front and centre in State and Federal politics and candidates were going out of their way to ensure White voters that their properties were not under threat from claims under their particular party's Aboriginal policy. Thus it was that Aboriginal rights became a potentially serious issue in the day-to-day lives of regional Australians – for the first time in 200 years. Ministers such as Clyde Holding, Gerry Hand and Robert Tickner had little option but to make public statements assuring voters that everything was under control and that justice and certainty would be achieved. This was the easy part; the difficult part was explaining to visiting international human rights representatives how the abominable living conditions, which were being beamed to a global television audience, could be explained, let alone justified, in this land of the 'Fair Go'. Very soon the debate turned from remote living conditions which could not be denied, to the evasive question of whose fault this disadvantage was – a debate which still rages and is unlikely to go away any time soon.

Returning to the late 1980's, it was clear that the loud protestations of fiery public performers like Charlie Perkins and Marcia Langton were starting to be taken seriously. This reached fever pitch when Opposition Deputy Leader Tim Fischer, a rural landholder in New South Wales, was moved to refer to an emerging "Guilt Industry" by which he meant a concerted effort to orchestrate a feeling of moral obligation on the part of Whites to right past wrongs through policy change. By 1987 the Governor General, Sir Ninian Stephen moved to refer to the Bicentennial celebrations in the following terms: "The Government believes it is essential we come to the Bicentennial Year, to recognise that 200 years of European settlement comes after 40,000 years of Aboriginal history. The Government will explore how best to reflect that recognition and the obligations which this involves for the whole community". The assembled crowd at the opening of that Thirty-fifth Parliament on 14 September 1987, may have gathered that the 'recognition and obligation' that her Majesty's representative had referred to, may just have carried the seeds of change in the moral compass of the nation.

This sense of change was enhanced by Prime Minister Hawke's call for all Australians to acknowledge 200 years of injustice to Aborigines when they ponder Aboriginal "demands and suggestions that to us may seem outrageous". He was referring, amongst others, to Charlie Perkins demand (as the most senior Aboriginal bureaucrat) for an instrument of Aboriginal rights that had legal standing. At the end of Parliament in 1987, Minister Gerry Hand prepared politicians for the coming Bicentennial Year by tabling his "Foundations for the Future" document which seemed to give Aborigines "the means, as never before, to determine their own future as part of this nation", clearly dampening any call for a separate First Nation as the Canadian Inuit had proposed.

The Hawke Government, like the Fraser Government before it, was wary of the implications of a Treaty and considered terms like "compact or makarrata", all the while making it clear that they had no intention of negotiating a treaty that implied an internationally recognised agreement between two nations. Brennan believes that what the government wanted was "a new and lasting era of mutual understanding and co-operation with our Aboriginal and Torres Strait Islander fellow citizens". Thus national Land Rights should be regarded as a historic dream that wasn't going to happen in the real world of contemporary politics.

Although the Bicentennial Year of 1988 is slowly passing into recent history, it remains an important point in time when Australians (perhaps for the first time) were asking the serious question of what we have to celebrate as a nation. Hawke in his National Press Club address in 1988 saw the occasion as a decisive point in the process of "national identity, national responsibility and national maturity" accompanied by a reassessment of the past, which would be of the greatest value to Aboriginal people. He added that his Government's commitment was not simply "some form of window dressing for the Bicentenary, for consumption overseas". The fact that he should feel it necessary to make such a disclaimer was taken to indicate that window dressing was precisely how many voters saw it. Hawke was at pains to counter

## THE PRESENT: SEEKING AN AGREEMENT

the guilt industry notion when he added: "The Australian people should never be asked to accept that their entire history as a modern nation must be predicated on the notion of a collective and irredeemable guilt". The political speech-writers of the day were faced with the unusual challenge of appealing to conflicting sentiments simultaneously. This didn't stop the Shadow Minister for Aboriginal Affairs, Chris Miles, from conceding that "many Aborigines feel a sense of alienation because of what they see as a lack of acceptance by other Australians". He then made it clear where the Coalition really stood: "The Coalition is keen to improve relationships between Aboriginal and other Australians and for this reason will firmly oppose a treaty", which he said would undermine cohesion. So here we had both parties agreeing on moving forward as one nation but that a treaty would hinder this goal.

In 1987 the Parliament had sought agreement on the wording of a resolution which recognised the Aboriginals as valued members of the Australian society. The resolution affirmed, among other acknowledgements, "the entitlement of Aborigines and Torres Strait Islanders to self-management and self-determination subject to the Constitution and laws of the Commonwealth….". Hawke and Howard agreed on most of the wording but Howard wanted the self-determination further qualified with "…..in common with other Australians". Brennan says that, at best, this amendment was ambiguous, suggesting that the entitlement of self-determination was universal but exercisable discretely by separate groups. At worst, Brennan regards the amendments as "ruthlessly assimilationist" excluding the Aboriginals' choice of a traditional lifestyle. The Opposition were very wary of alternative interpretations of the term "self-determination" and had insisted that "self-determination lead to self-sufficiency". In the end, the Hawke resolution was lost, described by Brennan as Parliament being "cheated of one of the rare opportunities" for finding common ground on a just settlement on Aboriginal claims.

By the end of 1988 Hawke had described a treaty as "an umbrella document providing direction and perspective to all areas of policy" – a treaty between Australians for Australians, all in the name of Bicentennial reconciliation. The Opposition saw it very differently. In Howard's words "a treaty must inevitably lead to claims for *national* (my emphasis) Land Rights and massive compensation". He saw it as "a recipe for separatism which would not result in the development of compassionate and sensible policies so desperately needed to overcome the situation faced by many Aboriginal people".

Meanwhile Galarrwuy Yunupingu, who was emerging as a strong credible voice in the Northern Territory, attempted a positive compromise to the Coalition's "One Australia" statement that year. He suggested that, "yes, there should be one Australia and Aboriginals should be part of it. But our part should be on our terms". Of course everyone had by that time noted that the Bicentennial theme of "Living Together" was neither a correct statement of Aboriginal history, nor a factual reflection of their present lives.

By 1990 the Hawke Government had established ATSIC as referred to earlier, to give Aborigines greater control over the administration of Government programs, subject to rigid financial accountability – at least that was the intention. Right from the start the fledgling ATSIC was to see, perhaps predictably, a clash between the new chair Lois (Louwitja) O'Donoghue who sought positive co-operation, from fellow ATSIC member Geoff Clarke, then also coordinator of the National Federation of Land Councils. Clarke saw ATSIC's function as administering government services, not negotiating a treaty and, as such, it couldn't be seen as the voice of the people. At about this time Michael Mansell, the Tasmanian Aboriginal barrister who had been welcomed in Libya by General Gadaffi as a kind of freedom fighter, accused both the Government and Opposition of colluding with others whenever the question of Aboriginal statehood arose, proclaiming "we are all Australians".

O'Donoghue's vision of ATSIC as "the beginning of a unique and productive partnership with the Government" did not take long to unravel, a downward spiralling process caused by dissention in its ranks about the worthwhileness of its charter, and by the immature and bullying behaviour of some of the "strong men" in its ranks. Fifteen years later, Howard, as new Prime Minister, decided to disband ATSIC, a decision supported by both Blacks and Whites who had long since detected that this peak body had developed into a farce of expensive proportions despite the gallant efforts of O'Donoghue to make the best of its constraining terms of reference. It should be noted that the new Rudd Government, while quick to bask in the accolades arising from Rudd's national apology to Aborigines, was less than expedient in getting ATSIC's successor-agency up and running. Nor did Howard, having done away with ATSIC, see any necessity to replace it with a more acceptable

## THE PRESENT: SEEKING AN AGREEMENT

successor. It took until 2009 for Tom Calma to propose the new national representative structure, as referred to later.

The frustrations of local Aboriginal leaders have led them to abandon the Australian legal process – they have come to regard it as a waste of time in their quest for legally-binding rights for their people. Brennan has noted how these frustrated but driven individuals have entertained "hopes that international initiatives, especially with agencies of the UN, will compel or at least shame the Government into agreeing to concessions and demands which are not forthcoming beyond the floodlights of global media." These Aboriginal malcontents had found the funds necessary to attend the annual meetings in Geneva of both the International Labour Organisation (ILO) and the UN Working Group on Indigenous Populations referred to earlier. Brennan reports from first-hand experience that in the nine years up to 1991, despite days of semantic discussion, not a single substantive agreement between Governments and Indigenous peoples has resulted from this expensive exercise. The ILO has witnessed a number of unseemly stoushes between Aboriginal leaders such as Geoff Clarke (on behalf of the National Coalition of Aboriginal Organisations) and government representatives such as Bill Gray (CEO of ATSIC) both purporting to speak on behalf of Australia. Since there are an estimated 300 million Indigenous people worldwide and none of them appear to have gained any benefits from these elaborate international gatherings, the Aboriginals may find it more rewarding to return to the domestic negotiating table. This however, will require what Brennan calls the "playing of endless word games" that do nothing for the alienated group who don't set the rules of the game.

Brennan makes the important point that in international law, self-determination has applied chiefly to "people emerging from the colonisation process being given a choice of future". He emphasises that self-determination is not for just any group, and that an inquiry is required first, to ascertain whether there is enough "homogeneity or unity or common desire" to hold the envisaged State together, and whether it possesses the resources and political capacity to succeed. Brennan stresses that self-determination carried with it "the entitlement to partition territory" and can only be exercised by a discrete territorial community. So full self-government is possible only for groups who are geographically separate. This means separation is inconceivable for scattered Indigenous peoples especially those who have inter-married over centuries. Irrespective of the academic debates and utterances of the warriors of the Culture Wars, the evidence is that the reaching of consensus on Indigenous rights seems as elusive in Geneva as in Canberra.

Having considered the whole continuum of Aboriginal futures options, perhaps it is useful to eliminate the more extreme views at both ends. At the dark brown end is Mansell's Central Australian Homeland run by his chosen ministers (with no ties to local country) running a newly-created Aboriginal nation as an autonomous and sovereign legal entity. This new nation, described in the *Weekend Australian* of 30 June 1990 would have "the common purpose of independence from the harshness of White control". It would have the capacity to "control itself without interference, raising its own economics, making and enforcing its laws and deciding its own future". That's one end; the other end of options is the complete assimilation into the general society and the associated total loss of identity as an Indigenous people – customs, religion, tribal networks, links to country and dreamtime stories: In essence, the disappearance of an identifiable people.

Somewhere between these 'all or nothing' alternatives is a gradation of culturally-intense identities which are available on a non-mutually exclusive basis, i.e. no either/or choice is necessary. Near the centre of the identity continuum is the economically independent Aboriginal family which appreciates and maintains its cultural values, sends its children to the local suburban school and collects the same middle-class welfare payments as everyone else. These centrists have made an effort to overcome educational and health disadvantage – a difficult task for the first breakaway families, not without its generational traumas, but a voluntary one reflecting free choice.

Each family accepts that several of their kin made different choices with different outcomes for their well-being. In this way Aborigines will gain equity and justice without existing as a separate people geographically or legally. We shall return to this matter of selective personal identity in Part 3 of this review.

For a scholarly consideration of the conditions pertaining to lasting treaties and agreements, the book by Langton *et al*, 'Settling with Indigenous People' (2006), gives one of the best insights into co-operative futures.

# THE FUTURE

## PEARSON'S POWERFUL PROSE

In analysing the decade ending 2010, then considering the future, we can gain a useful overview of problems and progress by using the Federal Government's framework based on key indicators of Indigenous well-being, as detailed in "Overcoming Indigenous Disadvantage" (2003). That report gives a factual basis for a point in time, which is described in statistical terms. It deals with the accepted policy areas of population growth, health, longevity, crime, substance abuse, housing, education and other recognised bureaucratic spheres of control. These statistics are important in that they present undeniable quantified data. Not that such attempts at sophistication of available information are not open to different interpretations, on the contrary the "So what?" question often looms large and the mode of data collection and basis for conclusions are predictably challenged. We shall return to this Constraints Report.

In choosing Noel Pearson as formulator of ideas on Aboriginal well-being, it must be said that as an 'ex-Mission boy' with an inherently fearsome intellect, he has shown a unique ability to use his boarding school education and legal training to construct a rare balanced view of Black/White relations. His self-generated personal contact with leading international thinkers on the human condition and its causes, has allowed Pearson to develop the self-confidence required to challenge both the government and his own people and to re-examine the voracity and appropriateness of their values and culture. He bridges the cultural gap like no other leader– Black or White, has done to apply these important concepts as subsets of each of the three sequential time zones or eras.

The present author has chosen to use as the basis for his futures study, the policy areas reflected in Pearson's first collection of papers (2009). This choice is made after long consideration of alternative subsets of policy and the choice is made primarily because of the way Pearson's overview of Aboriginal life and prospects, approaches these subjects 'from the inside' rather than from external controlling interests' viewpoint.

In acting as the lightning rod between competing philosophies, Pearson has predictably been at the receiving end of criticism from two camps, each being equally comfortable psychologically with their traditional worldview. When an individual writes with the combination of knowledge, intellect, passion and articulation which Pearson brings to bear, criticism and dismissal by those he aims his comments at, is predictable. Pearson's earlier articulation of his views could easily be branded as radical, emotive, even unreasonable. Coming at a time (1980's) when even minor deviation from a subservient response from Aboriginals could be branded as 'radical', Pearson's views were born of frustration with the lack of action on Aboriginal well-being and carried the emotions of watching his Hope Vale people slipping backwards while the Australian nation prospered.

While the above may appear as a character reference which glosses over possible flaws and ennobles his positive values, Pearson stands head and shoulders above other Indigenous spokespersons based solely on his irrefutable logic. For this reason his views and values are used here as a basis for policy consideration, based on press clippings filed by the present author over the past 20 years. The more significant of these appear in Pearson's compilation of selected writings titled "Up from the Mission", launched in June 2009 and followed a month later by Peter Sutton's remarkable memoir "The Politics of Suffering" to which this review will return.

The present situation is overviewed by Pearson under the headings:

- **The Mission** – an inside family view of life on the Mission and how Aboriginals lived in the 1960's and 1970's.
- **Fighting Old Enemies** – the fight for and gaining of Native Title.
- **Challenging Old Friends** – a forceful approach to his own community to accept higher behavioural norms, following the negative effects of passive welfare payments.
- **The Quest for the Radical Centre** – a proposed program for Cape

York, economic independence and the Federal intervention.
- **Our Place in the Nation** – a review of peoplehood and a national agreement.

Looking at the way Pearson has grouped his 38 papers, written over the period 1993-2009, into the above five parts, he suffers the same dilemma as the rest of us, as to how best to evaluate Indigenous affairs in 'bite-sized chunks'. As a result, many of his papers could equally logically have been allocated to alternative sections of this review.

Why this consideration of topic classification warrants special mention here is precisely because it is a good example of the problems of complexity of Aboriginal affairs which have frustrated many potential contributors to the national debate on alternative futures. The body of factual knowledge and values can be considered as a layered cake which can be sliced and diced from different angles. There is probably no single best way of cutting this body of information into sensible policy building blocks, although integration of elements into an approach, to which individual Aboriginals can relate, holds most potential. In his own way Pearson has done that with his Cape York Agenda which is an integrated step-wise regional program which can act as a microcosm of the national remote Indigenous community situation and its improvement.

In this Part 3, the present author attempts to use the Pearson building blocks (individual, discrete but inter-related topics) as identified issues of significance in defining both the present situation on Indigenous well-being and suggesting positive outcomes where applicable. The manner in which the present author overviews Pearson's take on the current Aboriginal situation, is such that it gives both Pearson's own suggestions and values (sometimes radical, sometimes unique, always informed), and this author's response to Pearson's comment.

These views of Pearson's were forged at a time, from 1983, when he was much affected by the politics of Left and Right, of Labour and the Coalition and were needed to guide Black thinking through the murky waters of the academic 'culture wars' in which intellectuals and commentators in the media interpreted history and contemporary situations very differently. He was confident enough to give the Prime Minister personal advice, telling Howard, in a letter before the 2007 election, that he had the opportunity to change Australia in a fundamental way by applying a 3-part strategy which could shift the nation:

1. "From symbolic and practical reconciliation to the recognition of

Indigenous people within a reconciled indivisible nation.

2. From a repudiational republic (which is Australia's current default direction) to an affirmational republic; and

3. From a welfare state to an opportunity state".

Pearson believed that the basic problem with the conservatives was that they were "too unwilling to recognise the importance of culture and identity to Indigenous Australians". He wanted Howard to agree that Australia had dual foundation stones – the first was the Indigenous heritage and overlain on that was the British heritage.

In summary Pearson's view considered poverty to be a four-pronged issue – income, education, health and shelter. The debate should centre not so much on what the problems of poverty are but rather how to evaluate the perceived benefits of optional solutions.

One would like to think that Pearson is one of those rare individuals who, in Kipling's words can "walk with kings nor lose the common touch". In practice he has been very good at articulating his people's issues at the highest level, but back home the people with the common touch are not yet ready to follow Pearson out of "passive welfare" despite this being his often-quoted basic cause of virtually all ills.

It is Pearson's challenge to his kinsmen to shake themselves out of their inactive stupor and face facts on disastrous, but apparently locally acceptable, norms of behaviour, which has led him to lose friends among present Indigenous community leaders. Having created a strong negative image of passive welfare (sit-down money) and an equally strong positive image of "the right to take responsibility", Pearson's 2009 book repeats these two ideas many times throughout his collated papers.

It is not possible to assess the worth of Pearson's ideas without constantly reminding one's self of why his opinion often carries so much more weight than virtually all other Indigenous commentators. As referred to earlier, here we have "the real deal", the Antipodean equivalent of "log cabin to whitehouse" rise, without actually arriving there at this stage. His powerful imagery of his parents, grandparents and mentors on the Hope Vale Mission, the work ethic, the Lutheran Church, the Brisbane boarding school, Sydney University and his later law practice, all combine to convince the reader that there is nothing lacking at basic intellectual level. He is objective enough to acknowledge not

## THE FUTURE: PEARSON'S POWERFUL PROSE

just his Indigenous identity but also his Mission identity and the positive values he took from that. Growing up in a house where the only books were the Bible and Martin Luther King's story, he was moulded by the dual forces of Christianity and Black Justice. In 1987 Pearson comes to the view that Aboriginals who want a decent future for their children "are searching for a place in mainstream Australian society that doesn't exist". He is saddened by the fact that Aborigines have failed to adapt to a 'White way of life' but have also failed to maintain the values and achievements of their own culture. This rejection of both Whitefella and Blackfella education is what he believes has left them in a moral and economic vacuum.

Like many observers before him, Pearson comments at length on the effects of alcohol on his people. However he does a much better job than most analysts at explaining the strong group identity and allegiance which bind his addicted fellows. Pearson's essay titled "Hope Vale Lost" which elicits his emotions on visiting his parent's old home at the Mission and experiencing the drunken violence in his once happy boyhood town, is a minor classic in Australian writing. His surprise, dismay, anger and feeling of helplessness portray a national conscience which hasn't yet fully surfaced. The present author still retains an underlined copy of the press clipping when this account shocked the nation in a 2006 Weekend Australian newspaper. Perhaps the most powerful paragraph of "Hope Vale Lost" is that in which mayor Greg McLean invites a large delegation of bureaucrats and leaders to a roundtable meeting. White officials always visit in mid-week and don't sleep over, but the mayor in a media coup invites a delegation of local primary school children to present their views. Says Pearson: "In plain English the children pleaded that they wanted drinking and violence in their community to stop". This is Pearson power at its best.

The second seminal paper in Pearson's book "Up from the Mission" is titled "Our Right to take Responsibility" – a 30 page analysis of the causes of, and proposal for, the Indigenous poverty trap. The central thesis of that paper is the concept that taking responsibility is a necessary condition for the right to self-determination.

Pearson's answer to the question of just what are the attributes of the dysfunctional remote communities, is:

1. Shortest lifespan of any Australian group.

2. Worst health in Australia.
3. Suffering from diseases not found in other groups.
4. Lowest participation in education.
5. Over-represented in juvenile justice system.
6. Highest violence in any community.
7. Highest alcohol abuse in Australia.
8. Highest sexual abuse of young girls.

Many disadvantaged communities the world over suffer from several of these afflictions, but the number and severity of negative well-being indicators among remote Aboriginal communities is extreme even by third world standards.

What Pearson terms the "cultural pathology of grog" has become the basis for a new identity for binge-drinkers. This has by now become so entrenched as a social grouping, that fellow drinkers can be expected to challenge the (new) Aboriginal identity of any drinker who attempts to evade their obligation to contribute grog money. Thus the ancient trait of sharing food for group survival becomes a deadly life-draining dependence on alcohol for group survival.

A second and equally debilitating aspect of group grog purchase as a new cultural attribute of the men in the community, is the pressure put on wives, mothers and grandparents to supply the money required for grog from the household budget. There are both Blacks and Whites profiting from this paralysing group collusion including publicans, carriers, air-charters, boat operators, taxis and shop owners selling methylated spirits to confirmed alcoholics. It is Pearson's view that calls for arrangements to allow moderate drinking at community canteens is unrealistic – total bans are what are required in his opinion.

Alcoholism is but one, albeit deadly, aspect of the passive welfare community's problems. Financial dependence and drunkenness feed off each other, leading to seriously different proposals by community leaders on where to intervene in the cycle of degradation. The Howard Government's "Intervention" in Northern Australia in 2007 aimed to tackle several social problems at once – paedophilia, education, housing, alcoholism, domestic violence and health. This far-reaching and very expensive correctional action strategy was not a thoroughly planned and phased program, but rather a political imperative triggered by a clear, comprehensive and evidence-based plea from the female Public Prosecutor of the Northern Territory to act urgently on totally unacceptable community norms operating in remote communities.

The present author predicts that without realistic and on-going attention to economic independence based on individual wealth-generation, the intervention cannot raise the afflicted from their depravity.

Pearson sees the original Indigenous hunter/gatherer livelihood as a 'real economy'. This was followed by the Mission era which in its own way was a real economy in the sense that its members, like those of the hunting society, had to contribute personal effort to survive – alone and together. Since 1967 when Aboriginals were recognised as citizens and when the stockmen's wage-rise caused widespread unemployment in the bush, communities on reserves have lived in an artificial economy.

Pearson, having blamed passive welfare for virtually all the present ills in remote communities, has examined this phenomenon in detail over the past decade. Some of the common problems of passive welfare he lists as follows:

- It is a poor substitute for participation in the real (mainstream) economy, psychologically, socially and economically. The welfare payments are insufficient to live on properly...passive welfare confines the recipients to his or her stagnant environment.
- It pacifies recipients rather than invigorating them into social, political and economic action to secure a better deal for themselves and their children.
- It reproduces these same problems in following generations.

The above three problems arising from passive welfare lead on to a community mentality which causes the following mindset, according to Pearson:

- People start believing that the solutions to their problems actually lie with others outside the group, namely the government.
- Individuals fail to take responsibility for themselves, their family or their community.
- People promote the victim mentality within their group.
- Individuals come to expect outside assistance without any internal or

personal effort.

- Resources (funds) made available to people are not valued and as a result, welfare money can be wasted.

Pearson makes no claim to be the first to appreciate these effects – they are well known he says, but this recognition had not brought corrective action until recently (2008) when government announced that Commonwealth employment programs (CDEP) would be phased out as of 2009. Why this welfare re-assessment is important is that, in combination with substance abuse, this form of paternalism could easily spell the end of traditional social values in these communities. One is left wondering whether the values of responsibility and reciprocity that were engendered by hunting and gathering, could be re-kindled by small-scale cropping, gardening and herding.

Looking at the income-generating jobs on the Cape at present; mines at Weipa (bauxite) and Cape Flattery (silica sand), arts at Lockhart River and isolated beef production on some Native Title stations, the full potential of the area would need to be assessed before resource exploitation could be accepted as a future prime source of wealth for Aborigines.

The human carrying capacity of Indigenous lands needs to be viewed in the general context of rural industry decline in regional Australia. The drift to the city has been accelerating for thirty years, country towns have been dying, schools have been closing and doctors have been leaving for a long time now, and Aboriginal communities are also suffering from the same decline in infrastructure and services as everyone else in regional Australia.

So where should communities suffering from dispossession, trauma and racial discrimination seek their future? The answer is in the mainstream economy according to Pearson, but in a way which does not abandon culture. The links to community, country and culture can be maintained by what Pearson calls "Orbiting", meaning participating first in external education and training, then in the migratory labour market where the real economy jobs are, but all the while returning to Homeland communities to uplift them with new skills and wealth-generating capacity. Pearson reasons that racism is not really a disability and should not be treated as such. Racism, if regarded rather as an impediment to personal progress, can be overcome by demonstrative evidence of competitive capacity in the labour market.

Using the same phrase as the present author's "Fair Go" paper, Pearson

## THE FUTURE: PEARSON'S POWERFUL PROSE

says the idea of 'get over it, get on with it' is not realistic when the depth and extent of personal trauma is recognised. He maintains that the crushing and destructive generational influence of trauma, is underestimated by those who simplistically suggest 'getting off your backside and getting a job' is all that's required.

The concept of racism is so sensitive that its sensible consideration is pre-empted by political correctness which repeats the belief that "all men are created equal". In practice it is not the inherent equal value of groups that is important, but rather whether there is the strength of identity of one's clan or tribe that allows members to exhibit a tolerance and acceptance of other's, which in turn produces non-discriminating treatment of these others. So we must seriously ask ourselves whether over-emphasis on cultural identity breeds an unconscious exclusivity in outlook – a sort of reverse racism.

Racism doesn't actually matter until it causes differential disadvantage. For instance, the fact that the Jews see themselves as the Chosen People, might be of no consequence if they did not use this 'chosen by God' assumption to treat their neighbours in an inhuman way. Are Aboriginals racist, but powerless to enforce the pre-eminence of their ancient traditions?

Rather than racism being the roadblock, the lack of a sense of responsibility may be at the heart of current social stagnation or retrogression. Pearson is big enough to attribute his original recognition of 'taking responsibility' as the key to community progress, to the Indigenous premier of Greenland, Lars Emil Johansen who visited the Cape York Land Council in 1994. Johansen told the locals that self-determination was hard work but that it is in fact "the right to take responsibility" – a phrase which Pearson consistently repeats to this day.

It is on this point that Pearson causes discomfort among his Cape York peers, challenging them with questions which they have probably never asked themselves:

- Do we really want to take responsibility?
- Do we want to do the hard work of self-determination?
- Are we sufficiently unified to fulfil our responsibilities?
- Are we prepared to show leadership and build consensus and overcome division?

He knows that the current answer to these questions is 'no' and he's still waiting for the community leaders' answers. The present author notes in his "Fair Go" paper that traditionally, Indigenous people had no experience in, or need for, democratic co-operation in social strata above the immediate family or clan level.

Pearson asks why the Aboriginal Medical Service doesn't talk to the Land Council and why the Legal Service and the Housing Co-operative head in different directions. He knows that until his people get serious about self-help through cohesive unity, they will remain at square one.

Beside responsibility, the need for accountability (to themselves) is a necessary ingredient of progress. He doesn't say so, but Pearson knows that the misuse of allocated funds and the treatment of official audits as a necessary evil, need a major overhaul. Ticking the right boxes on the official returns is a pale imitation for real accountability as a community response to how expensive taxpayer resources are applied.

"Can we not see that passive welfare is really a threat not an asset to our people?" asks Pearson before he goes on to use his classic sarcastic question "Who doesn't want *labour-free income*?" (my emphasis).

Several of Pearson's most recent insights into combatting poverty come from his contact with acknowledged international sociologists and other leading thinkers on the global human condition. One such contact was at the International Conference on Social Norms which he organised through the Cape York Institute for Policy and Leadership, which he had founded in partnership with a university and a number of socially-active businesses.

This conference set out to examine social norms as the communities' guideposts to acceptable behaviour. This emphasis on norms arose from Pearson's realisation that the life-threatening behaviours he had observed in his previously happy home town, were likely to remain unchanged until a new realisation of what's okay and what's not, was accepted by community leaders and members.

Norms, normal behaviour and normalising standards have long been at the centre of vigorous education debates and, in fact, form the very foundations of ethics as the basis of national values. Clearly Aborigines don't have a monopoly on slipping social norms. Many social commentators might suggest that some aspects of White Australian and Migrant behaviours also warrant an urgent review of community norms.

# THE FUTURE: SUTTON'S SUBTLE SUGGESTIONS

## SUTTON'S SUBTLE SUGGESTIONS

In mid-2009 Peter Sutton produced what must be one of the most insightful books on Indigenous life and values in Queensland. Titled "The Politics of Suffering" this work is a summary of 40 years of hands-on experience of an anthropologist whose life on outstations and in Cape York communities, makes him uniquely placed to explain the Indigenous situation to outsiders. As such, it should be compulsory reading for all bureaucrats and politicians in this field.

As one of the few Whitefellas to get the tick of approval from Marcia Langton, as reflected in her preface to the book, Sutton's experiences and views now need to be integrated with Noel Pearson's main themes of economic independence and taking responsibility. The differences between these two experienced writers are mostly differences in emphasis rather than substance. Sutton stresses the neglect of child welfare in the priority given to rights, treaties and identity by ATSIC and Native Title drivers. Pearson stresses the need for wealth-generation as the starting point for community betterment, but both writers are wary of the dead hand of customary practice as the prime constraint on improvement of well-being.

The present overview must of necessity take very seriously the evidence-based views and proposals of Peter Sutton whose unique experiences and professional studies set him apart from other contemporary commentators. The following summary is the present author's attempt to glean the most significant of Sutton's ideas, as a guide to future Indigenous policy and process.

Sutton can be put in context by considering what Marcia Langton says of his work: "He threw down the gauntlet and asked Australians to reconsider the contrast between progressivist public rhetoric about empowerment and self-determination, and the raw evidence of a disastrous failure in major aspects of Australian Aboriginal affairs policy since the early 1970's. His legendary state of calm and his curious, amused visage as he watched events… had been replaced by sadness and a worried, hesitant caution. Aurukun was transformed, he tells us, from 'a once liveable and vibrant community…..to a disaster zone'. Such honesty in the vicious world of Aboriginal politics is rare, and coming as it does from a respected White professional with a distinguished record of impartial observation, it is a powerful corrective to the romantic, misinformed fabulations about Aborigines as a special kind of 'noble savage'. Too many [of the communities he visited] are places of the kind of tragedy that turned him from dry observation to engaged argumentation. He tackles throughout the book the problem of the sanctity of 'cultural difference'." His cutting logic is liberating and vivid. Langton praises Sutton's 'humanist reasoning' and expresses the hope that bureaucrats and politicians reading his book will apply such humanism to their own writing. "Much of the tragedy, misery and death" suggests Langton, "has been caused by the inability of so many of Professor Sutton's contemporaries, to imagine Aboriginal life with all the normal trappings of modernity. Such a vision does not exclude 'culture' but it certainly does include life-enhancing circumstances".

What Langton is reflecting here, in her praise of Sutton's values, are probably her own (changing) priorities over time. The dilemma of Indigenous leaders who are pressured to choose between a rights/treaty/identity agenda and a family well-being agenda, shines through from both Langton's and Pearson's writings.

It should be remembered that Sutton writes against a personal background of a young anthropologist, so keen to help families escape the constraints of officialdom and the missions, that at great cost to his professional career, he acted as a labourer, helping Wik people build their own outstations where they could once again live with dignity on their own country. So he comes to the situation at Aurukun (and Hope Vale) as an accepted family member – as a brother/cousin who the families look to for help. As one who was taken in as a son by local Elder Victor Wolby in 1976, it was in this adopted capacity that he watched how, after 1985 when a regular alcohol supply became available, assault of women, children and Elders increased to the extent that nearby residents referred to Aurukun as 'Beirut". When his adopted niece was repeatedly bashed by her boyfriend and others, then savaged by dogs, then pack-raped, then hung herself, Sutton became even more committed to child welfare as his priority.

When Sutton arrived at Aurukun in 1973, he found Palm Island to be the

## THE FUTURE: SUTTON'S SUBTLE SUGGESTIONS

most violent community in the region but by 1990 Aurukun was as violent and dysfunctional as Palm Island. The point of this comparison is that the Wik people of Aurukun, who had what Sutton calls 'among the most benign postcolonial experiences', fell victim to alcohol despite never having been dispersed from their home country. Palm Island by comparison was a 'penal colony' where all trouble-makers were deposited and kept under Mission and Police control.

As with the present author, in 2000 Sutton decided comment on Aboriginal policy could no longer be left to Aborigines. He was well aware that 'Whitefellas were increasingly unwelcome in exposed positions of the Aboriginal political front line'. He'd decided that by 2000 it had become necessary to have 'all hands on deck.' At this stage Sutton had realised that the widely-held belief that dysfunction had resulted from loss of land, children, women and self-respect, just wasn't true – at least not in the case of the coastal Wik people of the Aurukun area. The local Mission, established in 1904 by German Moravians, had always accepted the seasonal migration of families back to their country and only a small minority of the Wik-Mungkan language group had had their country included in pastoral leases that refused them access. Sutton's attempt to explain the significance of the long-held 'liberal consensus' on Aboriginal affairs, forms the central issue of his book, indeed it is his subtitle. In essence his approach is to reject:

1. Politicisation of health and housing.
2. Insistence on recognition of customary law.
3. Formal reconciliation as an official mass agreement.

He identified what he termed 'compassion contests and toughness contests' – a political game in which each policy advocate tried to prove that they were less racist or less 'bleeding–heart' than opposing advocates. He unmasks these efforts as 'exercises in pursuit of one's own virtue....' To his surprise he found that his seminal public lecture in 2000 bearing the same title as his book, drew evidence of a 'widespread thirst for a new candidness' and a ready acceptance of the need to accept the massive failure of Aboriginal policy to date. What had been acceptable aims and processes in Indigenous policy for 30 years and agreed to as the new progressive approach in 1970, was now (2000) being rejected and replaced by a new reality.

## OVERCOMING DISADVANTAGE

In his honest, heartfelt and unqualified frankness on the causes of current degradation in communities, Sutton recognised that unsympathetic critics could use his frank statements against his own positive motivations. In short, he contended that many of the important issues which Indigenous Australians face today, arise from 'a complex joining together of post-conquest historical factors of external impact, with a substantial number of ancient, pre-existent social and cultural factors that have continued, transformed or intact, into the lives of people living today.' He contends that the way in which these (cultural) factors are maintained is through child-rearing and it is in childhood that the damage of violence takes place. In other words, Sutton's experience leads him to believe that the causes of contemporary disadvantage go far beyond the impacts of colonisation, Missions and Police.

Sutton states that this blaming of the Whitefellas has been 'a sustaining fiction', one which the masses accept because they can't handle 'the subtlety of the truth'. He maintains that the silence about the full range of causal factors of community breakdown has suited those at both ends of the political spectrum. The time of no debate and no freedom to speak out is over for Sutton and in an unusual parallel of views he mirrors many of the points hinted at cautiously by the present author in the "Fair Go' paper of 1998. Since the 1970's, honest criticism of Aboriginal customs and norms has been taboo. Equally, the personal attacks on non-Indigenous commentators have caused a vacuum in the political debate – almost as if, in repeating Sutton's words, 'one's ancestry determines what topics one is allowed to speak on in public.' While such constraints have discouraged many informed non-Indigenous commentators from risking accusations of 'patronising', a more serious outcome of this silence on unacceptable behaviour, has been the inability of the courts to prosecute violent offenders because of the repeated refusal of witnesses to 'say it as it is'.

The frustration and empathy for abused children, which drew Sutton to break his silence, was being felt by the general public after the Alice Springs public prosecutor Nanette Rogers, appeared on national television to state forcibly that 'enough was enough' and that the courts simply could not function under the ruling 'blanket of silence' on child abuse in 2007. Prime Minister Howard found it politically expedient to announce the National Emergency Response as a reaction to the 'Little Children are Sacred' report

## THE FUTURE: SUTTON'S SUBTLE SUGGESTIONS

on child abuse in the Territory. Howard used this response to put (ex-army) Mal Brough, Minister for Indigenous Affairs, in charge of the Northern Territory Intervention. Brough was just the man to confront the strong men and the gang boys on their own terms. Repeated failure of consultation and negotiation led Brough to use the only tactic they understood – cut off the money and the grog. The abusers of children, women and the elderly had had a free run for many years, ruling by fear and subordinating the communities to their new norms.

In one sense this was the hinge of history for remote Territory communities, in another sense it had the makings of a monstrous disaster in which the army took over social organisation, and health authorities threatened involuntary sexual examination of females, notably juveniles . When the army's Norforce confronted the local gang leaders, it became clear that the time for meaningless discussion was over and the dawn of a new era might just be upon the lawless outback settlements.

Lifelong hands-on anthropologists like Sutton must have watched this belated knee-jerk reaction by government with a mixture of amazement, concern, relief and disbelief. The term 'of too little, too late' had often been applied to official programs to 'fix Aboriginal problems.' Now the question seemed to be: 'was this too much, too early?'. The Rudd government proceeded with the (modified?) Intervention and its results cannot easily be clearly evaluated. Sutton seemed to regard the whole Intervention exercise as a risky shock treatment which may just initiate 'unplanned outcomes' for the powerless members of this broken society.

Crucial to Sutton's approach to the future well-being of Indigenous people, is his stance on culture and Land Rights. After a lifetime of trying to nurture languages, Land Rights, visual arts and social organisations, he now makes it very clear where his priorities for communities lie. His starting objective on policy is not to correct unjust distribution of power, or appease sectional interests, or to preserve what is left of Indigenous culture, or even to maintain the old form of links to land. Predictably this puts Sutton at odds with most of the culture/Native Title warriors. However, he explains that while these issues may be serious, they are not his first consideration: "*The first consideration, instead, must be to focus on those conditions that are conclusive to the emotional and physical well-being of the unborn, infants, children, adolescents, the elderly, and adult women and men*" (my italics).

Sutton says it is remarkable that so many in mainstream Australian society regard respect for cultural differences and racially-defined autonomy as more important than children's right to love, health and safety. This seems to indicate that White Australians have somehow been led to believe that political values are more important than moral personal values. This can surely only be the result of decades of propaganda on political correctness born of collective guilt. When such artificially-induced 'respect' for another's culture and autonomy, combine with value-free gangland rule in remote communities where fearful silence and closure to outsiders are the rule, the worst human urges are given free reign.

At the heart of corrective action at local level was the fundamental problem of child welfare being put in the 'too hard' basket – in Sutton's words: "The political glamour attracted by those who struggle for rights and justice has long outshone the small glow emitted by those who are at the coalface of the caring business, the ones who dress the wounds of battered women in remote clinics at three o'clock on Sunday mornings…" It is this reality which makes him put "considerations of care before considerations of strict justice as a matter of principle". Sutton is prepared to face complaints about flawed justice if justice comes at the expense of care. This may mean that vested interest groups cannot be appeased in many cases. So be it, says Sutton.

Here we have the hands-on anthropologist with a White upbringing, aligning himself with the legally-trained mission boy (Pearson) in pushing for caring over rights, for innocent children over strong men, for decency over dominance. We are dealing here with universal truths and human values that override local vested interests, powerplays, and political point-scoring. Pearson's shock at visiting his once happy mission town only to find it a hellhole, and Sutton's dismay at the suicide of a pack-raped young girl, arise from the same wellspring of raw humanity which cries: "Stop – this cannot go on". Such basic moral emotions transcend the nonsense of political correctness and cultural humbug and reach out to the most fundamental of human instincts – nurturing, as the very essence of group survival.

Decades of policy based on cultural relativism (accepting all cultures as unique and valuable in and of themselves) in which Aboriginal culture and tradition were freed from judgemental European mores, came at a cost to

## THE FUTURE: SUTTON'S SUBTLE SUGGESTIONS

unprotected individuals. This cultural relativism grew out of the over-reaction of governments to the myth that all Indigenous societal ills had been caused by White impacts. Indigenous spokepersons were able to get away for decades, with labelling concerned White helpers as patronising, condescending do-gooders whose guilt-ridden past caused them to display what Sutton calls 'saccharine sympathy'.

At issue here is how best to enable good social policy to lift broken people from depravity. Sutton: "We have long been told that the emotional and physical health of Indigenous people will not improve until their social justice needs, property justice needs, treaty needs, formal reconciliation needs and compensation needs have been met, and by implication, that the heart of people's problems and solutions lies in politics and law." This stance means that by definition, the reformers who save the people from all the social ills afflicting them will be the legal eagles, the promising politicians and the fund-based bureaucrats.

Such an assumption is anathema to Sutton who doesn't mince his words when such imagined saviours are put forward: "This unscientific mumbo jumbo beggars belief. It relies on a kind of magical cause–and–effect relationship, as if a treaty between 'races' will keep children safe in their beds at night. It is understandable only as a career-enhancing tack taken by those who espouse it. Unfortunately, some such careers can depend functionally as much on the perpetuation of a sense of victimhood in the population, as on any evidence of healing, if not more so." His call is for caring measures which ensure the human rights of freedom from abuse, sufficient diet, adequate medical care and the right to economic and spatial mobility as the real needs. He contends that these basics must receive priority over "increasingly stratospheric rights and international covenants."

Above all, Sutton calls for "the creation of conditions where Indigenous people have enough incentive and motivation, and enough capacity to change, to make important improvements in their own lives. Large numbers have done so." Neither coercive programs from government nor do-gooders' moralizing, can motivate individuals who need to handle their own emotions and finances. This is why Sutton pleaded for a personal, not a race, approach to individual improvement.

OVERCOMING DISADVANTAGE

# SIGNIFICANT EXTRACTS FROM SUTTON

Some justification should be given for the extent to which Peter Sutton has been quoted in this review. In a way, Sutton is uniquely placed because he brings three decades of close personal experience of living with Aboriginals, he speaks three Cape York languages, has contributed to fifty Land Rights claims and his book 'Native Title in Australia' is probably the most respected non-legal source on this issue. Importantly, Sutton's deep emotional commitment to the Aboriginal cause has not prevented him bringing a new view to sensitive cultural issues and challenging the current wisdom on policy. Having observed the impacts of government policy and societal decline since 1969 Sutton, above virtually all other observers on Cape York, offers policy-makers an innovative re-think of embedded ideology.

Sutton's fellow Cape York spokesman, Noel Pearson, complements rather than competes with his proposals, with differences in emphasis. One of Sutton's more important contributions is his exposure of the damage done to progress toward well-being, by silence and omission of vital information on cultural matters. He doesn't allow the pain which this causes, to divert him from the long-overdue need for honesty as the necessary ingredient of progress. Pearson has done a similar thing in challenging his people to take responsibility and stop blaming others for their predicament.

The above introduction to Sutton's philosophy and how it complements Pearson's, reveals his importantly different priorities in Indigenous affairs. What follows below, is an extract of further pertinent concepts from Sutton's approach in the sequence of his experience on consensus, rage, culture, violence, politics, customs, anthropologists and reconciliation. (As with other writers on complex inter-related social problems, the reader senses Sutton's struggle to identify bite-sized chunks of information in a readable sequence.)

Under the heading 'After Consensus' Sutton identifies the progressive politics that established the liberal consensus which he blames for three decades of faulty priorities on departmental structures at the expense of well-being. He maintains that the right to be free of violence, abuse and ignorance was ignored in past policy-setting. This 1970's political consensus became far removed from reality, although as Sutton puts it: "It is still evident in Central Australia and its outstation Melbourne, where dissent from Whitlamite values can still be policed by ruthless criticism and attempted public humiliation, or by careful omission".

## 1. Outstations and Policy

The record shows that when anthropologist John von Sturmer was at Aurukun in the 1970's, the outstation movement started as an attempt to reconnect clans with their land and give them back their identity of origin. This movement was to play a crucial role in Indigenous affairs. It was seen by some as the saving of the people, by others including Aboriginal councillors, as a 'dangerous and divisive return to tribalism'. Outstations were to increase in the Aurukun region until up to 300 people were spending each dry season out on their own country. This trend was not to last however, and by 2008 nobody was using the outstations.

This rise and fall of outstations wasn't occurring in other regions to the same extent, nevertheless the concept of small scattered groups living 'on country' remains an important and contentious issue in service delivery and infrastructure investment. Where outstations serve as dry-out (recovery) centres, their role is strongly defended and contrasted with larger violent alcohol-fuelled settlements.

While the mixed fortunes of outstations were being played out at the end of the 1980's, Noel Pearson had been holding many beach meetings with Cape Elders, trying to develop a new legislative base for Indigenous administration. At a meeting at James Cook University on 13th July 1990 the first $300 was collected to start Pearson's Cape York Land Council – a milestone which Sutton appears to give special significance.

The 100 page legislation submission from Pearson to State Government, had been withheld from Premier Wayne Goss by his minders for two weeks until just before a scheduled meeting between Indigenous spokespersons and Goss in May 1991. Kevin Rudd was Goss's Chief-of-Staff at that time and was influential, according to Sutton (who edited the submission), in cancelling any further meetings with Goss on this matter.

At that time (1991) the question Sutton asked was, "Why did this descent into a seriously dysfunctional state (of Indigenous communities on the Cape) coincide with liberal progressive policies" or rights agendas, new autonomy, improved services, infrastructure and income. The answer became clear after journalist Tony Koch of the Courier Mail and Noel Pearson brought the extent of the community disaster to public attention in a strikingly vivid way through the popular press.

By 2002 Rosemary Neill's factual depiction of dysfunction gave impetus to deeper examination of the situation. Her book "White Out: How Politics is Killing Black Australia" led to serious think-tanks analysing possible causes of community disaster and the right wing Bennelong Society was established to develop policy. "The media discovered 'Aboriginal community dysfunction' in 2001 and then rediscovered it in 2005-06" says Sutton.

## 2. Dysfunction

By this time (2005) many commentators were wondering about the future of ATSIC as the peak Indigenous advisory body, since conditions in remote communities were not being attended to and personal tragedies were increasingly being reported. The previous code of silence was rapidly disintegrating. When senior leaders in ATSIC were charged with serious criminal offences while an increasingly long list of issues was being exposed by an enlivened media, political action was required.

Sutton's catalogue of issues at that time, warrants recording here:

- Welfare dependency
- Community autonomy (and secrecy)
- Organisational corruption
- ATSIC's future
- Frontier history wars (black armband/three cheers)
- Racial differences in health and longevity
- Low school attendance
- Declining literacy and numeracy
- Substance abuse
- Violence against women
- Child sexual abuse

## THE FUTURE: DYSFUNCTION

- Customary law as criminal defence
- Staying, leaving or orbiting from 'ghettos'
- Mainstreaming services
- Gang warfare
- Public rioting
- Entry permit system in closed communities
- Restrictions on media access
- Future funding of remote settlements
- Expectation of massive migration to the city

Apart from Indigenous art exhibitions and the opening of swimming pools, the 'good news' stories were hard to find as a counter to this overwhelming catalogue of disaster. The crunch came when Nanette Rogers, the Alice Springs Prosecutor, put the record straight on national television in 2006. That interview, referred to previously in this overview, became a sort of turning-point in the national debate. Thus, while the reality had taken a while to reach Canberra and the national psyche, Cape York had already taken serious corrective action, starting with alcohol control and Pearson's repeated insistence that passive welfare payments were 'the root of all evil' – a stance which Sutton knew to need qualification.

It was becoming clear that anthropologists' apparent dislike for certain basic truisms over the years, had caused them to conveniently ignore two fundamental issues in their reports: the cultural factors affecting mental health, and the way sexual behaviour had altered over recent decades. This selective blindness was somewhat overcome by the studies of David Martin at Aurukun in 1993 and David McKnight's work in 2002 on Mornington Island.

Sutton points out that "truthfulness is not necessarily a good uniter of people and that most people in our society are more easily bound by simple fictions which avoid upsetting our sensitivities". He recalls the Aurukun of his early 1970 years. Child abuse was very rare, women were full-time child-rearers, men worked at mustering and running a butcher's shop. Some worked as motor-mechanics, others logged and sawed timber to build local houses. Women worked at the local shops and hospital and helped at the school; vegetable gardens were tended and irrigated. If not a scene of domestic bliss, then at least it was a functioning community, very far removed from the hellish atmosphere of the "Beirut" he returned to after 2000.

It was this strong feeling of Paradise Lost, which drove Sutton to point out that all the Treaties, Reconciliations and Stolen Generation reports would do nothing for the toddlers in the bush. Sutton's conviction was worded as follows: "My certain feeling was, though, that the wave of unusual honesty and self-examination in Indigenous affairs that erupted in the 2000's needed to proceed a while longer before the future would become any clearer". What he probably meant was that the untruths and political silliness which had emphasised victimhood for so long, would not dissipate overnight and required a sustained recognition of Indigenous shortcomings to balance the convenient blaming of government, before a new rationally-based pride and self-respect could drive sustainable communities.

This awakening of a more nuanced realisation of the causes of the bad community situation was a far cry from the previously accepted views on causes. These views were to a considerable degree based, perhaps unknowingly to many, on the seminal work of Charles Rowley, published in 1966 under the title; "Some questions of causation in relation to Aboriginal affairs". Central to Rowley's thesis was that the Aborigines had no pyramidal structure of social organisation and that Aboriginal custom should be encouraged if it was the will of the people and didn't contravene Australian law. Rowley regarded the largely unspoken Australian 'caste barrier' as the basic cause of disadvantage – a constraint which was to be removed, at least officially, by the Racial Discrimination Act of 1975.

More than any other recent writer, Sutton identifies simplistic racially-biased causation theory as the prime source of delay in developing and activating rational corrective policy. Referring to the 'blame game' based on post-colonial discrimination, he says, "Even people of apparent sophistication can publically subscribe to causal accounts that are an insult to the average intelligence". He cites the failure of obese parents to save their children from malnutrition being blamed on government as an example. "What enables the purveyors of such pap, and those who swallow it, to so suspend their normal critical faculties?" he asks. There are literate and well-educated people who seem prepared to support the view that Aboriginal dysfunction is primarily caused by governments' goal of discrediting Indigenous people and taking from them their land, culture and identity. At least this is Sutton's view.

[In a somewhat radical departure from supporting Sutton's opinions, the present author cannot avoid the unspoken question of what greater benefits might accrue to Aboriginal personal well-being if these so-called cultural losses did occur, i.e. is it just possible that fully mainstreamed Aborigines would be better off than their cultural bush cousins? We shall return to this unsettling concept in the final chapter.]

The point needs to be stressed, when evaluating Sutton's experience-based opinion, that the vague and cosy view which suburban White's may have of remote communities, requires a large dash of realism. If by 'community' is meant an ethos of mutual support and giving priority to the common good, many, perhaps most, such settlements deserve a very different connotation. This is why Sutton uses Peggy Brook's 1993 term 'outback ghetto' to more honestly portray the reality of remote communities. The Howard government found it necessary to designate 73 communities in the Territory alone, as in need of urgent social intervention in 2007. This is at odds with the self-perception of the inmates of these ghettos who in an oral survey, thought health standards were 'good to excellent' despite the fact that such a 'culturally appropriate' situation is seriously at odds with international health standards.

In Cape York, Pearson dates the start of community dysfunction at the early 1970's when both grog and some form of 'sit-down money' became entrenched. His repeated claim that 'passive welfare' caused the social decay, has been supported by many, although there is probably a more widely-held view, including that of Sutton, that this is only one issue, albeit a very significant one, in a situation that requires much more than removal of this passivity.

Attempts to break out of the poverty cycle in remote settlements have repeatedly failed, leading Colin Tatz in 1990, to refer to 'administrative myopia': "No one learns from the past, no one listens, no one learns, and hardly anybody stays around long enough to osmose anything. Everybody re-discovers the wheel". Sutton agrees with Tatz's frustrated claim and finds it odd that when Pearson is able to arrange for a small group of Cape youths to pick fruit in the Riverina, this is somehow welcomed as a notable breakthrough in mainstreaming and orbiting. Sutton points out that this was done back in the 1960's when South Australian and Territory pickers were used. This begs the important question of why it is necessary to invite Pacific Islanders and European backpackers to work the Murray-Darling orchards when Australia has unusually high unemployment among its youth, some close at hand.

The epidemic of alcoholism and drug misuse is more understandable in Sutton's experience when individual's history of dispossession, discrimination, enforced assimilation and devaluing of the male roles, are taken into account. But he emphasises that Land Rights have not led to improved well-being despite government efforts to improve schooling, housing, health and diet.

This brings the debate to the point where the nation must seriously consider the necessity or otherwise of what Sutton calls the 'parallel universe based on race, not need…' meaning expensive duplication of services simply to maintain separate ethnic identity. So the huge amount of funding appropriated to a range of services and structures prefixed 'Indigenous' must now come into sharper focus in economically tough times for government. Now the serious evaluation of the real cost and thus policy support of duplicated expenses becomes a significant fiscal issue, not just a 'culturally appropriate' policy.

## 3. New Opinions

Sutton quotes Trevor Satour, a Cairns Aboriginal who 'let it all hang out' in the press in 2001 when he challenged the Apartheid-like dual system: "Whether or not the separatist path has been a total failure and historic dead-end, it is surely time to rethink our focus and priorities….there comes a time to face truths…*one either reinvents oneself to be useful or one ceases to exist*" (my emphasis). We shall return to this bombshell in the final chapter since its evocative sentiment is at the heart of future policy. Ever since the policy trend of emancipating the individual in the early 1970's, as Tim Rowse pointed out in 2000, there has been a move toward communalising self-determination and not interfering with culture and customs.

Rowse uses the unusual title of "Culturally appropriate Indigenous accountability" to introduce the idea of loyalty to family as a man's first priority. He questions the validity of some so-called traditions, which he believes are 'Indigenous social forms that are recently developed and consciously contrived'. One wonders whether he extends his doubt to Indigenous art in its present commercial form as well.

Sutton believes that prior to 2005, policy was developed on the assumption that government could ignore the serious incompatibility of modernisation and traditionalism in its purer form. This pretence at compatibility he refers to as the 'Coombsian contradiction' – a concept we deal with elsewhere. Ethnic diversity has great potential to culturally enrich the national population but in the absence of tolerance and the presence of unacceptable behaviour, such diversity easily breeds discontent and even conflict where ethnic groups live in close proximity.

Under the heading of "The Trouble with Culture' Sutton reminds us that the valuing of culture is actually a Western concept. When he arrived in North Queensland in the early 1970's, the word 'culture' was rarely heard but within a decade it had become the buzz-word of liberation politics. Soon posters saying 'Keep Culture Strong' were appearing in government buildings at outback settlements. Indigenous leaders started asking outsiders to respect Aboriginal culture and in time many came to believe that culture would somehow save their society. Says Sutton, "My generation's insistence on the value and power of culture, has given it an exaggerated credit rating. Traditional culture, as something to be preserved even at high cost, has been overrated".

This sentiment is at the heart of future policy-making, or rather, it should be. Other experienced observers are less inclined to express this view, largely because of the Holy Grail status acquired by things cultural. Nevertheless, while remaining a sensitive issue, the urgent need to put culture in its 'correct' place in the policy debate requires that it must be removed from the 'Too Hard/Too Sensitive' basket.

The wishful thinking that the restoration and maintenance of culture will somehow regain lost dignity and will ensure respect from non-Indigenous countrymen, requires a serious re-think if the culture warriors are not to mislead their devotees any further – as Satour said 'change or die'.

In this consideration of the role and usefulness of culture, evaluation of Aboriginal stories and their implications for decision-making, become a major subset of the cultural debate. Unsurprisingly, when examining the age, validity and meaning of stories, one enters the same irrational world as Western religious fundamentalism – a world where doubters and questioners are unwelcome and easily labelled enemies of the faith. This is a pity in a people whose ancient culture, so heavily reliant on generational knowledge transfer, uses the oral tradition. In recent years a big effort has been made to record regional stories of The Dreamtime in books and on videotape or DVD as a means of preserving and spreading these verbal archives. Gauging their significance and worthiness of preservation, involves the same abstract values as the preservation of ancient languages, many of which are highly prized.

Changes in cultural values have recently been recommended by some Indigenous spokespersons – a move which is related to Pearson's call for an uplifting of behavioural norms in their society. These community innovators recognise the way in which unacceptable behaviour is increasingly being justified on a cultural basis, and they are determined to demonstrate that much of the violence and abuse was never part of their culture.

For grandparents whose Mission upbringing makes them considerably more literate than their offspring (and gives them their important work ethic), the devastating downward spiral starting with foetal alcohol syndrome needs action – now. These oldies value their traditions and country but the virtual loss of their grandchildren has become unbearable. This is why it was the old women who set up the alcohol roadblocks to their community – not the strong men or the police, but the matriarchs in desperation.

## 4. Culture's Future

So where should we go with culture? Perhaps Stanner was right when in 1979 he stated somewhat categorically "There is a sense in which The Dreaming and The Market are mutually exclusive". If he is correct then the question becomes, as stated earlier in this review, "How much and what form of culture and tradition is required to motivate, identify and keep grounded, future individuals of Aboriginal descent?" This surely is a personal judgement, like how much religious faith do we need to see us through?

The idea of culture and tradition must be juxtaposed to modernisation and mainstreaming but not in a mutually exclusive way. In the same way, the concept of 'assimilation' in which the dominant culture replaces the minority's culture, may or may not be a negative or pejorative term to those affected. It has become almost impossible to have an objective debate on the assimilation issue without preconceived good/bad values being attached to what advocates or adversaries consider the virtues/dangers of mainstreaming. Mounting evidence supports the long-term logic of assimilation when it is understood to imply access to mainstream services and structures as the basis for improved

# THE FUTURE: CULTURE'S FUTURE

well-being. The claim that such absorption by the dominant (but multiracial) culture will necessarily be at the expense of minority culture, just isn't true as shown by the vibrant Italian, Greek and Aboriginal communities maintaining their identity in Australian cities. In an Indigenous population of whom over 80% already live in towns and cities and largely inter-marry with other ethnic groups, it should not be difficult to encourage regional Aboriginals to assimilate for their own family's benefit – even if it means calling assimilation something else, like 'joining in'.

While on the subject of urban myths, Sutton cites the general view that the Aboriginal death rate in custody is far greater than that of non-Aboriginals. Not true, says Sutton, quoting official statistics to show that these rates are in fact the same according to the 1991 Royal Commission. Sutton asks, "In whose interests are such stories passed on?" Whose indeed?

The same myth applies to those who still believe that the Indigenous population is 'fading out'. John Taylor's 2001 studies in Central Australia produced credible estimates of a 2% Indigenous annual growth rate, suggesting that this race in that region would double their numbers in 50 years; Yarrabah in Queensland would double to 6,000 by 2051 and Arnhem Land would reach 34,000 in the same period.

Sutton tries to explain mainstream Australia's disinterest in Indigenous welfare by way of what he calls 'compassion fatigue' which not only makes many Australians unshockable, but starts to match the 'tragedy tolerance' of outback residents. In this situation, 'suffering' becomes relative and less than emotive. As for causality of Aboriginal disadvantage, Sutton regards Richard Trudgen's 43 primary reasons for 'secondary symptoms' (personal outcomes?) as seriously lacking, as stated in Trudgen's book "Why Warriors Lie Down and Die" published in 2000. This attempt at explaining causation is 'deeply flawed' in Sutton's estimation. He suggests that too many professed causation accounts are simplistic and often untruthful, not because untruths are stated but rather because of deliberate omissions even when these are widely recognised as clearly causal of dysfunction. At the same time Sutton warns of continent-wide generalisations (e.g. All Aboriginals…..). The recognised differences in function and progress aren't always related to the intensity of impact of non-Aboriginal settlement as is often assumed, but can arise from pre-colonial tribal differences and environmental variations. As an example he quotes Marcia Langton's "Too Much Sorry Business" in which she states that many Aboriginal communities in the Territory had never been dispossessed of the land and yet "…..the grog is crippling these same Aboriginal people".

## 5. Causation and Blame

The obsession with blame has led most spokespersons and bureaucrats to avoid certain subjects. For the Aboriginal representatives there was "a blindness to the ancient need to pursue family loyalties over essentially foreign ideologies such as the doctrine of the common good". For the administrators, their over-sensitivity to reviving the 'blame the victim' criticism, results in what has become politically-correct (actually incorrect) avoidance of sensitive subjects. Both groups of spokespersons must thus take the blame for seriously deficient causation statements. A case in point is Sutton's question of whether or not a high level of personal violence was normal among pre-colonial Aboriginals. The predictable search for selective evidence on both sides, makes such questions impossible to answer objectively, given present racial sensitivities.

The use of sorcery as an excuse for deaths is another issue which Sutton has experienced as recently as 2007 at Aurukun and Pormpuraaw. While ever such superstition is resorted to in homicide cases, the perpetrators will continue to hide behind this perversion of justice. Such beliefs are not easily deleted from the communal memory, so a generational change may be required before an alternative education system can overcome this primitive belief. [In essence this form of causation is similar to that used by those who claim that violent deaths were the will of Allah or God.] As part of the program to curb violence, sorcery needs special attention, notably when it is subsumed in customary law as an add-on to Australian law. Part of such a program is the critical re-examination of the way traditional life has been romanticised as what Sutton sarcastically calls, "a time of peace and harmony." The truth is that the present violence doesn't match new acceptability standards and as Sutton points out, such a historic whitewash "does no justice to the evidence and no service of historic truthfulness towards the very people one may admire and respect".

The historic violence referred to here is not limited to violence against women but includes sizable massacres as recorded by both Stanner (1969) and

# THE FUTURE: CAUSATION AND BLAME

Strehlow (1969) in the late 1800's where up to 100 men, women and children were recorded in Mission records as having been massacred in inter-tribal attacks in both Central Australia and Cape York. Sutton points out that there was apparently no accepted sense of revulsion at physical injury and he suggests that such squeamishness is a concept of the West, foreign to early Aboriginal hunter-gatherers.

Sutton's study of 100 homicides in the Wik region of the Cape shows that between 1890 and 1960, most deaths occurred during personal conflicts in which sexual jealousy seemed to be the prime motive. These records, in the Aurukun Mission Diaries, also show that after 1960 there had been 22 male deaths from homicide, followed by a quiet period (1960-85) in which no homicides were recorded, then a violent period up to 2006 with 17 deaths. Of note is the fact that the percentage of female homicides rose from 53% in the Mission era to 73% after that time. Pre-Mission female rates are estimated at 44%. Today, reinstating the old traditional control system, while attractive to some who are aware of the current power vacuum, is probably impossible in practice. In any case its 'totalitarian and violent' elements should, in Sutton's experience, no longer be supported. His plea is for a better understanding of how violence is learned (and accepted?) by the growing child, as well as how and why adults have become so violent. As to causation, Tatz makes the contrarian statement that the basic cause of current violence was not colonisation but decolonisation. By this he means exposing vulnerable communities to the power vacuum after the Missions closed.

Sutton makes the important observation that a number of Fourth World peoples throughout history, have reacted differently to similar impacts of external domination. He suggests that the degree of differential collapse of societies such as the Maoris, Aztecs, Aboriginals and even ancient Britons, was determined by pre-existing inherent differences between these cultures themselves.

## 6. Health

Under the heading of 'The Disease of Politicisation' Sutton takes Anderson and Loff to task on their conclusions on Aboriginal health, despite these being published by a respected international medical journal: "That a journal with the historic reputation of The Lancet would stoop to publishing propaganda like this was incredible." Their sin was to insist that it was the lack of an Aboriginal voice in health policy which was responsible for the 'appalling disparity' between Aboriginal health and others. In answer to this groundless assertion, Sutton lists precisely what, in his opinion, are the actual causes of Indigenous ill-health: "Culturally embedded behaviours….that have a direct impact on health…..include absolutely basic things like domestic sanitation and personal hygiene, housing density, diet, the care of children and the elderly, gender relationships, alcohol and drug use, [violent] conflict resolution, social acceptability of violence, cultural norms to do with the expression of emotions, the [low] relative value placed on physical well-being, attitudes to learning new information and attitudes to making changes in health-related behaviour." Suggesting that lack of Aboriginal representation is the cause, while leaving out these well-established behavioural factors, can only be explained as a conscious decision to put these cultural matters in the Too Hard Basket. Why does such a long extract from Sutton warrant quoting here? Because this list covers the essential issues at the heart of dysfunction and represents a checklist of issues in urgent need of understanding and corrective action.

On the question of incompatible practices and society's tolerance of harmful customs, Sutton's reminder of Malinowski's warning in 1913 is timely: Condoning any behaviour simply because it's traditional has been a serious mistake, leading to favouring custom at the expense of human welfare. Such warped priorities may be traced back not only to primitive peoples, but to the Christian crusades and Mohammedan invasions.

This relates to the idea of conscience – a modern concept built on taught values of right and wrong. Stanner, that renowned scholar of Indigenous culture, wrote in 1963, "As far as one can tell from outward show, the formations of conscience among Aboriginals are not strong". He seemed to infer that behaviours and reactions were instinctive and possibly survival-oriented in the Territory people, rather than enculturated by learning.

Enculturated behaviour apparently formed the basis of the old power structures – a form of social control fondly remembered by Elders of Sutton's acquaintance. Such values seem treasured by the old, but feared by the young. Says Sutton, "I haven't met too many women who have a nostalgia for the old patriarchy" in which the old men controlled regional boundaries, marriage, sorcery, payback injury and even execution.

Of significance in the sphere of racial separatist politics, is the important survey by Stephen Kunitz in 1994 in which American, Canadian, New Zealand and Australian 'special health service entitlements' to Indigenous people were compared with universal entitlements. Kunitz suggested that the targeted funding and the health of people with special needs, irrespective of race, was more important in improving health overall, than the relation between transfer of funds to racial control bodies. Sutton seems not to support Kunitz's deduction that Aboriginals are at the bottom of the ladder of international life-expectancy specifically because they are the only Indigenous race which has no formal treaty with its national government.

## 7. Housing

Much publicity has been given to the housing shortage as a prime cause of Aboriginal disadvantage. Together with health and education, housing has often been proposed as the starting point for breaking the dysfunction cycle.

Sutton points out that the useful life of Indigenous housing is very short – about seven years in fact. Pride in home ownership has repeatedly been seen as the way out of such destruction but, as Sutton points out, crowding has a number of 'culturally appropriate' elements to it. Social priorities, family responsibilities, a culture of sharing and personal safety, all contribute to the general tendency to overnight 15-20 persons in many remote area houses. Whether provision of more houses on its own, would reduce density for any substantial period seems unlikely.

Sutton notes that when Aborigines move to town and adapt culturally to suburban living, such change is regarded by observers as 'going White.' This, says Sutton, is to "falsely racialise" an adaptation that people in many countries have made for centuries – "We were all nomadic hunter-gatherers once."

## 8. Victim Blaming

In recent years the so-called Health Gap (between Blacks and Whites) has received so much publicity that most Australian adults can now repeat the official longevity gap – 17 years (2009). In seeking causes for the racial gap in health, the main difference of opinion is between the so-called 'Structural' and 'Agency' causes, a dichotomy of causation proposed by Kowal and Paradies. In this separation it is suggested from workshop responses of health workers, that the structural causes were listed as factors such as the historical context, the current health system, the prevailing culture, the funding situation and the remoteness in which health services had to be delivered. Staff who held this structural or organisational view did not accept the alternative Agency or Human causes of unacceptably poor community health. 'Agency' concerns are behaviours of individuals – almost all of which were regarded as 'politically incorrect' according to Kowal and Paradies. They found: "Participants were more likely to blame the system, and were reluctant to nominate Indigenous people's choices or actions as the cause of their ill-health. This ethos of political correctness is clearly a response to victim blaming" – a stance regarded as racist. Sutton insists that causation and blame should not be confused.

One of the constraints to changing traditional attitudes is that change is regarded as contrary to 'the law' – that timeless constant customary way of doing things. Sutton maintains that "the law never changes, whether to accommodate new circumstances, new knowledge or for any other reason". Strehlow believed that factual learning by young people was actively discouraged by Elders in Central Australia. This learned inability to move with the times, has become a serious brake on well-being and is perhaps akin to continued strict biblical interpretation by Christian fundamentalists who refuse blood transfusions and refuse early abortions even when the mother is in a life-threatening situation.

Returning to the sensitivity of 'blaming the victim' as a politically incorrect opinion, Sutton holds firmly that it is quite untrue to attribute moral culpability to those whose cultural practices and personal choices are believed to cause ill-health. The current author notes that sensitivity on this matter has become a major source of evasion of the truth on causality of ill-health. In reality it's not primarily the system's fault, it's the individual's responsibility to behave in a healthy way.

Sutton maintains that there must be some psychological attraction to protecting the victim from blame – somehow it allows the purveyor of this stance to take the moral high ground. This position easily becomes the political group's comforting assurance that their policy is morally defensible.

Meanwhile, all this does is encourage some outrageous behaviours which have long been known to undo the hard work of professionals committed to better health. As Gary Johns has remarked: 'It's not more rights, but more good behaviour, that is needed.' Sutton quotes Gary Robinson of Health Research in Darwin, as finding that, "Even in the short term, the capacity of individuals and their families to alter aspects of 'lifestyle' may be decisive in achieving any degree of effect in treatment". What Robinson is saying is what all experienced health workers know, i.e. that the benefits of medication and treatment will seldom result in wellness without behavioural change. In practice the social changes recommended for wellness promotion are often interpreted by local leaders as diminishing the community's own power and thus its autonomy and self-management.

Sutton warns against the recent practice of employing Aboriginal medicine men to complement hospital medical staff. He sees this well-intentioned concession to cultural medicine as seriously self-contradictory for staff who are trying to bring about changed behaviours for wellness. If the custom of instilling a belief in children that fatal diseases are caused by sorcery, is to be replaced with factual evidence, the traditional 'doctors' need to be removed. Sutton points out how Christian Science in the 1800's taught similar mystical causes of disease, thus spiritual causation of the Black Death in Europe is also widely recorded. Indigenisation of today's health system in Northern Australia may well slow the gains being made in Aboriginal health.

## 9. Customs and Cultural Relativism

Reference has already been made to Cultural Relativism as a vehicle for defending the virtues of even the indefensible elements of dysfunctional cultures. Sutton admits that many specialists working with Indigenous people took such relativism beyond its reasonable limits. "Many of us have recoiled from these" he says.

Over the decades, Cultural Relativism has been successfully used as a counter to Social Darwinism which explained and justified domination by the 'fittest'. Fittest in this sense, usually meant that those with the best weapons could apply racial prejudice and ethnic superiority even where it was morally absent.

The theories of anthropologists such as Franz Boas initiated a wide and long debate on the scientific basis of tolerance of cultural difference. In time, what had been regarded as the valuable concept of relativism, actually failed because of the practical unacceptability of some customs which clearly constrained the progress of well-being. In the case of Australia, this was reflected, for instance, in attempts to find a place for Indigenous law in the legal system, or a place for traditional healing in medicine.

Ken Maddock, an experienced medical researcher, was moved to note that "Unless some hard thinking is done about what customary law is, and what its recognition would entail, any political initiative in its favour may end in tears and disillusion." Sutton sympathises with attempts to indigenise the law, but his experience leads him to conclude: "With all due respect, the potential here for inconsistency and breathtaking contradiction seems plainly obvious." The practical situation is that in the present era, most Indigenous people move in what is called 'inter-ethnic social space' (big words for mixed community) and everyone is obliged to operate in co-operation with people of other races. This means doing away with inconsistencies such as those found in laws applied to Aboriginal homicide where over the years, according to Justice Martin Kriewaldt, the penalties on Aborigines (for murder) "have been consistently lighter than penalties imposed on White offenders.

Sutton asks whether White Australian's "repugnance to payback wounding, genital mutilation of minors and promised under-age marriage is just bourgeois squeamishness….. or evidence of an oversensitive disposition?" The short answer seems to be 'No', these practices are morally indefensible and the past efforts of anthropologists to sanitise their accounts of primitive societies has helped to enculturate the 'noble savage' image referred to earlier. In defending Aboriginal identity as an essential element of future well-being of this group of Australians, the impact of ethnic separatism on national social cohesion, needs to be evaluated. In many developed countries which have received immigrants and refugees of diverse ethnic backgrounds, the benefits of either social cohesion or multicultural freedoms have had to be balanced. The problems of general acceptance in Britain, of Migrant enclaves with ethnic schools, churches and community centres attached, ultimately caused the head of the UK's Commission for Racial Equity to declare in 2004, that full-blown multiculturalism had been 'pronounced dead.' Since this gentleman Trevor Phillips, was born in Guyana, his statement could hardly be written off as just another White racist comment.

The cultural warriors engaged in the media's multicultural wars, easily make the mistake of taking the factual evidence as moralistic feel-goodism, i.e. the comfort that comes from taking the high moral ground in defence of powerless victims suppressed by mean dominant others. Sutton lists several lines of attack, including 'the evils of colonisation, Western power, racism of pale-skinned people, wrongs of patriarchy, police violence and the oppression of minorities', as examples of crusader-type motivation. He makes the interesting observation that surveys and voting patterns show a consistent trend in which racial intolerance by Whites, increases in proportion to Whites' amount of contact with Blacks. In this way the do-gooders can easily empathise with remote people without the reality of having to experience racial behavioural differences at close quarters.

## 10. Reconciliation – one more time

The whole idea of reconciliation has already been alluded to in this overview but its relation to the perpetuation of racially-based separatism (Apartheid?) warrants wider consideration against the background of Sutton's sentiments on race relations.

Many who support racial separatism put a higher value on ethnic identity than on social cohesion. When the great Reconciliation Bridge Walk in Sydney took place, there were opposing demonstrators with placards reading 'Not in Our Name', just as when Prime Minister Rudd delivered his 2008 Apology on behalf of government, detractors insisted that they had nothing to apologise for. Sutton notes that few voters seemed to be aware that all the States had already made their 'colonial' Apologies, as had the ACT and the Northern Territory.

Perhaps, as Paul Keating said, "That's about as good as it gets" and Australians are left wondering whether and when a national Indigenous Forgiveness Movement might be formed, perhaps along the lines of the South African Truth Commission under Bishop Tutu. So too, with reconciliation via a Stolen Generation Apology, National Sorry Day or Stolen Wages Compensation, the population is left wondering when and how Australians can get over these historic issues and move ahead together. Then the idea of whether we progress together or separately, brings up the questions of unity and identity and how these are to be reconciled. Sutton quotes Pearson as saying that "you don't have to be a campaign Aboriginal all your life," meaning individuals also have the choice of putting the past behind them and joining the general flow toward personal prosperity, so well deserved by coming generations.

Earlier reference has been made to the fact that representation through a pyramidal or hierarchical structure is foreign to Aboriginal clan structure. With this parochial background it should not come as a surprise that clan members elected to representative bodies act in the best interests of their family. In Sutton's words, "Elected representatives who do the right thing by the rules of Aboriginal cultural practice, are principally there to speak for their own and to maximise the benefits flowing to their own constituents, their own mobs, more than to a higher collective structure….." In spite of such local priorities, some in ATSIC (the former peak national body) had visions of this body having the potential to act as an emerging Aboriginal government with continent-wide influence. This in turn could lead on to secession of a sovereign land claimed under the law.

Reconciliation, if taken to its practical conclusion, would need Australians to reach consensus on two basic matters which Sutton refers to as 'justice and remorse.' He says that in Aboriginal society, as opposed to the Judeo-Christian tradition, emotions such as remorse, conscience and guilt do not play a role in dispute resolution. Sutton accuses commentators who assign these feelings to Indigenous actions, of unfounded Eurocentric value judgements.

Formal reconciliation agreements can be expected to embed racial separateness into future relations. This may be predicted to work against the much-sought-after unity and cohesion in the Australian population. Division has been partially caused by the way in which successive governments have competed to expand the number of organisations dedicated specifically to Aboriginal welfare. Most of these carry the prefix 'Indigenous': sport, health, housing, social benefits, all leading to a duplicated set of national services. The reasons for this doubling-up of bureaucracies is clear enough – political do-goodism seen to be supporting the disadvantaged, as befits an inclusive democracy. Sutton extends the list of duplicate institutions to Aboriginal staffing quotas in banks, QANTAS and even the Prime Minister's Department. He adds Oxford's Aboriginal Scholarships of 2008 to the separatist list. All

## THE FUTURE: RECONCILATION - ONE MORE TIME

this is regarded as part of the racial catch-up, which in turn is part of reconciliation. So far so good, but this parallel universe is proceeding concurrently with the same government's policy of mainstreaming of services, i.e. one service for all.

Sutton regards these policy contradictions as important because they have led to conflicting objectives, contrasting actions, competing funding and several layers of confusion by service deliverers and receivers. Structural segregation is based on "separation of rights and powers according to ancestry" in Sutton's judgement. This he says, is serious in the extreme because from separate recognition (of need) comes the exaggeration of racial difference and importantly, the assumption of racial inferiority. The crux of the matter here is that the powers, rights and benefits in the dual system are racially based, not needs based or demonstrated disadvantage based. This racial basis in turn, leads Sutton to remark that recipients of separatist policy largesse must be aware that they are receiving differential help because of their ancestry – they are not defined by their abilities or their personal disadvantage. He almost guarantees that the Aboriginal Oxford scholars will not be disadvantaged students but those riding on the back of privileged boarding school education. In a strange twist of logic, Sutton explains that recipients of the differential benefits of dualism, will not only extend racial separation but will forever have victim status – the victimhood which caused the dual system in the first instance. In this process of separation, non-Indigenous battlers become aggressive against injustice, imposed not on the basis of need or disadvantage.

All the attempts to improve equity are seen as part of reconciliation but the real reconciling of individuals is far removed from official declarations. As Sutton sarcastically remarks, "The system will do our morality for us. If we sign up, we're in. But we're not of course." Further, Sutton claims that "To hold out to those suffering the grim realities of certain Indigenous communities, the expectation that they will be safer, healthier and less arrested, because of the contracting of a formal Reconciliation package, is to offer them goanna oil." Peddling this grand national gesture as a cure for child abuse and domestic violence is 'dangerous mumbo-jumbo' in Sutton's estimation. Besides, it acts as a time-wasting diversion of focus and resources from the urgent actualities of dysfunctional communities.

What's happened with formal reconciliation is that it has morphed

OVERCOMING DISADVANTAGE

from an intended change of heart by individuals, to a bewildering array of 'management-speak' on capacity building, partnerships, whole of government, benchmarks, stakeholders, social indicators, measurable outcomes, role models and efficiency. This, says Sutton, is "the language of managerialist welfarism".

So what comes out of all the Reconciliation talk? In short, the basic need to offer disadvantaged people the choice of breaking out of their spiral of dependency and join the rest of the Australia nation – an inter-generational process.

# MARTIN'S MORAL MAGIC

David Martin wrote his Ph.D. thesis on the kinship of the Wik people at Aurukun in 1993. Since then he has written on Aboriginal economics, welfare dependency and local governance. In the process, he has developed not only a deep empathy for Aboriginal tradition and culture, but also an often-antagonistic attitude to right-wing/conservative proponents of mainstream education, employment and wealth-generation as the solution to community dysfunction.

Martin (2008) gives a very interesting account of sorcery in the Cape York communities and how it is used to explain sickness and death. His in-depth knowledge of the local Wik Mungkan culture has given him an almost unique outsider's understanding of the language and custom of the Aurukun region. Of special interest is his explanation of the way in which earlier traditional male initiation empowered young men who believed that they have literally passed through the gut of the Rainbow Serpent during initiation. The self-confidence which comes from being recognised as a man, influences initiates' pride in hunting, fighting and sexual prowess. Since the last (possibly final) initiation took place in 1970 at Aurukun, young males have been unmediated by the Elders.

An important observation of Martin's is that the Wik people see their culture and society as being left to them by their ancestors and not as traditions resulting from the efforts of creative individuals. It is this historic inherited attribute which makes their culture constant and unchanging. Martin does however indicate that, as Sutton has shown, this cosmology not only shows

## THE FUTURE: MARTIN'S MORAL MAGIC

regional diversity, but is somewhat fragmented and discontinuous, leading to interpretations that are individualised and even conflicting.

Why are Martin's writings of importance in formulating Aboriginal policy? Firstly, because he is one of a very small number of observers with first-hand knowledge of one clan over many years – to this extent he shares The Knowledge with observers like Sutton. Secondly, he has constructed one of the most plausible explanations of male Aboriginal frustration, although he doesn't dwell on the rage phenomenon. Thirdly, he analyses sorcery as an essential element of contemporary belief in a way seldom found in the literature. Finally, he is an important example of how culturists handle the dilemma of maintaining tradition in the emerging modern Aboriginal society.

Martin makes the important point that while initiation is no longer practiced at Aurukun, sorcery is still alive and well. He fails however, to make a clear statement on the unacceptability of sorcery in a modern law-abiding society. He seems to value sorcery's quaint historic origins and criticises those who want to eliminate it from the culture.

His macabre descriptions of women having to sit under the burial platform from which the fat of their decaying husbands' corpse drips, and his detail on greasy genitalia, does little to convince the reader that his studies carry meaningful messages for positive future policy. In reading Martin's elucidation of local language terms, a distinction needs to be made between their novelty and their usefulness.

Martin notes how Aboriginal youths who recently returned from Army Reserve camp, used their khaki fatigues and army boots as a new symbol of personal identity and power in the community – a sort of modern male initiation which demands respect. His apparent respect for Indigenous healers and sorcerers revives ancient European writings on sorcery, witchcraft and the Inquisition. He places much store in the way in which initiation produced male potency and how the discontinuation of this source of personal identity has caused a vacuum in male role-playing. The way in which initiation allowed males to draw on external (spiritual) sources of power, seems akin to the Christian Confirmation ceremony in which the taking of ritualised symbols ('Eat of my flesh, drink of my blood') allowed the new male, whose baptism was confirmed by communion, to take strength from the higher power. (Interestingly, the Serpent is not Satanic, but Sacred, in Indigenous belief.)

## OVERCOMING DISADVANTAGE

Martin, like Sutton, picks up on the significance of 'demand sharing' in traditional culture and how this has become a new element in substance abuse and the availability of women. He does little to follow Pearson's example of condemning this adulterated norm, but treats it only as a 'new' noteworthy phenomenon. In the same way, Martin chooses unusual terms such as 'ensorcellment' and 'ensorcelled' which suggests an almost pornographic fascination with mystical sexuality and his reluctance to call for the discontinuation of harmful superstitions, indicates an unrealistic commitment to some of the unhelpful spiritual values of the culture.

Perhaps Martin is a useful personified example of 'cultural relativism', i.e. valuing each culture as an antiquated belief system in a non-judgemental way. He seems to revel in how the sorcerer puts his victim in a trance, makes an incision and withdraws his blood, to be buried in a special container. The fact is that the older Wik people not only believe in sorcery, but act on the strength of these beliefs. He makes no pretence at the need for changing policy or the law, to protect the 'ensorcelled' victims. On the contrary, he goes out of his way to criticise Helen Hughes of the Centre for Independent Studies in Sydney who calls for such 'degraded' tradition to be replaced by the 'rule of reason'. Martin challenges the logic of Hughes (and Gary Johns of the Bennelong Society) and asks whether their own proposals follow this rule of reason.

In essence, what we have here is a working example of value judgements based on subjectivity and intuition on both sides, posing as rational judgement and objective science. The background to this conflict between scientists is important in evaluating future options. Martin takes the concept of 'demand sharing' from Peterson's 1993 work in the United States and takes the idea of alchemy (ancient attempts to turn base metal into gold) from Goldman (1985). He then uses these concepts in his attack on Pearson's 'passive welfare' objection, Hughes' 'economic mainstreaming' and Gary Johns' 'wicked policy.'

Martin employs the metaphor of the 'Philosopher's Stone' to infer that his adversaries, cast as alchemists, don't understand their 'base metal' – their Aboriginal community – which they hope to transform. It seems that Martin's central premise may be that Aborigines can't, don't, or are incapable of, being motivated by first-class education, skilled employment, home ownership, sober healthy diet, gender equality or the benefits of positive male models.

## THE FUTURE: MARTIN'S MORAL MAGIC

He accuses Hughes of having scant regard for the facts when assuming Aboriginals' views, motives and emotions. He goes on to credit Johns with at least assessing some of the anthropological literature but then criticises his "reductionist and motivated reading of it". Martin also takes Richard Ah Mat (a respected Indigenous spokesman) to task for claiming that modernisation is essential to cultural survival, without explaining his (Martin's) alternative to modernizing apart from his compromise referred to below.

His main criticism seems to be Hughes' and Johns' reliance on market mechanisms as the prime driver of transformation of Aboriginal values. He challenges their premise of the 'morally reformative character' of market-based solutions. One suspects that it is the way that Johns 'pathologises' Aboriginal culture and Hughes dismisses tradition as a drag on well-being, that conflicts with Martin's deeply-held respect for culture. The bottom line, in his view, is that "Those who are not adapted to modern society are (according to Martin's adversaries)....trapped in immoral cultures."

In challenging Pearson's call for Aboriginals to get off 'passive welfare', Martin claims that Pearson's plea for his community to get into the mainstream economy is actually morally, not economically, motivated. Martin also objects to Johns' 1997 statement: "The way to make them work is to stop treating Aborigines as exotica and regard them as being able to abide by the same civic obligations and respond to the same economic incentives as everyone else." One suspects that it is this concept of expecting people to work, which upsets Martin's view on choice of culturally appropriate lifestyles. Martin uses the rather weak example of fly-in fly-out mining labour contracts to illustrate why mainstream work is inappropriate.

Why is this spat between several knowledgeable commentators important? Because it is the basic conflict of worldviews on wealth-generation, as the cornerstone of Indigenous well-being, which has held back community betterment for decades. "Incentives, by definition are not culture or value free" claims Martin and thus the carrots and sticks which drive most Australians "cannot be assumed to apply equally across cultures". He regards moving away from kin and country as very confronting to remote-dwelling Aborigines. These Homeland connections are so intrinsic to personal identity, that such loss is not compensated for by relatively high wages, according to Martin.

This issue of migration for wages is currently at the centre of policy formulation and requires urgent attention. What Martin needs to do is to seriously differentiate between the needs of the older and younger generations. Interestingly, in 2008 he had joined with others in not accepting continuation of the present remote situation: "There is in my view an unassailable case for the transformation of remote Aboriginal communities – maintenance of the status quo is indefensible."

In his 2008 concluding remarks, Martin takes a shot at both sides of politics using his alchemist metaphor: "Where the Right have wished to transmute Aboriginal society from the base nature of communalism and social dysfunction, to the gold autonomous actors, the Left have proposed they be transmuted from the base state of anomie to the gold of the enculturated Aboriginal citizen. For the Left, the "Philosophers Stone" has been the granting of rights under the rubric of self-determination, whereas for the Right it has been the market. Both have their magical illusions."

Having dismissed both sides, Martin makes heavy work of formulating a compromise or alternative solution. He admits that change is urgently required but asks the 'difficult question' of what extent of diversity can be accepted or encouraged by a pluralistic (not multicultural but parallel) society when such diversity may reflect disparities in status. Martin notes how political debate has avoided consideration of the very different values which Aboriginal society bring to engagement with the non-Indigenous population. This avoidance, he says, "is a big impediment to cultural transformation and the means by which this is promoted". He then states the obvious, that unless Aboriginals are active participants and committed change-agents themselves, cultural transformation will be resisted by them. He predicts that in cases such as those proposed by Hughes and John's, their crusade will fail just like the Missionaries did, for this same reason.

In Martin's defence it should be noted that he is only considering small remote traditionally-oriented communities but still he seems to ignore the financial reality of providing good infrastructure and services to small scattered clan groups. The Martin-versus-the-rest cultural conflict should be used as a microcosm of the national policy position where no progress will be made before agreed national objectives and principles are laid down.

## ISN'T THE PROBLEM OBVIOUS?

At the risk of upsetting the sensitivities of the cultural purists, it is useful and necessary to consider if and how certain constraints to progress in Aboriginal well-being can be identified and dealt with.

In the process of trying to move things along at an acceptable pace, many in authority are frustrated enough to return to the dictum of "Get over it; get on with it." This invariably draws a familiar response from sympathisers for the Indigenous cause, always referring to the hurt and psychological damage suffered by a "broken people", and explaining that getting over past hurts is very difficult, indeed it is regarded as unrealistic.

As referred to above, Sutton, in his 2009 book, maintains that the good intentions of White interventionists have repeatedly been thwarted by old traditional norms. The doctrine of the Common Good which Western democracies take for granted as a moral goal, is overridden, says Sutton, by family loyalty. Similarly the belief in traditional medicine, blocks the co-operative use of modern health care. In addition, the acceptance of natural happenings as decreed by the spirits, makes it impossible for traditional people to even consider man-generated change. While Aboriginal religion is not alone in such fatalistic beliefs, the priority of family benefit above all else, makes nepotism a plus rather than the crime it is in the White man's world.

So too with physical violence which has probably always been a normal aspect of redressing personal grievances in primitive peoples. Sutton goes as far as to say that inter-personal violence, until very recently in some communities, is a "perfectly expectable system of self-help…..". He maintains that this is the reason why the Census of 2009 demonstrated that the Whites' attempts to curb community violence "have been a hopeless failure". What hope is there, he asks, for the next generation, if leaders and government don't take wide and assertive action against such abhorrent behaviour.

This view is supported by Stephanie Jarrett (2009), who says that the explorer Edward Eyre in 1840 noted that ill-treatment of Aboriginal women by their husbands, brought no helpful reaction from others, indicating that the weak and injured had to fend for themselves. The shocking aspect for Jarrett is that currently there are still thousands of cases of such traditional violence which give power to a small number of dominant males in outback Australia: "What shocks outsiders is often seen as ordinary by the communities." Across four States, Jarrett's statistics show violence, particularly against women, to be 44.1 times more likely (in hospitalisation terms) than in non-Aboriginal women. She contradicts many pro-Indigenous historians when she writes, "Insistent blaming of White colonisation as a primary generator of high Aboriginal violence, suppresses the uncomfortable fact that, within Aboriginal culture, violence continues to have strong traditional legitimacy." She deduces from this that reducing such violence to mainstream (White) levels "....*will entail further shifts away from traditional beliefs, norms, power structures and behaviours.*" (my emphasis).

Jarrett points out that: "Only very recently did Western democracies produce a system whereby violence was not legitimate – only self-defence is permissible as a form of violence in modern societies". She uses the example of Mornington Island where males, when away from the island, apparently do not behave violently, but on return take up their inculturated violence again. This apparent choice of behaviour is used by Jarrett to demonstrate that the violent tendencies of these men are not from inherited anger relating to colonial cruelty, but are conscious decisions which could and should be changed: "People tend to be as violent and as tolerant of violence as their culture expects and allows." Jarrett accuses the nation's thinkers and policy-makers of baulking at the task of implementing strategies which eliminate cultural violence: "Adjustment to the mainstream is not about taking anything from the Aborigines – it is about implementing policies and programs that reverse Aboriginal exclusion from mainstream culture…..".

This matter of the benefits or otherwise of mainstreaming is mentioned elsewhere in this review and is at the heart of gaining acceptance of future welfare policy. It is not new however and Jarrett is only building on the foundations laid by Noel Pearson when, in 2006, he convened an international conference on Indigenous Norms, having lost the earlier support of his own people through his strong policy statements about the need for Aboriginal men to shape-up and stop the degrading domestic violence and drunkenness which was killing his people at Hope Vale and elsewhere.

So why did it take these obvious things to be said by Pearson, for them to resonate with the nation at large? Firstly, because criticism from White "patronising" do-gooders was always going to be seen as interference by the oppressors. Secondly, because the grey-bearded men in black hats have not yet got the message that the strong-arm tactics of tribal standover men will not be tolerated in the emerging enlightened Indigenous democracy. Thirdly, because what used to be tolerated by way of financial benefits going largely to the families of dominant headmen, is fast becoming unacceptable.

# AUSTRALIAN APATHY – NO WORRIES

Time and again, potentially helpful initiatives are announced by government, promising improvement in health, housing, education or employment of Aboriginals. Time and again, when the media ask, "Whatever became of the such-and-such program/scheme/project?", the answer is the same: "There has been a slight delay in the implementation, but the matter is still a high priority" for organisations and individuals other than the current government. While government-funded Indigenous infrastructure and services have no monopoly on such obfuscation and blame shifting, the long-term observer, searching for reasons, can come to no other conclusion than that it's a lack of political will, reflecting an assumed apathy on the part of voters. A case in point is the 2007 example of Territory housing. Two years before, the Federal Government promised $26 M for 750 houses to Territory communities but by 2009 the public were informed that not a single house has yet been built for these desperate Indigenous families. While this lack of action caused some public concern, it was overshadowed by the simultaneous claim that 1000 new suburban houses had been completed or at least started, in the Prime Minister's electorate in Brisbane. After the usual denials, government had no option but to agree that bureaucratic complacency and creaming off funds by the Territory Government had clogged the delivery pipeline. While this example reflects on the Federal Government of the day, successive governments have produced similar non-results.

The truth is that most Australian voters have become apathetic about Aboriginal disadvantage, and governments reflect this lack of priority and absence of urgency. While reasons for this apathy are seldom mentioned in the literature and never in official reports, years of discussing this attitude with a wide cross-section of the White community in Queensland, leads the present author to suggest that the following opinions are commonly held as general views on why there is less than widespread enthusiasm for voters to support high government expenditure on Indigenous welfare:

1. Yes, these people have had a hard time in the past, but they've got to learn to help themselves.
2. Sure they're behind the eight-ball but they've got to get serious about working for a living like the rest of us.
3. They've got to get over being victims and get on with joining the mainstream economy and gaining a bit of self-respect from good honest labour.
4. Somehow they've got to break the cycle of depravity that they're in, maybe by getting the kids out of those violent and abusive communities and giving them a proper education.
5. The youngsters need to be given something useful to do, to get them into paid work or relevant training so that they can leave those toxic camps that just destroy their future potential.
6. There's no point in pouring more money into those remote communities; they just become more dependent and less likely to get real jobs.
7. They just wreck any decent houses that are built for them so it's just a waste of money building more government houses. Perhaps if they could own and pay for their own houses they'd look after them better.
8. The sooner they stop all this cultural stuff about having to be on their own country, the sooner they will benefit from employment and their own income.
9. How can they expect their kids to grow up properly on a poor diet such as white bread and Coke when they could get on with community gardens to produce a healthy diet of fruit and vegetables.
10. They put so much faith in their culture that the well-being of their offspring is neglected when they insist on staying in camps where

they are doing no more than seeking refuge from reality.

11. The incompatibility of tradition and modernity is holding them back. Nobody seems game to tell them that the reason their kids aren't interested in old ways and Elder's knowledge, is that they regard these outdated elements of culture as irrelevant to their modern future. This probably also applies to their lack of interest in clan languages.

12. Proper housing and hygiene just don't go together with what has become culturally accepted overcrowding. Home ownership can only succeed if group norms on hygiene and violence change.

Whether such views are seen as redneck or realist, depends on one's values.

# MAINSTREAM, SIDESTREAM AND SLIPSTREAM

The repeated call for mainstreaming as the solution to Aboriginal disadvantage makes assumptions on mainstream norms and opportunities relative to the current lifestyles of remote communities. Two important points need to be made about the virtues of the mainstream: firstly, the mainstream also includes geographic and financial disadvantage. Thus remote Whites with insufficient income to send their children to good schools also suffer the 'tyranny of distance' as Blainey called it. Secondly, the mainstream has its own serious dysfunction but of another type at another level. The ills of modern society are beyond the scope of this overview; suffice to say that 'Affluenza' as a threat to mainstream Western societies is having an increasingly negative effect on happiness and the meaning of life. The poorly understood dysfunction being caused by communications technology is but one instance of serious unplanned outcomes of modernisation on social cohesion and contentment.

This is the subject of another book, but in the context of Aboriginal futures, it behoves those who are enticing Indigenous people to get aboard the western gravy-train, to emphasise that within the mainstream are several very different side streams. John Armstrong in his 2009 book "In search of Civilisation: Remaking of a Tarnished Idea" explains the problem as follows: "Civilisation occurs when a high degree of material prosperity and a high degree of spiritual prosperity come together and mutually enhance each other…. Material prosperity is not in itself a problem. The problem is [that] we have material prosperity (or had until recently) beyond our spiritual competence to deal with it well." Armstrong goes on to demonstrate how everything from economic insecurity to climate change and the daily work/family conflict, all stem from the mismatch of material and spiritual prosperity.

Like the rest of Australian society, those Indigenous families joining the mainstream's 'real economy' will have the choice of lifestyles which best reflect their values, their hopes and their children's aspirations. The opportunities to drink, gamble, fight and steal are everywhere to be seen, but the opportunity to make good for their family, is much greater than was the case in small remote communities. The extent to which they want to continue their culture in the personal identity sense, is up to each family and in the mainstream of multiculturalism, Aboriginals can overcome the debilitating effects of victimhood and do what the other ethnic groups do – get on with life enjoying their own culture, if they choose.

# INTEGRATION – THE EUROPEAN WOGBOY'S EXPERIENCE

'Wogboys' is a term used by comedians of Greek extraction in Sydney and is used by Australian teenagers to refer to any non-Anglo-Saxon Migrants from Mediterranean countries. Liz Thompson (1993) has written a personal account based on interviews with forty Migrants from a dozen countries, recording their reasons for choosing Australia, factors causing them to leave their Homeland, how they settled in and the difficulties they experienced as integrated new Australians. She highlights the way in which different personalities experience varying degrees of difficulty adjusting to a new Homeland. She finds that the ability to settle, adjust and live contentedly, is an individual rather than a national or racial trait, but she also noted that people of colour do experience more discrimination. While these results are not surprising, they indicate that cultural adaptation by ethnic groups can be successful within one generation and is usually virtually assured after two generations,

## THE FUTURE: THE EUREOPEAN WOGBOY'S EXPERIENCE

provided parents do not insist on a high degree of religious ethnicity.

So how does the Migrant experience relate to Aboriginal integration into urban life? First, there is still a degree of reluctance on the part of many employers to treat Aborigines equitably in selecting employees. Such a claim is generally denied and is particularly difficult to prove. A recent Australian study which used fake Anglo-Saxon and ethnic job applications (Asian, South American names, photos and origins), found that even with similar CV's on qualifications and experience, there was a clear bias toward Anglo-Saxon and other European applicants across a range of industries in 2009.

However, over the past few decades large numbers of Aborigines have formed successful communities in several Australian cities of which Redfern in Sydney is the most well-known. The term 'successful' is a relative term in this context; i.e. relative to the indicators of well-being in remote communities. All over Australia successful small businesses run and owned by Aboriginals reflect both an ability and a willingness to join and compete in the mainstream economy as town-dwellers who inter-marry with other ethnic groups.

Compared to many overseas Migrants and refugees, most Aborigines have the advantage of a reasonable level of lingual understanding and share the same love of ball games as most Australians – in fact in at least two codes of rugby they are well represented and in Australian Rules they excel – some say they invented the game and there is convincing evidence to support this claim.

Many commentators would argue that Aboriginal integration is different from Migrant integration. When it is remembered that a large proportion of Migrants were the victims of outrageous wartime oppression, many having lost members of their immediate family, it is clear that empathy with victimhood cuts across ethnic lines and colour bars. Clearly the resultant trauma which these Migrants experience is paralleled by Aboriginal colonial history, but lacks the advanced civil history of most Migrant nations. This classical background favours easy integration.

By international standards, Australia is perhaps one of the most racially tolerant nations in the world. This doesn't mean that local outbursts of racial violence are unknown – on the contrary, recent race-based conflict in Cronulla has been widely reported. By and large, newcomers are well received provided their work ethic, responsibility and lifestyle are in harmony with the local norms. Many Migrant families told Thompson that it was in fact their perception of Australian tolerance that drew them here in the first place. Over the years Australia has gained a reputation for tolerant acceptance of others, but this easy-going Aussie attitude has its limits and is tested by violence, religious bigotry, indecent behaviour and lack of hygiene. The same line is drawn for Migrants, refugees, Aboriginals and fellow Ockers.

Because Australian society is so racially mixed (1 in 4 were not born here) this nation generally harbours few jingoistic traits – those ultra-nationalistic attributes which have given national pride a bad name. Thus while Australians value their military and sporting traditions, they revolt against the flag-waving violence of ethnic football fans in their southern cities. What they'd like, is for ethnic groups to value their own culture but to leave their historic conflict baggage in their Homeland. Similarly with urban Aborigines, the same norms apply and it is up to the families concerned, not to wait for complaints from outsiders or for police visits, but to pull their own transgressors up when norms are slipping. This lack of self-regulation has been an important cause of remote communities' dysfunction. Of course there are causes of causes as well, but failure of the Elders to stop the rot is the driver.

# THE ESSENTIAL CHOICES

In the section on Sutton and his priorities for progress, the current author canvassed the idea of the benefits of de-tribalisation – in the sense that loss of land, culture and language as generally understood, may not be terminal for individuals in this ethnic group.

In essence, Aboriginal parents must honestly answer the question: "What do we really owe our grandchildren, to give them the best chance of a happy and meaningful life in the mid-21st century?" This fundamental consideration leads to further questions on the perceived roles of land/culture/language in developing grounded, motivated and productive individuals. In answering these personal questions, the researcher easily points to the way in which all developed societies have historically gained quality of life by moving away from superstition, sorcery and the might-is-right dominance by a few. The ancient history of all European tribes shows how such enlightenment takes

## THE FUTURE: ESSENTIAL CHOICES

centuries and we are thus obliged to ask whether it is reasonable to expect that such a group metamorphosis can be expedited in a few decades of legal equity in the case of Australia.

We are confronted here with the most basic of value judgements in what some might regard as social engineering, but what is in essence a personal judgement on a national scale. One way of approaching the dilemma of the ideal 'cultural intensity' required for personal identity and grounding, is to follow the demographics and leadership profiles of Aboriginal role models. Hundreds of thousands of Indigenous parents have already voted with their feet and moved their families out of the toxic environment of remote settlements. In August 2009, the State Minister for Aboriginal Partnerships told ABC radio that 75% of Queensland Aboriginals now lived in our cities. Sutton tells us that whereas in 1986, 46% of Indigenous partners nationally had married non-Aboriginals, by 2006 this percentage had risen to 71.5%. As Sutton puts it, "It will not be too many more generations before most Australians share some Indigenous ancestry". The figure for out-marriages in Sydney in 2006 was 82.3%. The lowest out-marriage rate was in the Territory where only 8.5% of females and 4.2% of males married non-Indigenous partners according to the Australian Census. Interestingly an earlier census (1996) showed that 86% of children of inter-racial marriages were identified by their parents as Aboriginal and the question is often asked whether this decision was ethnically or financially based.

If one considers the rates of urbanisation and inter-racial marriage, it is not surprising to find that both of what demographers call 'push and pull' factors, have been at work for some time i.e. fleeing from violence, abuse, ignorance and poor health and seeking refuge in safe, healthy well-serviced urban environments. In deserting their Homelands and clan relations, informed parents and young adults are placing a higher value on well-being than on tradition – just as Australia's vast racially-diverse population of overseas Migrants have done. Some might argue that other ethnic groups do not have the strong links to land that Aboriginals have. This may be true from a historic perspective, but as Aboriginals become more educated they increasingly realise that in a fast-changing world, tradition and culture must adapt if their offspring are not to accuse them of letting them languish in a timeless ghetto where service and infrastructure can never be justified as cost-effective.

Several writers have used the fictional comparison of two imaginary States

– Utopia and Dystopia, to characterise the attributes of progressive and regressive societies. Without repeating the features of each of these options here, it is reasonable to suggest that Aboriginal Australia currently has such a choice. In the past, public debate amongst the culture warriors has almost always focused on small remote communities at the expense of the other 75% of the Aboriginals. The figures quoted above for out-marriages and urban dwelling, strengthen the view that focus needs to shift from the remote minority and deal with the majority in the same way as all disadvantaged groups are provided for, based on need, not race.

Essentially the special requirements of remote dysfunction need to be decoupled from overall policy affecting those who are of, or choose to claim, Aboriginal descent. In their personal situation, individuals may choose where they want to live and how much culture and tradition they want to maintain. Government needs to make clear its policy objectives regarding separatism and geographic isolation. It also needs to get serious about supporting those wishing to move from Dystopia. Such movement may require more than personal initiative to produce the motivation to move. A simultaneous alternative change is not a geographical move but a move toward Utopia on location, i.e. a socio-economic change of norms, values, action and wealth-generation at regional Indigenous centres. Both types of movement are driven by the aspirations of the people themselves. In all cases self-sufficiency should be the essential goal.

# MINING: TAPPING INTO THE MOTHER LODE

The opposing financial positions of mineral extraction companies and local Indigenous peoples, have enabled government to set social benefit conditions for approval of mines. This was not always the case and several of the earlier approvals were limited to conditions which, while paying unheard-of sums to Aboriginal landholders, did little to improve local well-being.

Altman and Martin (2009) published the best overview to that date, on the agreements between mining companies and Aborigines. This timely publication was of particular import at that stage of community development, because mining represents virtually the only large source of wealth-generation in remote Australia, unless carbon credits become a significant reality. This is particularly the case in Western Australia and the Territory but is emerging as a major issue in the development of new bauxite mines in Queensland south of Weipa. To date, the Weipa and Cape Flattery cases have demonstrated how mining could benefit locals on the Cape. However, there is now a strong case to significantly alter the way agreements are structured and implemented.

Martin's chapter in the edited collection of papers with Altman, examines the sustainability principles of present and future agreements. This follows the call by Indigenous Affairs Minister Macklin (2008) to ensure that the agreement "structures the governance of these arrangements to ensure financial benefits create employment and educational opportunities for individuals and are invested for the long term benefit of the communities". This should not imply that companies to date have not operated useful training programs, on the contrary a few instances can take credit for fitting many young Aboriginals for employment in the 'real economy'.

In principle, the agreement by Aboriginal leaders to the mining of their country, accepts that the large social benefits accruing from a mining agreement outweigh the physical damage to proscribed areas sacrificed to open-cut mining, beneficiation infrastructure and transport requirements. Culturally and financially, these have been very difficult decisions, especially where sites of special significance, even 'sacred', have to be weighed against income, training, schools, clinics, bitumen roads and water supplies. The extent of the dilemma faced by the Elders is demonstrated by the fact that to win their case for Native Title they originally had to prove not only their continuous connection to the land as their traditional country, but also that they fully intended to continue living on that land in the traditional way.

Martin's experience with Century Zinc Limited (CZL) near Karumba in Queensland's Gulf, provides a good example of how apparently well-intentioned conditions failed in practice, to benefit the local community in the planned way. The Elders could be forgiven for being confused about who they were dealing with and thus what the company spokesmen's commitment was worth. Century Zinc was a subsidiary of CRA, later purchased by Pasminco which in turn was reconstituted as Zinifex. Normally agreements legally bind all future owners of the mine to the agreed conditions. Importantly the conditions also bind all subcontractors on the mine site. In this case, two special purpose bodies were set up to deliver the community benefit package which was expected to transfer $20m to the landholders over 15 years.

By 2002 the first 5 year review of the Zinifex agreement exposed the unworkability of the committee structure – "unwieldy, uncoordinated, inefficient and too resource intensive". The arrangements at Zinifex provided for the establishment of six Aboriginal corporations to be responsible for a range of community activities funded by mine income. By the time the first two years of the agreement had been completed, four of the six corporations failed to report and as a result, they became ineligible for further funding. Three of these ineligible bodies represented the Waanji Native Title Group on whose land the actual mine was situated. Martin regards these problems as "entirely predictable compliance failure".

Why is this example of importance in considering future options? First, because it shows how difficult it is to match up the largely opposing cultures of resource-based capitalism and a traditional non-accumulative sharing culture. Second, it illustrates the conflicting pressures of different legal frameworks – the Native Title Act, which insists on maintaining traditions, and the Indigenous Land Use Agreements which encourage wealth-generation from industries such as beef production. Third, this example exposes the difficulties faced by those who are driven to improve economic Aboriginal well-being and those who see maintenance of tradition and custom as the basis for defining what activities and sources of income are 'culturally appropriate'.

In essence, mining and its profits, offer virtually the only significant present basis for halting out-migration from some northern regions. The Pilbara of WA is a case in point, where the need to move away for family survival reasons, has been potentially negated by income from iron ore. No other remote area industry has so far been able to offer community income sufficient to prevent the need for Pearson's 'orbiting' – migratory workers earning a wage elsewhere then returning to support their communities. Martin quotes Bourdieu the French sociologist, who contrasted the narrow singular worldview of 'doxa' based on unquestioned, self-evident, natural adherence to one customary view, with 'heterodoxy' which accepts several views as well as dissent and even, non-acceptance of the traditional worldview. At the heart of this problem of choice, is the fact that under Native Title, the claimants rely on customs, law and tradition as the basis of ownership. So the question arises as to whether a move from this traditional basis weakens or nullifies their title claim. The most recent reaction from Government, pressured by experienced Native Title negotiators, indicates that both the original criteria and the process of title determination required, and had received, a long-overdue make-over.

This is in contrast to the trend in recent years for Native Title as a property right, to become diminished, to a point where the 'fungibility' (use as financial equity) of the land is close to zero. Even in the case of 'Indigenous Freehold' as a belated new class of tenure, lending institutions are unimpressed with this form of equity or borrowing guarantee. Thus, as referred to earlier, it was not unexpected when in 2008 Minister Macklin called for the restructuring of financial agreements in mining, to allow for capital accumulation by the communities concerned.

Martin uses the term 'sustainability' in the sense of on-going community benefit, when referring to the need to restructure mining agreements. In truth, no economic system based on a finite mineral ore-body can be 'sustainable' and many mines have a life of less than 30 years – in the case of Zinifex, a possible 15 year life based on present estimates of the size and rate of extraction from proven reserves. So Martin needs to answer the question of where the Waanji people go when the zinc runs out, as it surely will.

The gallant attempts by some writers to explain how the needs of capitalism and traditionalism can be met in one agreement, are often less than convincing. Martin's recognition of the inter-cultural nature of the values brought to the agreements, seems to overstate the importance of traditional values in a society which, for its own survival, really has little option but to modernise. Advisors need to make a much clearer distinction between the needs of the older (unchanging) generation and the needs of the younger (mobile) generation who show little interest in the Elders' culture but recognise the need to move to where universal well-being standards beckon.

To Martin's credit he appreciates the need for new societal norms but seems unable to relinquish the notion of the precious culture being lost – so he has 'five bob each way' and tries to structure agreements to ensure that capitalism protects traditionalism. The real answer lies in using mine income to educate, train and mobilise the coming generations so that they are not

## OVERCOMING DISADVANTAGE

trapped in the pathetic (as in pathology of violence) isolated enclaves of unnecessary disadvantage. The empathy with the dying culture shown by virtually all anthropologists who have intimate personal contact with remote communities, is not only understandable, but admirable from a humanitarian viewpoint. However, the emotional baggage which some anthropologists bring to the negotiating table needs a clear-eyed view of the reality of the future. This is not to devalue culture but to recognise its appropriate place in the psyche of the people concerned. If tradition can add richness, sense of belonging, pride in identity and self-confidence, without constraining the potential of individuals to contribute to both their individual good and the common good, a win-win combination can be achieved. The way to make this happen is to have a clear appreciation of the factual situation:

- Remote communities make up less than 25% of the Indigenous population and require different transition procedures.
- The majority of Indigenous people live as an ethnic subset of the broader Australian population and like other groups, deserve support based on degree of disadvantage, not race.
- There is a requirement to accept that the ancient links to country need to be re-interpreted to what is necessary to meet global well-being indicators.
- Irrespective of who is responsible for sustainable land use and environmental quality, the same scientific principles apply to threatened species, water quality, the misuse of fire and greenhouse emissions on all land. [On a recent visit, the present author learned that this mine will close in 2021]

These facts can be related to the major diamond mine in the Kimberley where the Argyle Participation Agreement makes special mention of how the traditional owners "insert their cultural forms and presence onto the mine site" – a statement to which the cynics might add : "provided production and costs are not adversely affected".

Martin tells us that there is a 'developing, if contested' literature on how Indigenous organisations can be made to operate more effectively (objectives achieved) and efficiently (costs minimised, outcomes maximised). He quotes an impressive list of researchers who have proposed good governance

## THE FUTURE: MINING – TAPPING INTO THE MOTHER LODE

principles, which space does not allow exposition of here.

As mentioned previously in this overview, historical Aboriginal experience in hierarchical governance is virtually non-existent. Martin suggests that what he calls 'intense localism' (family power) actually forms the core of how their organisations work. This apparent need for what amounts to expensive and time-consuming family consultation, not only makes consensus-finding very difficult but must now be seriously re-examined as an acceptable process in the transition to modernity. This family dominance of the democratic process has led Indigenous leaders to be so over-cautious about being seen to speak for others, that the development of generic principles, objectives and values has been a non-event. It's as though each mob has its own scriptures, akin to Christian cults which proclaim a unique interpretation of The Word, but which on closer inspection reflect nothing more than the outpourings of a charismatic egotist whose position is entirely dependent on his (always a male) edicts.

A good example of the dilemma faced by Aboriginal leaders in finding acceptable representative structures is the August 2009 report by Tom Calma on proposed new structures for a peak Indigenous body to advise the Rudd government. The Calma report was constrained by the government's insistence that the new body would have no decision-making or service delivery powers, so it was not surprising to find that Calma concentrated on not repeating the failures of ATSIC, disbanded by Prime Minister Howard because of waste, ineffectiveness and "big man" politics. The Calma report relates to mining agreements and their future effects on self-management and communities taking responsibility. In setting guidelines for approved mining agreements, government needs to come clean on its self-management objectives. By using the ATSIC disaster as a reason (unstated) for denying Indigenous people the responsibility of self-management, government is further encouraging welfare dependence or at least Whitefella dependence.

In an earlier (2003) statement Martin, referring to mining agreements, claimed: "I suggest it is totally inadequate to leave the construction and management of organizational management principles solely to the Aboriginal people concerned and to a domain of supposedly uniquely Aboriginal values." He further claimed that if good governance is central to Aborigines' engagement with society at large, then the broader values and practices of that society must be included.

The present author couldn't agree more with Martin when he claims that there are compelling arguments to leave distinctively Aboriginal process within the Aboriginal realm where it rightfully belongs, and not be tempted to embed these values into organisational mechanisms. He quotes several researchers to support his statement that, "It is therefore not defensible to resort to an unexamined notion of cultural appropriateness, or one of a notionally autonomous domain of Aboriginal culture, in determining the core principles by which effective Aboriginal organisations should be established and operated."

Jon Altman of ANU has been studying the effects of mining income on Aboriginals since 1983 in the Territory. By 1994 he could report the medium term social impacts, and by 2008 he was able to use Australian case studies in a United Nations overview of agreements between corporations and communities. He concludes that forms of hybrid economies (capitalist/traditional) can be recommended as an interim measure during the cultural transition era. The boom-and-bust cyclical nature of the global minerals market, makes mining corporations more than a little cautious about over-generous expenses in their operations. Indigenous communities need to be cognisant of periodic commodity price collapses as an integral feature of mining, when making optimistic claims on their share of profits. Equally, short mine life needs clear recognition.

# INDIGENOUS ASPIRATIONS

If the present author reads the current aspirations of the majority of today's regional Indigenous leaders correctly, there often appear to be several concurrent goals which most of them have in mind:

1. Self-management as a basis for self-determination in predominately Aboriginal regions.
2. Resource-based employment as a basis for family wealth-generation through primary industry and value-adding.
3. Education which gives the coming generations the opportunity to

## THE FUTURE: INDIGENOUS ASPIRATIONS

    break out of their remote disadvantaged situation and prepare them for competitive mainstream employment in the real economy.

4. Housing, social infrastructure and services sufficient to enjoy lifestyles appropriate to a developed nation – requirements which would require restructuring of scattered small communities into larger cost-effective serviceable populations in the region.

5. Health services sufficient to bring all major indicators of well-being up to the standard of the rest of the nation.

6. Preservation of language, culture and ceremony in a manner which maintains Indigenous identity at various levels desired by different individuals, without constraining personal choices on lifestyle and wealth generation.

7. Indigenous ownership of land and homes sufficient to give financial security to landowners and to maintain links to clan country by those who desire such ties to country.

This generalised simplification of needs is not new or complete in detail, but it offers a set of worthwhile goals for communities throughout the vast savanna spaces of Northern Australia.

To date, much has been written about the causal factors leading to the current worsening Fourth World conditions in remote communities. While such a blame game may be important to the culture warriors writing for intellectual journals, the current climate of awareness and urgency demands actions and solutions, rather than more debate.

Improving the lifestyle and well-being of Indigenous families' will require at least two guiding principles:

1. Distinguish between remote, town and city families' needs, desires and choices.

2. Allow and support individual families' choice of appropriate location, employment, schooling and home ownership.

Margaret Thatcher was ridiculed when, as the Prime Minister of Britain, she declared that in practice there was no such thing as a society, in the sense that in a genuine society, individuals put the common good ahead of family benefit. In his recent book, Sutton, the anthropologist with 40 years of intimate experience of Indigenous settlement life, seems to agree with

## OVERCOMING DISADVANTAGE

the Iron Lady's view, using priority of the common good as the guide to individual's behaviour: "There can be no assumption that such places (Cape York communities) have an ethos…..of the common good." Sutton's long experience also convinced him that "There can be no assumption that such places are unified communities where mutual support beyond members of one's own particular kin group is the order of the day." [It is a little-known fact that Thatcher was the first European Polititian to warn about climate change.]

# OBJECTIVES AND POLICY SETTINGS

A mid-2009 official report indicating that conditions in remote Indigenous communities are becoming worse rather than better, added to the evidence that basic changes in policy required urgent attention. On the basis of the concepts and values considered in the present overview, the following proposals, though not necessarily original, are submitted by the present author as objectives, together with a combined set of italicised policy settings for consideration by Indigenous leaders and government:

1. Recognise that historic treatment of Aborigines has resulted in White guilt and Black anger which, while affecting the older generation, does not cause inherent behaviour patterns or personal incapacity which cannot be overcome through generational change. Such recognition allows young individuals in both racial groups to overcome past perceptions and it offers the opportunity to turn the page and start anew.

   *This recognition translates into policy which excludes special provision for historic disparity.*

2. The momentum for improving well-being in remote communities can come from breaking out of the poverty cycle by starting with large scale residential schooling for the next generation. The advantage of urban residential schooling over new boarding schools provided in present communities, is that children in their formative years will have the advantage of experiencing and adopting the norms of mainstream Australia only if exposed to the urban situation. Whether

## THE FUTURE: OBJECTIVES AND POLICY SETTINGS

such education causes the coming generations to 'orbit' (in Pearson's sense) back to their communities, may not be important to their futures which are increasingly likely to be in urban society.

*This objective translates into policy which facilitates participation in residential schooling.*

3. Investment in remote communities will be more cost-effective and more helpful to the people if it is concentrated at population centres of sufficient size to offer modern infrastructure and services, notably health, primary schooling, basic skills training and appropriate housing with water, electricity and sewerage. Such effective concentration will eventually end the use of outstations except where these act as successful recovery refuges for small numbers of disabled individuals.

*This objective translates into a policy of population concentration, excluding timely and humane treatment of the elderly on country, if that is their preference.*

4. Government services will be combined and offered to all citizens on the basis of need irrespective of race. Such indiscriminate support will make special provision for remote communities in consideration of costs and inconvenience. Under such needs-based policy all urban dwellers will receive support relative to their personal capacity and disadvantage, irrespective of their ethnicity. Similarly, all remote Australians will receive support related to individual disadvantage.

*This objective translates into policy which doesn't discriminate between ethnic groups, by providing services on a needs basis.*

5. Health services will be supplied on a rational scientific basis without parallel input from traditional medicine. The use of traditional medical treatment will be the sole choice of individual clients. Health services will include an efficient and cost-effective network of remote clinics and transport arrangements to specialist facilities in large centres. Special health information services will improve community understanding of the effects of lifestyle and habits on health status.

*This objective translates into policy which properly funds a broad and on-going community health education program which excludes traditional medicine.*

6. Special services will be made available to develop irrigated community vegetable gardens and orchards in remote areas as the most effective way of overcoming poor diet, food related ill-health and high food costs related to imported fresh food.

   *This objective translates into policy which establishes and funds ongoing local food garden expansion and maintenance.*

7. In remote areas, home ownership and family pride will be supported by local housing schemes which use local labour and local materials whenever these are available and managed under sustainable resource use. Legal arrangements will be made to ensure that freehold or 99 year leasehold can be applied on Aboriginal land.

   *The objective of home ownership translates into policy which introduces new legal arrangements on Aboriginal land.*

8. Financial support systems will make provision for the differential needs of the old, young and disabled. Such support will recognise that the psychological needs of the older generation include a range of traditional and customary activities which are central to their sense of belonging. Distinction will be made between practices identified as harmful to well-being or community cohesion, and practices conducive to a positive ethnic identity. The needs of the young include first-class schooling and a non-violent home setting. The extent to which young people are educated in traditional knowledge and custom is a matter for the parents and the Elders to negotiate. The needs of the disabled in remote areas will be met on a non-racial basis with financial support dependent on individual need. All disabled individuals will enjoy the same services.

   *Such financial support systems translate into policy targeted at the needs of both old and young Aborigines as determined by themselves.*

9. The concept of autonomous Aboriginal Homelands will be augmented by a land productivity policy which encourages sustainable resource use as a source of wealth-generation within the mainstream economy. The concept of land as a reserve for traditional Aboriginal use will be re-considered relative to the potential of primary industry and

## THE FUTURE: OBJECTIVES AND POLICY SETTINGS

commercial tourism.

*This objective translates into policy which ensures productive and sustainable land use which benefits all Australians.*

10. Cultural centres will be established where cost-effective size populations in remote areas justify such community investment: Art, dance, language and music will be nurtured as cultural manifestations of shared tradition. Services will be provided to bring these arts to the wider population with a view to increasing appreciation of Aboriginal culture, enriching Australian diversity and generating wealth from cultural effort.

*This objective translates into policy which gives priority to rigorously prioritised building and staffing of cultural projects.*

11. Government policy will encourage a mainstreaming of Aboriginal education, health and training and will reduce funding for those activities which encourage separatist development of infrastructure and services. The prime objective of this policy will be to strengthen the Indigenous contribution to the Australian economy. This will be done without diminishing the respect and pride which Aboriginals have in their most ancient of cultures.

*This objective translates into policy which avoids funding racially-separate services and facilities wherever combined action can be arranged.*

12. The concept of culturally appropriate services and employment will be phased out with the aim of offering more opportunities for Aboriginals active in the future workforce and society. In future all activities considered ethical, useful and productive will be open to all ethnic groups.

*This objective translates into policy which regards all mainstream services and employment as appropriate to Aborigines.*

13. Customary Law will be phased out from the legal processes used in Aboriginal areas to allow for consistent judicial equity across the whole nation. The inequities arising from the legalisation of practices such as payback wounding in Northern Australia (or genital mutilation in Islamic societies) are incompatible with a just and equitable legal system.

## OVERCOMING DISADVANTAGE

*This objective translates into policy in which all courts apply only recognised Commonwealth and State Law and do not recognise Customary Law or Custom as part of, or complementary to, such recognised law. This objective also translates into policy which makes it clear to Aboriginal (and Islamic) communities, that ethnically-based custom will not have legal standing in Australia.*

## Summary of Aims

None of the above proposals are new, but taken together they offer a policy platform which can:

1. Allow Indigenous Australians to maintain a pride in their identity while benefiting from mainstream well-being.

2. Bring to an end the nationally-embarrassing social situation in remote Indigenous communities.

3. Allow coming generations to enjoy the benefits of first class education and the well-being which comes from employment in skilled occupations.

4. Position government to produce cost-effective social infrastructure and services conducive to a policy of non-discriminatory social welfare delivery.

5. Provide a framework for Australia to overcome historic divisions, socially harmful conflict, international embarrassment on sectional poverty, inefficient land use, extreme social dysfunction and outdated racism.

# SECTION TWO
# ROOTS AND WINGS

# PREFACE

Section 1 concludes that the objectives of Homeland development are unclear and that policy-makers have failed to agree on the role of culture and traditional identity in future well-being.

There is a growing tendency for academics, cultural leaders and media spokespersons to assume racist motives when observers of the Indigenous situation suggest, even in gentle terms, that contemporary wisdom on identity and culture may benefit from re-consideration. Past reactions by Indigenous leaders to suggestions from others, that cultural respect can't be assumed, has led to such unhelpful negative reaction, that many otherwise-useful contributors to Indigenous well-being have either been intimidated out of the debate or have made a conscious decision to apply their talents to more appreciative social groups. It should be emphasised that while the generational hurt, which has caused this angry victimhood, is well understood, its negative effect on the next generation does them no favours at all. What follows in this overview, invites respondents to build on positive emotions and to appreciate the realities of the opportunities which are available to the grandchildren if handled constructively.

It is the author's plea that Indigenous spokespersons exercise the same tolerance of alternative opinions as most Australians and Migrant groups have developed. Perhaps many Indigenous leaders are unaware that the less-than-enthusiastic public embrace of many Indigenous assistance schemes, may often result from the over-precious portrayal of programs which are light on self-sufficiency and strong on traditional culture. The time for a realistic review of Homeland identity and its implications is now.

Finally it should be emphasised that the approach taken in this review in no way seeks to diminish Indigenous Identity. Lest the purists once again interpret alternative views on Aboriginal culture as a re-emergence of colonial attempts to eliminate traditional identity, it should be reiterated that the values proposed here have only one objective, namely to support modernisation of culture for the sole purpose of securing the sustainable well-being of future generations of Australia's First People.

Responsible parents will give their offspring both roots and wings.

# A RECONSIDERATION OF INDIGENOUS IDENTITY AND WELL-BEING

## INDIGENOUS IDENTITY – JUST WHAT IS IT?

What follows in this first section is a response to Leah Purcell's SBS-TV program Black Chicks Talking (10/11/10) which asked several successful women how they felt about their Indigenous Identity. This is a case study with broad implications.

Currently a lot of time and money is being invested in promoting the cultural identity of Indigenous people. Many observers are asking what drives this activity? Have its benefits for adherents been critically evaluated, and what will it lead to in terms of well-being, racism and social cohesion in Australia?

Perhaps even before these questions are considered, the fundamental question of what this identity actually consists of and means to its adherents, is probably a useful starting point. Like all things cultural, quantification and codification of identity is not possible. What can be measured is the monetary value to individuals of qualifying for services differentiated by race and the income foregone due to job discrimination.

In attempting to define the Indigenous identity, outsiders need to be aware that, like migration, there are push and pull factors which both push individuals away from the dominant White culture, and pull them toward the minority Black culture. The opposite is also true. The push factors may include historic maltreatment, current discrimination and a perception of non-acceptance socially. Pull factors may include a sense of belonging based on past hard times, fellow suffering, family support and nurturing, connectedness through relatives and special financial benefits.

## OVERCOMING DISADVANTAGE

Adherents to Indigenous identity need also to be pragmatic about the benefits or otherwise of this identity for their offspring's future well-being. They have the responsibility to ask what their embraced identity and its associated cultural values will contribute to future adherents' happiness, standard of living, work ethic, financial security and economic independence. In addition, they need to ask whether their identity includes the concept of "cultural appropriateness" of jobs, entertainment, personal relations, religion and spiritual experiences.

Some Indigenous leaders have advised their offspring and others to enrich their lives by inculturating the inspiring, noble, exemplary, time-tested values and achievements of other cultures. Indigenous adherents have been encouraged to broaden their appreciation of international humanitarian enrichment and compassion, by encapsulating these global thoughts, inspirations and guideposts to life into their Indigenous connectedness.

It seems important to see this external cultural enrichment as a plus rather than a dilution or diminishment of Indigenous-ness. Those who suggest that, on its own, traditional Indigenous culture suffers a paucity of enriched modern human values, are easily accused of racism and lack of cultural respect. This is as unfortunate as the accusations of anti-Islamic racism made against those who make suggestions that Muslims should speak out against their brethren who proclaim death to the innocent in the name of Allah.

It behoves Indigenous role-models and spokespersons to recognise what contributes to personal and community well-being and to help their group modernise their culture and behaviours so as to recognise all those attributes which favour improved well-being as being 'culturally appropriate'. This broadening of the ambit of cultural comfort has the potential to facilitate the rate and extent of beneficial outcomes from joining the less-restricting mainstreaming.

Such beneficial outcomes will not be assisted by any emphasis on Indigenous separateness, whether cultural, geographic or economic. South Africa demonstrated how the artificial re-creation of tribal identity and autonomy can almost guarantee future discrimination. Leaders will do well to focus on tolerance, mutual respect, co-operation and partnership when promoting Indigenous identity and pride. Noel Pearson's leadership on this matter of modern Indigenous identity has brought criticism from those of his people not yet ready to take the personal responsibility necessary to make the transition to the modern Australian mainstream. While this transition is difficult for remote adults, it should come easily to the young who have been schooled in the ways of modern living through their increasing educational mobility.

On a number of choices available to Indigenous Australians, their leaders ignore or postpone the balanced proposals offered by Pearson, at their peril. The adults need to clearly distinguish between what cultural connection they feel and what intensity of connection will best serve their offspring's well-being.

Finally, before individuals decide that their Aboriginal duty requires them to believe certain stories and accept the sacred nature of their clan country connections, it would be as well to interrogate the family tree and estimate the extent to which Indigenous DNA dominates their bloodline. Aboriginality in its true sense, cannot simply be claimed by empathetic associates. Either it's the real thing or it's all in the mind – which may well be enough for seekers after connection who feel rejected by new Indigenous countrymen.

In the predicted future reduction of Indigenous financial benefits, the proportion of individuals identifying with the race may well change. Members of the tribe may then be pleased to know that membership is reversible and can be formally discontinued voluntarily.

The Apartheid experience can be instructive for Indigenous leaders. Outsiders commonly see Apartheid simply as a means for the Whites to avoid being swamped, by limiting the Blacks' land ownership to reserves. It was in essence an attempt to reverse modernisation by recreating tribal Homelands ruled by appointed chiefs complete with specially reinvented totems, insignias of tribe, declarations of chieftain authority plus tribal dress and language. Even original place names and historic sites were resurrected to indicate that each Homeland was the real ancestral home of the 11 language groups so reconstituted. Some, like Mandela's Xhosas and Zuma's Zulus, had by that time moved significantly toward an urbanised Western lifestyle, to the extent that their original reserve country had become a parking lot for old folks and fatherless families. The official drive to make people feel different, tribal and connected, overrode all. The fundamental difference between the South African and Australian Blacks' situations was the former's legal incapacity to own homes outside their Bantustans. Not surprisingly the first thing they did after gaining majority rule, was to break out of the geographical and cultural constraints of Apartheid. Clearly a job, a house and the kids' education near medical services, usually outweighed any tribal Homeland allegiance. There is a message in this for the Australian culture warriors and the message is simply – don't let the push for Indigenous identity get in the way of future well-being.

At the heart of the dangers of over-emphasis of traditional identity, is the extent to which it can label work ethics and competitiveness as un-Aboriginal. It is this fundamental humanitarian norm which causes Pearson strife among many of his own people of Cape York, as reflected in the Wild Rivers saga.

To return to South Africa, the Apartheid government made significant efforts to develop self-sufficient tribal areas. The combination of insufficient size, inadequate work ethic and violence resulting from breakdown of social fabric, led predictably to failure of many planned production schemes. While many would challenge this comparison, the factors mitigating against successful Australian Native Title Lands are probably not too different from the Bantustan case.

So if Leah Purcell's guests in Black Chicks Talking were feeling tribally ambivalent, they're in good company.

Darren Clarke, a professional photographer, set out on a 10-year project in 2000 to document "What it means to be Australian". By his 11th year, he admitted, "The longer I do it, the more confused I become". Is this perhaps not surprising in our multi-culture on a huge continent, or is this just another way of saying that the central question of what being Australian means has an infinite answer – infinite in the sense that we are an amalgam of independent, confident, free-thinkers, not harnessed by any orthodoxy which constrains our natural will to be ourselves. In essence, in our being Australian we have consciously 'unbeen' members of our earlier colonial or Migrant tribes whose historic, racial and religious shackles we have long since cast aside.

This never-ending search for identity and sense of belonging creates havoc for political leaders trying to read the public mind. In attempting to define what we stand for, our leaders repeatedly misread the healthy breadth of opinion and end up with paradoxes of their own making, as shown by the spread of views in regular opinion polls. Such diversity of views often causes political leaders to take a strong stand on a chosen identity which is often more pretence than conviction. This pretence goes as far as pretending that we respect (love?) all people irrespective of their culture and, that rednecks can't be tolerated, that boat people all deserve sympathy, that all Aborigines deserve empathetic support, that all religions warrant equal respect, that individual freedom overrides public good, that a fair go should protect slackers, that all Migrants should be equally welcome and that politicians don't need any real-world experience outside the party machine.

Add to these common assumptions, the propensity of parties to 'backflip and flip-flop' in an effort to mollify the Left, and Australia ends up as a value-free political zone where conviction by leaders has no role. In her 1998 maiden speech to parliament, Julia Gillard, former Prime Minister, said "For far too long public debate in Australia has failed to nourish or inspire us. For far too long it has been limited to the day-to-day monitoring of the health of our economy rather than the morals and goals of our society. The end result of this political cycle is a weary people who no longer believe what politicians say and who think the politicians saying it do not even believe it themselves." Bring on the carbon tax.

## FUTURE INDIGENOUS RELIGION

The late-2010 report which claims that the Australian Islamic community already boasts over one thousand Aboriginal members, begs the question of how modern Aborigines should continue, adapt, replace or dispense with their traditional land-based religion. World-wide, Islam is the fastest-growing religion. In the West, Buddhism grows fastest while in Australia only 13% of nominal Christians are church-goers. Over 80% of Aborigines tick Christianity as their census religion.

Despite these statistics, the recent increase of Aboriginal Islamists from 600 in 2001 to 1000 in 2010 warrants serious consideration. Many religious conversions reflect both pull and push factors (to use migration terminology) and both these forces may be implicated in the Aboriginal trend which has been given a high profile by Anthony Mundine, the Aboriginal world champion boxer following in the steps of Mohammed Ali.

## OVERCOMING DISADVANTAGE

The historic success of Christianity on the Australian mission-field is patchy and covers the whole continuum of religious conversion. Missions varied in their approach to Aboriginal religion and its associated totems and language. In many cases the potential converts were virtually forced to accept Christianity and denounce their Indigenous beliefs as pagan and anti-Christ.

Predictably this involuntary conversion of the young particularly, caused serious friction within Aboriginal families. In time, many of the urbanised Aborigines became regular members of suburban Christian churches, while remote communities often practised both traditional customs and Christian beliefs.

Over time, most Aborigines had no option but to accept the reality of the loss of their land with its sacred sites and ancestral spiritual connections. However, rather than seek a spiritual home in the Christian church, many fell between the two religious traditions available and for several generations their youth grew up with a confused dichotomy of beliefs which didn't provide a dependable value system sufficient to form a moral basis for that cohort.

So, as contemporary urbanised Aborigines might seek the normal spiritual compass required by most humans, they have a wide choice of established religions in Australian society. Such choice is probably more emotional than rational and may unconsciously be more influenced by negative memories of past Mission Christianity than by positive adherence to new conversions.

So why would present-day Aborigines adopt Islam in preference to say Buddhism or even a rejuvenated Christianity as embodied in ecumenical churches such as Hillsong, Fred Noff's son's new-look Wayside Chapel or some of the musical Happy Clappers of evangelism? This is a complex question but the escape into happiness was boosted by the rising popularity of black humour in TV programs such as 'Deadly Funny' in which, mostly female, Aboriginal comedians present stand-ups which expose very important nuances on social issues.

For many Aboriginals, Islam may be more readily defined by what it is not, rather than by what it is, i.e. it doesn't represent Christianity, it represents an alternative. Perhaps what it does represent can be sorted out later; meanwhile what we do know is what we don't want, given our family's painful experience at the hands of the Missionaries. Yet for other families, their experience and opinion of the Christian Missions is very different. Their grandparents and

## ROOTS AND WINGS: FUTURE INDIGENOUS RELIGION

parents were taken in by the Missions, protected from police and squatters, taught to read and write, introduced to the 10 Commandments and the Golden Rule, shown how to grow vegetables, work with cattle, ride horses and how to do domestic house work, including hygienic care of children. Their Missionaries sometimes respected Aboriginal language and culture but were convinced of the benefits which Christianity could bestow on their condition and their sheer humanity.

Perhaps it should be asked whether Aboriginals who have lost their spirituality or at least their religious connection, are any different from any other seekers after a new spiritual home. Perhaps the differences are personal and individual, rather than racial and ethnic. Perhaps it can be assumed that seekers after spiritual truths usually look for certainty, strength of support, guidance in decision-making and response to prayer requests. Of course religion is never a rational exercise although the most useful religious allegiance might come from a conscious search for a spiritual home which meets real needs. What, for instance, is offered by Christianity, Islam or Buddhism? Many seekers may be surprised to find how much commonality of values there is between Christianity and Islam. Buddhism however, differs in a fundamental way in having no God or Allah but focuses on self-improvement and harmonious inter-personal relations.

In simple terms, there are four kinds of religion: natural, organised, revealed and institutionalised. The original Aboriginal religion stems from fear and respect for natural phenomena and objects. This was the same for the author's Stonehenge clan's respect for the power of the sunrise. The Aborigines moved towards an organised religion with its moral code, rituals, song and dance, totems and sacred sites. Whether they proceeded as far as a revealed religion depends on whether they interpret their stories as coming through a messenger from a supreme being. These stories contain moral codes and beliefs, which act as the basis for the conduct of both spiritual and social matters. Both Christianity and Islam depended on messengers (Jesus and Mohammed) who were central to the three Abrahamic religions. The certainty which came from their immutable holy writs, was both useful and comforting to adherents and did away with the need to make personal judgements. However, if some Aboriginals are seeking a replacement value system, perhaps a system which recognises no superhuman controlling power, might more effectively fill their need. Buddhism has no commandments, laws, dogmas or threats of punishment. It teaches simply that the 'highest wealth is contentment' and that contentment comes from service to others. It replaces greed with self-discipline, a well-trained mind and the getting of wisdom. It teaches the universal truth of patience, tolerance, sympathy, humility and kindness. Christianity and Islam would make similar claims but a long history of Holy Wars has caused many to re-assess their allegiances.

At the risk of offering shallow representation of religious choices as a spiritual supermarket, it should be recognised that modern parents have an obligation to help their offspring find the form of spiritual guidance which offers their different personalities guideposts and a compass to a fulfilled life. If their future spiritual home can be more than a refuge from reality, but can provide a foundation for a confident and productive life, then contentment will be within their reach.

So today's Aboriginals would do well to find out why mainstreamers are abandoning Christianity in favour of other worldviews and why the vast majority of them avoid Islam as their alternative and seek contentment elsewhere. Perhaps they could evaluate Anthony Mundine's stated reasons for adopting Islam. Islam's avoidance of alcohol would be hard to beat as a real plus for both Black and Whitefellas.

# SELF-GOVERNING HOMELANDS – BE CAREFUL WHAT YOU WISH FOR

Having lived for 30 years under the Apartheid regime, and having lectured on sustainable Homelands for nearly 20 years, perhaps I may be allowed a few warnings.

Nobody has asked my advice but my experience compels me to bring a few pointers to the notice of the proponents of separatism in Australia. While many Indigenous leaders would claim that their goal is mainstreaming and not separating, I note an easy vagueness about the status, governance, rights and well-being which may or may not come about in future Native Title lands. These lands potentially constitute significant proportions of sovereign Australian territory and as such can contribute vast resources to the national economy.

At the risk of being accused of historical irrelevance, I submit that there are lessons to be learned from the previous story of official attempts to restore tribal identity in modern South Africa. While it is not appreciated by many commentators, what happened in South Africa after 1948 when the Apartheid government took over, was in fact the most formidable social engineering of the 20th century. While Australia does not have the same passbook system or legal limitations to geographic home purchase, it certainly suffers the social hangover of forced removals, declared Aboriginal reserves and family breakup.

It is instructive to remember that the Apartheid government policy had the noble goal of equal but separate freedoms. South Africa's Native Reserve system was set up in 1909, some by the same colonial governors who were lurking around Cape York. Segregated Native Locations near South African cities were legalised in 1923. The development of Australian Aboriginal reserves followed much the same path, the big difference being that the discrimination in South Africa was legislated after 1948. Australia followed its own legal path, doing away with the earlier laws against mixed marriages but maintaining its permit system for entry to reserves – this time for Whites. This exclusion of one race from another's territory is a strange regulatory appendage to Australia's enlightened legal system. Permits are a Coombsian hangover from the 1960's which attempt to preserve Indigenous culture and tradition. While Nugget Coombes developed the idea for preservation purposes, over the years it allowed widespread social dysfunction on reserves, DOGITs and Native Title lands to reach dangerous, almost irreversible proportions, without outside scrutiny. In effect, intended cultural protection led to child abuse rarely paralleled in the modern world.

We do not need to dwell on these negative and internationally embarrassing elements of separate development. What we do need to dwell on is twofold: what do we do about it and how can we plan for a sustainable Indigenous population? It behoves all Australians to support the practical efforts to close the gap in health, housing, education and well-being, and to support COAG in its agreement to a decadal Indigenous budget of over $4.6 billion, which reflected the need felt by the nation to act decisively.

However, the planning of sustainable societies on Native Title country remains in urgent need of an Indigenous equivalent of Labour's 'Light on the Hill' – an agreed, clear road map of how such sustainability is to be arrived at. This requires an understanding of the elements of a sustainable community and of the attributes of the members of such a society.

The literature is rapidly becoming overloaded with sustainability proposals, fuelled mostly by the recent realisation that climatic change has not only idealistic implications but also survival values. Unfortunately the media have concentrated on the environmental elements at the expense of the deeper more causal elements of socio-economic trend as reflected in behaviour, consumerism, earthly lifestyles and ultimately in the society's definition of success.

Indigenous organisations have now been offered the unusual opportunity to demonstrate that they have sufficient vision not only to overcome the backlog of well-being, but more importantly, to show the rest of this nation how future sustainable societies can be planned for, educated for and implemented for, in a way which surpasses the shallow and outdated Western consumerism of the previous century.

To many, aiming so high may appear visionary pie-in-the-sky, but to those committed to the reality of a need for sustainable lifestyles as a necessary basis of national survival, its goals are not only achievable, they are essential. The process starts logically with inculcation in the young, of the values and behaviours which characterise the sustainable society. In practice such ideals will come to nothing in the absence of a planning framework that creates the setting for a peaceful, productive, frugal and contented community. Community leaders and planners will need a good dose of realism to recognise and appreciate the limitations to their Homelands' wealth-generation capacity. Equally they will require acceptance of the need for mobility in both education and employment, while not overlooking the local value-adding capacity of community enterprise.

Leaders and planners must learn from past failures, from projects that didn't deliver and from funds squandered on unplanned outcomes. They must identify honestly and fairly, the causes of previous policy failure and then use those findings to improve success factors going forward. Each community is different, but realism demands that the extent and intensity of current dysfunction be recognised and appreciated before wishful thinking again produces inevitable failure. Detailed analysis of age, health, capacity and expectations of individuals will allow for factual estimates of possible success in uplifting the community's well-being. There is no place for uncritical optimistic group-think in this societal planning process. A brutal honesty, which produces unwelcome answers, is sometimes required to break out of old accepted cycles. Part of the process is acceptance of incapacity to change in the long-disadvantaged adults, as is recognised in the position of elderly people.

# WHAT CAN WE LEARN FROM APARTHEID – APART FROM WHAT NOT TO DO?

We can learn that policy which encourages the development of separate, race-based Homelands should teach us the following lessons:

1. Indigenous leaders are attracted to the concept of separate development because of the perceived benefits for themselves and their families.

2. Leading families interpret policy as accepting the principle that financial and decision-making benefits need not extend to the common good of the intended broader community.

3. Leaders and spokespersons can be expected to use historic, cultural and religious arguments to the full, in negotiating benefits for their community, giving them an un-democratic advantage over other racial groups competing for the same national benefits.

4. Proponents of Homelands can be almost guaranteed to over-estimate the human carrying capacity of these racially-based areas in which other races have no or diminished rights.

5. Successful communities arise only from the effort required to achieve economic independence, without which neither well-being nor respect accrue.

## OVERCOMING DISADVANTAGE

6. Homelands without mobility of learners and workers are most likely to fail.
7. With out-migration of the majority of able-bodied workers and wealth-generators, the residual Homeland community suffers demographic breakdown of social fabric and family cohesion.
8. Stratified residual communities dominated by the very old and the very young, cannot function as balanced social entities.
9. The cost and disadvantage of remoteness are such that cost-effective servicing of community needs is not possible on a comparative cost per capita basis.
10. Homelands with unreliably low numbers of productive individuals can only be continued as sheltered economies outside the expectations of the mainstream on real economies.
11. Protective separation in Homelands encourages escapism from economic reality by providing generational refuges from the expectations of productive modern communities.
12. The exaggeration of the value of customary tradition in isolated Homeland communities reduces the motivation of emerging generations to modernise toward well-being. Instead, the young can be entrapped in a culture of ignorance and uncompetitive behaviour.
13. The mindset of Homelands separatism, encourages the concept of racial difference and its associated expectation of special treatment. Such tribal identification mitigates against social cohesion nationally and as such, reduces the potential benefits to Homelands of productive partnerships and co-operative effort.
14. Divisive attitudes are encouraged by the race-based isolation of Homelands in the absence of inter-racial mixing and appreciation of universal humanitarian values and norms from a young age.
15. Both proud personal identity and the psychological comfort of connections to country, can be maintained as personal groundings by urban communities geographically distant from clan country.
16. Policies and benefits which are race-based, contain the seeds of division, dissension, discrimination and comparative discontent.

17. Policy which bases rights and benefits solely on non-racial needs and disadvantage, almost always gives more equitable outcomes in the long term.

Those who claim that the Apartheid policy was not comparable to the Australian Native Title policy would do well to develop a mind-map of how local Homelands are planned to grow into sustainable communities. Such an exercise soon shows that, just as with the Apartheid policy, the proponents of the current separatist policy, lack the vision to avoid what the South African government referred belatedly to as 'unplanned outcomes'.

Indigenous policy presently needs more than vague wishful thinking about the imagined Utopia of self-governed Homelands, by whatever name. While the tendency to demonise the male stereotype in remote communities must be avoided, there is sufficient factual evidence to validate the view that the level of dysfunction is so injurious as to disallow the description of many of these settlements as "communities". The reason for this is that in real communities, individuals actually feel a commitment to the common good – and an obligation to the betterment of all. No group, which allows the violence, substance abuse, and maltreatment of the innocent, is a community. The dog-eat-dog world of the Apartheid townships and rural slums must not be allowed to find further footholds in Australian Homelands.

Those responsible for the planning of sustainable Indigenous Homelands must heed the international lessons and stop pretending that because Australia is unique, different, ancient and without precedent, it cannot learn global humanitarian lessons. Human nature, human aspirations, human frailties and the human spirit are universal and knowable as a basis for progress in Australia.

# CAN HOMELANDS REALLY WORK?

It is understandable that practical operatives who deal with the daily realities of alcoholism, violence, abuse and unemployment, have little time for big-picture ideologists and well-meaning academics offering arm-chair advice on Indigenous policy. Those concerned with the here-and-now urgencies of community dysfunction just want to focus on fixing the immediate local problems. Their focus is on protecting the innocent from the on-going threat of harm from males who have long since fallen between the accepted norms of both societies.

It may be that the urgency and scale of this community rescue effort has already engaged the total available effort of those on the front-line and those supporting them with personnel and funds. This has left a vacuum in the policy planning effort, causing a degree of *vagueness on goals and objectives*, sufficient to result in directional misunderstanding and even conflict between Indigenous leaders. Government has attempted to keep the peace by trying hard to be seen to be meeting Indigenous wishes and at least not be perceived as oppressing the disadvantaged original landholders. In the process, realism on the actual probability of Homelands being viable entities within the nation's economy, has been replaced with a vague and impractical empathy supporting an unworkable ideology which produces hardly anything.

While the urgent betterment work on practical community well-being must continue to be strongly supported, unless the hard truths of wealth generation are faced and acted on, vast amounts of financial, material and emotional capital will continue to be spent on an unworkable system of Homelands which will almost certainly become refuges for the uncompetitive and parking lots for the old folks.

Strong vibrant communities cannot be developed in the absence of significant self-generated income. There already appears to be general agreement that Indigenous people need to grasp the nettle themselves and commence the required transition process in earnest. Without adequate income from natural resources (mining, grazing etc.) or value-adding (art, tourism etc.) Homelands populations could shrink to the point where only retirement villages remain. So how good an investment are larger schools and hospitals in the Homelands, relative to alternative investments elsewhere on Aboriginals' behalf? This fundamental question needs immediate attention.

The implications of the transition to modern Aboriginality and the urgency of its implementation, don't appear to be a priority for many Indigenous leaders. Presently we are headed for the loss of yet another generation, once again based on the pretence that well-being can be attained in non-productive bush communities. Whose job is it to administer the required large dose of realism?

# INDIGENOUS DEMOCRACY – WHAT'S THE PLACE OF THE FAMILY?

The author suggests the following truisms on Indigenous governance:

1. Aboriginals have traditionally only known social organisation which includes representation at clan or family level. There has never been a governance hierarchy.
2. Funds allocated to community well-being projects often confined benefits to one or two powerful families, to the detriment of others in the community.
3. Aboriginal leaders nominated onto representative bodies probably believe that they can be forgiven for acting as though their first duty is to ensure that their family is the prime beneficiary of government funds.
4. In the application of tribal law, payback and non-lethal spearing involves whole families, not just the original combatants.
5. Democracy as a universal system of voter-based equity, does not function within a framework of family loyalties and patronages, as operational subsets of power within the community.

These claims of empowered parochialism have led some informed observers to suggest that unless and until family loyalty is replaced with the common good, Indigenous communities cannot be seen as ready to govern themselves under a democratic system of self-government.

Predictably, such opinion brings accusations of racism or Hansonism or other redneck-isms. But the uncomfortable question remains: can tax-payers be expected to continue funding preferred family benefits? Or is another governance structure required for equitable and efficient fund allocation to future Indigenous programs?

In practice, a change to genuine common-good democracy, may also entail a reconsideration of the Elder system of decision-making. Does the process whereby Elders are recognised, fit a democratic model, and if not, could a different system offer a worthy alternative? The Democratic purists will claim that an unqualified one-man-one-vote system cannot be violated or qualified. Others, experienced in the traditions of group-governments and customary law enforcement, maintain that the Elder system still gains widespread acceptance in remote communities. This conflicting view begs the question of whether it is feasible or desirable to use a different system of governance in remote communities where tradition is strong. This in turn leads to the basic consideration of whether the Aboriginal subpopulation within the Australian nation should be governed separately and differently from the rest of the population.

The alternative is to differentiate policy, not on the basis of Aboriginality, but on a practical basis of disadvantage related to distance from services. In this way support is related to need, irrespective of race. This would eliminate the present inequitable system under which urban Aboriginals, with no more need than other suburban poor, and with the same access to services, are recipients of an illogical support system which has only one criterion – ancestry. Like the House of Lords in a way.

Because this differential policy has become ingrained for decades, any major change away from race as its basis, will need to be given forward notice of, and phased in, in progressive stages which recognise the needs of the older generations.

# WHITEFELLA CULTURAL IDENTITY

With all the recent writing on the importance or otherwise of Aborigines preserving their identity and sense of belonging, the question of the Whitefella's identity looms large.

Few writings challenge the old White Australian identity as well as Peter Conrad's scathing criticism of Hugh Lunn's "Words Fail Me: A Journey through Australia's Lost Language" in The Monthly (11/2010). Conrad forcefully suggests that "the mean, empty, conservative self-image" of the 1950s Australian is a damaging throwback which prevents the present generation from modernising, tolerating and appreciating cultural diversity. The old post-colonial identity does nothing to fit the upcoming generation for a different and changing world and serves only as a nostalgic refuge for those stuck in their inflexible time-warp. Conrad accuses Lunn of leading a 'peasant's revolt' against multiculturalism and the dilution of Australian integrity. It was this habit of belittling excellence years ago, which led to decades of contented national mediocrity, says Conrad. Global isolation had led to blinkered, bigoted and linguistically impoverished Whitefellas incapable of embracing global humanitarian values and tolerances. The extent of support for Hansonism made Howard recognise how widely-held these narrow views were and caused his government to move further to the right.

The truth probably lies somewhere between the polarised views of Lunn and Conrad, but this example highlights the need for a more serious effort to reach consensus on the values and aspirations of both White and Black Australians. The way the old and somewhat narrow Australian identity has broadened in recent decades, has allowed for a more diverse and inclusive self-image and identity, as reflected in the Boatpeople debate.

Is it too much to ask that Indigenous Australians make the same identity move as the Whitefellas, for the same reasons and benefits? Perhaps it is too much, especially for those trapped in the twilight zone between traditionality and modernity in remote locations where ingrained toxic norms prevail. For the more enlightened youths who have had the rare privilege of having inspiring teachers urging them to accept career challenges, both push and pull factors encourage them to move to greener pastures. The early realisation that the White suburban society also contains bad elements in its violent downside, no doubt makes these transitory youths accept the realities of contemporary Australian society and its potential underbelly element. Eventually, the newcomers come to recognise that by world standards, the general level of Australian well-being is high and that strong and informed individuals can and do thrive here, as in few other countries.

# COMMNUNITY NORMS – WHAT CAN WHITEFELLAS OFFER?

All the criticism of the decline of community norms in isolated Indigenous settlements begs the question of the status of Australian behavioural norms generally.

## OVERCOMING DISADVANTAGE

Crime and court records on just a few parameters of social well-being are sufficient to demonstrate the dire state of what used to be valued as indicators of an advanced society. Limiting the evaluation of societal attributes only to alcoholism, drugs, gambling and domestic violence, it has long been clear that Australians and their governments value personal freedom so highly that the nation ends up living with unacceptable trends in civilised behaviour.

Parliament has continued to pass laws which legitimise the sponsorship of sport at all levels by beverage companies which continue to encapsulate alcohol consumption as the essential element of the good life – the norm for successful modern individuals. Similarly, the disastrous effects of compulsive gambling on family financial security, continue to proceed legally as if this behaviour is not only okay but is a human right to be defended. The divorce rate, having risen to about 40%, has been assisted by legal changes in family law and reflects the increasing emphasis on individual freedom of adults including women's rights, irrespective of the impact on children. Departmental reports indicate that the increase in divorce rates plateaued in 2001. At the same time, the treatment of domestic violence and the expansion of safe houses for women and children, does little to change the norms and ethics of Australian society in general.

Without wanting to be seen as taking the moral highground or ursurping individuals' value judgements, the contemporary moral and ethical norms in Australian society don't auger well for the envisaged sustainable society of the future. This being the case, the relative dysfunction from which responsible Indigenous families in remote communities wish to escape, needs to be seen in a comparative context. Families' potential move from Dystopia thus doesn't necessarily lead to Utopia or anything vaguely similar. This is because the differences between the two societies is not absolute but very much relative. The message for new adherents to mainstream Australian culture (if there is such a thing) is that survival and prosperity are largely dependent on the individual's integrity and determination, rather than on one's ethnic background or cultural baggage. Just do it.

In attempting to help Aboriginal people improve their standard of living, the shortcomings of the mainstream society are brought into stark relief. Sociologists seem to distinguish between culture and civilisation, the latter being characterised by its ordered architecture, advanced fine arts, an independent justice system, educational institutions, civil behaviour, absence of violence, sanitary systems, and reliable food and water supplies.

Culture on the other hand relates not to civil organisation as such, but rather to the beliefs and values of society, whether advanced or not. Recent decades have seen the reverse of civil behaviour in several First World countries. This trend to "uncivilised" behaviour is exhibited in the form of violence, selfish public behaviour, disrespect to the law, abuse of the innocent and damage to property. A different but related form of civil reversal is the religion-based expansion of suicide bombing.

On another related matter, the downside of freedom of choice is going to require serious consideration for the emerging modern Indigenous society. The 2010 report of the Australia Institute prepared for Citibank Australia, makes revealing findings on what the behaviourists call 'behavioural economics'. This is the study of the extent to which individuals choose to make illogical financial decisions, including their home loans, insurance, healthcare and transport.

It is now time to ask whether freedom of choice on life's decisions could be, should be, must be, open or constrained by incentives for those on the lower rungs of society. This question is particularly relevant to those Indigenous people and others who have demonstrated a propensity to make bad choices. Allowing individuals the freedom of choosing, as Milton Friedman and Frederick Hayek have proposed, presupposes a capacity to move beyond the desires of primitive urges, to a level of responsibility that minimises the burden on the Welfare State. Perhaps the guiding principle should be: choose whatever you like as long as others don't have to support you.

# MARGARET TURNER'S STORY

In a beautifully presented coffee-table book titled "Iwenhe Tyerrtye", co-written with Veronica Dobson, Margaret Turner has told a story of what it means to be an Aboriginal person. As a Central Australian woman who was awarded the Order of Australia in 1997 for services to language, culture and interpreting, Margaret was identified by AIATSIS as the person most likely to ably define Aboriginal identity. The National Library and the Australian Government supported her publication.

Turner's chapter and section titles reflect the building blocks of her identity structure: "Born to be; Relationship to Land; The Generations; Dreams and Story; Ways of Telling; Sacredness of Kinship; Touch Feelings; Mourning; What Land Means; Recovering our Land; Healing; Ancestor Trees; Food from Plants; Stories from Plants; Respect for Animals; Once the White People Came; Language; Land, the Real Teacher; Teaching is a Sacred Thing; The Elders; Two Cultures can hold each other together."

The literary merit, technical perfection of the graphics and sheer humanity of the story with its ancient authenticity, leads the reader to admire this portrayal of Indigenous identity. However, its subtitle –"What it means to be an Aboriginal person" needs careful interpretation, especially since in the final chapter headed "Two Cultures", she recognises the need to move on from a culture she describes so beautifully.

Turner tells us she's an English-speaking Catholic and she is seeking ways of encouraging the two cultures to complement each other. Importantly, Turner is not calling her people to return to traditional ways, she asks only that they preserve and respect their culture through language, the arts and dance.

So why is Turner's book significant? Because it is one of the few literary attempts to express the meaning of Aboriginality in its original authentic form, driven neither by academic egotism nor by political opportunism. No doubt the purest culture warriors who write in city publications, are disappointed by Turner's love of English and comfort in Christianity, but she is a beacon of tolerance, respect and admiration for parallel cultures.

I'm sure Turner would like Australians to do with her stories what they do with Shakespeare's stories – preserve them, teach their lessons to the children and take the best of them as guides to living with your fellow humans as respected co-operators. This modernising of the Indigenous world view in no way nullifies the desirability of elderly Aborigines in remote areas living out their days in the psychological comfort of their traditional culture, without obliging the next generations to forego the well-being offered by alternative lifestyles. So perhaps we need to ask whether we understand DNA's role in social development as part of the Nature/Nurture debate.

The debate about the relative importance of inherited and learned attributes of personality is as old as the original Greek philosophers. It is usually referred to as the Nature/Nurture debate because it contrasts inherited with learned personal traits. In the sphere of Indigenous policy, it becomes a significant element of the basic assumptions underlying proposals to improve well-being.

Past policy may have assumed that Indigenous offspring inherited a limited capacity to accept Western norms. Over the years, the increasing number of examples of successful transition, famously personified by Charlie Perkins who is reported to be, but actually isn't, the first Indigenous university graduate, suggested otherwise. Soon the unexpected capacity of educated individuals was credited to their mixed heritage and the European DNA which this contributed to the intelligent hybrid vigour of the offspring. Examples of transitioned full-blood Aboriginals were difficult to find and confirm, but it soon became plain that their absence may be more closely related to lack of motivation than to lack of innate intelligence. Indeed, anthropologists soon recognised a unique native intelligence which had developed over millennia of survival in a harsh environment, unrelated to the attributes assessed in Western IQ tests.

The research on inherited IQ is pertinent to the present debate. The documentary "Race and Intelligence" (SBS 28/11/10) predictably caused cautious racial comment. It has been shown that racial origin of skeletons can be identified from bone DNA. Prof Steven Jones has shown that on average, US Blacks carry 20% of White genes but that the brightest Blacks don't necessarily have the highest proportion of White genes. Prof James Flynn of Otago NZ studied the rise of IQ of people in 30 countries over a period of 50 years and reported an annual average increase of three points globally. This rise was twice as rapid in Blacks as in Whites. The ability to think abstractly was the most obvious improvement factor in IQ scores. It seems agreed that contemporary IQ tests reflect adaptation to modern thought patterns rather than innate intelligence. Achievement of Asian schoolchildren above that of Whites in both America and Australia may reflect parental aspirations, support and recognition rather than superior innate ability.

## DNA AND MODERNITY – GIVE CREDIT TO YOUR 'NEW' GENES

Central to Indigenous policy are the earlier assumptions made on Aboriginal disadvantage and capacity, as limitations to their being able to benefit from educational opportunities. One school of thought holds that their inherited hunter-gatherer DNA precludes capacity-building in individuals, to the extent that Aboriginals require or at least deserve, both different ways of learning and more time to reach achievement milestones. The other school of thought maintains that learning ability is largely learned rather than inherited, and its proponents quote many successful examples. This latter approach assumes that over 70% of Aborigines are now urbanised and out-marrying from their ethnic group. Their inherited capacity and their exposure to modern education, can and will allow them to compete with mainstream job-seekers if this school of thought is correct.

This conclusion is at the centre of government decisions on differentiated financial support for those who tick the Centrelink box identifying them as Aboriginal or Islander. It is not clear whether the government's assumption is that because these individuals carry some Indigenous DNA, they deserve extra help. If this is the assumption, then taxpayers can justifiably ask at what level the Aboriginal DNA becomes a disadvantage, and after how many generations of urbanisation and out-marrying can Aboriginality be claimed to disadvantage its inheritor.

Statistics on heredity and mixed parentage are difficult to obtain and may not be comprehensive enough to estimate the extent of pure Indigenous DNA. Anyone questioning the rationale of the present flexible definition of Aboriginality can expect accusations of playing the old 'eugenics' card – a 19th century study of racial purity practised extensively in the British colonies to classify individuals of mixed descent as full bloods, half-castes, quadroons etc…

Today, one's eligibility for Aboriginal status appears to have little to do with the individual's actual Aboriginality if this is measured by inherited Indigenous DNA. This arbitrary qualification would not be serious if equally poverty-stricken non-Indigenous battlers did not feel they were being blatantly discriminated against. The sooner a needs-based policy replaces this race-based policy, the sooner Australia will move toward genuine egalitarianism.

Peter McAllister of Griffith University has recently come up with useful information showing why being called Black should actually be taken as a compliment. He explains why the AFL player Lance Franklin who was recently subjected to racial taunts in Tasmania, can hold his head high. It can be shown that Aboriginal ability to 'read the ball' comes from their exceptional eyesight.

## ROOTS AND WINGS: DNA AND MODERNITY

One optometrist told McAllister, that only one in 5000 people can read the bottom line of the eye chart and that, of all his patients over the years who tried to read that line, Aborigines were the only ones that succeeded. This confirms Fred Hollows assertion made three decades ago, that healthy Aborigines could see about four times better than other Australians on average. This observation was also made by European whalers in the 1800s who reckoned that their Aboriginal crewman could spot a whale further with their naked eye, than the Europeans could with their telescopes.

Running, however, stands out as the Indigenous achievement of note. Archaeologist Steven Webb, calculated from the shape, depth and distance between fossilised footprints unearthed in Western New South Wales in 2003, that 20,000 years ago one individual was running at 37 km/h, arguably faster than Usain Bolt, the current Jamaican world record holder. So why do sprinters of West African ancestry hold over 90% of the fastest times in the 100 m? Apparently it's the combination of longer legs and much higher ratios of fast-twitch to slow-twitch muscle than Europeans, that makes the difference. African-Americans have been breaking the 10 second barrier since 1968 while the first Caucasian to do so was in 2010. The only other non-West African to achieve this speed is Patrick Johnson, an Aboriginal-Irish man from Torres Strait.

McAllister makes the telling point that the old racist assumption that brawn develops at the expense of brain is just not true. When William Thomas, Protector of Aborigines Victoria in 1841 recorded the amazing five-foot leaps of the locals in the original Marn Grook football (the precursor of AFL) the assumption was that these noble savages had traded physical prowess for mental capacity. McAllister stresses that such assumptions are proven wrong by the similarity of all brains and that the idea that Indigenes are lower down the evolutionary scale, stems from a (possibly deliberate) misunderstanding of the evolutionary process. From this interpretation we can infer that the low representation of Aboriginals in intellectual careers is a matter of disadvantage and opportunity, not innate capacity, as demonstrated by dozens of Aborigines and African-Americans succeeding in many professions.

This Australian debate about intellectual capacity won't go away until enough time has elapsed for even more Aborigines to demonstrate their prowess in the professions, starting with legal and medical achievement.

OVERCOMING DISADVANTAGE

# PRIDE IN WHAT WE HAVEN'T ACHIEVED

All the world's cultures have developed through staged advances from their caveman origins – the author's included. The contemporary Indigenous cultures of Africa, Asia, the Americas and Scandinavia, either started modernisation, or progressed more slowly than migrating newcomers toward modern lifestyles. In some cases there may have been a deliberate consideration and rejection of 'progressive' changes. In other cases, rejection of new ideas was based on conscious protection of valued traditional norms. A third group of cultures may simply not have been mentally able to take on the innovations on offer from the newcomers. Or perhaps the 'inability' was financial – to purchase the saws, draught animals, bolts or roofing iron needed for the change.

Examination of the material progress of Australian Aborigines, African San Bushmen, Scandinavian Laps or Arctic Inuit (Eskimos) shows different rates of acceptance of firearms for hunting and of motorised transport. As a result, the rate at which each tribe impacted on the environment differs. Similarly, the degree to which each tribe took up modern schooling and medical services, largely determined the rate at which their people progressed toward modernity and its benefits and moral hazards.

In an environmentally-threatened world, the benefits of non-development are writ large. In this situation, Indigenous peoples still living a traditional life easily claim the moral high ground which comes with minimal resource depletion and pollution. The question now arises as to whether the Indigenous cultures offer an improved role model for more consumptive societies. The answer is yes, but only in some aspects of their social economy. The prime reason for this limited application of hunter-gatherer systems to contemporary Earth, is population pressure. There is general agreement among ecologists that a wide range of harvest systems can remain successful while ever human population remains low. Aboriginal hunter-gathering is no different but is probably unable to sustain contemporary numbers. Thus was born ESD – ecologically sustainable development, based on maximising food production while minimising environmental impact.

## ROOTS AND WINGS: PRIDE IN WHAT WE HAVEN'T ACHIEVED

So what can modern Western culture take from traditional Indigenous culture? The answer is twofold – respect for Nature and the importance of unselfish sharing or 'doing unto others'. This brings the cultural evaluation debate to the question of valuing a culture for what it hasn't done to progress its well-being.

As the old saying goes, virtue may be no more than a lack of opportunity, or in this case, capacity. We do not need to be reminded that the original Green Lobby, after the publication of "Silent Spring", used the Indian chief Seattle's statements on Nature as their battle-cry – Man belongs to the Earth (not vice versa). We'll also ignore the sound evidence that Chief Seattle's published speeches were written much later by a White man.

# THE IMAGE OF PRIMITIVISM: CAN IT CONTRIBUTE TO RESPECT AND ADMIRATION?

In their effort to emphasise difference and cultural identity, many Indigenous leaders have allowed themselves the dubious luxury of relying on primitive imagery in clothing, body painting, dance and music, to define who they are in the public square. It is not clear to outside observers whether this uncivilised image was meant to say "This is us, we're the oldest culture, we demand respect." or whether the message was "Inherently we are still primitive and as such we deserve special support." Perhaps both. The cynical reaction of many mainstream outsiders seems to say "yeah yeah, but we all know that this effort to exaggerate Indigenous identity is actually financially based – no difference means no special handout." This scepticism has become referred to as Hansonism.

Repeatedly the problem arises as to how (and if) we can really compare and value cultures which are actually incomparable. Originally, the ancient cultures of the Eastern Mediterranean – Greek and Roman, were compared with the great antiquity of Asian civilisations. Then in the 1960s the awareness of Indigenous cultures expanded to a point where "pre-civilised" cultures gained recognition. The problem was, and still is, that while these very early primitive cultures were interesting and significant as points in time along the evolutionary path of human societies, they were not taken seriously as valued contributors to sustainable contemporary well-being or improvement of the human condition.

The comparison was often made between symphony orchestras and corroboree clapsticks, between Shakespeare's writings and Dreamtime stories and between technological and campfire lifestyles. Accusations of elitism and snobbishness usually accompany this holier-than-thou viewpoint and are predictably countered by dismissive claims that it was precisely the unacceptability of the 'primitive', which drove the progress that eventually led to enlightenment.

The alternative theory on delayed civilisation among Aborigines, is the view that, like the Neanderthals, this line of human development was inherently incapable of taking the next progressive steps. Are there not enough examples of full-bloods being able to take on Western ways when given the opportunity, to attribute this theory to biased racism?

## COLONIAL THANKSGIVING DAY

Do Indigenous leaders ever ask, "Where would we be today, had the British not included Australia in their Empire?" The answer is two-fold – either we'd have been invaded by another European or Asian country or we'd have continued hunting and gathering until today when we would represent the latest in uncivilised cultures.

If the world's other hunter-gatherer societies' histories are any guide, the past 200 years would have made negligible difference to our progress towards a wheel, a smelter, a plough, a firearm or a draught animal. So which alternative pattern of our development would have been most beneficial to our people? Ideally a benign co-inhabitor of our vast and diverse continent – a new occupier who recognised our stage of development in 1788 and who valued our knowledge and culture sufficiently to appreciate that their own civilisation had been through ages of stone, bronze, iron and steam, never forgetting that that they usually had to wait until newcomers showed them how the wheel worked and how metals could be smelted, moulded and forged.

## ROOTS AND WINGS: COLONIAL THANKSGIVING DAY

The ideal newcomers to the Great South Land would not have forced their religion onto us but would have valued the way our land-based religion had sustained us and our country for over 40,000 years. They would have appreciated the subtle nuances of our ancient languages which were attuned to the country and its sources of sustenance. They would have recognised the healing properties of our medicines and respected the complex linkages of our family moiety. They would have recognised and valued the virtually pristine productive state of our land and seascapes.

Once we had realised that both peoples were previously Migrants and came to the Great Southland in different eras but shared a caveman heritage, we could both benefit from mutual exchange of knowledge. It would not have taken us long to learn the benefits of hunting with guns, keeping animals and birds for food and fibre, and the huge increases in grain production from sowing crops and planting orchards of high yielding fruits. Irrigated vegetable gardens would secure our seasonal needs for easily-obtainable fresh greens. Together we would have found a way of limiting their cattle and sheep to stocking rates light enough to give the newcomers an income without destroying the productivity of our landscapes.

With respect to social cohesion, we would have suggested that they bring enough of their own women to satisfy their needs and that they co-operate with us in developing a respectful inter-racial society based on a non-violent acceptance of cultural differences. This cross-fertilisation of our gene pool, together with our willingness to learn new ways of benefiting from a better living, would have helped us progress toward a society in which education, health and general well-being would form the basis of a recognised nation in our own right.

In time we would have developed a unique religion, forged in the Australian landscape and encompassing global humanitarian values. Its' Genesis stories would be as credible as those of all the great religions, but it would focus on the Golden Rule and would make no reference to God's chosen people, guilt, redemption or heaven. To this extent it would be a Bush Buddhism.

Our original tribal law would have been amended to develop an equitable and just form of democracy which respected women, Elders and youth. Our emerging nation would empathise with refugees, welcoming the victims of oppression in other countries and offer them a new home if they were willing to meet just two simple conditions: earn your own keep and respect your neighbour. Unfortunately history didn't turn out their way. Greed, ignorance and lust won the day. But the question of "where would we be?", is still well worth pondering.

In this regard, Sam Watson's 2010 play "Oodgeroo - Bloodline to Country", is worth evaluating as a metaphor for colonial inheritance. Sam is a nephew of the late and great Kath Walker, the Noonuccal writer from Stradbroke Island and runs the Aboriginal Studies Centre at UQ in Brisbane. He has recently made a name for himself as a writer and now playwright and takes his bloodline connections to his ancestors very seriously. One suspects that to give depth to his writings, he has invented new insights into tribal stories. He relies heavily on the emotions of historic martyrdom and plays strongly to the victimhood of past generations. His tendency to blame the White invaders for the myriad of ills afflicting his mob, leads him to invite the present dysfunctional community to seek refuge in tribal lands, in dreamtime Utopia and in the psychological escape from modern reality.

All this would be harmless enough if Sam's considerable literary influence didn't dilute the already-wavering efforts of young Aborigines to participate in the mainstream and uplift themselves from what appears to the outsider as the rusted-on victimhood of tribal people.

If Sam's objective is to make a name for himself as purveyor of the victimhood of depravity, he has done well. If his almost pornographic depiction of past wrongs was meant to capture the emotions of his public, he can be pleased with his efforts.

However if, as an Aboriginal leader he hopes for a bright future for his broken people, he would do well to put his future efforts into a much more positive and constructive invitation to his next generation, to modernise and put their culture firmly in an appropriate positive context.

Sam needs to learn from the way Jewish or Afrikaner martyrdom and hatred have led to a surreal isolation and non-acceptance of those who are so blinkered by historic 'preservation politics' that the benefits of cultural tolerance and pluralistic values, have passed them by. He makes the same mistake as some other Indigenous activists, of allowing their historic bitterness of victimhood to dominate their proclaimed will to help their people. As self-appointed spokespersons for the historically oppressed, they have repeatedly failed to adequately answer the seminal question: What's best for our grandchildren?

The basic tenets of the world's great religions and the universal teachings of modern humanitarian values, hold the greatest promise for Aboriginal youth. Surely it is obvious that tolerance, respect, co-operation and plural values offer more potential than parochial tribal martyrdom.

# COMMUNITY TRIAGE AS A PRIORITY-SETTER

Experience has shown that while uplifting the whole community is a valued ideal, realistic evaluation of the differential capacity of each individual to respond to support for behavioural change, is necessary.

It may seem insensitive to suggest a three-way division of receivers of financial support but clearly the efficiency of expensive betterment will be centrally dependent on realism about personal capacity. Historically, triage originated during wartime in Europe when wounded soldiers were delivered to the field hospitals and a quick decision needed to be made on whether each individual would: i) survive without treatment, ii) die even if treated or iii) probably heal with treatment.

Today's hospitals rarely advertise their use of triage as a process in emergency departments (or euthanasia in geriatrics) – they just get on with it. How different would it be if social services and well-being personnel assisting remote communities actively used age/health/motivation criteria to appropriately channel funding in such a way as to focus hope on the most hopeful. Such picking of winners may seem crass, but physical and mental incapacity of the majority of adults needs to be faced if betterment projects are not to fail once more.

The triage concept is applied indirectly to all in the Australian health system and has current application to all population groups. The selection process is subtle and often unspoken, but clearly older persons increasingly have expensive surgical treatment withheld on the basis of age, chances of recovery or costs. In the same way, decisions on where Indigenous health funds are most effectively allocated, involves medical and economic realism on value for money – *viva la triage*.

# A DECLARATION OF INDIGENOUS RIGHTS

## RESPONSE TO THIRTY CONCEPTS

In 2007 the United Nations General Assembly adopted its Declaration on the Rights of Indigenous Peoples. In 2009 the Australian Government formally agreed to support this Declaration. Article 43 refers to the Rights constituting minimum standards for survival, dignity and well-being of Indigenous people.

The published summary of the Australian Declaration which re-words the Declaration's 46 articles for local application, has done a comprehensive job of spelling out Rights but does not refer to responsibilities. The present author's response to the Australian document, which was distributed by the Australian Government in its "Indigenous Newslines" of October 2010, is to propose a parallel Declaration of Responsibilities.

To appreciate the background to the Declaration's agreement between Indigenes and Governments, it is necessary to return to 1957 when the International Labour Organisation first brought Indigenous Rights to the notice of United Nations. Brennan's seminal text "Sharing the Country: The case for an Agreement between Black and White Australians" of 1991, is required reading for those wishing to contribute to the Rights/Responsibilities debate.

It behoves government to consider the place of Responsibilities which accompany Rights before underwriting the application of the Declaration of Rights document in the Australian context. It is also important to appreciate the context and qualifications of the Australian Government's support for the UN Declaration on 3rd April 2009 (the full document is available at www.humanrights.gov.au). A close examination of the responses of successive Australian Governments over the past 40 years shows repeated hesitation to commit to agreements which include the concepts of autonomy, self-determination or independence.

There is a need for clarity and agreement on the implications of the current Declaration's intent when considering the following 30 UN Rights concepts:

1. Self-determination
2. Right to be treated equally
3. Live according to our values and beliefs
4. Employment Rights
5. Traditional health practices
6. Freedom from cultural destruction
7. Determination of our own political status
8. Extra assistance for vulnerable people
9. Right to revitalise our culture
10. Decision-making powers through informed consent
11. Better engagement
12. Control over our own lives
13. Compensation for land loss
14. The goals of the Declaration
15. Right to maintain our own laws
16. Right to determine how and if our country is developed
17. Right to spiritual connection to country
18. Right to assistance to ensure we enjoy the Declaration of Rights
19. Rights to apply equally to men and women
20. Respect for cultural differences and values
21. Wrongs of the past that continue to affect lives
22. Declaration to enhance relations
23. Using the language of Rights
24. Effective engagement based on mutual respect
25. Right to determine Indigenous membership
26. Binding treaties like the Convention on the Elimination of Racial Discrimination

27. Declaration is for survival, dignity and well-being of Indigenous people
28. Use of the Declaration to lobby for policy reform
29. Action to be taken to make sure Indigenous people can realise the Rights in the Declaration
30. Right to protection of the environment on our country.

There is scope for serious disagreement, even polarisation, on the practical implications of virtually all the above 30 concepts in the Declaration of Rights. The following is a consideration of the way in which logical interpretation of each of these concepts could form the basis for a Declaration of Responsibilities of a people who are now largely in transition.

## 1. Self-determination.

Acceptance of self-determination and self-government require a clear understanding of the self-sufficiency implications of this form of autonomy. The idea would be more acceptable if it could be assumed that the self-determined people gained the respect of the nation through the pride which comes from economic independence and productive self-sufficiency. Self-determination should never be taken to mean land and community development determined solely by Indigenous interests and values.

## 2. Right to be treated equally.

This equality has two sides; the one is equal opportunity, the other is equal responsibility to use and benefit from equality. If it means treated equally and not specially favoured because of past disadvantage, such equality could be a positive challenge to personal advancement.

## 3. Right to live according to our values and beliefs.

The acceptability of this 'culturally appropriate' approach requires clarity and agreement on the extent to which the said values and beliefs are beneficial to future generations of both Indigenous and other groups. Enough Indigenous leaders have called for an urgent updating and modernising of cultural mores, to give momentum to this matter. The extent to which negative stereotyping of abusive males has damaged the nobler view of Indigenous values, needs urgent rectification. Similarly, the use of sorcery and certain spiritual beliefs could benefit from a rigorous identification of the most appropriate beliefs for modernising generations. In addition the place of secret business in modern law may warrant reconsideration. Acceptance that The Law cannot in fact remain immutable now, becomes an essential element of moving forward.

## 4. Employment Rights.

This is a contradiction in terms since employment in Australia is almost totally dependent on competence. While cases of discrimination are still reported, its origin and the history of alleged unreliability of some past Indigenous labour should not be overlooked. The development of a dependable work ethic has long been regarded as the key to higher employment. There are no Rights to employment of individuals who don't deliver the goods output-wise and this applies to all job seekers. Job-readiness of people doesn't change overnight and for this reason several companies and departments operate staged up-skilling programs for all staff.

## 5. Traditional health practices.

Indigenous medicine is of great interest to many health authorities and the wisdom of the millennia is respected where outcomes justify the treatment. The fundamental test of the physical benefits of Indigenous medicine is of course the extent to which actual healing occurs, compared to the rates from Western medicine. This measurable outcome must be distinguished from the psychological comfort which particularly older people, gain from Bush Medicine even in the absence of wellness results – a sort of Blackfella's placebo effect. Some traditional treatments may even be shown to be detrimental, especially to infants' health. A thorough longitudinal study may identify positive, neutral and negative cures among the current Indigenous practices as a basis for support or otherwise of this form of alternative medicine. The same applies to Asian and Eastern alternatives. Until then, snake-oil may prevail in some remote communities.

## 6. Freedom from cultural destruction.

Such destruction must be assessed within the considerations suggested under issue #3 which propose taking only the best from the past and benefiting from leaving some less positive elements of culture in the past. All cultures have strengths to be built on and Indigenous culture has several laudable attributes, notably those cultural mores which provide a shining example to non-Indigenous people of childcare and family networking, nurturing and mothering responsibility. There is however increasing confusion on what exactly constitutes Indigenous culture and its contemporary strengths. Once this clarification of "the right stuff" is agreed, the actual disbenefit of the "destruction" referred to, can be evaluated. It should be noted that the proponents of non-Indigenous Australian culture would have similar challenges in clarifying and codifying their values in a diverse nation of individuals.

## 7. Determine our own political status.

This sentiment is found in virtually all cohesive peoples with a common identity. The political reality is that Sovereign States have the power and the responsibility to develop the level of inter-group cohesion required for a functioning democracy which values diversity, tolerance and equity. Over-emphasis on group identity and separateness based on distinctive tribalism, has been shown throughout history, to fragment national cohesion and to fracture productive co-operation. The Apartheid system demonstrated this outcome in an extreme form.

Indigenous Australians are advised to weigh the benefits and disbenefits of separateness, if that is what high political status implies. The value of societal cohesion, unity of purpose and productive co-operation, must not be underestimated by group leaders intent on progressing their group, irrespective of ethnic distinction.

## 8. Extra assistance for vulnerable people.

This principle has been virtuously used in many countries, including Communist countries, because of its humanitarian validity. The Declaration mentions the elderly, women and children as vulnerable, but the general health situation of adults in remote areas begs the question of how 'the vulnerable' should be defined. This matter gets to the heart of self-sufficiency. Ill-conceived support for irresponsible adults can easily encourage the wrong behaviour. In this context, the real causes of 'self-disadvantage' need a rigorous examination.

## 9. Right to revitalise our culture.

As referred to in #6 above, the cultural elements which warrant revitalisation require consensus to ensure that the nation builds on the best, drops the unhelpful and de-emphasises those traditions and beliefs which future generations can well do without. The same applies to other cultures and religions, so there is no racial discrimination in this proposal.

## 10. Decision-making powers through informed consent.

The idea of involving Indigenous people in decision-making through availability of full information and community consultation is sound and long overdue. The addition of consent as an essential element of negotiation, is less straight-forward since it presumes powers which may not, and should not, be allotted to the local community. This is the case for all landholders as citizens of a democracy in which Government holds certain "Crown Rights" which relate to natural resources and compulsory acquisition of land for public purposes, e.g. new hospitals or rail corridors.

Holders of Native Title land have probably yet to come to terms with the power of the State over all land, including Freehold. At the same time, the lack of financial equity and thus of fungibility for fund-raising purposes of so-called Indigenous Freehold tenured land, needs correction.

The state powers referred to here should never be used as an excuse for insensitive bureaucratic attitudes toward land-use, infrastructure or service provision. This is particularly so on clan country holding ancient spiritual significance related to respected ancestors.

It can be predicted that the ownership/consent/compensation issue will not be easily solved by government edict. Meanwhile Indigenous landholders would do well to accept that certain historic laws are in fact not as immutable as the Elders may have presumed.

## 11. Better engagement.

As a motherhood statement, better engagement can't be faulted. However the practical inference of this Right appears to be that the lack of consultation by others has disadvantaged Indigenous people. This would be correct.

Good engagement with government and other groups is clearly a two-way process which is centrally dependent on trust, agreement of objectives, clarity of procedures and reliability of partners to fulfil their side of the engagement.

Engagement is re-visited in #24.

## 12. Control over our own lives.

This Right implies that Indigenous people have lost control of their aspirations and choices, due most probably to discriminatory policy and government procedures. All citizens accept a certain amount of control within the democratic process. Choices and behaviours are justifiably constrained by laws and regulations which focus on the common good – the greatest benefit to the largest number for the longest time.

It will be useful to ascertain which controls are currently perceived by Indigenous leaders as affecting their life choices. Examination of real-life cases may indicate that incapacity to make positive choices originates more from personal motivation than from preventative policy or the attitudes of others, notably employers. There is no doubt that racial discrimination still occurs in some spheres of Australian society. What Indigenous leaders need be wary of, is the real danger that any day now, their own over-emphasis on racial distinction and Rights could predictably be interpreted as racist. This perception is strengthened by Indigenous insistence on Rights and entitlements based clearly on race rather than on need.

## 13. Compensation for land loss.

Over the years the fundamental concept of 'land ownership' has brought a wide range of perceptions at the United Nations Working Group for Indigenous Peoples. In the Australian political arena, there have been several attempts by different governments, to regard differential spending on remote infrastructure and services to Indigenous citizens as a planned form of compensation. Doubt about the probability of irresponsible spending of cash compensation may well be justified by past experience, including the way the Rudd Government's $900 global downturn (GFC) incentive to all taxpayer families was applied to public spending in 2009.

There is no way monetary payments can appropriately compensate for land loss and, as a result, the chances of reaching an equitable consensus on such payment remains near zero. This matter should be finalised by offering infrastructure and services with tangible long-term benefits to remote communities in need of education, skills training and health care, at regional centres.

## 14. Goals of the Declaration of Rights.

The objectives of this U.N. document summary are not clearly spelt out although its potential uses are described. The basic goal seems to be to clarify which Rights Indigenous people desire to have encapsulated within Australian governance if not within the Constitution or a Treaty.

It will strengthen the achievement of Rights if the current Declaration is read in parallel with this author's proposed Declaration of Responsibility (See following: Proposed Declaration Of Indigenous Responsibilities Related To Rights). Ideally, the Declaration of Rights document will be comprehensively expanded to include the positive actions which reflect how the exercise of each Right also relates to non-Indigenous citizens and the responsibilities and limitations of encouraging a distinctive Indigenous identity.

## 15. Right to maintain our own laws.

Of all the Rights demanded by the Declaration, Indigenous law is probably the most contentious. The reason for this is plain to most in the legal profession and it centres on the need for one legal system for all citizens within the Australian democracy. This presumed self-evident truth is far from accepted by many Indigenous leaders, based largely on their personal experience of the White legal system and its bitter outcomes for them.

Attempts to operate parallel Westminster and Indigenous legal systems have met with mixed results. The rate of re-offending is no better under Magisterial/Elder courts. The comparatively lenient penalties imposed by these courts are currently being regarded as insufficient deterrents. However,

ROOTS AND WINGS: A RESPONSE TO THIRTY CONCEPTS

this hybrid justice system is not what many Indigenous leaders have in mind when demanding their own customary law. Opponents of such law compare it to attempts by some Australian Muslims to legitimise Sharia law in their communities. Such attempts have failed to date, due largely to the abhorrence of some practices to mainstream ethics. A distinction needs to be made between the ethical acceptance of practices and the inherent problems of operating dual laws within a national justice system. In essence, the acceptability of Indigenous law within the Australian justice system cannot be properly evaluated as a generality and requires examination of specific offences and penalties.

## 16. Right to determine how and if our country is developed.

This Right goes to the heart of the concept of land ownership in Australia. *How* land is developed is subject to environmental impact regulations which must apply to all Australian land. This is of particular importance where endangered biodiversity is threatened. Under Local Government procedures, all land is subject to land use zoning which restricts the use of each portion of land for residential, agricultural, industrial or biological reserve purposes. Without such zoning, orderly planning for population growth and conservation cannot proceed. In many cases, multiple land use can not only be justified, but can result in more effective ecologically-based planning.

Government has a quadruple responsibility for providing residential land, industrial land, food production land and bioreserve land. Within these goals, independent Indigenous land use decisions may be in conflict with the Government responsibilities and as such would cause unacceptable inequity and irresponsibility.

As to the determination of *if* the land is developed, the non-use of food production potential of agricultural land has serious implications especially when Indigenous population growth is twice the national rate. Under such conditions, the preservation of large tracts of productive land for traditional purposes only, is unlikely to gain approval of either planning authorities or pragmatic Indigenous leaders who value ESD.

## 17. Right to spiritual connection to country.

As with the Right to Indigenous law, the Right to land links needs evaluation in the light of contemporary reality, while respecting historic spiritual connections.

The central proposition here is the extent to which ancient religious beliefs could be, should be or must be proclaimed as immutable truths without which future generations will be the poorer. This spiritual grounding finds a parallel in the modern trends in Western religion where dependence on faith has steadily diminished. Whether the emerging deity-free value system is serving the contemporary mainstream society well will continue to fuel the moral debate.

Indigenous leaders generally find it helpful to their land claim cause, to emphasise spiritual connection to country, even to the point of insisting that it is a survival necessity. This claim is however, disproved by the successful urbanised Indigenous communities. Nevertheless, the purer culturally-remote communities deserve different transition timelines to achieve comfortable mobility from clan country.

As with other ethnic groups, Indigenous communities have demonstrated how they can develop generational links to new country, as evident for instance at Cherbourg in Queensland where they have overcome the historic negativity of removal from country and today pride themselves on their motto "Many tribes, one community".

In demanding continued spiritual connection to country, it behoves Indigenous leaders to confront the question of what will be best for the grandchildren, honestly and pragmatically. In the same way as the Israelis require a re-think on being God's Chosen People, or the Afrikaners required modification of their Biblical support for Apartheid, Indigenous leaders need to take growing scepticism on religious claims seriously.

The spiritual strength originating from ancestor landscapes can no doubt be maintained without living on country or even regularly visiting country. Perhaps an Indigenous equivalent of pilgrimages to Jerusalem or Mecca warrants consideration as an interim transition position in modernising Indigenes' religion, the vast majority of whose members record Christianity as their religion in the census.

It should not go unnoticed that critics of the way in which spiritual links are used to strengthen land claims, reflect a growing cynicism of what outsiders perceive as exaggeration of beliefs which have been demonstrated as non-essential to survival, respect or well-being as sought by the Declaration.

## 18. Right to assistance to ensure enjoyment of Rights.

Clearly this Right is open to such broad interpretation as to be unhelpful to those seeking to support Indigenous identity. For instance, where the line should be drawn on tax-payer investment in Indigenous cultural infrastructure and services, is seen very differently by various cultural groups and governments. The reasons for this diversity of views are several-fold and include comparative benefits for all groups resulting from selective ethnic exaggeration; 'costs to taxpayers'; disunity arising from discrete group loyalties; multicultural competition or even conflict; adverse influence of some Rights on productivity; self-sufficiency; respect from others, and danger of encouraging the 'gravy train syndrome'.

Whatever level of assistance to enable the enjoyment of Rights is forthcoming from government, unless it is tapered and diminishing in the longer term, it will justifiably be regarded by the Australian population, as artificially propping up one selected culture at the economic expense of others. This may sound harsh but unless self-sufficiency is part of self-determination as it is in all other Australian sub-cultures, both respect and support can be predicted to fade. In the meantime special assistance in overcoming disadvantage is urgently warranted, notably in remote communities.

## 19. Rights to apply equally to men and women.

This concept stands out among all Rights in the Declaration, as perhaps the best example of modernising tradition to meet contemporary expectations. In his 1998 paper "What constitutes a fair go for Aborigines?" this author asked why mainstream feminists were silent in their shrill demands, on the obvious and most dire need of Aboriginal women – a question which still awaits an acceptable answer.

What is different about this claimed Right is that it is perhaps the only one which has no customary base or traditional history. Without inflaming the ongoing debate among the literary culture warriors on domestic violence in traditional Indigenous society, it should be noted by all, that much of the problem-solving in the sphere of substance and sexual abuse, has been initiated and maintained by Indigenous women. Informed observers on these matters state forcibly that few community women will miss the declining old patriarchal control system which they suffered previously. Whether 'secret business' of both genders has a future under the new deal is for the people affected to decide.

## 20. Respect for cultural differences and values.

This matter has been touched on in several points above but it is necessary to seriously consider the meaning and ambit of respect as a regularly emphasised demand by Indigenous leaders. Some Indigenous writers would have the mainstream believe that respect should be automatic for 'the world's oldest continuous culture'. This ancient basis for respect may only maintain support up to the point where this culture is perceived to be a brake rather than a facilitating framework for the well-being of its future members. Antiquity alone may be an insufficient basis for respect, to the extent that there is a growing expectation by mainstream Australia, that respect actually needs to be earned. A parallel exists in the Catholic church expecting respect for its Inquisition history – evil pervades the centuries.

Two responses to perceived lack of respect are called for: updating or modernising the culture, and demonstrating civility through practice of universal humanitarian values, lifestyles and behaviours which embody the Golden Rule by whatever name.

The same requirements for respect apply to all cultures in Australia – without tolerance, co-operation and mutual appreciation of difference, no Migrant culture gains acceptance or respect. By comparison, Indigenous culture has much to contribute to Australian peoplehood but it must be ever-mindful of the dangers of its distinctiveness becoming intolerant separateness, which loses respect.

Because they're the country's First People, Indigenous Australians have a special claim to recognition above and beyond the recognition afforded to Migrant cultures. However they should be careful not to mistake this recognition for licence to ignore social unity. Nor should they focus on distinctive separation as if it necessarily contributes positively to their peoples' own future well-being. To this extent the place and role of culture demands very careful examination, because being 'too precious', invariably loses friends.

## 21. Wrongs of the past that continue to affect lives.

The perception of the extent to which past discrimination and dispossession really do incapacitate the present adult population of Indigenous people, is a serious matter deserving of national consideration. Much of the mainstream rationale behind the simplistic view of 'get over it, get on with it', ignores the permanent psychological damage to the self-image and self-confidence of affected individuals. An essential caveat to this empathy is that the young need not necessarily inherit these negative historical influences. Through early exposure to a modern, positive education system, Indigenous people have a real opportunity to put the damaging past behind their offspring and allow the coming generations to start with a clean sheet. Self-respect is learned and is not inherited, although the jury is still out on inter-generational trauma.

## 22. The Declaration will enhance relations.

This claim should be deleted as it makes unfounded assumptions on the acceptability of many of the claimed Rights. It can be stated without fear of contradiction, that enhanced relations between Indigenous and other Australians, will come only from productive, co-operative ethical behaviour on the part of both population groups. No group can demand respect, since respect comes from trustworthy responsible co-operation, and enhanced relations develop from the resultant mutual respect.

Enhanced relations between population groups emerge from just treatment and equal opportunity but also from the acceptance arising from performance. In sport and to a lesser degree in the arts, many Indigenous names have become legendary, not because they are ethnic but because they 'delivered the goods'. This will increasingly happen in politics, medicine, social well-being, literature and the law, wherever larger numbers of Indigenous professionals demonstrate capacity, skills and determination to improve the human condition of their kinfolk. In time, their pride in being a particular tribal man or woman will probably be overtaken by their greater pride in humanitarian service which is recognised globally in the mould of Mandela who rose above tribal identity to international recognition of the goodness of Man.

## 23. Using the language of Rights.

This is an unusual phrase, which reflects the concept of the primacy of Rights as a pillar of future well-being. The language of Rights is unlikely to impress the outsider unless it is clearly and continuously spoken in association with the language of Responsibility and of Obligation. The apparent need for Indigenous leaders to stress Rights at this stage of their people's development is understood and appreciated against their background of colonial inequities. At the same time, these leaders should not be naive about the reception that over-use of the language of Rights can expect from the mainstream who currently are having a relatively hard time financially, compared to the level of affluence they'd become used to since the 1960's.

It is a well-established historical fact that group cohesion is strengthened more by martyrism than by any other factor. Historical hardship is not an Indigenous monopoly and can be easily found in both the Australian convict heritage and the persecuted European Migrants family history. The language of Rights has its origins in historic persecution, thus language or religious groups who succeed and prosper, all have one thing in common – a demonstrated capacity to match their Rights with their obligations to the broader society. Ultimately the term "un-Australian" refers not so much to what Anglo-Saxon Migrants hold dear, but rather to what global humanitarian societies have come to respect.

## 24. Effective engagement based on mutual respect.

The rules of engagement in a civil society are well understood in advanced countries and have been referred to in #11 above. There is however another context in which engagement requires consideration, and that is the extent to which engagement is a two-way process built on mutual contribution and productive input. Engagement cannot realistically be used as a one-way process where the give-and-take has become largely take. Engagement is the process by which population groups contribute to the common good. Since the 1970's when certain bureaucrats suggested rather crudely that Indigenous people 'stop complaining and start working', this uncalled-for advice was seen as insensitive to the past trauma suffered by those concerned. However, in 2000 when the same sentiment was expressed by an Indigenous leader, but this time in terms of the Right to take responsibility, it was regarded by the mainstream as bold and insightful – calling it as it is.

Engagement in its productive sense cannot be achieved without respect. Respect in turn, cannot be achieved without positive performance, and positive performance cannot be achieved without sufficient work ethic to gain economic self-sufficiency. A much more structured effort is required to 'get over it' than is currently applied to remote communities. It is more complex and time-consuming than the quick-fix experts realise.

## 25. Right to determine Indigenous membership.

It is not without good reason that politicians tread cautiously on the subject of who should qualify for Indigenous benefits. Politicians are well aware of the permanent hurt caused by the race classification used under the Apartheid system and for good reason they avoid such tests as the pencil-through-hair abomination used to identify African Blacks.

As a result of the sensitivity of this racial identity issue and the inherited guilt complex arising from it, Australia has arrived at the internationally unique system whereby prospective recipients of Aboriginal and Torres Strait benefits need only tick the box at Centrelink. The fact that this option is selected by over 80% of mixed marriages in urbanised communities has led to 'gravy train' accusations which in turn have elicited Hansonite comparisons, both of which require a more nuanced view than the simplistic good guy/bad guy connotations.

Nobody blames Indigenous individuals for using whatever benefits the law provides for, and non-Indigenous beneficiaries of other welfare schemes are judged similarly. However, the sooner benefit approvals are not based on race, the sooner pride and equity will return and motivation toward self-sufficiency will be encouraged.

Apparently the law accepts anyone as Indigenous if they can show at least minimal inheritance and acceptance of membership by a clan or family. There have been many instances since colonial times of White sympathisers being accepted into the tribe, sometimes through a traditional initiation ceremony, sometimes through marriage. What is required today is to discontinue race-based benefits which are not only discriminatory but also demeaning.

## 26. Binding Treaties like the Convention on the Elimination of Racial Discrimination.

Australian Governments have a history of avoiding binding Treaties or Declarations. A case in point is this UN Declaration on the Rights of Indigenous Peoples which New Zealand, Canada and the US also declined to sign when it was first put up in September 2007 – a position which Australia reversed in April 2009.

While the Commissioner for Indigenous Social Justice at the time regarded this declaration as "the most significant achievement in the protection of Indigenous people's Rights…." celebration of its implementation in Australia should be postponed until a number of practical and equity issues have been agreed on.

Similarly, the extent to which the UN Elimination of Racial Discrimination actually affects Indigenous well-being, is both variable and one-sided. It has become a common perception that racial discrimination refers to Blacks oppressed by Whites despite the global evidence indicating that racism comes in all colours.

At its most fundamental level, racism is a tribal xenophobia based apparently on fear of others – of those who are different, usually in religion and language, but not necessarily in colour. In Australia's case, as in the US, colour difference has prevailed as the basis of racism since colonial days.

Sensitivity on racial discrimination in Australia has reached the point where logical decision-making and appropriate benefit provision has become irrational. Fear of being seen to 'play the race card' has discouraged mature policy formulation at least since the 1980s. The response of the Howard Government to Hanson's easy win as an Independent, demonstrated the shallow double standard of political convictions on appropriate racial policy in modern Australia. The political silliness associated with even sensible questioning of the equity of some race-based payments seems to be reflected in the simplistic and unfounded assumption that, "If you're not for us, you're against us". This childish polarisation finds a parallel in the present-day Climate Change debate where the moderate middle-ground between the true believers and sceptics has disappeared, due to an almost religious bigotry on unproven certainties.

Indigenous leaders today have a special responsibility to help break down what appears to be a rising level of racism among their own people. The equity situation is complex in the present transition phase of modernisation of Indigenous lifestyles – a process which will take at least another generation. Perhaps Indigenous people are not sufficiently aware that racism goes beyond policy-makers or mainstream power-brokers and includes exaggerated self-perception of tribal distinctness and its resultant exclusive attitudes. It follows that inability to practice inclusive co-operative social intercourse, can cause others to respond in kind. Outsiders may justifiably ask where contemporary racism starts.

Australians as a nation have gained an international reputation for tolerance and acceptance of people of other races. This acceptance has always been contingent on Migrants' willingness to 'play by the rules' and carry their share of communal obligations. Indigenous Australians will do well when proclaiming that they're different, distinct, ancient, and thus special, to appreciate their ultimate dependence on the mainstream and thus the need for social cohesion in a unitary State. The co-operative partnership envisaged does not require a diminution of personal ethnic identity, but it does require a deep appreciation of the enrichment which other cultures can bring to a culture which lacks the literature and advanced arts of others. (Perhaps this is why Noel Pearson is apparently translating Richard III into his tribal language as I write. BR)

While comparisons with South Africa may seem facile, Australian Indigenous leaders can take lessons from the recent economic and social deterioration of that country due largely to discrimination against the most skilled professionals and to the political end of the Afrikaner people, resulting from their exclusive attitude to other races.

## 27. The Declaration constitutes the minimum standards for survival, dignity and well-being.

'Standards' is probably not the best word to describe the essentials of racial survival and dignified well-being, although the intended meaning may be clear enough.

The Declaration by no means ensures achievement of any of these goals, while the proponents of survival need to be clear on what it is that they wish to survive. If it is survival of a proud people with their culture and traditions intact, then the values system which characterises these people needs to be understood by all, in its updated modern format. Given the fact that the vast majority are urbanised and out-married, those same proponents will need to articulate what essential values and attributes they wish to preserve.

Dignity as an outcome of Rights, is hardly a self-evident consequence, since dignity comes as much from personal effort as from Rights. Rights enable but don't produce. Similarly with well-being, Rights simply set the stage, but the performers have to produce the motivation, skills and acclaim that are necessary for success. Any examination of the attributes making up the National Well-being Index shows that under the present combination of policy, regulation, Rights and mainstream attitudes, Indigenous families can and do succeed. The successful families were never held back by the lack of a Declaration of Rights. The opposite is also true, i.e. that a Declaration will do nothing for the individuals who choose to escape the real world of economics and to seek refuge in unproductive tradition. Examples abound in both camps.

## 28. Use of the Declaration to lobby for policy reform.

Are the proponents of the Declaration seriously suggesting that the basic shortcoming of present Indigenous policy is the lack of Rights? They would be hard put to identify a single instance of policy which is detrimental to Indigenous well-being caused by the lack of Rights. Many cultural purists would no doubt disagree with this statement. A wide range of informed opinion seems to agree that if Indigenous policy needs reform, it is not in the Rights department but in the group equity department where reverse discrimination could currently be the weak link. This is not to say that the policies underpinning housing, health and education could not benefit from a review of implementation procedures. In addition, policy relating to land use planning and economic development, clearly could benefit from urgent attention. None of these need more Rights, just more responsibility and acceptance of democratic obligations.

## 29. Action to ensure Indigenous realisation of Rights.

It is true that action is required, not only to ensure realisation of Rights but also to ensure acceptance of personal and group obligation. Australians have become used to the political cost-shifting game between levels of Government. In the present case we have the game of responsibility-shifting in which one societal group pretends that Rights can only be enjoyed when the authorities take action to ensure that this happens. Clearly the onus is on the Rights-holders to make policy work in their favour. Invoking the Nanny State only encourages dependence and the negative vibes of victimhood.

## 30. Right to protection of the environment on Indigenous land.

The origin and intent of this claimed Right is not clear. If it relates to mining, the normal Impact Study procedure is applied. In each case, the broader community benefits are weighed against the environmental disbenefits. Since mining has been virtually the only large source of potential wealth in the Native Title lands, vision and balance are required by those Elders who are in decision-making positions. Compulsory acquisition should never be seen as discriminating specifically against Indigenous landholders since it applies to all landholders, including mainstream freeholders, as referred to in #16.

Perhaps this author has misunderstood the intent of this Right but it appears juxtaposed to the Wild Rivers conflict over the negative effects of protection on planned Indigenous economic development.

## Assessing Rights

In evaluating the above Rights, it is useful to go back about a decade. In 2011, Noel Pearson commented at length in the press on Julia Gillard's speech to parliament on social trends and individual responsibility. The burden of his message is his long-held view on the Right to take Responsibility. Pearson has often referred to the *Left's* propensity to stress Rights and the *Right's* focus on Responsibilities. Once again Pearson criticises government for usurping Indigenous leadership and responsibility, so robbing Indigenous leaders of the opportunity to exercise precisely the responsibility which Gillard was calling for.

As a focus for future well-being of Indigenous people, their leaders would do their people a much greater favour if they concentrated on corrective actions, based not on the UN Indigenous Rights Declaration, but on the UN Declaration of the Rights of the Child and on a new supplementary articulation of responsibilities. The rationale of the above responses to the 30 issues, is embedded in the following 'Declaration of Responsibilities'.

# PROPOSED DECLARATION OF INDIGENOUS RESPONSIBLITIES RELATED TO RIGHTS

"We, the Indigenous people of Australia, having had our Rights acknowledged by the Australian Government in April 2009 through acceptance of the United Nation's Declaration on the Rights of Indigenous peoples (UN 2007), now propose a Declaration of Indigenous Responsibilities."

This Responsibilities document proposes to clarify for Indigenous people, the societal obligations which parallel the Rights document. The number of each responsibility (R1-30) coincides with the Rights number in the associated Declaration. The overlapping concepts necessitate a degree of repetition.

## RESPONSIBILITIES

R1. The process of Indigenous self-determination will focus on self-sufficiency, economic independence and commercial partnerships with mainstream Australia.

R2. In applying our Right to equal treatment under the law, Indigenous Australians will work toward equality of benefits through an on-going reduction of special race-based benefits until parity with mainstream Australia is achieved and our pride as equals is restored.

R3. In exercising our Right to live according to our values and beliefs, Indigenous Australians will be responsible for modernising and updating cultural values and traditional behaviour to ensure that our values are appropriate to contemporary Australia and the well-being of our future generations.

R4. We acknowledge that having been accorded equal employment Rights, Indigenous Australians have the obligation to educate and up-skill our people in order to compete in the mainstream job market.

R5. Having won the Right to equal health services, we acknowledge our responsibility to promote and practice healthy diets and lifestyles among Indigenous Australians. In addition we accept the responsibility to phase out those elements of our traditional medicine which cannot demonstrate recovery rates similar to those of Western medicine.

R6. In our efforts to salvage our living culture, one of the world's oldest, we accept the responsibility for the development of cultural mores compatible with other Australian sub-cultures to the extent that rich co-operative cultural diversity is achieved. Such compatibility includes Indigenous standards in gender relations, women's Rights, substance abuse, domestic violence, voluntary marriage arrangements, respect for other religions and respect for the law under the Constitution.

R7. In our participation in the determination of our appropriate political status within the unitary State of Australia, Indigenous people will not only accept our share of the need to promote social cohesion nationally but will also accept our share of responsibility for ensuring cultural harmony in Australia.

R8. Indigenous people accept the obligation of protecting the weak, nurturing the disabled, caring for our children and the aged, ensuring parental responsibility in a manner comparable to international humanitarian norms.

R9. In re-vitalising our culture, Indigenous Australians undertake to harmonise the values and behaviours of our culture with the universally accepted humanitarian values of Australia's other sub-cultures.

R10. In seeking both consultation and our people's consent to policy decision-making, Indigenous Australians accept the powers of the nation's three tiers of Government to make over-riding decisions in the national interest, notably in the sphere of natural resource exploitation.

R11. In seeking better engagement with Government and non-Indigenous bodies, Indigenous Australians accept the obligation to conduct negotiations in a spirit of goodwill between mutual partners intent on achieving the objectives of engagement which reflect both equitable and efficient outcomes. Engagement will be activated in the knowledge that fair outcomes involve trade-offs and compromises rather than winner-takes-all.

R12. In seeking to implement our Right to have control over our people's lives, Indigenous Australians accept that the freedoms of citizens of the democracy are constrained by the effect of the personal freedom of individuals on the well-being of other groups in the unitary State. To this extent Indigenous leaders have the responsibility of clarifying with their people the boundaries of personal control of individual's lives. Rather than a Declaration of Independence, the Rights document could be interpreted as a Declaration of Inter-dependence.

R13. In seeking compensation for historic loss of Indigenous land, our people will recognise the validity of compensation being offered in the non-cash form of targeted Indigenous infrastructure and services in remote Australia. In addition, we accept that the level at which direct monetary compensation is agreed to, can never adequately reflect the loss suffered.

R14. In contributing to the clarification of the Declaration of Rights document, Indigenous Australians accept the responsibility of focussing on Net Social Benefit as the ultimate goal of the Declaration. As such, we are obligated to work co-operatively toward using our declared Rights in such a way as to form an integral contribution to the national economy and society. Such contribution will assume our full engagement in the Australian education, health, legal and wealth-generation systems. In fully participating in these mainstream activities, we accept that the personal retention of Indigenous identity is the voluntary Right of each individual.

R15. In negotiations on benefits or otherwise of maintenance of Indigenous law, we accept the responsibility of harmonising our laws with the Australian legal system to the extent that anomalies on culpability and appropriate penalties, are equitable between all population groups. We further acknowledge our obligation to discontinue those aspects of our traditional law which are not appropriate to the operation of a single national legal system of which we are a part.

R16. In exercising our Right to determine how and if Indigenous country is used, we are mindful of the need for, and power of, national resource planning and the Government's obligation to exploit national resources for the common good. We accept the responsibility of participating fully and constructively in environmental impact studies and their interpretation in the best interests of both our people and all Australians. We accept that non-use of resources may have detrimental outcomes for our people, while recognising the significance of conservation of rare and threatened species.

R17. In pursuing our Right to maintain spiritual connection to country, Indigenous Australians acknowledge the potential benefits to our people, of reconsideration of the appropriateness of some of our original religious beliefs relating to spiritual ancestral landscapes. Such review will be based on Indigenous experience of the successful urban dwellers and will respect the need for pragmatically updating religious practice as all the great religions have done throughout history. In the evaluation of beliefs and practices regarded as appropriate for our future generations, Indigenous Australians will give special attention to the future significance of sacred sites and secret business. In our efforts to maintain spiritual connection to country we will be ever-mindful that the vast majority of our people are now both urbanised and inter-married with others who have no claim to clan country and ancestral land links.

R18. In seeking assistance to ensure that our people can enjoy their declared Rights, we recognise that the initiative and capacity to implement our Rights, is primarily the responsibility of Indigenous Australians ourselves. We accept that the vision, motivation, practice and enculturation of Indigenous Rights must come from the people who themselves desire to be acknowledged as a productive, self-sufficient, ethical and co-operative subset of the Australian nation.

R19. The application of equal Rights to men and women in our society is a welcome departure from our earlier patriarchy in which gender inequity was the norm. Indigenous Australians accept their obligation to enculturate women's Rights into our teachings going forward, and expect all ethnic groups of this nation to do the same, irrespective of religious background.

R20. In developing a respect for our culture among non-Indigenous Australians we accept that it is our responsibility to respect equally, cultures and values of other ethnic groups of our nation. Our goal of a non-racist Australia obligates us to reciprocate the cultural respect which we desire of others for our ancient culture.

R21. In dealing with colonial history we will undertake to present a fair portrayal of the positive and negative influences of colonisation on Indigenous civilisation.

R22. In our efforts to use the Declaration of Rights to enhance relations with other Australians, Indigenous people will accept their responsibility in nurturing understanding, acceptance, respect and partnering with other groups and individuals. We will do this through an education system and home environment which emphasise the values and attitudes which enhance mutual benefit through respect and trust between equal partners.

R23. When using the language of Rights in our efforts to gain parity with mainstream Australia, Indigenous people will continually be mindful that with Rights go Responsibilities. This realisation will temper our internal values and our dealings with outsiders. Our obligation to take responsibility for our people's future well-being will always serve as the counter-balance to our enjoyment of Rights. To this end, we undertake to also use the language of Obligation when using the language of Rights in our negotiations with other Australians. In this way we aim to build respect from others on the basis of our demonstrated responsibility and self-sufficiency.

R24. Indigenous Australians will make special efforts to overcome our previous image as a dependent people. We will do this through a patient ongoing emphasis on contemporary education of our youth. If this requires distance education or educational mobility to settings conducive to good learning and health, we will encourage and seek support for availing our youth of the best education Australia can offer. We appreciate that mutual respect can only be achieved among equals and we accept the challenge to bring our young people up to parity with the mainstream.

R25. Having the Right to determine our own Indigenous group's membership, we have the responsibility to challenge our members to accept enlightened social norms. We undertake to make it clear to young and new members, that our pride in being Indigenous, stems from the extent to which we shall in future, embrace enlightened universal norms of behaviour and values appropriate to a future multicultural Australia. We undertake to critically examine the further application of race-based welfare schemes which demean our people as potentially equal citizens. As the preferred alternative, we will encourage our members to use the expanding needs-based support schemes available to all Australians. This will eliminate the long-held negative view, that a majority of our members claim Indigenous identity primarily for financial reasons – claims which are made by large numbers of individuals with little or no Indigenous inheritance or clan country.

R26. In the implementation of anti-discriminatory legislation and conventions aimed at eliminating racial discrimination, Indigenous Australians will remain mindful of the fact that racist behaviour may emanate from both advantaged and disadvantaged groups. Awareness of reverse racism will drive an internal Indigenous campaign to ensure that in our effort to strengthen our Indigenous ethnic identity, we do not inadvertently extend the racism which we aim to eliminate.

R27. To pursue the triple aims of our Declaration of Rights, namely, Indigenous survival, dignity and well-being, we shall focus on the differential factors which produce these prime outcomes. We understand 'survival' to mean the perpetuation of the people with Indigenous origins but also with a modernised culture appropriate to the needs of the future Australia. Our people understand that modernisation of our culture, tradition and behavioural norms is essential to our survival as a viable and competitive subset of Australian society. We accept that the achievement of 'Dignity' by any ethnic group is dependent on more than Rights. This is recognised by our leaders who encourage all Indigenous people to appreciate that our dignity in the eyes of others, must be earned through behaviour, performance and achievement. We accept that no dignity comes from antiquity or uniqueness in and of themselves. We have the obligation to teach this as a key value of our emerging modern people. Our third aim, namely well-being, is acknowledged as an outcome of both our Rights and our own initiative. Indigenous Australians do not expect Rights *per se* to produce well-being and we undertake to develop the understanding, skills and motivation to achieve self-determined well-being.

R28. In the process of using our Declaration of Rights to lobby for policy reform, Indigenous Australians recognise that under current policy, our progress is seldom if ever constrained by policy that is in need of reform. We believe that some of our people's diminished capacity in the near past, was partially due to discrimination and disadvantage. However, we appreciate that contemporary policy gives us new opportunities to overcome the historic stereotype and to compete on an equal footing as proud modern Australians. We undertake to develop an understanding amongst our people that while policy reform was required in the past to remove discrimination, our progress now requires Indigenous initiative to grasp new opportunities.

R29. In calling for action to be taken to enable our people to realise the benefits of their declared Rights, Indigenous Australians have the obligation to initiate such action primarily within our own membership. We appreciate that Government has the responsibility to both enact enabling regulations and to ensure their implementation. However, we equally appreciate that few benefits will accrue to Indigenous Australians unless a 'self-starter culture' of independent individuals is inculcated in our emerging generations.

R30. Our claimed Right to protection of the environment of Indigenous Homelands will be largely in our own hands. We undertake to work within the bounds of regional planning and impact assessment of development, and we acknowledge Government powers to resume land with compensation, in the national interest. We further undertake to develop our land in a way which is guided by rigorous consideration of the benefits of balanced development and conservation, for the Net Social Benefit of our planned sustainable society. The most urgent Rights in need of attention in contemporary Australia are contained in the UN Declaration of the Rights of the Child.

# THE ESSENCE OF ISSUES AND RECOMMENDATIONS ON INDIGENOUS FUTURES

After drawing on 150 sources of information on the past, present and future, Section 1 of this compilation concludes that a series of fundamental policy questions require answers. It identifies three issues – Separateness, Culture and Governance as the essential policy spheres requiring clarity and agreement – in effect, an Overvention for the Intervention.

The author maintains that the public debate needs to focus on a vision for the future of Indigenous people within the Australian nation. In recent years the extent and urgency of remote community dysfunction, has focused on the practical improvement of housing, education and health, as well as addressing substance abuse and domestic violence. While these essential elements of well-being warrant concerted and ongoing corrective action, the author has identified fundamental policy weaknesses in central elements of separate development, traditional culture and self-determination, which warrant special attention.

With up to 40% of States such as Queensland being claimable under Native Title, the need for land use planning, including the development of business cases for sustainable communities, looms large as an emerging priority.

The consolidated list of 'Policy Issues' arising from Section 1, covers the following:

A. The benefits and disbenefits of "mainstreaming", that is, the adoption of modern Western lifestyles and values.

B. The long-term community future for those choosing to remain in remote settlements.

C. The spiritual benefits or otherwise of Indigenous people remaining on their clan country.

D. The benefits and limitations of teaching of "The Knowledge" to younger generations.

E. The possibility and desirability of selective updating and modernising of Indigenous culture and traditional behaviour.

F. Religious beliefs relating to country, and the spiritual benefits or otherwise thereof.

G. The need for a Treaty or formal Agreement between Indigenous people and government.

H. The advantages or otherwise of parallel use of Indigenous law and medicine within the Australian justice and health systems.

I. The sequence and means by which the cycle of dysfunction in remote communities can best be corrected.

J. The incorporation into the $4.6 billion Closing the Gap program of COAG for the present decade, of proposed details of Indigenous self-determination structures and principles.

K. The development of a Land Use and Business Plan for that 40% of the total Australian land area which is available under current Native Title claim conditions.

L. The equity and effectiveness of current special Indigenous financial support in urbanized communities already supplied with mainstream infrastructure and services.

M. Determination of a clear and agreed rationale for taxpayer support for Indigenous cultural enhancement and promotion.

N. The development and implementation of community food production schemes in regional and remote areas.

As a basis for policy formulation to address the above issues the following demographic and ethnic overview can form a starting point for policy deliberations:

The population statistics of 2010 suggest that the Indigenous population totals just over 516,000, of whom some 360,000 are urbanised to the degree of having access to a wide range of mainstream services. The extent to which Indigenous people marry out of their ethnic group, varies from 8% in Arnhemland, to 83% in Sydney, averaging over 70% for the group nationally. This rate of out-marriages has increased significantly in recent years, the Cape York case of Aurukun reflecting an increase from 43% in 1986 to 73% in 2007.

The ABS statistics indicate that over 80% of mixed marriages claim Indigenous status and that 87% record Christianity as their religion. In addition, the birth rate among Indigenous Australians is approximately double the national average, bringing the latest estimate of our Indigenous population to 798,000 (ABC 26.03.19). Several indicators of well-being of Indigenes are significantly worse than the national average i.e. longevity, health, substance abuse, crime and education. Marked differences occur between the well-being of urbanised and remote communities.

# SEEKING ANSWERS

A useful method of initiating incisive debate on societal issues is to propose recommended actions to achieve a preferred outcome for each issue, with accompanying rationale, then invite critics to offer better alternatives.

The proposed action on each issue listed below is given in the paragraphs commencing with "**In essence…**"

## Issue A: Benefits of Mainstreaming

Mainstreaming as a concept, is prone to various interpretations and would not be an issue if there were not several Indigenous leaders opposing mainstreaming as a perceived threat to identity, culture and distinctiveness of their people.

The goal of mainstreaming was originally to encourage Indigenous citizens to take advantage of the regional and metropolitan lifestyles enjoyed by the rest of the Australians. As such, the opportunities in education, health and housing in urban settings offered comprehensive upgrading of Indigenous well-being.

In practice the problem was not the offering of choices but rather the providing of the means by which remote families may gain mobility, education and the capacity to relocate to adequately serviced centres. A distinction needs to be made between the more healthy and functional young individuals and the variously dysfunctional others whose ability to respond to capacity-building requires realistic acceptance of diminished physical and mental capacity, largely due to substance abuse.

**In essence**, the potential benefits of working families joining the mainstream far outweigh the alleged disbenefits to identity and tradition. Under these circumstances, policy should be amended to strongly encourage an increasing proportion of remote people to join urbanised Australia. The desire of elderly people to remain on their country is understood but our ability to care for the aged population requires realism, empathy and enlightened selection of economic priorities.

## Issues B and C: Remote Futures

Currently many remote communities don't meet even a minimum of well-being criteria, but several cultural reasons are given to justify the ongoing habitation of small isolated communities and outstations. The reasons centre on tribal peoples' essential link to the spiritual country of their ancestors.

The impossibility of servicing these scattered clans in a cost-effective manner is obvious, leaving authorities with three options: leave the camps unserviced, subsidise services, or convince the clans of the family benefits of moving to centres with good services.

**In essence**, isolated camps need to be discontinued except where outstations are being successfully used for safe retirement or rehabilitation of substance-abuse patients. Generations of Indigenous urban dwellers have demonstrated how families can flourish and remain grounded by their culture without having to live on their original country. Special provision must be made for old folks who desire to live out their days on country, as an interim measure.

Acceptance of the reality that cost-effective health, housing and education in isolated settings cannot reasonably be expected to reach standards required by future generations, is overdue and requires early policy change.

## Issue D: Teaching the Knowledge

Two opposing trends are currently leaving Indigenous youth feeling guilty and confused about The Knowledge, i.e. that traditional body of knowledge passed on by the Elders in the form of storytelling through which contact is made with the ancestral spirits and totems. Family obligation networks (the Moeity) are explained by the Elders and survival knowledge on bush foods and medicines is transmitted on country, but widespread enthusiasm by transitioning youth seems lacking.

This knowledge has both cultural and utilitarian values and is belatedly being urgently embedded in modern databases by scientists, anthropologists and sociologists. However there is a rapidly decreasing core of Elders able to teach the next generation, and there is apparently only a small minority of young Aboriginals committed to becoming the carriers of tribal knowledge. While reliable data is difficult to obtain, anecdotal evidence from Northern Australia reflects diminishing knowledge-transfer activities, despite heroic efforts by an ever-decreasing number of Knowledge men and women.

**In essence**, the rapidly disappearing sources of Knowledge must be urgently tapped and recorded for posterity while the imposed duty on young Aboriginals to learn and transfer cultural information, should be reconsidered and both guilt and failure of responsibility of the young, should be removed from generational expectations on knowledge transfer.

The reason for reducing the obligation to carry and perpetuate knowledge is that such information is unlikely to improve or contribute to the well-being of future generations, the majority of whom are urbanising and outmarrying. Both the old and the young must be secure in the knowledge that what remains of their traditional information is being urgently and diligently recorded and stored for future use.

## Issue E: Updating Culture and Tradition

The sensitivity of cultural matters and the virtual demand for respect for tradition, immunises cultural debate against logic and reason. Despite this ingrained defence of tradition, several Indigenous leaders have called for an updating and modernisation of Indigenous cultural values. They distinguish between those elements which carry inherent positive values for their people into the future, and those less helpful elements and traditional behaviours which can be left in the past without loss to future enculturation.

There has been a strong call by several spokespersons, male and female, to break away from the negative effects of sorcery, paternalistic control, arranged marriages of young females, witchcraft affecting children's health, sanctioned domestic violence, peer pressure to contribute to substance-abuse and acceptance of child abuse by men in some communities.

**In essence**, the need to identify the most positive and useful elements of accepted cultural mores and traditional behaviour has become urgent. This is especially so, in view of the way dysfunctional behaviour is used by the media to stereotype Indigenous males in a way which infers that alcoholism, domestic violence and welfare dependency are somehow cultural norms, which they are not.

What is required is an unambiguous statement of agreed values by which Indigenous people can stand as the cornerstones of their beliefs going forward. In this way they can build on the best from their past and embrace new enlightened elements, which increase the relevance of Indigenous culture to contemporary Australia.

## Issue F: Religious Beliefs relating to Country

This issue relates to B and C, but encompasses religious freedom as a fundamental right within the Constitution. If the land-based belief system of the first Australians requires both preservation of, and access to, clan country, then the diminishing of either of these conditions may be considered by some to constitute a breach of religious freedom.

**In essence**, within the land laws of contemporary Australia where freehold has usurped Indigenous community ownership, it is probably not possible to restore original conditions and access. On Native Title land, the more pressing issue is servicing remote people rather than historic beliefs on clan country.

## Issue G: Need for a Treaty

For several decades, Indigenous supporters have maintained that their people's future cannot be clarified or agreed to, without a formal Treaty (by whatever name) between the Federal Government and the People concerned.

This is not strictly true, since a range of binding policies, regulations and procedures are available as a lasting basis for Peoplehood. The prior technical argument that the Treaty can only be signed between two sovereign States, carries no weight in this case. However, the advantage of a formal agreement would have the very real effect of removing misunderstanding and ambiguity about goals from the debate on Indigenous futures. This is so, because the wording of the agreement would require clarity on the rights and responsibilities of both parties and would include economic and tenure principles which included fungibility (tradeability) of assets.

**In essence**, an Agreement would bind both parties to the common understanding of self-determination and its economic base. As such, it should be on the Parliamentary agenda and could be an Addendum to the constitution.

## Issue H: Indigenous Law and Medicine

In recent years there has been an increasing tendency for service agencies to trial the parallel use of Indigenous custom in both legal and medical practice. While different in their application, both these forays into Indigenisation of services aim to increase positive participation and better outcomes for the communities concerned.

In the case of the dual legal system where the magistrate and two Elders examine the offender, there is often serious difference of opinion on the worthwhileness of the procedure. Evidence over several years indicates no improvement in rates of reoffence, and much criticism centres on the lighter sentences imposed under this Elder system. This does not however, infer that more user-friendly legal processes cannot contribute to greater justice for Indigenous people. There is general agreement that present excessive incarceration rates must cease.

In the case of allowing Indigenous medicine men into remote clinics or regional hospitals, evidence of improved recovery rates is virtually absent. Medical staff point to the overwhelming effect of changed lifestyle, diet and substance-abuse on health improvement, without which pharmaceutical treatment produces little benefit.

**In essence**, a comprehensive evaluation of the effectiveness of Indigenisation of courts and hospitals is required to assess the need to remove these procedures from government services, unless clear benefit can be demonstrated.

## Issue I: Sequence of Poverty Cycle Correction

The cycle linking poverty to education, birth control, health, housing, diet and income, is a widespread global phenomenon, notably in Africa, Asia, South America and the Middle East. Authorities in many countries have attempted to break the Poverty Cycle by choosing to improve one element of the causal relations, only to find that progress is limited unless several contributing factors are improved simultaneously.

In the Australian situation, the position of the urban majority is functionally different from that of the remote communities. It can be argued that all urban dwellers should be supported equally on the basis of need, irrespective of race. Since the urban communities are significantly less dysfunctional than many remote communities, their service priorities require fundamentally different structuring.

Urban dwellers benefit from decidedly better education, health and employment choices. The bush-dwellers suffer a social breakdown so intense that many experts see no alternative to removing the children from the most toxic camp environments. These children require improved primary schooling before acceptance of boarding school places. The effect of Foetal Alcohol Syndrome on learning ability is vigorously debated, but many Indigenous leaders see educational mobility as the essential action in breaking the cycle. Generalisation and stereotyping has unfortunately moved the focus from the individual to the community, but there are more than sufficient role models among the boarding school successes, to endorse this practice. Difficult as it is to accept the reality of adult resistance to change, service providers in remote areas have repeatedly had to admit the failure of alcohol, drug and violence policies. Theoretically there is a strong case for saving the young, dealing with the adults and making the old folks comfortable where they are happiest. This means acceptance of generational change, which invests heavily in the youth, accepts a large degree of non-reversibility in adults and values humane treatment of the elderly.

Several leaders have suggested that the youth can become capably self-sufficient through good education in the mainstream, to gain meaningful employment after which they may return to serve and progress their Homelands. In reality these privileged "breakaways" can only be expected to "orbit" back to their communities if conditions and opportunities there are comparatively attractive – compared to the urban mainstream to which they have been exposed.

Improving housing and medical facilities will not overcome dysfunction until a generational improvement in social norms is allowed to change the combined negative elements, which feed off each other. Those who recommend the closing of toxic violent communities are easily accused of racism and lack of respect for culture. In practice, the opposite is often true, i.e. that racism is perpetrated by those who defend the indefensible, ignoring the fact that no system which violates children, warrants respect.

**In essence**, the poverty cycle can probably only be broken by starting with a comprehensive education system encompassing mobile learner's outside dysfunctional homes and communities.

## Issue J: Self-Determination Structure for COAG Investment

This issue relates to the Treaty issue but builds on the $4.6 billion decadal investment in 'Closing the Gap' – a 2008 document which de-emphasises culture and self-determination, but concentrates on on-ground action to improve the human condition, irrespective of location.

The admirable intentions of all governments to focus on improvement of physical facilities and services are to be applauded. What is needed now is a parallel focus on the governance and responsibility required as cornerstones for a Homelands framework for community improvement.

**In essence**, the envisioned biennial monitoring of progress of the Indigenous strategy by the Productivity Commission must also report specifically on Self-Determination under the ambit of its 'Governance and Leadership' section.

## Issue K: Land Use and Business Plans

A number of States have nearly half of their land area claimable under Native Title. Although these claims have taken an average of *nine years* to process, the need for consolidated planning of land use and business cases is becoming serious.

To date, the increasingly vast portions of Native Title lands have been difficult to consolidate into an integrated Land Use Plan because of ever-changing boundaries. It is not clear whether each claim can operate effectively as a separate and economically independent planned Homeland. Nor is the position on holding freehold title by individuals clear.

There is a strong case to replace the old communal ownership system with the individual freehold model, which encourages efficiency through competition. Without this change, Hardin's 1968 classic 'Tragedy of the Commons', looms large as a highly probable outcome. If the assumption is that land with food production potential should be commercialised, then the location of biodiversity reserves and residential zones should be decided and mapped. If Homeland residents are to gain the respect they seek, this will only occur through individual economic independence. Many Homelands in Central and Northern Australia have very low productive potential. As such, their communities will have only two options, i.e. to mobilise their labour-force or move their expanding population to where the jobs are. Such socio-economic restructuring requires forward planning if wasteful infrastructure investment in non-viable Homelands is to be avoided.

Obviously the possibility of alternative sources of income can contribute to remote family income – arts and tourism are cases in point. However, realism on the question of available job numbers leads predictably to most workers migrating.

The record of attempts to establish Indigenous businesses is patchy and less than impressive. The reasons for this are complex, although weak commitment to a productive work ethic, inadequate market research and the negative influence of subsidies, repeatedly appear in final reports of faltering businesses.

**In essence**, the present laudable Partnership arrangements encouraged by enlightened leaders and by government, need to be developed within a co-ordinated commercial Homeland framework with emphasis on sustainable land use and commercial business principles.

## Issue L: Urban Equality

This issue is touched on in several previous issues but it warrants a separate concise statement of intent and rationale.

The central element to building self-respect and pride among urbanised Aborigines and Torres Strait Islanders is not simply having a secure job, but being seen to be economically independent, self sufficient and competitive in the mainstream.

The way to achieve pride through independence, is to challenge innovative individuals to shed previous financial support and to demonstrate personal capacity. This cannot be done without appropriate education and orientation, but given the opportunity, increasing numbers of Indigenous men and women have demonstrated political nous, business acumen, and philosophical insight of the first order.

It would be criticised as ultra-Right Wing to advocate a total discontinuation of Aboriginal eligibility for racially-based financial support and training preference in urban settings. However, the case for support being limited to those citizens disadvantaged by remoteness and lack of employment opportunities, is not only strong, but holds significant promise as a driver of upliftment of an emerging urban generation of achievers. This proposal is not new, nor is it divorced from Pearson's belated call to stop passive welfare. The changes envisaged are such that a phasing-in period is required, with a transition process in which hardship exemptions require consideration.

**In essence**, financial assistance policies must move from a racial to a needs (and disadvantage) basis. The transition process requires careful, comrehensive planning, but until it makes significant progress, dependence will dominate and a medium-term phase-out of support can be justified.

## Issue M: Cultural Support

For decades, the extent to which taxpayer funds should be devoted to cultural preservation of particular ethnic groups has been an ongoing debate.

The general consensus holds that Migrant groups should be expected to preserve and enculturate their own traditions and religions. Indigenous culture is regarded differently, not only because of its antiquity and inherent reflection of Australianness, but because it offers a psychological grounding and sense of belonging to a largely dispossessed people who are custodians of one of the world's oldest living cultures.

As such an ancient culture and as a stabilising identity, Indigenous culture itself is often seen to warrant respect. Such respect distinguishes clearly between the positive, useful and inspiring elements of this culture's language, art, dance and kinship networks, and the more recent negative elements, which debase its original values.

**In essence**, while cultural identity and intensity is a very personal matter, formal support by government for individuals should be in line with government's commitment to multiculturism or parallel cultures, with short-term focus on cultural infrastructure such as planning approval of cultural centres and places of worship. The extent to which the teaching of Indigenous languages is supported financially by government, should be determined by whether one northern Australian language selected on the basis of both the number of speakers and the degree of development of the language, is the most effective approach. All other languages should be supported independently by their communities with the help of their commercial partnerships.

## Issue N: Community Food Production

Food gardens and orchards are central to Indigenous peoples the world over. Those descended from more recent hunter-gatherer societies, tend to gather rather than garden. With the persistence of remote populations and decrease in availability of bush tucker, the need for augmentation of natural diets makes the planting of food crops an obvious alternative. Considerable success has been achieved in the expansion of Indigenous marine industries, notably off Arnhemland, but also off Cape York. These Saltwater People are better served than their inland cousins who have become over-dependent on poor-quality high-priced community stores as the only local sources of 'fresh' fruit and vegetables.

Despite early demonstrations of successful community gardens by the Missionaries and Chinese in several regions of remote Australia, serious commitment to homegrown food is only found in a few communities. Limitations of climate, water supply, pests and disease, all impact on food sufficiency projects, but the main cause of past failures appears to lie in a lack of commitment to the task. This is adequately demonstrated by those working groups who have overcome natural hazards and persevered with the production of well-adapted food plants, including the domestication of the more productive species of bush-tucker.

**In essence**, the potential for community gardens should be revisited, success factors identified and serious ongoing financial and technical support given to food security based on local effort. This action should be the first step towards independent sustainable communities in regional and remote locations. While the reasons for the failure of earlier attempts (such as those by

Queensland's DPI in Cape York) may be valid, the political will to overcome those factors must now be invoked. Many successful permanent gardens on outback stations testify to the biological feasibility of the task. While Indigenous people in urban settings are able to benefit from higher quality and lower-priced food than their remote cousins, there is also a strong case to encourage community gardening in towns, based on costs of better diet plus social and health benefits. This movement is to be strongly encouraged among all population groups, as it was in the 1990's by the Landcare movement.

# END NOTE

The author contends that the foregoing recommendations not only cover most of the major aspects of Indigenous policy, but that they may offer a somewhat more comprehensive and balanced proposal for the nation-wide policy debate. In many aspects of policy-making, there is probably no single best proposal, however, this list of essential principles and practices offers a nuanced framework for factually-based consideration of an interlocking series of rational building-blocks. These could replace the fragmented, defensive statements ensuing from government, when challenged on the embarrassing lack of progress in Aboriginal well-being.

It is the author's sincere hope that Federal Government will consider these proposals and respond positively to the concepts offered.

# SECTION THREE
# CONVENIENT HALF-TRUTHS

# INTRODUCTION

This third Section follows "Extracts from Past, Present and Future" and "Roots and Wings" which examined Aboriginal history and sought guidelines for rights, responsibilities and identity in modern Indigenous Australia. The third Section is a compilation of broad ideas on civilisation, racism and cultural adaptation which, in combination, may help to clarify future Indigenous directions. The concepts included here re-cap some of the basic issues introduced in the first two sections, but bring up to date the cases of Noel Pearson, Gary Johns and Andrew Bolt which have been highlighted in the recent media focus. If the Sections appear fragmented that's because they are, but each major concept forms a spoke in the wheel of Indigenous progress.

This series of ideas attempts to juxtapose political expediency with the most appropriate policy proposals and seeks to bring new light to the complex issue of Indigenous Carbon Projects, as potentially the biggest remote income source after mining.

In essence, this Section urges the maturing of racial sensitivities, as a basis for gaining Indigenous well-being at a greater rate than is occurring under the current circular political debate, which leaves certain locations in places like Alice Springs stuck in the Third World.

Before dealing with the Indigenous issues in this Section, it was thought useful to first consider other earlier 'tribal' groupings such as Africans, the Irish, Anglo identity, early Christians and Islam. All of these disparate groups can contribute to understanding race relations in Australia if we remember that we were all Migrants once.

# MESSAGES FROM CONTEMPORARY CASE STUDIES

## BACKGROUND

Section 3 covers a range of concepts which may have been touched on in a previous sections, but which warrant consideration as building blocks of a broader Indigenous policy framework. As a compilation of ideas, this Section makes no pretence at constructing a sequential narrative with cohesive logic – instead it offers discrete concepts drawn from personal examples – concepts which hopefully can be used to guide the present debate on Indigenous futures.

In selecting these case studies, the author encourages Indigenous leaders to challenge their own (entrenched?) assumptions, rather than tell them what an outsider thinks is good for them. The over-sensitivity of cultural issues and the political silliness which comes from an unspoken White guilt-feeling, makes it difficult for outsiders to be taken seriously, let alone credited with understanding of the remote victim's situation.

As a social refugee from Apartheid, it is hoped that the author's experience of modern tribalism, fabricated separatism and over-valued identity, give insight into how concocted 'preciousness' works against the well-being of coming generations.

This Section pays special attention to religious trends and implications for both Indigenous and other Australians. It builds on the consideration of ethnic identity, as introduced in the previous Sections, and attempts to expand the narrow racist debate beyond the old Black/White dichotomy. The author is at pains to credit Australians with accepting all races who meet the behavioural and productivity norms required to make a modern democracy function as a tolerant inclusive society.

*The threefold crucial issues of culture, separatism and governance*, identified in the first Section, are expanded and assessed, using recent media examples, and the role of Indigenous carbon trading responses is presented in a new light.

The Section concludes that, without critical evaluation and policy action on joining the Open Society, Indigenous disadvantage is likely to continue until the constraining effects of out-dated values are appreciated. In advocating a move to join the mainstream, this Section does not imply a single best outcome for Indigenous society, but emphasises the need for an agreed overall outcome which provides for a continuum of nuanced personal achievement in keeping with the capacity and motivation of a wide range of individuals, whose ability to accept challenges varies greatly according to their personality, background and situation.

In an attempt to distill the basic meaning which may be gleaned from each topic, every sub-section ends with a **Message**, reflecting the author's suggested implications of each subsection. Readers will no doubt have their own messages.

# WORLD'S OLDEST: THE HADZA OF TANZANIA

DNA testing of the Hadza hunter-gatherers of northern Tanzania near the cradle of humanity in the great Rift Valley of Africa, indicates that their 100,000 year old family tree probably makes them the oldest living group of humans.

This tribe is surrounded by other African tribes who cultivate crops and herd cattle and sheep. During big droughts these neighbours seek game and forage in the Hadza lands – a refuge which caused the renowned author Jared Diamond to proclaim that adopting agriculture was the worst mistake in human history.

For the Hadza, game, fruit and tubers are their food, the sun is their god, grass huts are home and the outside world doesn't exist. When agriculture came 10,000 years ago, they kept hunting and remained in groups of 20-30 as the survival family size. Beside their hunting spears, bows, arrows and axes,

## CONVENIENT HALF-TRUTHS: THE HADZA OF TANZANIA

plus their cooking pots, they have no material possessions although at least the women have been persuaded to wear clothes. Their long history is one of preserving their lifestyle over the centuries while other regional population densities grew, crop-based settlements expanded and cities were formed. Finally nations were established around the Hadza.

During their long existence, the Hadza have never known war, never been invaded and never been converted by missionaries. They have survived famine longer than any tribe on earth and today they still benefit from the rich wildlife of Africa which evolved after the geological separation of Africa from Gondwanaland. Interestingly, the women dig yam-type roots and gather Baobab fruit so closely related to the ancient foods of Australia. One of the few signs of the Iron Age influence, is the arrow-head nails they have bartered for honey from their more advanced neighbours.

Culturally, the Hadza have no wedding ceremonies, no funerals and no religious gatherings. It appears that the reason for their record period of survival as hunter-gatherers may be that their country is so unsuited to agriculture that it has never attracted agricultural invaders. However, in recent years, population pressures on neighbouring lands have caused several influxes of cattle-keeping tribes into Hadza lands.

One of the first Hadza to receive a school education, is a man named Baalow who now speaks English and encourages tribal children to attend school and learn bushcraft after-hours. Michael Firkel, reporting for the National Geographic, got to know the Hadza and records how he came to envy them for their freedom from possessions, from social duties, jobs, bosses, schedules, taxes, debts, laws and worry. However, these freedoms were somewhat outweighed by high infant mortality and a short average lifespan. Overall, Firkel's experience made him wish that there was some way to "prolong the reign of the hunter-gatherers, though I know it's almost certainly too late."

Why would we want to prolong this reign of the primitives? Because it marks an evolutionary step in our development as humans, and because in a crowded, polluted and hungry world, we sometimes long to return to primitive sustainability – a condition no longer attainable with our present population pressure.

Has the tool-making animal got too big for his intellectual boots? Many informed thinkers believe that it is the power of imagination which places humans above the other animals. The ability to contemplate the future has tempted these big-brained apes to imagine that they must have both a purpose to this life and a meaningful afterlife. Does he ever ask whose bright idea this was, and what evidence there is, that either meaning of life or afterlife are valid? Just as Man is said to have invented God, he's invented conscience, free will, purpose and the life hereafter. All these come, not from their innate validity, but from Man's imagined superiority over others in his co-evolved animal community. Aristotle suggested that philosophy was born of Man's sense of wonder. Let's remember that.

Halfway across the world from the African Hadza are the last of the rainforest primitives in South America. The author was privileged to visit the ancient Amazon habitat of the last of the 'uncontacted tribes' in 1992. Many of these, estimated at about 100 tribes, live in the Brazil/Peru border area. With zero contact with modern society, these most primitive of races are rapidly being threatened by large dams, timber harvest and oil exploration. The last of these hunter-gatherer's are surrounded by other tribes who experience increasing outside influence and whose children move to the outside world for education and work.

When first contacted, Amazonian Mashco-Piro tribal women were terrified of disease, of being killed and of their children being taken into slavery. The anthropologist who made this first contact deduced that these fears arose from inherited stories from ancestors elsewhere who had been in contact with the Spanish Conquistadores. Today so-called 'social integration projects', organised by resource extraction companies, threaten the time-honoured values and lifestyle of these gentle people.

A distinction needs to be made between the effects of oil and heavy metal pollution on health, and the extinction of a culture, as issues which warrant international intervention. In 1992 in the central Amazonian city of Manaus, where the two mightiest rivers meet, the author debated the Indian futures with the locals, recognising the parallels with Australian traditional cultures and their future. There seemed to be general agreement that submitting the children of the forest-dwellers to more generations of primitivism, was difficult to justify if human well-being was to be given priority over the 'living Museum' value placed on the culture by some anthropologists.

The romanticism of 'savage nobility' seems to come a poor second to rational progress, when the world's obligation to the primitives is weighed in the moral balance. Not that this overcomes the inevitable sadness of losing an ancient living culture. We have little moral option but to make every effort to preserve in books, film and video, the language, ceremonies, medicine, spiritual customs and domestic techniques, as a permanent valued record of what we are helping hunters to move on from. Their transition must be gradual, voluntary, empathetic and healthy. They must be protected from exploitation, abuse, mental pollution and loss of identity. In the process of transitioning, the differentiated needs of the old and the young must be a major feature of the on-going adaptation. Much as we may wish to perpetuate the 'crude' but sustainable lifestyle of the Indigenes, we shall fail in our duty as custodians of human well-being, if we allow exploitation to overrun these forgotten people.

## Message

Where one's own culture stands on the list of oldest cultures, is less important than the cultural values it offers future generations.

# EVOLUTIONARY SUCCESSION

It seems that a number of Peoples are very selective when they claim their place as 'first inhabitants' on various continents. Being very spiritually close to their fellow Indigenous animals, Aboriginals share the same respect for animal spirits, as their counterparts among the Eskimos (Inuit), Laps and San Bushmen.

Somewhere along the animal evolutionary journey, humans branched out from their mammalian ancestors and, with their newfound tools and weapons, developed a physical dominance using fire, spears and traps to prey on other animals. In Africa's Rift Valley, this sequence is well documented over the longest period on earth. In Australia the early humans recognised several animals as their ancestors, both spiritual and apparently in familial lineage, producing a complex animal/human ancestor story.

## OVERCOMING DISADVANTAGE

In time, when White newcomers staked their claim through 'sovereign' annexation, both Indigenous people and animals came under the newcomers' control. Whether the Indigenous humans had usurped the Indigenous animals' freedom was of no consequence to the earliest migrants, nor did those 'invading' humans consider that the animals had any rights not to be killed even while they were regarded as spiritual relatives and fellow beings of much greater antiquity.

In Africa, the evolutionary ladder has an additional rung represented by well-organised Black invaders of hunter-gatherer country, the former being war-like farmers and cattle owners. The hunter-gatherers of Africa include the San Bushmen who practice a similar animal/human spirituality to the Australian Aboriginals, with close familial links to the large antelope which they prey on and pray to.

Professor Karin O'Dea of the Sanson Institute of the University of South Australia, has been studying the 'therapeutic potential' of traditional hunter-gatherer diets and lifestyles for the past 30 years. She studied the Mowanjum people near Derby and in 1978 was able to demonstrate a high rate of diabetes. Today cardio-vascular and kidney complaints add significantly to the diabetes problem. All these issues are lifestyle-related and their early age of onset and severity are increasing.

O'Dea can show that when the traditional lifestyles kept people lean and fit, they were free of these conditions. She has demonstrated that temporary return to their former diet and exercise, gives dramatic improvement in all the major risk factors, even after only seven weeks on their traditional diet.

These geographical examples of human/animal connection, expose the natural dominance of the more advanced evolutionary types and the later 'arrogance' of the civilised cultures. The authority for this arrogance was their self-fabricated religious belief that they had divine right to have Biblical 'dominion over' all the creatures of the Earth, which Victorian England assumed to also include perceived lower human forms.

It took several centuries for modern humans to query their god-given assumption of rights over (non-religious) animals. Roderick Nash in his seminal study 'The Rights of Nature' (1989) gives the most persuasive logic yet published, on why First Peoples should re-think the voracity of their claims as martyrist invasion victims. Nash casts a dark cloud of doubt over the scientific basis for many of the claims of the United Nations Working Group on Indigenous Peoples Rights in the age of Gaia and animal rights.

## Message

Irrespective of racial, tribal or genetic affiliations, a future sustainable society will be required to live in harmony with the environment it depends on. This will require respect for all life-forms, irrespective of human pretence at superiority born of religious bigotry.

# RACISM: THE IRISH BARBARIANS

It has become so common to read of racist Whites demeaning Blacks, that whenever the term 'racist' is used, other cases of racism tend to be overlooked. To restore the cultural balance, it is worth considering the Irish experience.

Centuries ago, the English kings sought to bring all parts of the British Isles under English control. Attempts to separate historic facts from popular blarney, generally indicate that although Ireland is credited as the geographical centre of origin of Christianity in today's UK, the ruling English regarded the Irish as unteachable wild barbarians. This perception led to a form of racism which translated into violence which the English believed was the only thing that this primitive tribe understood. Centuries of punitive rule didn't only consolidate and harden Irish identity but caused emigrating peasants to transfer their attitude of being 'agin the government' to their new home colonies.

It is not unreasonable to see this background of persecution as a major driver of the tendency of ex-convicts to fraternise with the Aborigines who they recognised as fellow tribal victims of Imperial repression.

It is not drawing too long a bow to identify kindred spirituality between today's shenanigans on St Patrick's Day and celebrations of Aboriginality in Australian cities. In common we find that the cohesion of martyrism and alcohol-assisted escapist behaviour, yield at least temporary release from the generational trauma of oppression. The belittling tenor of both Irish and Aboriginal jokes reflects the same demeaning motive and its unconscious flip-side – the demonstration of the Imperialists' superiority. The old Irish song refers to 'the strangers came to teach us their ways; they scorned us for being what we are ...'

The importance of the Irish story is that the invaders didn't have to wait for colonisation of Black Africa or Australia to find barbarians – they were at the gate. This original racism spread later in a religious form when the Crusades went forth in the name of their God to demolish the Islamists. This holy racism was not against barbarians, for the English were well aware of Muslim initiatives in science, mathematics, astronomy and written language. This time, it was the sure knowledge that God had ordered this conquest for the glory of Christianity – a conviction which Aborigines were to find was firmly held by their invaders and their missionaries.

## Message

The idea of racial superiority has a long history and pre-dates Black/White relations. Racism was originally a subset of survival strategies of small groups and has no place in a modern, diverse society. Racism comes in many colours, and it needs to be exposed as a 'weakness of pride' in emerging group identity. Over-zealous tribal patriotism carries the seeds of separatist racism which needs to be guarded against in a plural society.

# THE ANGLO-CELTIC IDENTITY IN AUSTRALIA: A MAINSTREAM MYTH DIMINISHING THE IRISH

Indigenous individuals wrestling with personal identity may be comforted to know that the mainstream as a group is nowhere near consensus on who exactly they identify with in historic terms. The lure of the oppressed Irish origin is strong enough to cause several researchers to pursue their roots, examining nearly 50,000 Migrants from 1848 onwards in their efforts.

The original Irish larrikin image has faded as Irish Catholics have filled posts of Prime Ministers, High Court judges and Governors General. Since earliest times the Irish influence was never confined to inner-city ghettos, but was spread by rural labourers and tradesmen right across the land. Richard

Reid, curator of the exhibition titled 'Not just Ned: a True History of the Irish in Australia', tells us that Australia is 'the most Irish country' outside Ireland. With half a million Irish settlers arriving before 1921, these people were not as destitute as those who made the cheaper trip to the US. So early in the 20th century they were 'too many to ignore but not enough to take over' as Patrick O'Farrell put it.

Why is this colonial Irish identity important to Indigenous people today? Because whereas back home in England, Ireland was regarded almost as a foreign country, here in Australia the Irish found a new and real United Kingdom where equity of the mixed up White tribes produced a polyglot of more tolerant groups than was the case back in the old country.

Siobhan McHugh, the oral historian, found that many among the Australian Irish whom she interviewed, displayed a "strong sense of apartness". These individuals were "brought up on a diet of Irish oppression, they'd not met Protestants before age 21 and lived in pockets of social apartheid right up to the 1960s".

In parallel with Indigenous Australians who were Aboriginal first and Australian second, these Irish Catholics identified very much as Irish first and foremost. They did not identify as Anglo-Celtic's and regarded this term as patronising and misleading, misconstruing their core culture. Helen Trinca suggests that the Anglo element may have gained more traction with decades of Irish out-marrying, but Irish pride in being subservient to no other race remains alive and well – as can be gleaned from any of Tom Keneally's St Patrick's Day speeches.

Most observers will be quick to insist that the Aboriginal case is very different from the Irish as far as ease of integration goes, but there are lessons from the Irish progress in Australia. The first lesson is not to let a narrow historic martyrism and its associated hate/anger get in the way of teaching children the benefit of 'doing unto others'. The second lesson is that there is a different but valuable type of pride which can arise from contributing to rich diversity, understanding, tolerance and an acceptance of religious alternatives.

## Message

Whatever your tribal heritage, its' lasting value and appreciation will be determined by how it contributes to, and tolerates, others' tribal values.

OVERCOMING DISADVANTAGE

# CHRISTIAN CHILDREN AND ANCESTRAL COUNTRY

There is no such thing as Christian Children says the religious contrarian Richard Dawkins, only children brainwashed by Christian parents. Dawkins' claim has predictably outraged religious parents but the debate has highlighted the hypocrisy of those demanding the closure of Islamic schools – the Madrassa, where young Muslims are 'indoctrinated' with Islamic (Sharia) law and total submission to the will of Allah as reflected in the teachings of Muhammad. In a basic kind of way this doctrinal teaching is little different from the 'holier-than-thou' values conveyed in Christian Sunday Schools when referring to the Crusades and their God-given intent, e.g. the hymn 'Onward Christian Soldiers, Marching as to War'.

Why might debate about children's right to choose their own spirituality, be of particular significance in contemporary Aboriginal Australia? Because Christian parents somehow just know that it is their duty to prevent their offspring from becoming lost souls who are unaware of the Living God and all that such faith entails. Over the past half-century this conviction has weakened somewhat, as evidenced by declining church attendance and the great debate on religious studies in schools, a debate which contrasts the benefits of teaching religion or ethics, offering students and parents an either/or choice.

Urbanised Aboriginals are offered the same choice, but remote Aborigines still wrestle with the Bible/Bush dichotomy. The complex uncertainties arising from the meeting of the Christian/Animist belief systems, have been a moral burden for Indigenous leaders ever since the Mission days, when the all-knowing Soldiers of God knew what was good for those who were still in the dark.

The literature records many real-life attempts to rationalise the contrast in spiritual beliefs on the old and new worlds (see Section 1: Missionaries: heroes or villains?). Today the conversation has moved on from focussing on comparative belief systems, to the rights of the child, particularly the right to follow their own choices in spiritual matters, including a deity-free option.

In this way, the driven parent who is intent on giving their offspring a framework for psychological security, guidelines for integrity and a clear

## CONVENIENT HALF-TRUTHS: CHRISTIAN CHILDREN

distinction between of right and wrong, instinctively goes for what worked for them. The flipside of such parental guidance is protection of their children against what didn't work for them – like many of the less than charitable demands of the Missionaries on their Aboriginal inmates.

So, do modern parents have an obligation to expose their children to a range of belief systems or even to the non-belief systems of informed humanitarianism? School records apparently indicate that the affirmative group is expanding rapidly and that the ethics class preference is very popular in contemporary public schools, while the church schools go their own way.

Meanwhile, back at the camp, there is a parallel drive to re-invigorate Indigenous culture and to strengthen the concept of Sacred Country among the young. In this 'spiritual crusade' there is urgent action to record the Elders stories and document the knowledge before it is lost forever. Sad stories of the last individuals to speak certain languages, give gravitas to the moment.

So today's Indigenous leaders are faced with the complex choices of policy direction which must consider the slowly-changing (and conflicting) benefits of cultural options. Many of the religious realists are pessimistic about the survival of Indigenous belief-systems as real living religions or spiritual values. They admit to the inevitability of largely Animist religions being replaced in the future scientific era. They also believe however, that the ancient land-based beliefs offer a historic and cultural richness which is not only well worth preserving but, without which, the whole nation would be poorer as a potentially sustainable society.

One question can't be avoided any longer: "Isn't it possible to preserve in literature, the rich cultural heritage of an ancient oral religion tied to country, while also offering the descendants of that culture, a modern global humanitarian values system, as a guide for contemporary living in a grounded urbanised society?" If the answer is no, please tell us why, because Indigenous people have been left in limbo for far too long already.

## Message

Respect your Children's right to choose their own spirituality. Their religious faith or lack of, is their right, not yours. Offer them insight into spiritual options.

OVERCOMING DISADVANTAGE

# CULTURAL CONTINUA IN ABORIGINAL AND MUSLIM AUSTRALIANS

As discussed in Section 2 "Roots and Wings", there appears to be a growing interest in Islam among urban Aborigines. Superficially, the Indigenous and Islamic cultures may appear to have very little in common. In practice, they both have the capacity to practice their traditions and express their cultures, across a range of intensities. So just as the Islamists identify at least four levels of traditionality and modernity across their membership, so Aborigines can identify a range of mainstreaming and traditionalism across their urban and rural communities.

With an increasing number of Aborigines converting to Islam, it is worth examining the way this culture has fitted into Australian society. First, it is necessary to appreciate that the cultural diversity within Australian Islam comes from over 70 different nations, the largest of which originated in Lebanon (29,000) and Turkey (23,000). The total Australian Islamic community numbers 282,000 or about half of the Aboriginal population of 516,000.

There is a danger that those converting from Christianity, are unaware of the close theological ties between Islam and Christianity as two of the three Abrahamic religions; Judaism being the third. Because Islam is 530 years younger than Christianity, it adopted much of the Old Testament, the Christian creation story and all its characters from Abraham to Moses, Noah, Jonah, David and even Solomon. The two religions, as the world's two largest, share many common beliefs and values. Where they differ fundamentally is in the Islamic non-belief in Christ as the Son of God.

While Indigenous 'religion' in Australia has its own complex genesis story, it has no history of inter-faith conquests and expansive conversions as Islam has. Long before the first Crusades in 1095, the Islamic Empire had spread militarily from Mecca across Syria, Egypt, Central Asia, Spain and various North African countries. By 1550 Islam had reached Java and Borneo but from the mid-1800s the armies of Christian nations had invaded many previous Islamic nations. By the end of World War I in 1918 the Western Allies had delineated several new national boundaries and granted independence, through the League of Nations (forerunner to the UN), to several Islamic countries in the Middle East and North Africa.

How does this Islamic history relate to the present-day Aboriginal situation? It serves as a living example of how, despite bitter historic struggles, most Muslims in Australia can and have, adapted to mainstream values without losing their culture's core values. Abdullah Saeed in his book 'Islam in Australia' (2003), gives what is probably the best description to date of how integration without loss of group identity can work.

Because of the level of development of the Indigenous people at the time of settlement, Aboriginal culture was not perceived as being able to contribute 'enlightened' ideas to others, the way Islam did. Many in the Western world are unaware of the contributions of Islamic civilisation to global humanity. After translating the Greek, Persian and Sanskrit writings into their Arabic *lingua franca*, they developed the numerals used globally today and they produced the decimal system, Algebra and Astronomic instruments. Their Chemistry, Medicine, Geology and Music advanced over a 700-year period until the 1300s, by which time Islamic civilisation's contribution to human progress was arguably the greatest of all previous civilisations.

This rich legacy contrasts sharply with the narrow negative connotation of Islam by many uninformed Western critics, who focus on the violent deeds of a very small minority of extremists who see terrorism as their personal path to heavenly glory. While different in style and threat, the Aboriginal community, like most communities, contains a minority of individuals whose hatred and anger over past events, leads them to demand separatism and an imagined cultural purity, which wants no White influence on their beliefs and traditional way of life. The reasons why there are no Aboriginal terrorists, bear thinking on but will not be entered into here.

At the core of Islamic belief, is that the God of Muhammad is the same as the God of the Christians and the Jews (Quran 29:46) but his followers are in two streams – the Shi'is who claim direct descent from God's Messenger, Muhammad, and Sunni who believe that succession of leadership must be based on merit, not on ancestry and direct descent from Muhammad.

The great majority of Australian Muslims are Sunni and both groups have their own mosques and schools. The Shi'is are largely from Iraq, Lebanon and Iran, while the Sunni originate largely from the other 70 Migrant

Islamic nations. The Aboriginal clan connections have a different base, being characterised by their ancestral tribal country, so when an Aboriginal Elder announces that he is a proud Yalanji or Aranda man, he refers to his rainforest or desert people with no differentiation of ancestor 'deity' but rather of his local creation story, his ancestors, both human and animal, as reflected in his totems.

Just as Islamic subgroups have followed different paths of advancement and acceptance of non-Islamic elements of lifestyle, so Aboriginal clans have taken on Western ways in varying degrees. The rate of change seems related to both their remoteness and their earlier removal from clan country to mixed reserves such as Palm Island, Woorabinda or Cherbourg.

The series of recent terrorist and suicide bombings in various countries have developed a strong negative perception of Islamists in those countries who have opened their immigration doors to them over decades. Since the late 1980s, after Ayatollah Khomeini issued his *Fatwa* (demand for killing under Islamic Law) against Salman Rushdie's book 'Satanic Verses', a popular fear of violence has developed which expanded the negative Western perception of Muslims, now portrayed as 'aggressive, violent, intolerant, fanatical, barbaric, uncivilised, murderous and bloodthirsty' (Saeed's words).

This tendency to assume the worst about a group, based on the actions of a small minority, also appears in the Aboriginal context, but differently. The tendency to generalise about the group in negative terms because of pockets of uncivilised behaviour, needs to be tempered with factual evidence on the numbers involved relative to the racial population as a whole. Thus, while it is right to focus attention and resources on eliminating unacceptable behaviour where it causes community dysfunction, it is wrong to tar the whole group with the same brush.

In the same way, the leaders of the Australian Muslim community are at pains to point out that the worst-case scenarios of forced marriages, enforced dress codes, polygamy, genital mutilation and other old Islamic customs, have almost been eliminated from local Islamic custom. The same applies to the crime rate among young Muslim men, which statistics show is actually no greater, proportionately, than in other ethnic or mainstream populations in Australia. Fear and hatred by some in the public, of Islamic boat people and of women who wear burkas or even just a headscarf (hijab), reflects an illogical intolerance based on false assumptions about peace-loving people who happen to have the same religion as a few egotistical, violent maniacs detested by both Christians and Muslims alike. The basic problem is disaffected youth, a cohort which occurs in most cultural groups.

The imagery of clothing and even facial hair, seems to be important in both forming public perception and in staking a claim for one's identity. Why, one might ask, does Patrick Dodson, a boarding school-educated Black man from the bush, insist on wearing a long grey beard, a big black hat and a band of Aboriginal flag colours on all public occasions, even when he became professor, public intellectual and senator. We must assume that he is imbued with making the point that he represents the proud clearly-defined original nation in which wise Elders have long beards and do not remove their hats indoors. Similarly for the Muslims of both genders who want to make a personal statement on behalf of their tribes. All tribes believe that they have something to be proud of, even if it's only their having survived historic conflict. Social cohesion may not be important to all players in a multi-culture but the ability to integrate into the national society has become a serious issue for both Muslims and Aboriginals, especially in the past decade. The secret seems to be in enjoying the openness without selling your soul, so to speak.

Criticism for not integrating, is based on two very different rationales for these two very different groups. In the case of Islam, Australians fear that increased isolation could lead to 'hotbeds of terrorism' (to quote local radio shock jocks). This radical mindset is spread through separate schools, separate mosques and separate languages, at least in the minds of the integrationists. Aboriginals, on the other hand, are seen to cost both themselves and the nation, by remaining isolated, distinct and generally in need of special support.

So, in both cases, the answer seems to lie in the mix-and-match approach to culture and mainstreaming, in a way which allows the integrating beneficiaries to gain from both worlds, as the Greeks and Italians have done within the great polyglot that is modern Australia. John O'Grady writing as Nino Culotta, put it well in his book 'They're a Weird Mob' many years ago. His message to Migrants and other joiners, was that we should not take ourselves too seriously as cultural beings, but join the easy-going Australian family, which reflects the humanitarian good in all cultures – the good which probably drew us to this country in the first place.

The difference between the global Migrants and the Aboriginals is that the latter have no 'old motherland' elsewhere, with which to identify outside the Great Southland. This means that Aboriginal grounding must be local, in lieu of pilgrimages to Mecca, or Lourdes, or Stonehenge, or the Parthenon or Colosseum (or even the Voortrekker Monument!). Both groups accept that to respect and honour one's ancestors and culture, one doesn't have to live on ancestral land or even practice certain *in situ* traditional rituals. At the same time, Muslims will always attempt to say prayers five times a day (which is why Australian universities have installed prayer rooms) and Indigenous city-dwellers will often teach their children Dreamtime stories, on a daily basis.

Australian critics should note that while Islam is against many Western behaviours which Muslims regard as decadent, they do not protest in street rallies against bars, night clubs, casinos, nudist beaches or gay Mardi Gras. They apparently don't see it as their Islamic duty to attempt to change Australian society, but rather they adopt an attitude of 'live and let live'. When Aboriginals demonstrate, they do so for one basic reason: justice. Mostly they ask for no more than equal treatment and just decisions on their land.

Any rational attempt to assess the comparative success of competing cultural groups, stands the risk of either gilding the lily or further oppressing the victim. In the present comparison, observers will want to know why radical Mullahs, who are known to encourage their firebrands to rise up against the infidels, don't get a public mention on this account. The answer is that they are an insignificant element in an overwhelming climate of goodwill amongst Australian Muslims who probably also detest these deviants as odd-ball egotists, but aren't able to say so.

With well over 80% of Aborigines ticking the Christianity box and with Muslims praying to the same God by another name, the glue of original spiritual cohesion should be considerably stronger than it presently appears. Australia has work to do.

## Message

No governments or group leaders have the right to infer individuals' appropriate intensity of ethnic identification. To each his own, with no implied guilt attached to ethnic dilution as a personal choice, i.e. religious mixed-marriages are okay.

# DIVERSITY IS NOT THE PROBLEM, INTEGRATION IS

In February 2011, a conference was held to encourage respectful dialogue between Australian cultural groups. This meeting arose out of growing public complaints that Muslims don't integrate, and the Gillard government was recommitting to multiculturism while several European countries were phasing it out.

This debate is central to several aspects of Indigenous policy relating to optional futures. The president of the Australian Imam's Council put his own slant on integration when he told the conference that those opposing multiculturalism, were making a veiled attack on democratic values, cultivating fear and undermining the stability of a civil society: "The freedom to observe one's faith, justice and personal freedoms, are the strongest guarantees for safeguarding security and stability of society and protecting human dignity…"

Most Australians are only too aware that religious groups which insist on strict dress codes and religious law, while being seen not to adequately condemn violence among their youth, are often less than welcome in a tolerant society. An unwillingness to participate in the educational, literary and social activities of the mainstream, needs to change before respect and acceptance are forthcoming from most tolerant Australians.

The SBS-TV series 'Immigration Nation' screened in January 2011, gave an interesting review of the stages of Australian change from the days of the White Australia policy to the large European migrations of the 1950s, then the influx of Vietnamese in the 1970s, right up to the present debate about Australia's optimal future population size. The ultimate issue seemed to be the extent to which a too-generous immigration policy could undermine 'the Australian way of life' as we know it.

## Message

Replace the multiculturalism debate with a personal decision on tolerance, appreciation of diversity's enrichment, and following the Golden Rule.

# ISLAM – WHERE DID IT COME FROM, HOW DID IT ORIGINATE AND DOES IT RELATE TO ABORIGINAL POLICY?

As the world's second largest religion, Islam started in the Arabian Peninsula. Islam's Holy Book, the Koran is based on the memories of an Arab man named Muhammad who heard God's (Allah's) voice commanding him to establish a new religion for all Arabs in 610AD. Muhammad never saw himself as divine but his keen interest in meditation allowed him to accept his role as God's messenger when he was spoken to by the angel Gabriel, in his cave on Mount Hira near Mecca – according to Islam's Holy Book.

For hundreds of years the Arabs had been persecuted, first by the Jews, then by the Christians. When Muhammad offered them a religion which could eliminate the evils they saw around them and at the same time offer the first coherent faith in the Arabic language, it was soon adopted. In time, the Islamic scribes produced the Koran (or Quran) of 78,000 words, arranged in 114 chapters (suras), which are arranged in order of decreasing length.

Muhammad died in 632 A.D. and it took Islamic scholars nearly 200 years to decide on and write up what they considered to be the genuine teachings of Muhammad, in Scriptures titled 'The Hadith'. This compilation is revered as second in importance to the Koran itself, which is accepted as the revelations of God (Allah) to Muhammad. Muslims also recognise three other books as partial revelations of Allah's will – the Torah of Moses, the Psalms of David and the Gospel of Jesus. The Koran however is revered by Muslims as the final and complete divine revelation, superseding all previous claims to truth including the virgin birth of Jesus, his divinity, his crucifixion and his resurrection.

In these disbeliefs, the Muslims joined the Christian sceptics of their day who distinguished between a historic man with good ideas and the Son of God. People were apparently attracted to Islam's power, simplicity and cohesion, but socially and politically it drew adherents because it represented a united Arab world-view and, importantly, it was presented in their own Arabic language, rather than the Hebrew of the Jews or the early Aramaic of the first Christians, or the later Greek of their Christian Gospels. Equally attractive were Islam's concepts of brotherhood and equality and the way it taught that acceptance of the faith, wiped out individuals' past transgressions.

In their search for 'anything-but-Christianity', today's Aboriginals could find Islam's tolerance, reverence for Indigenous language and humility, represented a more comfortable new spiritual home than the Missionfield of their Elders' generation.

## Message

Australian Islamists will do their children a favour if they let them chose their own contribution to national social cohesion by following S.109 of the Koran: "To you, your religion, and to me, my religion." Similar tolerance by Aboriginals traditionalists will benefit all.

# I WAS INDOCTRINATED

When I was five years old my parents sent me to a special religious school for one day a week. This morning class taught us that our religion was based on the Word of the Almighty and that its founders had been martyred by the soldiers of another religion in a faraway Holy Land. We were all taught to stand up against the Empire of Evil and to pray daily to our God.

Our holy prophet had been a messenger for God. He had come down from the mountain in the Holy Land and had gathered true believers around him and preached The Word, which told everyone to worship God, to pray regularly and to prepare themselves for the life hereafter when they would be rewarded for living a holy life.

We were taught about the great heroes of the religious wars between the two opposing faiths of the Middle East in ancient times. These wars went on for many centuries and included many warriors from overseas. During these times our religion had the scribes write our Holy Book which became the ultimate truth not only for individual believers but for kings, governments and schools. Our religion was the world leader in establishing universities and early scientific discoveries. Our houses of prayer became centres of learning and our religious leaders advised governments on how law-making must be based on principles recorded in God's word.

We were taught that we were God's chosen people, that our group had been selected to save the world, to banish evil from the earth and to spend our lives in service of God. When we grew up we had to attend religious gatherings every week and would be expected to follow God's instruction to care for the less fortunate. Each individual would be expected to dress and behave in such a way that was respectful in the eyes of God.

I later experienced the way in which our government and even our army, in times of war, would always have a holy man to pray at large gatherings and how, as God's representative, he would always call on God's help. When our soldiers went to war, we knew that this was a holy war and that God was on our side -- we were doing his work and sacrificing our lives for his glory. We would be rewarded in heaven (or paradise) so we would die knowing not only that we gave our lives for God's cause but that we would be eternally rewarded.

Later, in my teenage years I would be formally initiated into our religion in a ceremony which acknowledged my knowledge of our Holy Book. This ceremony confirmed the promise which my parents had made when I was born, to be one of God's children brought up in His light, according to His laws and to follow Him all the days of my life. So by the age of 15 my preparation for a life of faith was virtually complete; it was now up to me to follow God's ways. In my senior school years, at a school which commenced morning assembly with prayer and holy singing, plus religious service twice a week and religious instruction every Tuesday night, religion became part of my every-day life. All weddings and funerals were led by religious men who were very much respected in the community.

In my senior History class I learned for the first time about how conflict between different religions had been the cause of most of the world's great wars. First in the Middle East, then in South America, then in Asia and finally in Europe. We were taught how each emerging nation used religion to justify its cause, how Muhammadans and Christians clashed for centuries, how Christianity fought Animism and finally how different subsets of Christians fought among themselves and against the Jews.

One of the things I learned is that my religion is one of three religions which are called 'monotheistic' meaning they believe in only a single God. All three also have their roots in what is called the Abrahamic faiths, i.e. They regard the historic leader Abraham as the founder of their Islamic, Christian and Jewish religions. This means that the early days of the Middle East in the region of Palestine, all three religions recognised a common origin. This religious history is recorded in what the Christians call the Old Testament and for which Islam and Judaism have their equivalent holy texts.

I learned that the upbringing of Christians had convinced them of the Biblical truth of the new Testament, which is the story of Jesus Christ as the Son of God and Saviour of Man, whose role and significance are apparently seen very differently by the other two Abrahamic faiths. In fact Islam challenges the evidence that it was actually Christ who was crucified. Islam is based on the appearance of God to Muhammad, who acted as the messenger from God to Mankind. So important was Muhammad to the followers of Islam, that in later years they split into two groups; one claiming to be the direct blood descendants of Muhammad, the other claiming that such direct inheritance was not a necessary factor in determining the true Islamic faithful. These groups became known as Shiites and Sunnis respectively.

In later life I couldn't avoid the conclusion that I had been indoctrinated, i.e. subjected to one doctrine as the only true faith, and I began to wonder what gave parents the right to inflict their personal beliefs on their children.

Luckily my Methodist Sunday school in 1930s South Africa didn't preach death to the non-believers.

## Message

It behoves all religions to recognise that in their failure to expose their youth to other faiths, they too are guilty of indoctrination by whatever name.

# TOLERANCE – THE CRUX

Those taking the moral high ground on social cohesion, repeatedly return to 'tolerance' as the key to the Australian plural society's future success. This 'live and let live' attitude is widely-held and justifiably used by many religious and social groups, as a motherhood statement without fear of contradiction.

In practice, the appreciation of the tolerance mantra comes unstuck when competing cultures rely on selective evidence to gain community acceptance. In Western Sydney, the resistance against the establishment of a mosque and Islamic school, is based essentially on perceived evidence that such new infrastructure provides a base for potential terrorists who feed off the radical Madrassa-type schools and their extreme intolerant idealism. In this case, the good burghers of the Australian suburbs are seen either as intolerant bigots or the trusty defenders of democracy against violent minorities.

Meanwhile in Indonesia, the largest Islamic nation and also the closest nation to Australia, violent Islamic gangs are murdering break-away Muslims sects who diverge from the official main teachings. In this case the intolerance is internal to Islam, unlike the earlier violence against Christian followers in Indonesia. In both countries the local politicians play to the crowd, gauging the mood of their majority, rather than the morality or equity of the cause at hand. Once again the dependence of a functioning democracy on an educated majority is demonstrated.

## Message

Intolerance, however it is disguised, is the downfall of diverse societies. As such, tolerance requires special attention in the education system – it is the basis of respect for others' values, and it is found at the very centre of peaceful, culturally-rich societies. Its crucial function in an emerging diverse Australia is fundamental to the nation's future.

# WHAT DOES THE KORAN TEACH WHICH MAY MATCH ABORIGINAL ASPIRATIONS?

This question of what the Koran actually teaches has engaged religious scholars for centuries and it certainly won't be answered by the present author who only recently has studied the 1964 Oxford University Press translation of the Koran, by Arthur Arberry.

The first authorised text of the Koran was issued in 660 A.D. In essence it was a statement not just about God's instructions on how to live a good life but it repeatedly refers to the real messenger (although it doesn't mention Muhammad's name) and contrasts his teachings and authenticity with the Holy Books by previous messengers several centuries before, i.e. the writers of the Jewish Torah and the Christian Bible. In essence Muhammad was the true 'sceptic' in the original sense of the word. Not that there weren't previous doubters of the basic tenets of the Jesus story, but in Muhammad's long effort to devise a Pan-Arabic religion, he needed to convince followers of the false prophets who had earlier misled the people.

Rather than attempt an amateurish analysis of the Koran by a non-theologian, it may be more useful simply to quote a few extracts (S indicating Sura#) from this important scripture. In order of appearance, the following quotations have been selected using the Oxford Press's precise wording and unusual punctuation:

> S2: 80  And we gave to Moses the Book, and after him sent succeeding Messengers; and we gave Jesus, son of Mary, the clear signs and confirmed him with the Holy Spirit; and whensoever there came to you a Messenger with that your souls have not desire for, did you become arrogant, and some cry lies to, and some slay?

> S2: 105  And they say, 'None shall enter Paradise except that they be Jews or Christians.' Such Are their fancies. Say : 'Produce your proof, if you speak truly...... The Jews say, 'The Christians stand not on anything; The Christians say, The Jews stand not for anything, yet they recite the book. So too the ignorant say the like of them.

> S3: 17  The true religion with God is Islam (to be read with S59: 5 To you your religion, and to me my religion [a message to unbelievers])

> S3: 57  People of the Book! Why do you dispute concerning Abraham? ..... No; Abraham in truth was not a Jew, neither a Christian; but he was a Muslim and one pure of faith .....

> S3: 79  Whoso desires another religion than Islam, it shall not be accepted of him; in the next world he shall be among the losers.

S3: 138 Muhammad is naught but a Messenger ; Messengers have passed away before him.

S4: 38 Men are the managers of the affairs of women ..... Righteous women are therefore obedient ..... and those you fear may be rebellious admonish; banish them to their couches, and beat them.

S4: 155 .... and for their unbelief, and their uttering against Mary a mighty calumny (false charge) and for their saying, 'We slew the Messiah, Jesus son of Mary, the messenger of God' – yet they did not slay him, neither crucified him, only a likeness of that was shown to them. Those that are at variance concerning him surely are in doubt regarding him .....

S4: 169 People of the Book, go not beyond the bounds of your religion, and say not as to God but the truth. The Messiah, Jesus son of Mary, was only a messenger of God......

S5: 85 Now wilt surely find the most hostile of men to the believers are of the Jews and idolaters; and thou wilt surely find the nearest of them in love to the believers are those who say 'We are Christians.....'

S19:34 Peace be unto me (Jesus), the day I was born, and the day I die, and the day I am raised alive! That is Jesus, son of Mary, in word of truth, concerning which they are doubting. ...: 39: But the parties have fallen into variance 'among themselves.....'

No attempt is made here to analyse the important guides to living in these writings, merely to indicate the way in which Islam followed the original sceptics, long before Muhammad's scribes established his voracity using evidence from the original doubters of Christianity.

In modern Australia, most citizens are probably not concerned with the Koran's teachings apart from the extent to which they were suspected of encouraging violence against 'unbelievers'. Not that the Bogan's of Western

## CONVENIENT HALF-TRUTHS: KORAN AND ABORIGINAL ASPIRATIONS

Sydney and Cronulla would be expected to take much heed of their own Biblical support for the Crusades. In practice we are dealing with race riots based simply on testosterone-fuelled adolescents seeking an outlet for energy aimed at 'The Other'. Contemporary and earlier analysts have always suspected that all three Abrahamic Religions originated not so much from differences in fundamental theology as from emerging tribal identities which relied on scriptures in their tribal language to develop early political identity and patriotism. Language and holy books remain at the heart of national groupings to this day. In this way the Hebrew Torah, the English Bible and the Arabic Koran maintain followers who probably follow the language as much as the teachings themselves.

The extent to which multiculturalism should encourage parallel legal systems, came to the fore when the Australian Federation of Islamic Councils in 2011 called for government consideration of accommodating Islamic Sharia law into Australia's legal system. Their claim is that this law is integral to their culture and that denying its operation is unjust and impedes religious citizenship rights in a multiculture. The Islamic Councils see Sharia law as a natural subset of a legal pluralistic model.

As with the public perception of much of Aboriginal law, Sharia is seen as repressive and unenlightened, besides being regarded as causing potential legal problems with defence of unacceptable behaviour based on claimed cultural norms. In 2008 the Archbishop of Canterbury, in a show of religious tolerance, proposed that Britain consider incorporation of some elements of Sharia law which could allow Islamic courts to deal with non-criminal conflicts such as marriage disputes. This radical proposal received a resounding negative reception from the public, the government and even from the British Muslim Council.

Tim Soutphommasane, in his popular philosophic press column, is emphatic in warning against multiple legal jurisdictions in Australia and emphasises that all individuals, especially women, should always maintain their legal right to question and reject traditional roles and practices within their culture of origin. He goes further, insisting that multiculturalism should be about nation-building and not about encouraging communities to live in isolation from one another – or what Amartya Sen (Noel Pearson's hero) refers to as 'plural monoculturism'. There is clear evidence that inclusion of tribal or Sharia law in the Australian legal system, entrenches the concept of second-class citizens, and the law is the best example of where the line needs to be drawn on diversity's limits within Australia's social fabric.

## Message

Proponents of *jihad* and Sharia law should recognise the compassionate teachings of the Koran and admit publicly that their radical beliefs have political, not prophetic, origins divorced from the teachings of Allah. Similarly, the unseen political roots of some recently-articulated Dreamtime Stories, need to be appreciated.

# GENESIS AND DREAMTIME

When Pope John Paul II addressed the Aboriginals in Alice Springs in 1986 he made some interesting observations: "For thousands of years this culture of yours was free to grow without interference by people from other places. You live your lives in spiritual closeness to the land..... Through your closeness to the land you touched the sacredness of Man's relationship to God, for the land was the proof of a power in life greater than yourselves."

Many in the mission-field have attempted to show similarities between Aboriginal and Christian beliefs, but frankly the present author challenges several aspects of this (fabricated?) sameness. The reason for the rejection is the fundamental difference in 'belonging', between the two beliefs. It took the Christian faith 2000 years to move from a domination of nature ('dominion over') to the belated contemporary eco-friendly stance, driven more by a physical imperative of survival, than by a humble acceptance of spiritual equality. In this way, the concept of 'others' in 'Doing unto others', was only expanded to other creatures, very late in the faith's adaptation to modern realities.

Attempts to depict Jesus as the Great Dreamtime Figure, as Deacon Boniface Pertjert of Port Keats did, gives Christianity a natural spirituality which it doesn't deserve. In fact the missionaries were at pains (literally) to enforce the elimination of pagan beliefs which underlay the animal/human ancestry in the Genesis story of The Dreamtime: they had no Messiah, no God, guilt, sin or redemption. The afterlife concept was very much one of continued presence of ancestor spirits, not in a God-given heaven but right at home in their clan country.

The Australian Catholics, through environmentally-aware leaders such as Paul Collins, have tried hard and quite successfully, to pull their church out of the Dark Ages on ecological realism. This is a positive development but it is held back by the ill-informed Australian Catholic Council of Bishops, whose pronouncements on birth control, abortion, stem cell research, women priests and marriage of the clergy, do nothing to convince their modern parishioners that their faith is moving with the times. In fact, closer to home, in 2011, the media reported the sacking of the Bishop of Toowoomba for persisting with his calls for female and married priests.

When the Bishops, through the Committee for Justice, Development and Peace, issued their paper 'Christians and their Duty toward Nature' (undated), they saw the environmental movement as a sign of the times indicating 'God's call to the church to care for the Earth and its creatures as 'part of our faith, and consonant with our biblical tradition' in Stockton's words. The present author in 'Where Angels Fear to Tread' (Roberts 2009) has challenged this belated eco-friendly 'biblical tradition', suggesting the present awakening, springs not from tradition but from the modern pressures of an overcrowded, warming world.

Of much more use would be the church's focus on preaching the four attributes of successful modern societies, as referred to in Stockton's 'Landmarks: A Spiritual search in a Southern Land' (1990). These are listed as 'an asceticism' (self-sacrifice) by people who are socially and environmentally aware, namely:

- Compassion
- Patience
- Gentleness
- Simplicity

In one sense, these are the opposite of four of the original 'seven deadly sins'. In another sense, they epitomise the citizens of the sustainable society. Stockton would not be the first to identify what is required in a lasting society of caring and sharing people, who have low consumption rates and define success in non-material terms.

In scriptural terms, the writers of the Torah, the Bible and the Koran, would all claim these traits as cornerstones of their contemporary teachings. These four attributes don't quite cover the full gamut of virtues required, unless one reads 'simplicity' as 'opposed to greed', greed being the cause of many modern maladies and conflicts.

Stockton may be the only writer who has described in some detail, the attributes of an Australian society which would arise, if the future nation was built on the way 'the principles of Aboriginal law applied to the re-ordering of modern society.' This is a bold and challenging vision covering all elements of triple-bottom-line policy, and while its author is to be congratulated on a unique attempt to sketch the sustainable Australia, his credit to Aboriginal principles may sometimes be misguided and unfounded.

This brings our consideration of moral guidelines for progress, to our asking what ancient religious beliefs can really contribute to the future balance between Man and Nature. Thus, while the holy books of the great monotheistic faiths offer some useful guides to the good (moral) life, it really is time for a contemporarily-worded set of living principles (New Commandments).

Dawkins has published an example of suggested Commandment responses received via the Internet. These read:

1. Do not do to others what you would not want them to do to you (sound familiar?).
2. In all things, strive to cause no harm.
3. Treat your fellow human beings, your fellow living things and the (natural) world in general, with love, honesty, faithfulness and respect.
4. Do not overlook evil or shrink from administering justice, but always be ready to forgive wrong-doing, which is freely admitted and honestly regretted.
5. Live life with a sense of joy and wonder.
6. Always seek to be learning something new.
7. Test all things; always check your ideas against the facts and be ready to disregard even a cherished belief, if it does not conform to them.

## CONVENIENT HALF-TRUTHS: GENESIS AND DREAMTIME

8. Never seek to censor or cut yourself off from dissent; always respect the right of others to disagree with you.
9. Form independent opinions on the basis of your own reason and experience; do not allow yourself to be led blindly by others.
10. Question everything.
11. Enjoy your own sex life (so long as it damages nobody else) and leave others to enjoy theirs in private, whatever their inclinations, which are none of your business.
12. Do not discriminate or oppress on the basis of sex, race, or (as far as possible) species.
13. Do not indoctrinate your children. Teach them how to think for themselves, how to evaluate evidence and how to disagree with you.
14. Value the future on a timescale longer than your own.

The former editor of the New Scientist journal (A.C. Grayling) has gone as far as producing a godless Bible titled "The Good Book: A Secular Bible" which is offered as a non-religious guide. He avoids any mention of God, supernatural powers or the afterlife. Grayling's effort however, doesn't match Warren Bonett's humanist case in his "The Australian Book of Atheism" published in 2010. In reviewing Grayling, Roy Williams, the theological scholar, makes the interesting assertion that, "The acid test for the original inclusion of a given text in the first Old or the New Testament, was whether, at the time of publication, it had been accepted and acted upon by a substantial community of believers." If Williams is correct, then we have here the earliest recorded case of populist politics, i.e. what's in and what's out of our policy statements, will be decided on by using the pre-determined level of popular acceptance. Theological history tells us of many potential gospel stories, notably miracles, which were discarded by the early compliers of the Bible on the grounds that they pushed the limits of credibility beyond what the populace would believe. Francis Bacon may also have been right when he said, "A little philosophy inclineth men's minds to atheism but depth in philosophy bringeth men's minds to religion."

OVERCOMING DISADVANTAGE

## Message

Since eventually the Vatican's traditional teachings on women clergy, married priests and contraception, will have no place in a crowded planet, early acceptance of change could ultimately save both the church and its' followers. The recent changes being proposed by Pope Francis are welcome moves in the right direction. Meanwhile, most other religions seem to have recognised the inevitable progress of universal humanitarianism as a replacement for brand-name creeds and beliefs.

# CIVILISATION IS ONLY ONE GENERATION DEEP

Historians distinguish between cultures and civilisations, the latter being recognised by all the trappings of an ordered urban society. However, it is also true that without civil behaviour, the epithet of 'civilised' cannot be maintained simply by physical structures. Over the millennia, the record of the fall of civilisations on various continents, indicates that the decline in social norms and a rise in brutish and selfish behaviour can cause organisational failure in less than half a century. Social organisation can implode without intervention by invaders.

Chroniclers of social trends are fond of the phrase that 'civilisation is only skin-deep', meaning that the animal instincts of Man remain just below the surface. To support this warning, many examples of crude behaviour and group violence, easily come to hand. Since long before Plato and Shakespeare, this 'animal brain' dominance has remained a subliminal part of human fragility.

Closer to home, it is held that British colonisation of Australia brought the benefits of 'the two greatest forces for good' that the world has ever known – Christianity and the Westminster system of democracy. It is not difficult to appreciate the heartfelt conviction of both governors and missionaries, who 'knew' what was best for primitive peoples, even if it involved an initial period of 'tough love'. The benefit of hindsight allows us to evaluate the relative success of both governance systems and religions, but neither of these assessments allow much objectivity, and conflicting histories reveal an

## CONVENIENT HALF-TRUTHS: CIVILISATION...ONE GENERATION DEEP

unreasoned allocation of causal factors.

Why is reiteration of this historic journey important to contemporary Australia? First, because it stimulates the re-assessment of social cultures and religions in this nation of many traditions. Second, because it opens the possibility of developing a unique Australian sense of values and acceptable social norms. Third, it gives the opportunity to clarify and agree on national goals. Fourth, it offers a vehicle for assessing the relative importance of racial identity and social cohesion as pillars of well-being.

A cursory scan of the 'good and bad happenings' reported in the daily media, gives scope for optimists and pessimists, to peddle their opinions and editorials on Australian values. This offers a platform for both the Fair Go/Gallipoli adherents and the White Trash of Asia fraternity. Somewhere between these poles are many of the present Gen Y, who look forward rather than backward for their identity and meaning. Not that these mini-visionaries don't exist in both White and Black communities, but rather that Australian society hasn't yet clarified what it seeks by way of group identity, that feeling of belonging and personal security which comes from a diverse tolerant society with clear agreed values.

There is a tendency to differentiate between Migrant and Indigenous communities on the basis of need for separate policy on support. The perennial debate about the extent to which Aboriginal disadvantage is caused mainly by 'Colonial trauma' or also by self-inflicted social breakdown, is not likely to be concluded any time soon. However, this somewhat tiresome split in political views, still cries out for a much more serious and factually-based resolution, without which the victimhood martyrs and responsibility champions, will continue to fill our Letters to the Editor columns.

Noel Pearson puts it simply when he repeatedly claims that the political Left overdoes the Rights issues and the political Right overdoes the Responsibility issues. He is correct when he insists that, since this is not an either/or choice, the essential action is for Aborigines to embrace their Right to take Responsibility. This balanced approach forces those in transition from traditional to mainstream norms and lifestyles, to abandon victimhood in favour of the positive well-being of their offspring. In doing this, they move not to a Utopian future, but to a different future challenged by the crude 'un-civilising' pressures of Australia's current immature (Bogan?) social mores. Within this transition, is the important role of tolerance in individuals' decision-making, on the relative importance of group identity and wider social cohesion in their lives.

An appreciation of the shallowness of civilisation and the fragility of democracy, must be allowed to penetrate the thinking and actions of those narrow bigoted commentators who profit from highlighting intolerance and egotism. These spokespersons feed continued division in the world's most ethnically diverse nation. In the end, each parent must honestly answer the question of how best they can contribute to the future world of their coming generations.

## Message

Treat democracy as the delicate flower which it is, for if mob rule overrides individual rights, civilisation as we know it, probably has no future.

# WHAT DOES WESTERN CULTURE VALUE FROM ITS HUNTER/GATHERER ANCESTRY?

This is a question which is never asked in Australia. Why? Probably because the knowledge and beliefs of our caveman ancestors have been incorporated into or superseded by, more advanced thinking. Consider the following scenario:

The present author's tribe from Stonehenge is considering the organising of a Native Title campaign to regain control over our ancestral Anglo country which was invaded by the cruel Normans in 1066. These invaders had no respect for our language or culture and forced our mob to take on their religion, our sun-worship was banned and our children were forced to learn a new language. The invaders did appreciate our herbal knowledge for their food and medicine but they rode roughshod over our Druid creation stories.

We intend to right these historic wrongs and demand that England's First People have their Land Rights restored. The courts will probably require that we show continuous connection to the Stonehenge lands, a condition that we have good evidence for. If the court requires that we continue to live in traditional style and not disturb the country, we will probably have a problem.

## CONVENIENT HALF-TRUTHS: HUNTER/GATHERER ANCESTRY

Our Native Title barrister advises us that he has a slight problem finding successful precedents, having studied the history of invasion throughout both the Old and New Worlds. Our barrister has studied the earliest precedents since the first recorded invasions by Moses, then Joshua on behalf of the Hebrews, Jews and Christians. He has sought to use the violent expansion of Islam and the Ottoman Empire as precedents, but finds no examples of developed land being returned to first peoples.

We have decided that we shall have to fight for our ancestral country through the UN Working Group on Indigenous Rights. Unexpectedly, we have the support of Pauline Hanson who demands that she be recognised as an Indigenous Australian, having been born there. We hope to report back on progress, meanwhile let's consider the origins of our 'knowledge'.

Man's original knowledge can be extended back to 'Animal Knowledge'. For instance the Chacma baboons who the author grew up with in South Africa, used small quantities of *Euphorbia* leaves as stimulants, in the same way as humans use coffee. The leaves are not consumed as nutrients but as consciously-selected euphorics, as shown by the University of California.

Giraffes in the Kruger Park have learned to eat mouthfuls of clay-rich soil from termite mounds as a cure for upset stomachs. Elephants and rhinoceros do the same thing. Scientists found this clay to act as an effective binding agent and de-toxifier with significant absorptive properties. These compounds de-activate toxins which originate from bacteria, and act in the same way as kaolin used in human diarrhoea treatment.

Kenyan elephants in advanced stages of pregnancy have been observed wandering away from their herd to seek out the leaves and bark of trees of the *Boranginacea* family to induce birth. WWF scientists find that these plants contain substances which induce uterine contractions. Women in Kenya use a tea brewed from the same leaves for the same purpose.

Elsewhere in the world, the Venezuelan Capuchin monkeys squeeze the juice from a millipede over their bodies for protection against rainforest mosquitoes. Scientists found the millipedes secrete a potent insect repellent named benzoquinone. In Madagascar, Sifaca lemurs eat Tamarind tree leaves for several weeks before giving birth. The tannins in the leaves have been shown to stimulate milk production and kill gut parasites. In a controlled trial, tamarind-eaters had fewer failed pregnancies than others.

Chimpanzees in Tanzania fold the leaves of Aspilla plants and swallow them whole as a means of expelling parasitic worms which are a major source of illness. Californian wood rats fumigate their nests against mites, fleas and ticks by carrying Bay leaves into their nests and tearing them, to release insecticidal vapours. European starlings crush ants and wipe the formic acid into their plumage to kill external parasites. The acid acts as insecticide, fungicide and bactericide and contains the same repellent benzoquinone, as used by monkeys. Song birds, squirrels, cats and monkeys are also known to use 'anting' in the same way. Even caterpillars of the genus *Grammia* know to eat groundsel (*Senecio*) to kill parasitic fly larva in their bodies, using the pyrrolizidine alkaloids in the groundsel as an effective larva control agent.

This new science of Zoopharmacognosy is increasingly demonstrating that nature holds a vast, as yet untapped source of pharmaceuticals. It also shows that humans don't have a monopoly on 'knowledge'. (Cosmos 4/2011).

## Message

The values of ancient cultures should be appreciated as a form of historic cultural enrichment but should not be allowed to constrain modernisation and well-being of their contemporary adherents. For this reason, particular attention needs to be paid to 'culturally appropriate' limitations on acceptable wealth-generation, social behaviour and norms. In the process, adherents to traditional culture will do their offspring a favour by critically examining the usefulness or otherwise of certain aspects of their culture to their emerging modern generation. Many animal species beyond *Homo sapiens*, carry knowledge which has since been learned from them by modern man.

# INDIGENOUS LIFESTYLE CHOICES: HOW ESSENTIAL
# IS ON-COUNTRY LIFE?

Without clarity and agreement on the goals of Aboriginal peoplehood, it is unlikely that the well-being of Australia's first people will be assured. Several intensities of cultural identity are available as basic choices for Indigenous individuals:

First there is the tradition-driven goal of a dispossessed people regaining their Homelands where they keep their historic identity strong and practice only culturally appropriate lifestyles. They demand economic compensation for past injustices and insist on developing their own norms, justice system and spiritual land links. They teach their children the law, the knowledge and bush medicine.

Second is a less intense traditionality which values tribal history but accepts education and outside employment as necessary pillars of progress. This option encourages migration to off-country settings which meet the requirements of their mainstreaming youth. This worldview values cultural links to land as a psychological grounding rather than as an on-country lifestyle. The older generation recognise and respect the differential needs of the younger generations and appreciate the right of individuals to make lifestyle choices at variance with traditional norms. Equally, the young appreciate their seniors' inherent desire to live on country.

The third option is the dominantly mainstreaming choice, which accepts that a modern sustainable Aboriginal population will probably have virtually no reliance on remote clan country as a contributing factor to future Indigenous well-being. In this scenario, bush communities are gradually reduced as the old folks pass on, until the whole population enjoys the benefits of urban infrastructure and services. In time, the clan country becomes important primarily from a tourism and cultural preservation viewpoint, and contributes only marginally to wealth generation, social cohesion and community well-being. This entails land use planning on the same basis as all other regional land, where the level of harvest and protection, is dependent on universal principles of ecologically sustainable development for cattle, crops or mining.

Human nature and common sense however, continue to make the clear-cut pigeon-holing of Indigenous options into the above three choices unrealistic. At the same time the individual's choice of the mix-and-match elements which constitute a lifestyle, can be guided by social policy. Within the framework of national goals, government has three major levers by which the direction of progress may be guided:

## OVERCOMING DISADVANTAGE

1. *Education* and information to expand awareness of goals, community objectives and challenging aspirations.
2. *Incentives* to encourage beneficial change toward a contented, productive and peaceful society.
3. *Laws* and regulations as a socially-agreed set of standards and behavioural norms which form the basis for a vibrant democracy.

As a platform for the functioning of these policy tools, the concept of diverse nationhood needs to be understood and agreed on. There are many global examples of so-called Autonomous Regions enacted by law, which seek to respect varying degrees of self-government within culturally-recognised areas of the sovereign state. What Australia currently doesn't have, is agreed clarity on the level and form of self-government by future Indigenous people. One way of ending the present visionless fragmentation of Homeland development, is to recognise urban Aborigines as equals in urban settings and to support remote communities on the same basis as all other regional settlements, where market forces and individual choices determine internal migration patterns – as with the Sea Changers and the Tree Changers of the mainstream.

Just as the national population shift from the Bush has been driven for half a century by individual desire for a better life, so the urbanisation of Aborigines could have similar benefits. Recognising that some 80% of Australia's half a million Aborigines already live in towns, the perceived necessity for being on clan country is fast becoming a historic remnant of the tribal era.

Indigenous leaders, and as of June 2011, the 'new' National Indigenous Congress, need to be honest with their people about the reality of quality of life in the bush in future Native Title areas. These tribal countries vary greatly in wealth-generating potential and frankly many of them will never be more than third class cattle country. Assuming all communities accept that pride and self-respect can never be achieved without economic independence, land use planning might have to recognise, that in terms of wealth-generating potential, there is a human equivalent to what are distinguished as 'breeding or fattening country' in the beef industry.

In policy terms, What this means is that if COAG has $4.6 billion to spend on Indigenous well-being in the present decade, it could do a whole lot better for these people, by investing outside Homeland areas. While the figures may be somewhat rubbery, COAG's expenditure would be of the order of $400,000 per Aboriginal if the investment were spread among all, but it would increase to $1.2 million per Aboriginal if allocated only to remote people (15-20%) over the decade concerned. It would be interesting to hear from the 'new' Congress, how its members would suggest that this amount would best benefit their families.

If expectations had been higher for Congress outcomes, the matter of qualification for membership, would have been a real issue. The national press call for membership included some interesting wording ahead of the first Congress meeting on June 7, 2011 at the Homebush Convention Centre. The membership application to join the 'Congress Mob' requires applicants to declare:

'I confirm that I am a person of Aboriginal and/or Torres Strait Islander descent and (not *or*) who identifies as an Aboriginal or Torres Strait Islander, and who is accepted as an Aboriginal or Torres Strait Islander by an Aboriginal or Torres Strait Islander community. I further declare that the contents of this application for membership have been accurately completed.' The applications 'will be considered for approval by the National Board of the National Congress of Australia's First People's Ltd.'

The question now arises as to whether, given the above wording, the Board will blackball those of Indigenous descent who don't identify with, or are not accepted by, the community. As a point of law, the conditions will exclude persons of Aboriginal descent who have joined the Open Society and no longer associate with their traditional mob. With membership being 'at the complete discretion of the National Board', the rules now make it legal for full-bloods, who have chosen to identify with the non-Indigenous community, to be excluded. With such rules, an Indigenous equivalent of Labour's 'branch-stacking', becomes a distinct possibility, relegating descent alone, to a non-essential qualification. The cultural purists will have to decide whether this is okay and appreciate why government gave Congress no decision-making or service delivery powers.

As inaugural co-chair of the 2011 National Congress of Australia's First People's executive, Les Malezer's vast experience of international Indigenous rights, leads him to also give weight to responsibilities. He recognises both the very powerful economic forces opposed to Indigenous Rights, and the need for Indigenous people to meet their societal obligations. In Malezer's words,

## OVERCOMING DISADVANTAGE

"Indigenous people must find a way to present, in a cohesive and workable way, their ideas and proposals for a fair and just redress of their situations.... In this regard the Indigenous populations *need to focus on their responsibilities* (my emphasis), at the individual, community and national levels, to each other and collectively, if they are to achieve the elements of self-determination as identified in the Declaration [of Rights]". Malezer makes special mention (NIT 28/4/11) of the unhelpful personal and clan groups' internal disputes which diminish their successes in unifying 'under the goal of self-determination'. We shall re-visit the Congress later in this review.

### Message

Unless the traditional lifestyle is recognised as largely denying future generations an enlightened future, those advocating this cultural and educational retrogression could be held guilty of what may fairly be termed 'intellectual genocide'.

# ONE MORE TIME: WHAT VALUES DO WE STAND FOR?

Two decades ago this author asked what values a modern Indigenous education system would teach. This question was sent to every State's peak Indigenous body, with zero response. It's time to try again. Six State Education Departments listed, in order, the following in a survey by Clarnette in 1989, as the most frequently repeated values reflected in the values of their State Department of Education: Self-Esteem, Respect for Others, Co-operation, Social Justice, Honesty, Respect for the Environment, Respect for Truth, Kindness, Tolerance (and eight other values).

It was noteworthy that Departments did not list a number of the older entrenched values which many in the community probably regard as basic to good citizenship: Patriotism, Self-Reliance, Respect for Authority, Competitiveness, Resilience, Honour and Labour (Work Ethic). A further survey of school mottos includes the values of Truth, Bravery, Faith, God, Duty, Courage, Achievement, Knowledge, Toil, Power, Perseverance and

Endurance. Which of these do Indigenous educators include in the values which their preferred curriculum teaches?

The four core values 'proposed' by Wiltshire in his school curriculum recommendations, as the central pillars of Australian education (as listed in Section 1, Appendix II), warrant evaluation in the present context. The *italicised additions* are the present author's attempt to expand meanings which may be pertinent to Aboriginal consideration.

1. **Belief that each person is uniquely valuable, which requires Australians to commit to:**
   - Individual self-respect and pride in identity, *including respect for others' identities*.
   - Honesty and personal integrity, *reflecting universal norms*.
   - Care of others, *irrespective of race or religion*.
   - Open-mindedness to the views of others, *whether acknowledging our group's values or not*.
   - Social Justice, *which treats all groups equitably*.
   - Realisation of personal potential, *measured by capacity in a healthy, substance-free state*.
   - Initiative and enterprise, *built on skills available from the education system*.

2. **Belief in the sharing of responsibility to contribute to the welfare of our society which requires Australians to commit to:**
   - Co-operation, democratic processes and active informed citizenship, *as reflected by the mainstream*.
   - Ethical behaviour which is socially responsible, *and meets universal humanitarian norms*.
   - Respect for the variety of contributions which different groups bring to society, *irrespective of race or religion*.
   - Partnerships between home, school and community, *as demonstrated by the best schools*.

3. **Belief in the all peoples' shared stewardship of the Earth, which requires Australians to commit to:**

## OVERCOMING DISADVANTAGE

- Ecological sustainability, *which neither over-uses nor wastes resource potential.*
- Economic and social development for the benefit of all *who contribute to wealth generation.*
- International understanding and co-operation *on a democratic and free-market basis.*
- Processes which shape a better future *by reducing pollution and cost.*

4. **Belief that everyone needs knowledge and meaning, which requires Australians to commit to:**
    - Curiosity and questioning insight, *which is not constrained by tradition or custom.*
    - Logical, critical and reflective thinking, *irrespective of its effect on past beliefs.*
    - Intuition and creativity, *drawing on individual originality and insight.*
    - The search for truth, *even when it conflicts with our firmly-held views.*
    - Various ways of knowing and learning, i*n a search for an efficient data analysis.*
    - Lifelong learning *which continually expands our personal vision.*

Both mainstream Australia and ethnic populations would benefit greatly from school and college curricula which both taught and practiced these four core values. These values could act as a framework for global prosperity and peace, so all Australians could develop a sense of pride in personally preserving these aspirations.

The important question now is, "If the Indigenous education authorities do not embrace these core values, what values do they stand for?" Perhaps these educators accept the universal humanitarian core values reflected in these stated beliefs, but require an overlay of Aboriginality and its spiritual connections to the land.

## Message

While the valuing of a culture because of its antiquity, has a place in modern society, the clear identification of the actual pragmatic values from which

CONVENIENT HALF-TRUTHS: MEANTIME IN THE DREAMTIME

culture's behavioural norms stem, warrant both unambiguous articulation and a defined guiding role within the education system. Vague assumptions on values, cause loss of direction and confusion of objectives, especially in emerging plural societies.

# MEANTIME IN THE DREAMTIME

One of the reasons why most Whites probably place little value on Dreamtime Stories and the concept of The Dreaming, is the English word 'dream' itself. It appears that in 1899 the Arrente words 'altjira rama' were translated by Spencer and Gillen as 'to dream'. When in 1978 Strehlow, who grew up with these people (also called the Aranda) proclaimed the word 'altjira' to mean 'eternal', the proper translation should apparently have become 'originating from eternity'. So the central meaning of The Dreaming is a sacred, heroic era, long ago when Man and Nature came to be as they are. Nor does The Dreaming refer to either time or history, as understood by Whites. To that extent The Dreaming is what Whites understand as Genesis.

Deborah Bird Rose in her 1992 book 'Dingo Makes Us Human', explains that White Australians need to appreciate that The Dreaming encompasses the Aboriginal creation story, it's creative beings, other species, land features and the laws of existence. Importantly it includes the relationship between humans, animals and plants – an essential recognition of fellow creatures which is absent from Christian teachings. Part of the Aboriginal creation story is the way that ancestral beings moved between appearing in animal or human form. These beings moved across the landscape, shaping physical features and resulting in a country which had a story for every landmark. When elderly Aboriginal painters draw their sketches, they're often presenting a mental map of their clan country, usually depicting the travels of their ancestral beings, but also reflecting a model for present-day life. Most White viewers of these life-maps may see only a series of crude meaningless dots of dubious artistic merit, completely missing the deep totemic story being told.

The Elders believe that after the totemic ancestors completed their travels of creating landscape features, they finally indicated the clan country boundaries for their descendant line. In this way the ancestral spirits gave each creature its law and place in the landscape. Some of these ancestral beings are believed to have taught humans how to hunt, gather, make fire and survive.

Stockton (see next essay), in an unusual effort to explain the religious spirituality of the Aboriginals writes, "at length, after completing their tasks and overcome by weariness, they sank back into their original slumber. Some vanished back into the ground whence they first emerged, others turned into physical features of the landscape, leaving behind a trail of their life, the spirit children yet to be born in the form of their ancestors. Though immobilised, these Creator spirits did not cease to be alive, powerful and conscious. This creative activity continues through the life-force latent in their resting place, insights of significance to their story and in various transformations......as participants in ceremony and especially in their totemic ancestors."

The early colonials soon realised that the locals not only took their spiritual beings very seriously but allowed their lives to be ruled by them. Fear of the Debil Debil or dependence on the Lightening Brothers was very real, although the colonials missed the spiritual power of the corroborees which, rather than being dismissed as primitive pagan rituals, in fact were a serious participation in the creative acts of the ancestral beings, ensuring their continuation into contemporary life.

It has taken Christianity over 2000 years to recognise Man and Nature as what Elkin called "one corporate whole", which was later expounded in Lovelock's Gaia theory. The Aboriginal songlines reflect their eternal connection to Earth, and celebrate the deeds of ancestors in their country, for which their moiety allocates lifelong custodial responsibility to nominated individuals. The Christian equivalent might be Paul's text, "In Him, we live and move and have our being", except that 'Him' becomes country.

This author (Roberts 1973) had previously proposed that Christians could be converted from being 'dominant exploitative masters of the earth', to sustainable earth partners, by simply expanding their original (human) meaning of 'others' as in 'Doing unto Others', to include other living creatures. In this way, arrogance is replaced by co-operative partnership, in which the Biblical birds of the air and fishes of the sea, become partners in a human symbiosis – which is what Aboriginal spirituality is all about.

To a people whose personal ancestral stories are written on the landscape, desecration of the land is like ripping pages from their Bible. To them the land is their law, just as the Jewish Bible is called the law (Torah).

In his 1968 Boyer Lectures titled "After the Dreaming", Stanner maintained that no English words could adequately portray the links between Aborigines and their clan country. The Western connotation of land as an economic acquisition is abhorrent and leaves us "tongueless and earless" says Stanner, to their other world of meaning. Perhaps the most incisive exposition of Aboriginal belief as reflected in The Law, is that of Bird in 1984 in which she identifies four principles in their law: autonomy, balance, symmetry and response. She shows how, what Europeans called 'the law of the jungle', was in fact a much more nuanced and moral set of rules for living, than its European legal counterpart. In her 1988 "Jesus and the Dingo", Bird makes a persuasive case for wider Western appreciation of Aboriginal spirituality. It seems that both the believability and the societal usefulness of competing Genesis and Resurrection stories, suggest the need for a more serious assessment of The Dreamtime narratives. From all this it can be seen that Aboriginal reverence for both life and land has the potential to contribute strongly to future sustainable societies. As Eddie Kneebone, a Christian Koori said, "We don't go anywhere to worship – we're there!"

Silas Roberts seems to speak for the traditionalists when he sees himself as a tree rooted in his country, but adds that when uprooted Aboriginals lose their land, they also lose their culture and part of themselves. So it was not surprising that the 1974 Woodward commission first formalised the concept that it was not so much a notion of land belonging to people – as people belonging to land, as chief Seattle was said to have told the US President in 1856. It is for this reason that the disturbing of sacred sites was such agony for the people, who described the bulldozers as scraping the skin off their bodies causing sores (erosion) that would never heal. Listening to an Elder at Argyle Diamond Mine recently, the author was interested to learn that Indigenous workers were not only given special leave for 'Sorry Business' (funerals) but also for Walkabout.

It appears that the positive sense of grounding which develops from the life-giving spirit of The Dreaming, can easily carry the believer into developing a strong faith in this unique transcendentalism. This is said to be regarded as the way to Aboriginal salvation, at least on earth. The downside of this strong land link is however, an issue which observers have noted for many decades as a persistent brake on modernisation.

Stanner in his 1979 "White Man got no Dreaming", spoke of the 'metaphorical gift' of the Aboriginal, which gave them the ability to transcend themselves and to use their powerful imagination to 'stand outside oneself'. The individual is the metaphysician who is able to use his spirituality to override his physical being with its desires and priorities. Stanner maintained that it was precisely this transcendentalism which was the cause of the Aboriginals' downfall in the modern world: "So much of his life and thought are concerned with The Dreaming that *it stultifies his ability to develop*" (my emphasis). It was of course, this pantheism (animistic belief in spirits in Nature) which originally set Christian missionaries against Aboriginal beliefs, classing them as 'pagan'.

Today, Eugene Stockton suggests that much of mainstream spirituality seems ready to be enriched by a stream of Aboriginal spirituality – just as a river is fed by its tributaries. I admire Stockton's optimism but I fear that the water quality of this new tributary will not match the mainstream. Others believe that the opposite is true.

## Message

While all cultures deserve to have their creation myths respected for what they are, social acceptance, ethnic tolerance and cohesion will be enhanced by a universal inclusive attitude to beliefs on origins which respect differences and celebrate diversity.

# THE ABORIGINAL GIFT: SPIRITUALITY FOR A NATION

This is the title of a 1995 book, which is the work of the little-known (previously mentioned) archaeologist, Eugene Stockton. It is remarkable because it is probably the only Australian book by an Aboriginal chaplain and biblical scholar who has the insight of a Doctor of Divinity and a Ph D. in Science.

In his unusual blend of religion, science and sociology, Stockton takes us back to the fundamentals of Aboriginal religion, before he describes the valuable gift of "Dadirri". Dadirri refers to the well-spring of our internal togetherness which includes deep listening, awareness of peace and renewal of the spirit – a personal contemplation of self-awareness and being.

While the concept of Dadirri is apparently ancient, it was only publicly described for the wider community in 1988 by Miriam-Rose Ungunmerr in Compass Theology Review. Its focus on quiet listening which makes one whole, appears to be related to Buddhist meditation and Confucian reflection. Some observers perceive Australians to be "thirsting for this gift" – as an anchor and a grounding in today's uncertain and fast-changing times.

Stockton puts Dadirri into the context of Indigenous culture. Culture, he maintains, has core values, attitudes, goals and ways of thinking, all of which are expressed in behaviour and communication. Culture, he says, includes a 'dynamic for change' in new settings of social structure and economics.

Stockton makes the (contested?) point that the less one is aware of one's culture, the more one is subject to its all-pervading influence. As a result, says Stockton, the sense of identity, security and rootedness which stems from the enculturation of children, is actually what makes them what they are. He makes the unusual observation that growing up as a mainstream Australian he was unaware of his own culture – "culture is what other people had!" Cultures change over time because they are geared to survival of the people. One culture will borrow from another only when that which is borrowed is seen by the receiving culture to be conducive to its own goals. In this way, what were once regarded as threatening pressures (economic, social, technological) then become 'enabling adaptations' with survival value for the recipients.

The name 'Islam' does not occur in Stockton's interesting comparison of religious cultures in Australian history, but Saeed in his recent book 'Islam in Australia' reminds us that Islam pre-dated Christianity in Australia by many years, having been brought to Northern Australia by the Macassan fishermen from 1750. For 150 years these Muslims traded from what is today Indonesian South Sulawesi where the present author was able to see wooden effigies of ancestors proudly displayed on cave balconies in the Christian 'Toraja' region.

Returning to Stockton's Catholic worldview, we learn that the values of the missionaries tended to follow the Irish rather than the Italian Catholicism. This might not have been important if it wasn't for the fact that the Australian missions practised a decidedly *assimilationist* apostolate in which they looked forward to Aborigines "taking their pews in 'normal' parish churches instead of aiming at an Aboriginal enculturation of the Gospel" (my emphasis). The Australian church, says Stockton, needs liberating from this out-dated religious Imperialism. What Australia needs is a few trans-cultural prophetic individuals who can act as catalysts to merge the best of contributing religions into a thoroughly Australian faith. A spiritual ingathering of the people in a pluralist way could meld several honourable traditions into what I'll call a Downunder Doctrine born of the country.

## Message

Acceptance of all religious belief as an original response to fear in Nature, needs to be recognised as an apparent human need for a higher power than self. As such, superstition and the supernatural must be accepted as beliefs which can enhance or diminish human well-being, depending on individuals' conscious decisions on how myths are permitted to influence human relations and well-being compared to the benefits of modern science.

# DOWNUNDER DOCTRINE

Stockton's concept of a 'home-made' Australian religion, warrants serious thought if it is assumed that a large proportion of humans need and seek, a cosmic power to guide them through life's challenges. His idea of 'melding several honourable traditions' into a locally-appropriate doctrine, would make sense to many tolerant believers in a natural religion. The diehards in each of the Christian brand-name churches and in The Dreamtime clans, could be expected to stand firm on the core values of their traditions and would probably not entertain even a reasoned challenge to the actual historical truth of their myths. The majority of religious Australians would no doubt welcome an ecumenical inter-faith attempt to find common ground on values and for a 'generic' faith open to all.

Stockton's 'spiritual ingathering of the people in a pluralist way' offers the psychological security which is not found in purely humanitarian creeds.

However, the emerging pluralist 'core beliefs' would have to go beyond Stockton's 'Aboriginal enculturation of the Gospel.' Such new beliefs would have to break away from the man-made sacredness of Scriptures and stories, and would need to replace these with the 'sense of wonder' which Stockton refers to. This would need to replace the deity of each combining faith, with recognition of the universal cosmic spirit related to the undoubted wonder of the universe.

Whether such a deity-free organising power is sufficiently personal for many believers, depends on the individual, but modern society seems able to appreciate the wonder of Nature sufficiently to want to help in Nature's protection whether ordained by God or not.

So we might ask ourselves whether we can find a way of considering how we might combine the values in our new 13 commandments with the concepts in our new Charter of National Values as set out in the previous section. In essence, these two sets of values contain the answer to the fundamental question, "What should we teach our children?" We would like to think, as Stockton does, that the products of the pluralist spiritual construction resulting from our deliberations, would be uniquely Australian, but they will probably reflect universal truths about human goodness. In this way we could meld Aboriginal links to country with the best of St Francis' admiration of creation.

We might have to put up with the narrow pluralist accusation of a return to paganism and pantheism, but this time around there will hopefully be no threat of an Inquisition. For political reasons we would avoid the term 'Intelligent Designer', but we'd need to find acceptable words for Stockton's breakaway group from 'religious Imperialism'.

Stockton's search for 'trans-cultural prophetic individuals' offers a particular challenge and would probably eliminate those contemporary religious figures closely associated with church brand names. On the other hand we may be surprised by the closet ecumenicals who long to break out of their increasingly unpopular orthodoxy. Whether the new leaders need to be prophetic, is an open question. What they will need to be, is credible, in the sense of being able to articulate to an increasingly agnostic constituency, their vision of a clear and agreed set of values and beliefs for intelligent self-starters, as did Buddha and Confucius many centuries ago, without the help of a deity. Their focus would be on self-improvement and relationships based on integrity and humility.

## OVERCOMING DISADVANTAGE

Stockton's book is subtitled 'Spirituality for a Nation' but he doesn't use the word 'church' or 'religion' when seeking his 'thoroughly Australian faith'. The churchy connotations of some of his words could have too many outdated or irrelevant associations for most modern Australians, so the title and icon used to denote the new deal will require sensitive consideration. Perhaps there is an appropriate '-ology' or Code, Mandala or Nature connotation. In this vein Ken Wiltshire's 'Draft Charter of Values' has much merit.

The conversion of the original Tablets of Stone into i-Pad Screens, shouldn't be too difficult but the form of social gathering and communal activities will require flexibility and tolerance by the contributing sub-group traditionalists. As the tribal Elder said, 'I don't have to go to church, I'm there!' – but all cultures need people to gather and gain personal enrichment from communal activity. There would be advantages in avoiding expensive real estate, while public parks could enhance the natural element of Charter gatherings.

Beside living according to the Charter of Values, the adherents would easily develop objectives based on the Golden Rule and in this way they could organise good works in the community, just as our service organisations such as Rotary, Lions and Apex have done for decades. Importantly, the Charter of Values could have great potential in schools, to replace Religious Studies and Ethics in a way which puts universal humanism front and centre in children's formative years.

The initial election of leaders of the new movement would probably avoid Archbishops, Mullahs and Elders, in favour of those quiet achievers from community leadership, whose modernity, tolerance, informed opinion, service record and acknowledged integrity, made them inspirational leaders with the common touch, divorced from outdated organisations and systems.

It may be that the idea of a deity-free ethical movement will have to overcome the evidence that many humans seem hard-wired to believe in the supernatural. At least that is the finding of a three year $2.9 million research project by Oxford University's Faculty of Theology, as reported in The Times on 13/5/11. Professor Roger Trigg, the project leader, and his 57 researchers in 20 countries, found that people generally were 'programmed to accept a range of supernatural beliefs – monotheism, polytheism and pantheism'.

Stockton foresees a time in the future when many of Anglo-Saxon descent will take pride in claiming an Aboriginal connection, just as they have in claiming convict ancestry as a badge of honour. When the colonial mixing of racial genes eventually combines with modern inter-marriage with Aborigines, an emerging pride in being a member of the unique 50,000-year-old real Australian people could develop an unexpected ethnic pride which may well become widespread. These new fair dinkum Aussies may even come to regard their invader forbears as temporary sojourners in the Great Southland when viewed from the great arc of millennial history.

Stockton, unlike the present author who proposes merging the Indigenous culture into the mainstream, takes Les Murray's metaphor of the 'Common Dish' and looks forward to a new re-defined sense of belonging and of being Australians, "who can find their identity and unity around the Indigenous core of traits and who, rather than the money changers, might yet be the foundation of a truly great nation."

While the connectedness with a unique ancient heredity, may give a personal grounding and feeling of security, the values and behaviours which originally emerged from this link, may no longer necessarily be beneficial. Stockton would have modern Australians believe that the gift of Dadirri can be of special value in giving deeper meaning to a value-free and directionless contemporary existence in their modern consumer society.

It behoves individuals to ask themselves whether this concept is really of value, or whether it is nothing more than a product of Stockton's optimistic imagination. In fairness, the same could be asked of the gems offered by Buddhism, Confucianism and Christianity. There is no way of establishing the value of Dadirri for instance, without knowing the psychological needs and responses of individuals. However, attempts to assess Dadirri as a 'gift to the nation', opens the central debate on what it is about Indigenous culture generally, which could constitute a meaningful contribution to the current state of Australian 'grounding' overall.

Past attempts to evaluate such cultural gems, have generally been less than persuasive, at least to the great unwashed of the consumer society. Perhaps Australia needs to look again at what a sustainable society actually consists of, in terms of its expectations on social, economic and environmental issues. The short answer to assessing Indigenous cultural values for future Australians, is twofold: firstly, Aboriginal values have long been misrepresented as reflecting an inherently dysfunctional people, and secondly, the credos of eco-friendly non-consumerism are not unique to Aboriginals and can be learned from several societies, including early Europe. In truth, the practicalities of ecologically sustainable development (ESD) probably cannot be learned from older nature-based societies, in the sense that infrastructure, intensive food production and high energy use, are probably necessary elements of all future societies on a warming over-crowded globe.

## Message

If the new Australian plural society is to benefit from religious and cultural tolerance, narrow sectional worldviews will need to be replaced by the tenets of universal human goodness. Brandname religions will survive only to the extent that their tolerance and respect for the golden rule, nurtures caring and sharing of the people and their habitat.

# AND IF THE SALT SHALL LOSE ITS SAVOUR, WHEREWITH WILL IT BE SALTED?

Bernard Salt, a partner in economic consultants KPMG, is known for his thought-provoking interpretations of census and demographic data. His 2011 foray was into Australia's trend toward 'godlessness'. He estimates that at Federation, 99% of Australians believed in a god, but by 2001, surveys showed that over 20% of the nation did not believe in any god. God is losing market share to the Devil, says Salt, because the latter 'has a more appealing product and has slicker marketing techniques'. Why would Generation Y seek an afterlife when the present life is so good?, he asks before proclaiming 'Out with religiosity; in with hedonism, consumerism and me-ism', with typical Salty sarcasm

Salt is wrong in assuming that godliness and hedonism are the only alternatives. So, while he may be right when (tongue in cheek) he says that generation Y need a good depression or a war or both, to bring them to their senses, he misses the increasing signs of good, unselfish traits reflected by the youth – the godless do-gooders who have actually outperformed those from the era of the 1960s extravagances. When I saw 50,000 mostly-young volunteers lined up to clean houses after the Brisbane floods in 2011, I knew that Samaritanism was alive and well. Salt would do well to have another go at analysing what replaces godliness in modern Australia, even if he wasn't being serious in the first place.

## Message

Instead of ridiculing others' religious beliefs, recognise that individuals draw strength from different sources. Appreciate the fact that while faith recedes as science advances, a cohesive productive society can actually draw strength from a range of complementary beliefs.

# RACIAL VILIFICATION: ANDREW BOLT'S CASE

Journalist Andrew Bolt is known for his directness and tough questioning of public figures. In March 2011 Bolt wrote that several light-skinned Aboriginals had apparently made the conscious decision to officially register as Aboriginal, for personal gain. Bolt maintained that light-skinned Aboriginals of mixed parentage, have the option to identify officially as non-Aboriginal. As a result of their claimed Aboriginality, said Bolt, several individuals had won grants, prizes, awards and career advancement, based on their eligibility for benefits available only to Aborigines.

The persons named by Bolt, alleged that he had breached the Racial Discrimination Act and that they all in fact, had no choice about identifying as Aboriginal. It so happens that the plaintiffs in this case include an activist, an artist, a state Australian of the Year, an author and an ex-member of ATSIC. The charge was that Bolt's articles gratuitously denigrated these people on the basis of their race. One plaintive, under questioning, admits that some of her relatives do not identify themselves as Aboriginal, but in her own case, Bolt's article appeared determined to disconnect her from her Aboriginality. The court heard that Bolt's views were akin to the colonial eugenics approach, which led to the anti-Semitic Nuremberg laws of 1935, which in turn were used to justify the Holocaust.

So why is this racial 'storm in a teacup' worthy of public comment? Because it epitomises the unreasonable ultra-sensitivity with which the Racial Discrimination Act has been allowed to become ensconced in the national psyche. What happened in this case, was essentially that a journalist did no more than express his antipathy toward race-based awards and benefits. Apart from the fact that Bolt's major concern was that some of the awards in question should have gone to more deserving and more 'Aboriginal' recipients, his contention was that race-based awards were themselves racist.

There are of course the high-profile 'Deadlies' awards held annually in the Sydney Opera House which is organised by Aborigines for Aborigines to honour those who have contributed most to Aboriginal art, culture, sport and social service. In this case there can obviously be no criticism of the sympathy vote favouring Aboriginal nominees, as there has been in some Australian or Young Australian of the Year awards.

Legal opinion has it that the Bolt case should have been brought under the Defamation Act, not the Racial Discrimination Act. Such opinion also holds that it would have failed under the former Act, but had a stronger chance under the latter Act, even if financial rewards would have been smaller – several thousand dollars. In Bolt's case, nominally costing up to $1.5 million, the prosecution's pro-bono lawyers could have been ruined if they had been ordered to pay Bolt's costs. Bolt lost the case and did not appeal. A decade later, this case continues to make headlines as an example of how legally inappropriate the 'offence of offending' others on racial grounds is in Section 18c of the Racial Discrimination Act (1975).

So why was this case important beyond the defence of sensitive egos? Because it had potential to set new boundaries of free speech and it also had the potential to remove a whole suite of important cultural issues from the public debate. Nic Pullen, a media lawyer, maintains that it could open the floodgates for groups to sue other groups e.g. Middle Eastern or Pacific Islander or Asian groups, who interpret published statements as vilifying their region/language/culture/dress/customs.

Chris Merritt, legal affairs editor for The Australian newspaper, feared that the Bolt case would lead aggrieved groups to shun the mediation provisions of the law and proceed directly to court. Frank Zumbo, professor of law at

Sydney University, advised that there was already a widely-held belief within the legal fraternity, that it is easier to sue for vilification under the RDA than to base a case on defamation. Pullen also warned that the Bolt case will not only tend to shut down open debate but, instead of reducing racist and bigoted statements, will make mainstream Australians more resentful of some aspects of multiculturalism.

Is it stretching the comparison too far to liken court actions under the RDA by minorities claiming offence or racial vilification, to the killings by Islamists of those who are accused of demeaning Muhammad or the Koran, as in Danish cartoons? Perhaps it is drawing a long bow, but the level of intolerance and lack of cultural respect by another group, is similar.

In April 2011, an Islamic mob killed fourteen UN staff in their Afghanistan headquarters in response to a small American Christian Church of fundamentalists whose minister threatened to burn the Koran, as a show of opposition to terrorist attacks. Of course the scale and intensity of reaction is extreme in this case, but the root cause is similar to the intolerance of even nuanced but valid criticism by outsiders, shown by those who claim vilification in Australia.

The balance between free speech and racialism in a tolerant democracy, requires wisdom and insight from the judiciary, and unless a realistic line is drawn on what is appropriate for contemporary Australian society, race relations will get worse, not better under the RDA.

The relative level of blatant racism in Australia, continues to dominate the debate on the future of multiculturalism. Kevin Dunn of the University of Western Sydney conducted surveys on comparative racist attitudes among 12,500 Australians from 2001 to 2008. Second to Canada, we turn out to be one of the least racist countries on earth. Dunn found that an individual's level of racism was influenced more by their awareness of peer reactions, than by their 'ingrained biological impulses'.

Fewer than 10% of those surveyed believed that certain races were inferior or that races should not inter-marry. Pew International found this figure for belief in racial inferiority, to average 40% in Africa, Asia and the Middle East. Less than 5% of Australians believed the Muslim *burka* should be banned. In France, the equivalent figure is 50%. Importantly, Dunn found that education had been shown to overcome all racist biases, inferring that such bias was largely enculturated.

## Message

Base support on need, not race. Judge individuals on good works, not ethnicity. End tribal separatism. Encourage universal humanitarianism. Recognise global connection.

# "GOVERNMENT BANS GROG, TOBACCO AND POKIES": AN UNLIKELY HEADING

Unlikely for mainstream communities, but close to the reality of the NT Intervention, this heading is only quoted here as an attention-grabber for a widespread and serious Australian malady. Our national history tells us that mention of any form of prohibition, is derided as moralistic grandstanding and it 'never works anyway'.

Be that as it may, medical statistics repeatedly inform us that the Evil Trinity of alcohol, smoking and gambling, have each been costing this nation in excess of $5 billion annually, apart from the unpriced misery they inflict on families. Such enormous losses don't however, cause governments to legislate against these debilitating practices – except in some Aboriginal communities where government thinks that the White voters believe that prohibition is just what dysfunctional communities need. The reason? The level of violence and child abuse is unacceptable and needs firm action, at least according to the media beat-up which voters are exposed to.

So why doesn't dysfunction through substance abuse and gambling result in similar action in unstable mainstream communities? Because it's 'un-Australian' to interfere with the personal rights of individuals, and besides, it could seriously affect voting patterns. In any case, we mainstreamers regard ourselves not only as tolerant, but as an informed electorate, we are able to change behaviour when necessary, or through advertising campaigns which appeal to our integrity and better judgement. Really?

This nation has an unusual way of characterising unsociable standards. On the one hand there are claims that selfish, racist, violent or unfair behaviour is, 'un-Australian'. On the other hand official or community attempts to limit or control wild or irresponsible behaviour is also referred to as un-Australian on the grounds that such limits demean personal liberties in drinking, smoking and gambling, important indicators of our national lifestyle.

Perhaps it is not surprising in a young multicultural society, that who we are and what we stand for, are not yet settled. However, in the north of the country, other definitions of acceptable behaviours require that these also be 'culturally appropriate', a phrase used to define acceptable wealth-generating activities. In future it will be useful to drop the use of the term 'un-Australian' until the population has a stronger consensus of what it is that we stand for as a nation. Sociologists point out that it is high time that Australians recognise that, what they have been led to believe is somehow uniquely Australian, is in fact universal humanitarian behaviour. More and more, there is a global realisation of the centrality of human goodness and an understanding that this trait is expressed differently in different cultures. In this way mateship and fairness can be embraced by a diverse nation, which appeals to all cultures to follow the Golden Rule.

## Message

In all societies, personal stress leads a proportion of personalities to seek refuge from reality in temporary comforting behaviour. Accept this fact, and support policies which nourish the youth with love, understanding and positive role models, who can assist in developing more mature behaviour and greater personal integrity.

# PARENTAL EXAMPLE AND HEROIC DADS

Tim Russert's book 'The Wisdom of Our Fathers' (2006) includes many tear-jerking letters from sons and daughters about what they learned from their dads and how they were inspired. This reflects a segment of the American experience and leaves the reader wondering how different such bonds and respect might be for mainstream and Indigenous Australians. Clearly not everyone had a heroic dad in America and the same must be true elsewhere, but Russert's compilation of glowing letters reflects a universal facet of human nature – the child's need for love, for a role model, an exemplar and a guiding light in an uncertain world.

Did those of us who were sent to boarding school at an early age, miss out on part of our nurturing? Were dads replaced by other father figures? Were our senior peers unconsciously filling this role? Are we the worse for it or did it actually benefit our independence and self-reliance? More than any other question, the pros and cons of boarding school must be seriously debated and agreed on in remote Indigenous communities.

## Message

Since the dominant determinant of character is experiential, not genetic, parents have a responsibility to develop the capacity for both compassion and independence in their offspring by giving them roots and wings – a sense of safe-haven and an ability to follow their dreams elsewhere.

# LIONEL ROSE: SO WHAT'S THE BIG DEAL?

The big deal is that in Rose, Australia had the ultimate successful battler. From his family's tin shack on Jackson's Track near Warragul in Victoria, Rose, through sheer guts and native cunning, became world boxing champion in 1968. The communications records apparently show that 72% of Australian households tuned in to that fight – a record which stood until even more tuned in to Cathy Freeman's Olympic win in 2000.

So why did 250,000 Melbournians line the streets for Rose's Parade in 1968? Because Aussies are fair dinkum about giving the underdog a fair go irrespective of race or creed. When asked about pride in his Aboriginal identity, Rose replied "I haven't thought about it, I guess I'm just an Australian like everyone else…". Not only did he act as a very important role model for his mob, but Rose inspired all Australians with his amazing tenacity and dedication to his chosen career. His family say he never cared about money, he gave most of it away, he sold his title belts to boost his superannuation and gave one of them to Tjandamurra O'Shane, a youngster badly burned in a racial attack. He had earlier refused a very lucrative fight in Apartheid-ridden South Africa but he kept right out of politics. Later as a Country and Western singer he was again hailed as a local hero, before alcohol finally got the better of him.

Rose's spirit lives on and his iconic image burns brightly for Black and White Australians seeking inspiring role models for directionless youth. Rose did not blame the system or hate the ruling class, he did what all self-starters do; he decided early in life that his success depended on his own will and effort. On the way up, Rose never lost his innate humility, his courteous respect for others or his self-effacing demeanour. It was this combination of being a good bloke and a champion fighter, which made Rose one of the most widely-admired Aboriginals in history. The capacity of a mild-mannered youth to go 15 rounds with the Japanese world champion and win on points, touched the hearts of millions of Australians and lingers on to this day.

Allied to the emotions shown at the funeral of Lionel Rose (16/05/11), is the unexpected finding of Tony Curry (who writes as 'Murri in a hurri'), that Aboriginal NRL players score higher than the average of all NRL players in their percentage of high school completions. The completion rate across the board for all NRL players is 84%, while for Indigenous players it is 92%. We thought Tony was pulling our leg, but it seems that the same perseverance and self-control which made these lads stick to their senior school studies, is now paying off as the career drivers of the Indigenous NRL champions. The moral of the story is that both self-discipline and commitment are the essence of the battlers' success. Just do it.

## Message

Recognition and acknowledgement that successful battlers, irrespective of race, deserve to be enshrined as the essence of pluralism in a diverse society. The inspiration from disadvantaged individuals who achieve through perseverance, should forever be valued and taught as an essential Australian trait binding all races.

OVERCOMING DISADVANTAGE

# YOU KNOW GOODNESS WHEN YOU SEE IT: HARNESSING THE J FACTOR

Having researched the causes of, and possible solutions to, Indigenous social dysfunction for the past few years, this author has become sensitised to the basis for human well-being and how it is achieved. With this background, the author recently attended the sixtieth birthday party of Julie Arthur, one of his wife's friends. This would have been just another birthday gathering but there was something about the atmosphere of this group which seemed somehow very special. After several days of recognising that this gathering produced a warm inner glow, an effort was made to analyse the factors contributing to this gathering, with which everyone present seemed to want to identify.

In essence, this family atmosphere appeared to be juxtaposed to the social breakdown which the author had been studying, and it seemed to be built on three old-fashioned pillars: hard work, Christian fellowship and solid family values. The group included a wide range of colours, creeds, ages and accents. Somehow, without anyone mentioning it, each seemed to reflect their appreciation of a sense of belonging to this apparently solid nuclear family of four generations.

The generational continuity gave a sense of security in our uncertain world. From the Grandmother in her nineties to the three-week-old infant, there was a sense of grounding and permanence. Adding to the sense of family cohesion, was a sing-song led by the birthday-girl's sister, wearing the same dress which she wore as bridesmaid to her 60 year old sister. The fact that the dress still fitted, only consolidated the apparently timeless aura surrounding this family.

All those present were aware that this family had flourished financially on the back of the birthday-girl's husband – originally a New Zealand dairy farmer's son, well-acquainted with hard work, long hours and modest income. This work ethic permeates the whole family of builders, tradies, teachers and devoted mothers. As a group, this third-generation offers an inspiring example of intelligent, independent and productive members of society.

## CONVENIENT HALF-TRUTHS: HARNESSING THE J FACTOR

This commitment to self-sufficiency by these self-starters may even seem somewhat old-fashioned, in this era of ever larger proportions of young people applying for government support of some sort. Watching the girls of the family leading the line-dancing on the outside deck, belied their commitment to education and training as respected professionals.

The make-up of the birthday crowd reflected a cultural soup of accents and colours such that it would be surprising if, as a diverse group of global humanity, they didn't represent a great reservoir of emigrant tales, of victims of violence and of refugees from a range of political upheavals over the decades. As the beer flows, the music is turned up and the chatter grows louder, the observer gets the clear impression that what we're dealing with here is not irresponsible work-shy Bogans, but solid citizens who've seen hard times and have come to value the simple joys of life.

At the centre of proceedings is the birthday-girl, barefooted in very plain home clothes. As a quiet committed Christian, this slightly-built woman is known to spend her time unobtrusively 'doing unto others' in very practical ways. Along with all her grandmotherly duties, every fortnight she picks up a group of elderly ladies, most of whom live alone, and takes them to lunch at various restaurants. This has been going on for over a decade and looks like a permanent dedication – all in the name of 'loving thy neighbour'.

This unusual individual seems to have an infectious effect on all who associate with her – call it the 'J factor', which appears to inspire others to be their better selves. When the video show of J's life, as put together by her teacher daughter, screens a picture of J hugging two Aboriginal girls at their Gulf campsite, the caption reads simply 'Unconditional Love'. This sums her up in two words and looking around the audience, one notices a few teary eyes – tears of joy, of empathy, of recognition, which seemed to say 'we are so glad to be part of this mob, even if peripherally'.

At this point in the show, one perceives an unspoken realisation that what those little Black kids need more than anything, is what J can give. Suddenly it all comes together for those enjoying the glow of love exuded by the wonderful home-made 'This is your life' show, containing dozens of images of a life so well lived. Collectively we bask in the warmth of being part of an ordinary family which is so special.

The more analytical guests must have returned to their homes not only counting their blessings but perhaps also wondering how these blessings could be made available to their disadvantaged countrymen. So the author returns to his Indigenous research, inspired by a renewed vision of the other end of the social continuum.

## Message

Appreciate and nurture the precious role models in our society. Recognise and reward their vital contribution to the future stability of all our people, who are but one race – the human race.

# CULTURAL ADAPTATION

Norman Doidge, author of 'The Brain that Changes Itself' (2007), offers some useful insights into how Indigenous people and others might adapt to the changing world, and how their emerging new world may learn from their ancestral adaptations.

Doidge believes that the conventional view that 'the brain produces culture', is now inadequate. This is because generations of traditional activity have in fact changed the brain – altered the original brain's capacity to perform required actions. Such alteration presumes the *neuroplastic* capacity of the brain, i.e. its ability to alter its function according to physical needs. In his appendix titled 'The Culturally Modified Brain', Doidge explains that enculturation occurs through training in a range of activities – customs, arts, interactions, ideas, beliefs and technologies. Every sustained activity *including thinking and imagining*, has been shown by neuroplastic research, to change the brain and thus the human mind. As a result, we all have culturally modified brains and as culture evolves, new brain changes occur in the form of adaptations to our changing situation. This leads Michael Merzenich to proclaim that our brains are vastly different from the brains of our ancestors. At the same time, as shown by the Swedish researcher Anna Gislen, tribes such as the Sulu, a sea-gypsy tribe off Thailand, prove that generational custom can produce remarkable adaptations over time. In this case, the ability to dive to seventy-five feet unassisted, and to be able to see well underwater without goggles.

## CONVENIENT HALF-TRUTHS: CULTURAL ADAPTATION

All cultures have what are termed 'signature activities', i.e. those repeated actions which are central to the culture's lifestyle. These don't include the universally-evolved primitive abilities of walking, seeing and hearing. The signature activities may be hunting techniques, food preparation, dance, song or art, which contribute to developing a specially-wired brain.

The evolutionary psychologists maintain that all humans share the same basic brain modules (subsections) which evolved during the Pleistocene age (1.8 million-10,000 years ago) when we all lived as hunter-gatherers. These brain modules have been passed on, essentially unchanged genetically, but modified experientially by generations of differential activities. The archaeologist Steven Mithen describes this capacity as 'cognitive fluidity', which can be ascribed to plasticity of the brain.

So why is this cerebral knowledge of significance in the Australian Indigenous context? Firstly, because it confirms what we already know about the modern adaptive capacity of culture-bearers, and secondly, because it does away with the Imperial idea that some tribes (Black or White) are unteachable.

The brain modules which children use to read and write for instance, have been shown to have evolved a very long time before literacy arose a few thousand years ago. It only takes one generation to teach hunter-gatherers to read, i.e. a fraction of the time that is required for a new literacy gene to develop. It now seems clear that human capacity moved from cave painting 30,000 years ago, to hieroglyphics 5000 years ago, to modern writing 2000 years ago, through an adaptive learning process based on strengthened neuronal connections in the brain.

Sharing 98% of our DNA with chimpanzees, The Human Genome Project demonstrated that the vital difference between these two groups, is 'that gene which determines how many neurons we produce.' The neuroscientist Robert Sapolski explains that in the human embryo, cell division in the brain develops until we have about 100 billion neurons. In chimpanzees this process stops earlier, leading to their smaller brain and lower connectivity. Before the discovery of neuroplasticity, the Darwinian theory of evolution of species which claimed that adaptive evolution takes thousands of years, was accepted as the only way the brain could change, reliant on change mutations which, if they had survival value, were passed on in the gene pool.

Today it is known that when children are taught to read, the biological structure of the brain actually changes. According to Doidge, when the brain learns new tasks such as reading, the circuits connecting the brain molecules increase, and in the process, new changes occur in the existing 'hunter-gatherer modules'.

Under the heading of 'How will we Civilise our Animal Instincts?' Doidge broaches the sensitive subject of what he terms 'instinctual and intellectual activities'. He refers to Freud's suggestion that our brains have one section which we share with animals, and a higher, uniquely human section which inhibits the instinctive expression of predatory brutishness. Freud believed that civilisation depended on this inhibition, but also that if these instincts were too repressed, neurosis would result. Sport and competitive games can act as a practical replacement for these instincts. Doidge agrees that civilisation will always be a tenuous affair which needs to be taught in each generation and is always *only one generation deep* (my emphasis) at most. The plastic brain can also apparently allow brain functions which it has brought together, to separate again. This means that a regression to barbarism can occur at any time – as it seems to be doing in the Middle East and in parts of Africa presently.

Importantly in the Australian context, it appears from neuroplastic research, that the brain can be what Doidge refers to as 'caught between two cultures'. When moving from one culture to another, brain function can become either more flexible (accepting) or more rigid (fixed). This explains why human migration can be difficult, because as the newcomers learn new ways, they either lose their old ways – or they 'freeze in the past' and fail to adapt. Culture change can be very difficult for the adult brain, requiring huge amounts of brain re-wiring and consuming much brain energy.

When changing to a new culture, the behaviours learned when young, may appear natural, as if they were hard-wired at birth, but they have in fact been shown to be enculturated. In the mid-1900s the famed child psychologist Jean Piaget demonstrated that the capacity to perceive and reason is the same in all children – a universal process. Research has now proven that the observed differences in reasoning capacity between known groups, results from enculturation and not from genetic difference.

The fact that neuroplasticity declines with age is perhaps not surprising. As Bruce Wexler of Yale argues in his book 'Brain and Culture', as age increases, there is a natural tendency to ignore information which doesn't fit our established values and worldview.

Those with experience of old and young people in multicultural situations, don't need research to predict social policy outcomes. It has long been widely known that the young adapted easily and the old are more rigid. Many examples of individual Indigenous culture change, are well documented. As a basis for policy on Aboriginal well-being, the lesson is clear – give the young the opportunity to progress and adapt through education, and give the old folks the opportunity to benefit from their traditional situation with minimal demand for change.

## Message

Static cultures die. Adaptive cultures offer on-going strength and belonging to their adherents. Adapt or join history, but respect a varying degree of adult inflexibility.

# THE INFLEXIBILITY OF REMOTE INFRASTRUCTURE INVESTMENT

Part of the current dilemma for government, which has the responsibility to improve Indigenous well-being, is the degree of permanency which attaches to investment in expensive social infrastructure – housing, schools, hospitals, police stations and local government offices, all of which require a permanent water and power supply.

The adage of 'build it and people will come' is more than a little risky when applied to infrastructure in remote Indigenous communities. The flexible provision, or withdrawal, of human services is a much less risky investment than infrastructure, but with the exorbitant cost of remote buildings, the potential for government waste is huge. Long-term utilisation of infrastructure requires reasonable certainty on predicted population numbers; numbers in turn require an economic base in either commercial productivity or in government support.

As with decisions by mining companies on the options of building infrastructure or relying on fly-in/fly-out staffing in remote areas, government is faced with similar choices on expenditure. Flying out doctors, dentists, opticians, accountants, bankers, engineers and tradesmen, leaves police, service station owners and a few others as the only remaining full-time operatives. As a former outback resident, the author has observed the 'social sifting' process which accompanies growing inequity of services in remote communities, relative to their city cousins. Many writers have chronicled the decline of rural towns, the closing of banks and schools, the impossibility of retaining a permanent doctor and the demise of social organisations due to lack of numbers. The reason is always the same – lack of employment.

Indigenous planners and advisors ignore this message at their peril. Rather than repeating the unfounded confidence in community viability in emerging Native Title areas, planners would do well to consider long-term business plans and their income sources, before requesting government to build temples to the God of Community Development. As a vote-buying exercise, remote infrastructure investments often only have a very short shelf-life and as a result, it behoves Indigenous advisors to apply real vision, as opposed to political expediency, when proposing how remote Aboriginal well-being is best served with the funds available. The choice is largely between investing in staying or moving.

To this extent, these advisors' preference for one of the Indigenous Lifestyle choices, warrants careful deliberation. Equally, the relatively short life of many (not all) outback mines, needs realistic appraisal so that those with the 'mineral gravy-train view', look far enough ahead.

Planners also need to separate the emotion from the reality, when trying to reverse the long-established trend in population drift away from rural areas. The unemployment 'push factor' referred to earlier, cannot usually be remedied by government; it is driven largely by commercial market forces. Misplaced emotions, or the blame game, only serve to confuse those who actually have no sustainable future in the regions concerned. Sympathy with the inhabitants of dying rural communities makes emotive TV viewing, but does nothing to assist the locals. The equivalent in remote Aboriginal settlements, calls for even more understanding of complex social breakdown, far beyond unemployment. Under the circumstances, the advice that 'we must encourage the people to come back on country', can't be accepted at face value. The myth that evil

## CONVENIENT HALF-TRUTHS: REMOTE INFRASTRUCTURE INVESTMENT

urban destinations must be avoided in favour of the wholesome on-country alternative, has long since lost any traction, to the extent that at least in Aboriginal terms, the opposite is now often true. The Alice Springs town camps are an exception which beggars belief in this modern age.

The lesson for planners and advisors is: keep your options open, value flexibility highly, choose vision over expediency and in all priority-setting, make the requirements of the grandchildren your number one.

The risk of waste on inappropriately located infrastructure was again been highlighted by the $4 million Amata Substance Misuse Centre in South Australia which had no clients in its first seven months. Described by locals as an enormous white elephant staffed by people paid 'for doing bloody nothing', this most modern facility on APY lands is described by Jonathon Nicholls of Uniting Care Wesley as 'one of the finest pieces of infrastructure in a very disadvantaged community' but not used and a colossal waste of money. No doubt the State Department of Drug and Alcohol Services will be embarrassed into opening the facility for a range of uses, since being forced to respond to a damaging Federal report six months before.

## Message

Remote cost-effectiveness must be based on telecommunication and mobile service delivery. Large infrastructure investment reduces economic efficiency, leads to waste and it slows beneficial out-migration, while perpetuating geographic disadvantage.

# WHITEMAN DREAMING, BLACKMAN SCREAMING – A CONSIDERATION OF GARY JOHNS' 'ABORIGINAL SELF-DETERMINATION'

Johns' book (2011) had the potential to be a barbecue-stopper, particularly since it came out just as the Homelands movement and the cultural push, were giving new momentum to Aboriginal identity and peoplehood.

## OVERCOMING DISADVANTAGE

Among the significant points which Johns makes, three concepts stand out as the pillars of his philosophy:

1. Integration offers the only hope for Closing the Gap.
2. Separate development and self-determination have failed as policy objectives.
3. Economic integration doesn't demand that Aborigines leave their land, only that they become economically independent.

Back in 2008, Johns had doubted the efficacy of the Intervention when he wrote, 'Wicked problem or wicked policy?' Ever since, he has been asking whether the problem is actually that the preferred government solution to closing the gap is wrong. While he is right in claiming that many Aboriginal leaders 'misdiagnose their people's dilemma', Johns may be wrong to infer, as his sub-title does, that the Whiteman had this dream of Aboriginal separatism as a sort of generally-held mainstream view. He gives earlier missionaries and governments credit for protecting Aborigines and preparing them for the outside world, but he criticises these agencies for later 'abandoning their efforts in favour of self-determination'. History tells it somewhat differently and chronicles a patchy and contrary series of policies which usually give Nugget Coombs the blame/credit for encouraging the return back to traditional values and lifestyles.

Johns rightly denigrates the UN Indigenous Rights charter which purports to be some kind of remedy for the ills of the 'pathetic' remote communities. His insistence that it is not rights which they lack, but self-discipline and respectful behaviour, is supported by his judgement that, if other Australians showed prejudice, it was not against the race but against the bad behaviour and unacceptable norms. Only when the 'culture' offends common decency and/or the law, do outsiders usually draw the line.

Johns maintains that tribal Aboriginals no longer exist, a view which the Arnhemlanders and Tiwi Islanders would probably reject, depending on how purist the definition of 'tribal' is. He claims that entering the modern world would destroy their belief system – an outcome which many Aboriginal leaders would like to think, could be avoided. Johns seems to assume that an old culture cannot be modernised in a way which gives its adherents both the benefits of modernity and a pride in belonging to an ancient tradition. He appears to dismiss the benefits of 'taking the best from your past and building on it for the future'. He may be right of course, but many of us see cultural mores as guidelines to a grounded future, provided the un-helpful elements are dispatched to history.

The statement that: "all appeals to save the Aborigine in his original state, are doomed to fail", probably doesn't bring Johns into conflict with realistic Aboriginal leaders who recognise that Johns' 'pristine' society has had its day. Crucial to his argument on integration, is Johns' strong call for respect for Aboriginal culture and for their communities to take charge of their destiny. To the Aboriginal 'autonomy demands', he responds with his bombshell question: "What if this solution is the problem?" Johns challenges future capacity of the self-governing Aboriginal people to actually achieve well-being in a separate Indigenous Homeland setting. He accuses governments of being intellectually dishonest on this score and he maintains that it is the fear of being branded 'racist' that causes this lack of integrity.

Johns gives Galarrway Yunupingu both a plus and a minus for his insights – a plus for his observation that 'all around me are do-gooders and no-hopers', and a minus for wanting both the 'White man's economy and the Black man's culture'. The latter is an oxymoron in Johns' view, although he doesn't use this term. Wealth is not plucked or stolen, it is created, says Johns, when he infers that a non-traditional work ethic is required, rather than just a hope of another windfall. What he refers to as a *faux* culture and a *faux* economy, fall far short of the requirements of a sustainable modern society in Johns' estimation.

The push to recreate an Aboriginal society in remote Australia has led governments to condemn some 100,000 Aborigines to a 'living hell' claims Johns. Many leaders and politicians would probably prefer to play down the 'hellish mess' in the outback and seek support of those emerging little success stories in the Far North and the Cape. Sorting the realists from the idealists in this patchy situation is complex, but Johns' insistence that peer pressure usually smothers the few individuals who have enough initiative to seek a better life, is hard to fault.

It is important to note the change of policy in the Northern Territory, which allocates $160 million to the development of the Federal government's nominated 20 growth centres. These are to be financed by a $5.6 billion Federal infrastructure programme at the expense of closing 580 of the remaining small settlements, developed since the 1970's Homeland Movement. This centralisation is juxtaposed to the Yolngu People's submission to the Senate in 2010, which made a strong case against both moving and assimilation: "We strongly value our culture, law and links to country, and we do not regard our locational separation from the mainstream as equating to being disadvantaged". The report, "Working Futures: Remote Service Delivery" (2011), presented by the Northern Territory Minister for Indigenous Policy, Alison Anderson, and Pat Dodson's report on Homeland viability, should both help to settle this geographical conflict. If the Growth Centres Policy is perceived by the locals as another Stolen Generation or attempt at assimilation in the negative sense, more work lies ahead.

Johns' philosophy is based on his conviction that in their earlier tribal culture, Aborigines did not flourish, they just survived. He maintains that having to change and leave most of their traditions behind, should not be viewed as the tragedy which the cultural purists see it to be. On the contrary, cultural loss, he claims, "*is only a tragedy if what is given up is more valuable than what is gained*" (my emphasis). Johns doesn't say so, but I suspect he'd like to ask the up-and-coming generation to also make this same judgement.

"Part of the tragedy of the past 40 years is that the intelligentsia believed that what was given up *was* more valuable", claims Johns. He suggests that the big mistake of those who push separatism and cultural protectionism, is that they want it both ways for the Aboriginals – to be left alone and to receive the rewards of others' work.

Defending the indefensible must stop says Johns, for in his view, separatist traditionalism will kill many more Aborigines than the colonial forces ever did. "Why does the Left's 'social inclusion' exclude Aborigines?" asks Johns.

One reviewer of Johns' book has problems with Johns' general belligerent tone and his severe condemnation of just about everyone who has worked in Aboriginal Affairs. The reviewer judges Johns' outright rejection of traditional culture as excessive and unfair, and sees Johns' inadequate reference to the inhumane treatment of Aborigines in colonial times, as uncompassionate. In addition, Johns' failure to appreciate the Aboriginals' ideals of independence, identity and human rights, was seen by the reviewer as a fundamental weakness of his book. Johns' hardline ideological position was also seen as undermining the usefulness of his policy analysis.

The present author, while agreeing with Johns (and Sutton) that much of Indigenous culture has been over-valued, has taken a more conciliatory approach which rather encourages Aborigines to ask more questions about what is best for their grandchildren. His approach has been to encourage rather than denigrate, which is sometimes very difficult in an over-sensitised atmosphere in which expressing even the slightest doubt about cultural values can cause disproportionate attack from the purists claiming disrespect and even racism.

Let's hear it from the Indigenous leaders – where has Johns got it wrong?

## Message

It is not sufficient to be right when advising on ethnic futures. Without empathy and sensitivity, alternative cultural proposals lead to a retreat into, rather than an advance out of, encultured stagnation. People need to feel it's their idea to change, before they accept the need to change. No culture-bearers like to be told by outsiders what's wrong with their values.

# OUTBACK REFUGEES

The idea that Aboriginal families who make the conscious decision to move away from remote settlements, are in fact Migrants who are fleeing an unacceptable social situation, hasn't been grasped by many of our politicians. Rather than boat people, we have ute people who respond to the same push and pull factors as the overseas migrating families faced with a similar level of violence and personal persecution.

Compare the arrivals from Hopevale with the arrivals from Johannesburg; both reached the point where they valued more highly, those things that they are gaining by moving, than they valued those things which they were leaving behind. Both consciously forfeit the tribal home for the new home which offers a better future for their children. In both cases their move will cause a split in their families, an accusation of abandoning their ancestors and their tribe, and cause a claim that the leavers are neglecting their duty to help

## OVERCOMING DISADVANTAGE

improve the local clan situation. To break tribal ties, takes a conviction so deep that only the most self-confident can face the familial break, the cultural loss and friends' negative view of their move. I know this feeling.

It must be accepted that the movers have considered and decided on the futility of waiting for their local tribal situation to improve within a reasonable time – a time which perhaps unconsciously benefits the movers' children and grandchildren. In this way, the Hopevale resident is as realistic as the violence-threatened Jo'berger. Both have a strong enough sense of responsibility to their families, a sufficiently well-developed work ethic and the income-generating capacity to face the Open Society with confidence.

So the question must be asked whether in fact, it is the stayers not the movers who are letting the family and thus the tribe, down, albeit only at a later date. Clearly many stayers do not have the physical, mental or even financial capacity to move, and their situation warrants empathy not blame, but there are others who fail due to a self-imposed lack of will, which exhibits as a form of selfishness and irresponsibility. At the heart of migration, is the intangible and complex reality of that elusive sustainable community, which eventually divides the optimists from the pessimists. In this way the local pessimist is also the migratory optimist. When Moses decided to leave Egypt for the Promised Land with his mob, the same push and pull factors were probably at work.

So much for the theory of migration and its causes, but in practice the remote Aboriginal families are actually in a very different position from the Jo'burg Japie who meets all the criteria of a successful Migrant. The families from the Kimberley, Arnhemland, the Gulf or Cape York often, perhaps nearly always, aren't in a position psychologically, health-wise, skills-wise or financially, to even consider making the first move. Why? Because the accumulated disadvantage over generations has left them as uneducated, violent, abused and broken individuals – unskilled, illiterate and unmotivated – essentially unemployable.

So what to do? The argument that the town is safer than the bush settlements, or *vice versa*, misses the point that the real solution is removing the coming generation from what, too often, appears to be an incurably toxic environment. Such generational migration is in no way a 'stolen generation'. It could occur with un-pressured family approval, with good education as the key to ending the poverty cycle. When the situation is so dire that old women have to take it on themselves to blockade the community entry road against grog, then desperate measures are not only warranted but demanded. The alternative is for government to pretend it has the answer to the deadly accusation, "So you just let it continue and you fail in your responsibility to these children".

There are of course those who feel more than a little strongly about how beneficial some outstations have been. A good example is Dr Vicki Greeves who has made a comprehensive study of the Utopia Outstations in the Central Desert of the Territory. In the 1970s and 80s many Aboriginals were leaving the Territory towns, to escape the dysfunction which was increasing in fringe-dweller camps. In 1978 two tribes successfully claimed Utopia Station and the Elders decided that separate outstations were more appropriate to clan country settlement, than the development of a central town. By the mid-1980s, a total of 16 outstations provided 'home on country' for the Utopians.

Today there are about 10,000 people on Territory outstations, whom the government is attempting to socially engineer into 20 so-called 'growth towns' or regional centres. This transhumance policy arose largely from the official interpretation of the 2007 report 'Little Children are Sacred', which demonised the Homelands as 'repositories of toxic cultural practices' according to Greeves. This, she says is a nonsensical construction which undervalues the connection of people to country. Greeves is passionate about the fact that for over 40 years, the value of continuing to practice culture on country, has fallen on deaf ears in officialdom. Greeves asks why government doesn't respond to numerous research findings, starting with Prof Karen O' Dea's work in 1998, which clearly demonstrated the health benefits of the outstation lifestyle. She is especially critical of Minister Mal Brough's insistence that all outstations need to be closed down, and she asks the question: 'what will happen to land devoid of people?'. Greeves' reasoning on health benefits, is considerably more persuasive than her attempt to show how wealth-generation through eco-tourism and caring for country, could sustain the people. She is dismissive of those who suggest that outstations are too expensive to service, and that they encourage people to do nothing. She makes the important observation that there are great opportunities for growing food, but she doesn't concede that this initial goal could probably be more effectively achieved without outstations.

While it is pure coincidence that the name Utopia is juxtaposed to the Dystopia which is so tellingly used in comparative social constructions, Utopia's outstations must now be used as a national test-case of social well-being. Similarly, there is a need to evaluate Greeves' claim: "Many of us look to the Homelands as a source of cultural pride and the opportunity to live well on country". Presently, evidence supporting this view is both fragmented and contradictory.

## Message

Where individual families choose to live, should be left up to them. Coercion to remain in isolated settlements should be discontinued. The relative safety of the bush or the town is defined by behavioural norms, not geography. Outstations have limited specialised benefits and are very difficult to service effectively.

# SOME FAMILIES WENT TO TOWN – SO WHAT'S NEW?

Several years ago a South Australian academic came up with what is called a typology (or classification) of Indigenous families based on the extent to which some families move from settlements to join the mainstream for education and employment in urban settings. This was Maria Lane, who studied the way families migrated and formed new patterns of family structure. She ends up with five classes of families who are largely defined by their relative embodiment, work ethic and by their position (on a sliding scale) in higher education. Lane notes the increasing extent to which 'rising classes' gain self-respect and confidence, plus the prevalence of inter-marriage in these upwardly-mobile families.

Why is Lane's study important? Well frankly it is only being mentioned here because Pearson wants some of the Aboriginal academic 'elite' (such as Larissa Behrendt), to take note of Lane's findings – which surely are hardly a revelation, in fact have been generally known by most observers. The point Pearson is making is that the elite have lost contact with the desperate situation that the

## CONVENIENT HALF-TRUTHS: SOME FAMILIES WENT TO TOWN

'lower class' endure. If that embattled group didn't make up an estimated one third of the entire Aboriginal population, the position would be less urgent. What interests Pearson is the actual social process by which the movers and stayers tend to split the population.

Pearson allows himself some deep personal questioning like 'Am I perpetuating victimhood? Would I put my children through the solutions I propose for others? Do I have any justification for any double standard?' Here Pearson is dealing honestly with his personal soul-searching, which should be, but apparently isn't, characteristic of many Aboriginal intellectuals who leave their people behind in their aspirations. In Behrendt's case, she despises Bess Price, the Alice Springs Aboriginal leader who publicly supports the Intervention out of desperate practical necessity, not out of ideological fulfilment.

What Pearson seems to appreciate in Lane's social class analysis, is the record of Aboriginal individuals and families, who of their own accord since the 1940s moved from their settlements, took on menial work in town and left their next generation with an enviable legacy of education and a sound work ethic. From this, followed the family's continued insistence on good education as the basis for betterment.

So Pearson's heart-searching reflects a broader contemporary dilemma which should be, but probably isn't, felt by White leaders and policy-makers. The dilemma of moving ahead without losing identity, unfortunately does need a personal decision to re-define one's position on Lane's continuum, and this brings into play what sociologists refer to as 'readiness' – to move, to work, to be seen to be what some might see as abandoning one's roots.

In 1972 the present author, when visiting the Territory, used the opportunity of meeting Harry Giese, a leading NT politician in Darwin, to discuss alternative futures for the Aboriginals. At that time, Aborigines had only enjoyed formal Australian citizenship for five years and Giese had been studying the progress with Apartheid in South Africa. He could see a local need for both reserves and out-migration of those wishing to join the national workforce. In 1972, the mob led by Vincent Lingiari off Wave Hill station were still camped by the roadside, with a White female spokesperson ready to parley with passing visitors, including the author.

With this background, it is interesting to read Galarrwuy Yunupingu's recent account of how in the early 1960s his father had heard Giese (then Protector of Aborigines, NT) tell the mob gathered at Yirrkala store, that their families would be moved to make way for mining. Today the people of the region have signed up with Rio Tinto in an agreement which promises their children 'real education for real jobs and a real future'. In addition, a new Aboriginal mining company, with its own bauxite lease, was being established. In Yunupingu's words, "Our local communities today are fragile and a signature on a piece of paper will not fix that. But hard work and *targeting the needs of individuals will give each individual a chance*" (my emphasis). At last we recognise the primacy of the individual over the community.

## Message

Moving the focus from communal to individual motivation is the most important driver of family progress. The dead hand of the lowest common denominator must be removed, so that individuals with initiative are not held back. The first responsibility is to self, not the mob, and self-interest remains the prime change-initiator.

# BESS SETS THE RECORD STRAIGHT ON CULTURE

The spat between one of the Indigenous academic elite and Bess (Nungarrayi) Price after Bess publicly supported the NT Intervention on ABC's Q&A programme in early 2011, opened up an important debate among Indigenous policy-makers. The interpretations which others put on Bess's support for the Intervention, include accusations that she is assimilationist and supports the denial of human rights.

Critics need to understand that Bess is one of 11 children and her mother outlived eight of Bess's siblings. In one week, Bess's sister-in-law died of stab wounds in the Town Camp, a stepson was killed in an accident and her 14-year-old niece suicided at an Intervention community.

In her support for the Intervention, Bess states that she wants Indigenous children to 'live free of the fear of sorcery, of violence'. She wants men and

## CONVENIENT HALF-TRUTHS: BESS SETS THE RECORD STRAIGHT

women to be equal and she wants traditional culture to change so that Indigenous kids 'have what other Australian kids have'. What Bess doesn't want, is for city dwellers who call themselves Indigenous but live lives indistinguishable from other Australians, 'to tell us that our kids can't have these things because, in the words of the latest Amnesty International Indigenous representative to visit us, "It's all about staying on country and keeping culture and language". Bess says she wants to deal with the remote realities, not urban myths. Far from seeing the Open Society as a threat to her people, Bess sees it as a potential saviour from their Remote Hellholes.

Bess's husband, Dave Price, insists that it is now time for 'honest and intelligent debate' on the place of tradition and culture in future policy formulation. He quotes the telling story of where young girls stand today under the law: "In this country a 14-year-old girl can be threatened with a shot gun and raped by a middle-aged promised husband, and hear the judge tell the court that the accused didn't know that what he did was against the law; and another [girl] tell the court that she knows what to expect as a promised wife". This, says Dave Price, is the factual position, but what is of equal importance to him, is that there is not a peep from feminists, human rights advocates or the UN. Why the deafening silence, he asks: "Don't these moral crusaders want protection for the powerless?"

Dave Price states categorically: "We don't believe that Australian citizens have the right to use their un-earned taxpayer-funded income to destroy themselves and their families". He and Bess deal with hundreds of people from the Town Camps and from remote communities. They find that most of those with a responsibility for children, do support income management, stronger policing, alcohol restrictions, improved housing and other infrastructure being provided by the Intervention. According to Price, a survey by the Central Land Council found that over 50% of Aborigines 'supported the Intervention', some seeing the Basics Card (for food) as the saving of their families. However, Paddy Gibson, a local spokesman, claims that this 50% support, doesn't hold up when the individual questions asked, are analysed. He reports that 85% opposed the imposition of five-year home leases, 94% opposed the abolition of the permit system (allowing outsiders into communities), 78% opposed the scrapping of CDEP (dole work) and only 17% were happy with the performance of their government business manager. Gibson admits that the 50% approval could refer to the income management element of the Intervention, but claims that spending $105M on administration of the $150M fund of Centrelink funds in 2010/11, is a disgraceful waste. Clearly this assessment of the Intervention still has a long way to go.

Northern Territory politics has been spiced up in recent times by the registration and activation of the First Nations political party. The grandson of Vincent Lingiari, who famously led the walk-off at Victoria River, collected 10 times the number of signatures required to register a new party. Maurie Japarta Ryan, leader of the FN, managed to gain 3% of the vote in the NT's 2007 election and he predicted a place in future Territory politics for that 40% of the Territory's population who are Indigenous.

Unless Ryan gets a better reception by Aboriginal voters than the Congress of Australia's First Peoples did (where only 600 of its 2000 members voted for its leadership candidates in 2011) he may find that his people don't value his separatist politics as highly as he does.

## Message

Communities should desist from attacking their forward-looking members for being assimilationists when urgent change in norms is called for. Staying on country and keeping culture, must always remain subservient to giving children maximum opportunities. Promising young girls to middle-aged men must stop.

# THE NATIONAL ABORIGINAL CONGRESS

The 'readiness' idea was sorely tested when the inaugural National Aboriginal Congress (officially, Congress of Australia's First Peoples) held its first meetings in 2011. This new body arose out of the ruins of ATSIC, its predecessor, which despite Lowitja O'Donoghue's gallant chairmanship, allowed male arrogance and corruption to overtake the noble goals of ATSIC. The structure of the new Congress was set by government, it has no decision-making powers, no service delivery responsibilities or detailed objectives. Such constraints must have convinced most well-informed potential leaders to withhold their nomination as joint Chairman. So the Congress ends up with Les Malezer, a full-time representative on the UN Indigenous Rights Working Group for most of the past decade, as Congress Co-Chairman. His first move was to recommend abolishing the other Co-chair position so that he can lead the Congress agenda on his first priority, Indigenous Rights.

All Australians of good will would have wished the new Congress well, in the hope that the Aboriginal people agree on clear objectives and procedures for extracting that third of their people who still live in remote misery. Unfortunately, this goodwill was nipped in the bud even before the first meeting. Why? Because few believe that the structure, responsibilities and personalities at the top, carry any committed credibility for the task at hand. At that time, everyone was asking the same questions: who didn't stand for election and why not? Who did stand and what was the voting? More importantly perhaps is, why all the general pessimism? What drives the cynics, and isn't it just another negative beat-up by The Australian newspaper?

The answer may be found in the long list of precedents, recent inter-tribal spats and personal conflicts. At the heart of the early scepticism were the intractable conflicts which arise from race-based politics when the solutions are clearly needs-based and not race-based. At the centre of the confusion was the Indigenous lobby's non-acceptance of individuals' freedom to choose a new life for their offspring. It is the individuals' prerogative to choose something which they value higher than that which they are leaving behind. It is not for the culture vultures to insist that individuals have a duty to respect their ancestors by remaining on clan country. There is a religious parallel here – in the form of the inferred obligation for children to follow the spiritual convictions of the parents, but without the threat of hellfire damnation. Today's mobile working class largely dismiss the ancestral obligation as another myth, which while respected by the old folks, needn't, shouldn't and doesn't, leave the movers with any feeling of loss – on the contrary, it fulfils their new obligation to their children.

With Les Malezer and Jodie Broun as co-leaders of the new Indigenous peak body, we had a clash of the Titans waiting to happen. Warren Mundine and Noel Pearson sought a migration of their people to Lane's Open Society through serious attention to education, training, health and housing, while Malezer opposed the Intervention and focused on Land Rights and Self-determination. Broun wanted Congress to attend to broader issues like climate change. Is it any wonder the public were asking what such priorities do for the beaten-up and abused families in the bush? And they added: 'Thank God Congress has no actual powers'. The Congress had 2000 eligible voters of whom only 600 voted to elect Malezer and Broun. The Coalition of the day initially opposed the establishment of the Congress but later supported the concept of this body, set up in 2011 as a company to carry its own running costs after being funded for its establishment by a Federal allocation of $29.2 million for the first five years only.

It will help the process of gaining well-being through participation in the Open Society, if some of the most vociferous activists stop exaggerating their Aboriginality and being Stolen, and get on with the job of helping the multicoloured disadvantaged to become modern Australians. At the same time, nobody expects the 'campaign Aboriginals' to stop playing their racial game until the prevailing inducements and incentives are removed.

It is hoped that the National Indigenous Women's Alliance (NATSIWA) will play a major role in driving not only the gender agenda but the broader agenda of the new Congress. The 120 member Congress had early difficulty being accepted as being properly representative of the people who form its constituency. This can be sorted out in time, meanwhile most observers were calling for a fair inaugural period of the new organisation before writing it off as unrepresentative, toothless and government-designed. A special effort was made to ensure an appropriate gender balance in the organisation's three sub-structures, and past experience pointed strongly to the need for empowered women to contribute strongly to Congress recommendations to government. As the first Indigenous national body set up as a private company responsible for its own on-going funding, stakeholders watched with anticipation how Congress would fare after its seeding-funds ran out.

If the author could be allowed just one prediction on the future of the new Congress, it would concern irreconcilable conflict over objectives – on who we aim to be. In the end, the lack of agreement will probably be on the extent to which policy and action, aim to produce a separate, self-governing ethnic group strong on traditional values and customs, dealing only in culturally-appropriate employment and educating their children to speak their tribal language while practising their law and medicine.

Let us hope that the modernists are able to dissuade the culturists from a retreat to traditionalism at an early date in the life of the Congress. Such a victory for common sense could lead to an early demise of the Congress as a private company and save everyone from an unseemly personal power-play, in which monetary benefit for individuals can be eliminated early in the life of this artificial government-inspired structure.

## Message

Recognise that the educated urban dwellers have little in common with isolated uneducated Aboriginals. Appreciate that the priorities of dysfunctional communities are mostly survival actions to reduce violence and improve health. The National Congress on present evidence, is unlikely to improve well-being faster than the planned decadal COAG program will.

# POLITICAL TRAPS FOR INDIGENOUS PLAYERS

Mick Gooda and his Social Justice Commission didn't come to the negotiating table as political babes-in-the-wood. No, they are well versed in the cut-and-thrust of bureaucratic manoeuvring and polispeak. They had little option but to accept the Federal government's conditions that their Commission and its associated Congress, have no decision-making or service responsibilities. The Commission had to deal with a Labour government that inherited the controversial Intervention, which despite modifications still only produced minimal beneficial outcomes for the inhabitants of the toxic non-communities concerned. Real communities are committed to work toward the common good.

Successive Federal governments have avoided decisions on autonomy, self-government and independence. Equally, governments have not responded to calls for Native Title on freehold land. Much policy-making in Indigenous Affairs reflects a guilt complex which causes avoidance of any semblance of persecuting the victims. This growing fear in turn, has led to a plethora of short-term 'make-work' projects aimed at immediate employment in remote communities. It would be instructive to explore the details of project spending and outcomes achieved over the past two decades. In addition, it would be useful to examine the vision and broader structural goals which assumedly formed the framework for these project investments.

It would be churlish for critics to expose what appears to be a lack of direction and of basic convictions on policy goals, without acknowledging the complexity of Indigenous Affairs and without offering clear alternative policies. Nevertheless the need for clear agreed objectives is not only increasingly urgent but long overdue. What is required is not more motherhood statements which by definition defy opposition, but well-crafted details of settlement policy and modernisation procedures. These should include clear statements on rights and responsibilities of urban Aborigines as well as the governance and economic basis of Homeland communities.

The danger for the Rudd/Gillard years (2007-2013) was that the minority government would act even less decisively than its majority predecessors. Politically, Aboriginal policy draws considerably less public comment than several other popular sectors of Australia's politics, notably Gay Rights, Illegal Immigration and Boatpeople. Why is this? Essentially the apathy toward Aboriginal issues stems from their not being perceived as either a national threat or as an issue of potential national benefit. For many mainstreamers, the repeated reports of remote dysfunction and the lack of return on investment, have become both tiresome and a turnoff. They do not understand why Aboriginals don't seem to do what everyone else does – grab the opportunities offered and make your own luck. They diminish the significance and complexity of post-colonial trauma and social adaptation, and they generally see little real value in cultural preservation. In their simplistic view, the Aboriginals should get over it and get on with it, stop the hatred and complaints, and recognise that most Australians are having more than a hard time financially.

In this situation, it is difficult to see what approach the Social Justice Commission can develop to get its concerns on the national agenda. Some would argue that with $4.6 billion already committed, public debate is hardly necessary. What is necessary is public transparency on the operational objectives, future outcomes and economic plan for Aboriginal lands.

If the Australian mainstream are to get behind Aboriginal progress and to get value for their taxes, they need maps, business plans and production predictions. Unlike some minorities elsewhere, there is no cry for liberty, no threat of suicide bombing and no risk to public utilities from Aboriginal activists. Action on Indigenous well-being is thus driven solely by moral imperative, with few triggers for urgent action other than humanitarian obligation.

## Message

Ethnicity is a poor basis for choices on personal well-being. Over-emphasis on Aboriginality and claim to special treatment based on race, demeans capable individuals who seek only equitable opportunity, not race-based support.

# THE INDIGENOUS PRESS – STEPHEN HAGAN'S EDITORIAL EFFORT

Over the years, several bold attempts have been made to bring Indigenous views to the general public through targeted reporting in newspapers such as Koori Mail and others.

In 2011 we had Stephen Hagan's National Indigenous Times, published fortnightly with a circulation of 10,000 copies 'linking, empowering and advocating' by and for Indigenous people. It was then in its 223rd edition. NIT claimed to receive no government funding although all its advertisers except one, were government-funded bodies. Hagan stated that his editorial philosophy was 'that Australians can and should work together towards a common goal' – hardly reflected in Hagan's earlier infamous attempt to single-handedly appeal to the United Nations to force the Toowoomba authorities to remove the 'Nigger Brown' nameplate from the local rugby league grandstand. Nigger was in fact a very popular blonde, White rugby star who wore his quirky nickname with pride. This didn't stop Hagan ignoring the considered opinion of many of his fellow Aboriginals, including the late great Artie Beetson, that his trumped-up indignation was an embarrassing storm in a teacup.

Undaunted, Hagan also found it politic to publicly attack Andrew Forrest, owner of Fortescue Metals, for the way he had gone about the agreement on mining the Yindjibarndi land around Roebourne in Western Australia. Forrest's offer of $4 million in cash and $6 million in training annually, was derided by Hagan as "just another attempt at White assimilation"! The preservation of culture on the proposed mining leases, turned out to run a rather poor second to the alleged offer of 10 times Forrest's momentary offer, from the competing Rio Tinto Mining Company.

Against a background of Forrest's widely applauded Australian Employment Covenant, launched by Prime Minister Rudd in 2008, Hagan's attack on Forrest went down like a lead balloon. The Covenant had the ambitious goal of creating 50,000 new full-time jobs for Indigenous Australians nationwide. Out of the Covenant grew Generation One, a vibrant modern programme of youth encouragement for Indigenous people, including luminaries like Warren Mundine and Tania Major (Young Australian of the Year).

Hagan sided with the landowners who were demanding four times the Forrest offer, in line with other companies' offers in nearby Kimberley mines, accusing Forrest of attempting to con the locals by rigging the decisive Meeting of Approval at Roebourne. Hagan had set himself up, in a long and well-researched investigative piece in his own newspaper, as the saviour of his people, from the evil industrialists whom he perceived as manipulating the apparent support from the locals.

This case looked like going to the High Court but was an important real-life example of the complexities which arise when culture meets capitalism in a situation where one culture discovers vast resources which were of no value to the other and were actually owned by the State.

Strange as it may seem, Hagan's personal rejection of Aboriginal culture for his own family's well-being, is used by Gary Johns as an example of how informed individuals choose to opt out. Johns quotes Hagan as saying, "I re-prioritised my personal and family goals. I took those decisions knowing they were directly opposed to…. the shallow expectations of my extended family and friends…. This process was quite painful, as I stopped lending money to family and friends…. and declined requests for them to bunk down for the night at my residence…. It nevertheless gave me complete confidence to provide uncompromising safety and financial security for my family....". Johns says that later as editor, Hagan preferred to 'play the culture card' and to keep up appearances as a 'radical Black'.

The Hagan case is quoted here only because it personifies the experience of thousands of ex-tribal Aborigines who have reneged on their relatives for the well-being of their own families. In Hagan's case, the change in lifestyle is exaggerated by his tendency as a contrarian, to seek conflict and feed his ego by playing the central martyr role, defending his carefully selected oppressed mob and playing the Indigenous Rights card to the fullest. One is left wondering how his rejected homeless and penniless relatives feel about their rights and his obligations.

Hagan was however, big enough to give airtime to Letters to the Editor which ran counter to his personal biases. He presented both Johns' critical letter and one from Jerry Georgatos whose research on deaths in custody shows that 82% of deaths in custody are non-Indigenous, giving a total of 3,656 deaths in Australian jails between 1980 and 2010, a figure which Georgatos says is quite unacceptable. Never-the-less Aboriginal deaths made up 18% of all deaths, which was six times their proportion (3%) of the Australian population.

Hagan also reported that the 350 Aboriginals employed by Forrest's Fortescue Metals averaged salaries of $70,000 per annum, which was well above the Australian average salary of $52,213.20 (Average of Public and Private sector employees as at Feb, 2011 - Australian Bureau of Statistics).

In a long editorial in the National Indigenous Times, Hagan headed the piece 'Writing Aboriginal History' and described himself as a Person of the Year and multi-award-winning author and filmmaker. In what comes across as an unabashed case of Relevance Deficit, he tells us how other tribal Elders robbed his father of his claim to Native Title land near Cunnamulla and how the Land Council "kicked his father out of his tribe". Hagan then uses sloppy grammar to tell us, "I'm currently writing my Ph.D. as well as two other fiction books (!). How does a boy born in a fringe camp.... find himself 51 years later as an award-winning author and now editor of a national newspaper?", he asked. Hagan writes of how he declined the offer by both his lawyer and his wife, to write his life-story, but he lists all the books he's written. "We must be cognizant in telling our stories and exposing the truth, that we do not perpetuate racism…."(!). Hagan refers to Gary Johns' book on Self-Determination as "….this palpably insensitive book that has out-rednecked all racially intolerant authored works before it."

The above may seem harsh criticism, but the NIT was probably the most useful medium for debating Indigenous values and futures. Although its influence was significantly reduced by the discontinuation of its 'Letters to the Editor' in 2013. NIT has since moved online and still offers a useful service.

## Message

A national Aboriginal press can play a useful role if its editorials and opinion pieces reflect intellectual honesty and encourage individuals to modernise. The way in which this press reflects on tradition and future well-being, will determine its positive influence as change-agent.

# LET'S BE HONEST: GUILT HAS DRIVEN INDIGENOUS POLICY

Perhaps it is not clear to government yet, that policy which has as its main driver, the confected appearance of not oppressing the disadvantaged, is most unlikely to encourage internal migration into the mainstream. When conservative politicians are criticised for using terms like the 'Aboriginal Industry', the 'Guilt Industry' or 'Professional Aboriginals', the critics usually play the old 'blame the victim' trick. When Pauline Hanson claims to be Indigenous by virtue of her birth, the self-righteous mixed-blood activists cried out in horror. In this way the body politic has taken on almost sacred meanings of terms which play on the Whiteman's guilt. This is not the Whiteman's burden as the colonial Christians put it, but the guilt by generational association and the purist's idea that all the ills of present-day Aboriginals were caused by the Whiteman's forebears. This leaves the Australian Migrant population somewhat miffed as to whether they too have a cross to bear in all this finger-pointing. Somehow the Migrants don't seem to be credited with the fact that many of them fled oppression.

In a strange kind of way, the recent pride taken by White Australians in their convict ancestry, has produced a model for Aborigines to boast their mixed ancestry. After 200 years of ignoring and even hiding their convict connections, the pride which group martyrism brings, has produced a flood of genealogical enquiries to the well-advertised convict database. (The author must admit to a similar inner feeling, when learning of the pirate Black Jack Roberts, scourge of the high seas and hanged by the British in West Africa).

Slowly, but not so surely, the present generation of Aborigines are finding, recognising and appreciating their mixed heritage. So, whereas it had become customary for Blackfellas to emphasise their Aboriginal ancestors and not give the Whitefella ancestors an airing, times are a-changing and dark individuals with great-grandfather's of oppressed Irish or Scottish stock, are starting to give credit where credit is due. Stan Grant is a case in point.

These days DNA tests can identify the percentage of inter-racial genes in all of us and of course, these tests can play havoc with family trees, through proving new fatherhoods – a painful process for the offspring of enculturated ancestors. We now have an opportunity to find the truth and take pride in proving racial hybridisation, a process which invariably benefits the 'less-developed' bloodline.

## Message

Take personal pride in your ancestors; value individuals for their unique attributes. Seek universal goodness, irrespective of heritage, and value hybrid vigour.

# INDIGENOUS PLANNERS IGNORE NOEL PEARSON AT THEIR PERIL

Predictably, a people with no experience of democracy for the common good above clan level, has produced a number of very independent spokespersons. All of these largely self-assertive leaders, have the well-being of the Indigenes as their general objective. Unfortunately, this is where agreement seems to end. The problem of gaining consensus of goals and policies appears to centre on differential visions of the desired lifestyle aimed at. The most serious disagreements seem to be in the sphere of tradition and culture, more particularly in their role of influencing the extent to which mainstreaming (going White?) and the associated modernisation of Aboriginal culture, could or should determine the people's values and lifestyles.

In simple terms, leadership philosophies may be contrasted as modernists and traditionalists. In practice, there is a continuum of cultural intensity between these extremes, reflecting varying degrees of reluctance to leave tradition behind and move toward universal humanitarian values and lifestyles. The reasons for leaders' differences in vision are important, since they reflect basic interpretations of history, rights and victimhood.

Over the past two decades, Indigenous spokespersons have usually identified either with community Elders, or with educated city-based groups. Over the years, names such as Perkins, Langton, Yunupingu, Mundine, Dodson, O'Donoghue, Clark and Robinson were regularly reported in the press or seen on television. The great divide came between the realists, who accepted the inevitability of mainstreaming with its future benefits for well-being, and those idealists or captives of culture who seemed determined to maintain strong cultural identity and all its traditional behaviours, especially on country.

Since the mid-1960s Noel Pearson has slowly gained a broad-based but reluctant, recognition from both camps of leadership, based on his unusual ability to combine a number of talents. His Lutheran upbringing had developed his respect for the work ethic and Christian values. At boarding school he used his innate intelligence to compete intellectually, then he studied Law at Sydney University before completing his Articles at Liebler's legal firm, and being given his first public service job by Kevin Rudd in the Goss government.

Sutton, in his book, 'The Politics of Suffering' describes how Pearson held beach meetings with Cape Elders, then formed the Cape York Land Council with personal contributions from conference-goers in Townsville.

The question needs to be asked, why today all political parties and most intellectuals, quote Pearson as the most appropriate authority on Indigenous policy. Tony Abbott taught in Pearson's Cape York schools, Jenny Macklin supported Pearson's finance management scheme and Peter Beattie thought Pearson was the only one who had sensible ideas on Indigenous futures.

## CONVENIENT HALF-TRUTHS: PLANNERS AND NOEL PEARSON

One of the more insightful observers of Pearson's Cape York Agenda, is Ernest Hunter. As a medico with vast experience of Aboriginal health in Northern Australia, Hunter recognises the gap, not only between Aborigines' and Non-Aborigines' health, but also between remote and urban communities. Hunter has worked for many years among the Cape York communities, which Pearson is attempting to uplift. Before that, Hunter undertook a remarkable study in the Kimberley, on trends in Aboriginal suicide. In the 60's there was 1 suicide, in the 70's there were 4, in the 80's, 21 and in the 90s, 46. Hunter then traced the fate of those selected Aboriginal boys who attended an enlightened boarding school in a Kimberley town. He does not give the numbers of ex-boarding school suicides, but Hunter suggests that whereas the male : female suicide ratio was 2:1 in the overall Kimberley population, the shift in ratio to 4:1 among the school boarders reflects greater vulnerability of boys and lower vulnerability of girls. The boarder boys were at greater suicidal risk when returning to their dysfunctional communities, probably because of conflict regarding their role, and apathy within the community toward both the scholastic achievements and the broader values of their 'returning enlightened boys'. The girls, in turn, had probably learned self-respect and protective confidence allowing them to handle conflict better.

Indigenous Australians made up 26% (7600 individuals) of the National prison population, but only 2.5% of Australia's entire population, according to the 2011 report of the Australian Institute of Health and Welfare. Noel Gillespie, CEO of the Aboriginal Land Rights Movement, believes that the percentage of incarcerated is nearly 40, a proportion which had increased by over 50% in the past decade. (In fact 1,248 per 100,000 adults, to 1,892 in 2010). Gillespie identifies four reasons for this high incarceration rate:

1. Over-policing and targeting of Aboriginals
2. Social disadvantage and marginalisation
3. Entrenched and systematic racism in society
4. The cumulative effects of racism during school and early adult years

The present situation is an 'appalling indictment' of the justice system, reflecting a worsening of race relations since pre-Howard years, according to Gillespie. He cites the non-implementation of the 300 recommendations of the Royal Commission into Aboriginal Deaths in Custody, as the crux of present problems and he maintains that government statements that 'the issues are too complex to correct', simply reflect insufficient analysis and action by the authorities. To the outsider, Gillespie's indictment of the justice system, based on incarceration rates, appears to excuse the Indigenous community and its leaders, of any responsibility in maintaining social norms – as such, Gillespie seems to almost encourage bad behaviour.

The Minister for Mental Health in 2011, informed the public that suicide accounted for 4.2% of Aboriginal deaths nationwide and 1.5% of Non-Aboriginal deaths. The $274 million program titled 'Taking Action to Tackle Suicide' included $22.6 million for the component called 'Supporting Communities to Reduce Risk of Suicide' and also included access to Allied Psychological Services. The publicity given to the serious suicide rate in the Kimberley was central to these enhanced services, which now operate in partnership with the Aboriginal Medical Service.

Hunter's characterisation of himself as a non-Indigenous service provider within Pearson's Cape York Agenda, 'near the end of his career and not having the answer to remote dysfunction', undersells his important insights. As an empathetic medical practitioner specialising in mental health, Hunter recognises the extent to which traditional and historic factors mitigate against economic viability. In admitting that he doesn't know how to break the cycle of dysfunction, Hunter challenges others who profess to have social-engineering answers: "I think more experts who claim to have the answers should 'fess up that they don't." He recognises important differences between dying rural towns in regional Australia and toxic Indigenous settlements, suggesting that non-Indigenous rural people have both the capacity and the motivation to move when the economic viability of their Shire declines, but that Aborigines usually lack both these employment drivers.

Geographic mobility is not the same as creating viable remote settlements in Hunter's view, but he seems at odds with Gary Johns' insistent solution of 'moving and integrating' as the only solution to remote poverty and social disintegration. He hopes leaders like Noel Pearson and Bess Price can succeed in developing well-being in remote settlements, even if this requires nearly half the population orbiting out of their home country for education and employment. Hunter prefers Pearson's positivism to Nicolas Rothwell's negativism, but the reader gets the distinct impression that deep down he probably doesn't think remote communities will work as economic entities. He fears that the emphasis on good education will 'see a drift of the brightest young Aboriginal adults away from remote communities'. Hunter seems to regard this as a bad thing, and it is at this point that his philosophy parts from that of Johns and the present author. The sooner Pearson qualifies his orbiting concept, to apply only to communities with a reliable local economic base, the sooner agreement can be reached to avoid wasted investment and dashed hopes, in what will almost certainly become permanent rural ghettos that have no future as acceptable domestic habitats with a viable economic base.

So why is Hunter treated at such length in this analysis of Pearson's vision? Because he epitomises that rare breed of admirable professionals who have sacrificed more rewarding careers because of their sheer humanity. In addition, he acts as an exemplar of those dedicated specialists who focus so intently on what they do well, that they develop only a belated grasp of the big picture and the virtually vision-free policy framework within which they labour. This lack of clear objectives and agreement on the goals of Aboriginal policy, together with vague conceptions of what separate development implies for well-being, is precisely what the present author has identified as the key to implementing real and comprehensive betterment programs.

Hunter claims that the difference between Pearson and other Indigenous leaders is that Pearson has embraced a much more all-encompassing vision for his people. In particular he is the only leader, including government leaders, who has developed comprehensive policy which covers all three Pillars of Vision:

1. Development of an *intellectual framework* for social policy, based partly on the work of Nobel laureate Amartya Sen on individual capability enhancement.
2. Harnessing the *political will* to drive progressive change – a will which is too often lacking in other would-be initiators.
3. Providing what Hunter calls the '*Indigenous imprematur*' which gave traction to the welfare reform program in Cape York.

It has long been recognised that the Aboriginal birth rate is significantly higher than the national average. The Department of Health's 2009 report states that Aboriginal women's fertility has steadily increased since 1996. In

2009 their fertility rate averaged 2.57 babies per woman, compared with 1.9 babies for all Australian women of child-bearing age. The number of babies born to Indigenous teenage mothers, was five times the general Australian teenage rate: 7.9% of Aboriginal teenage females gave birth, compared to 1.7% for all teenage females in 2009. The rates of out-of-home care of children, i.e. officially removed from their families, was 10 times higher for Indigenous children than for others. Pearson uses the statistic of 80 children per month taken into custodial protection in Cape York, as a clarion call for action in this nominal regional population of 13,000 Aborigines.

Dr Loretta Kelly, an Indigenous senior lecturer at Gnibi College of Southern Cross University, has made a detailed study of 'closing the gap' in women's health and well-being. She suggests that Australia needs to take the UN Declaration of the Rights of the Child (1959) much more seriously, if Indigenous children are to benefit from the level of care that they deserve. This means less emphasis on Indigenous Rights and more focus on the children, who should be placed with those families who can best look after them.

Pat Anderson, a respected co-author of the 'Little Children are Sacred' report and later, chair of the Lowitja Institute in Melbourne, maintains that disempowerment and social exclusion have powerful negative effects on Indigenous health. It is on these grounds that she is critical of the Intervention in both its Coalition and Labour forms. She maintains that research 'with us and by us' is now regarded as best practice. Having been chair of the CRC for Aboriginal Health for seven years, Anderson has a particularly good grasp of the crucial role of lifestyle and behaviour in Indigenous health. As with Pearson, she maintains that all policies aimed at reducing disadvantage will fail if they don't increase Aborigines' capacity to take control of their lives. It is surprising that a committed individual with Anderson's grasp of the health situation doesn't make a strong case for removal of children from toxic violent family situations and emphasise the need to break the poverty cycle through educational mobility.

In all his early public pronouncements, Pearson had forever been careful to stress that he speaks of Cape York. He doesn't claim to speak for all the people on the Cape and he makes a point of not pretending to represent other Indigenous regions. He knows the sensitivity of regional tribalism, but at the same time his well-balanced grasp of global humanitarian values, often makes his proposals not only relevant but also most appropriate for many other regions' clan country issues.

Originally the Aborigines inhabited the whole country, then they were limited to reserves, then Land Rights gave back sections of their country and finally today they seek sustainable Homelands. 'Sustainable' has come to mean able to become permanently economically independent, which implies that those Native Title areas which cannot develop sufficient income generation, probably don't have a future as community hubs and should be run as any other outback property, in economic terms.

Pearson estimates that in Cape York, probably some 40% of his people will have to find their employment and thus their future, elsewhere. His hope is that by 'orbiting' back to their original communities, they can contribute to their well-being and maintain links to country. This issue of migrant labour needs to be built into the socio-economic planning for Cape York, Western Australia and the Territory without delay, if the heartache that comes from unplanned rural slums is to end.

The ongoing debate about whether the 'Bush or Town' situations are worse for families, won't end until it is recognised that when desperate and hopeless people move, they often take their poverty cycle with them. In other words, geography does not determine well-being – so the violent, uneducated and unemployed youth of the Alice Springs camps cause similar unrest in both town or the bush. Pearson recognises this in his efforts to break the cycle with education as the vehicle. As Martin Luther King said: "Don't ask a bootless man to pull himself up by his bootstraps."

Pearson has been critical of the debilitating effects of paternalism in past policy, but he also believes that in fact, there often is a place for paternalistic approaches where community mores have collapsed and value-free behaviour has taken hold of dysfunctional communities. Hunter says that Pearson occupies a 'lonely space' in which someone had to lay it on the line, and state the obvious, that "dissonance is critical to change", i.e. no dissatisfaction, no change. Pearson is perhaps the only one of his mob who is intellectually honest enough to say it as it is – of the people, for the people. In doing this he gets the cultural traditionalists offside, despite his strong call for Indigenous languages to be taught in schools.

In his approach to education, Pearson avoids the politics of envy, the claim of elitism and the us-and-them division, so often heard from others. Pearson embraces the values and behavioural norms taught at Australia's great private boarding schools and even spends his own money in sending selected individuals to gain such educational benefits.

The whole question of the timespans of delayed gratification, is writ large in both the climate change debate and in the sphere of self-improvement within Aboriginal communities. In an unexpectedly mathematical analysis of solving addiction problems, Pearson builds on the approach of the psychiatrist George Ainslie. In essence, this approach distinguishes between two mathematical curves reflecting change trends. In human adaptation terms, this comparison reflects on the biological responses to change, of individual personalities who gain short term or long term personal benefits.

It has no doubt occurred to many observers, that 'delayed gratification' is a concept central to the solution of both climate and drug addiction problems. The basic assumption is, of course, that the human race is worth saving – a concept which can never be challenged despite the fact that cosmologically, this assumption probably doesn't stand up as a necessary 'given' in universal futures driven by the physical laws of the cosmos.

In the above paper, Pearson makes heavy work of his exponential and hyperbolic curves, to explain why mere mortals tend to prefer the earlier, if smaller, rewards for appropriate behaviour. The 'hyperbolic discounting' apparently means that most of us are less sensitive to delays in rewards which lie far into the future – like death and cooler climate.

His critics might remark that Pearson's grandmother could have told him that, but the concept remains useful in understanding how we may avoid damaging personal choices, notably in drinking, eating and smoking. These are some of the things which Pearson wants action on, for the well-being of his people. Pearson does have a tendency to dress common sense up as deep philosophic truth, which is why he likes to quote the classics, like his reference to Aristotle who had a word for what we might call greed – *akrasia*, meaning weakness of will, which Pearson translates as 'self-defeating behaviour'.

An attack by Pearson on environmentalists in 2011, contained a number of concepts of importance to Indigenous carbon negotiators. In essence Pearson laid the blame for the subsequent, almost violent, polarisation of the voters, squarely at then-PM Gillard's feet – 'never were reforms prosecuted so ineptly'.

## CONVENIENT HALF-TRUTHS: PLANNERS AND NOEL PEARSON

The 'political chaos which has been unleashed' has resulted in 'a policy question, arising in the realm of science and reason, being debated in the realm of belief and medieval superstition by both leaders and citizens'.

With all the frustration he has built up as a result of Green preferences stymieing his push for development of declared Wild River catchments in Cape York, Pearson sees the local citizenry now given the choice between putting the environment or the economy first, with little attention to ecologically sustainable development (ESD).

Pearson's penchant for wordsmithing comes to the fore when he describes the opposing carbon tribes: "the regressive nature and direction of the contemporary debates are debased by antediluvian obscurantism on one side and millenarian Gaiaism on the other"! Pearson suggests that both sides are at fault, but he sees environmentalists as the prime culprits whom he says, in their extreme form, 'harbour dark thoughts about the necessity, if not the desirability, of the human population of the planet'.

Pearson has picked up the evidence that there is a strong correlation between support for climate action and individual economic insecurity. However, he falls short by not pursuing the population debate, especially because he would be well aware that his own people are growing at a rate twice that of the rest of the Australian population.

Pearson makes the further telling point: that the 'primary motor of change' [in individual well-being] is self-interest. But he points out that self-interest has long been anathema to policy specialists in Indigenous Affairs. He follows Adam Smith's dictum of free choice in stressing that the self-interest doesn't need to imply a mean selfishness. Pearson also draws on Amartya Sen's concept of choice being impossible without personal capacity, emphasising that many unhealthy Aboriginals in remote settlements, in practice have no choices. Individuals are unlikely to develop their earning capacity while discouraged by work-free welfare. Pearson insists that social income support must be conditional on taking responsibility for self-development.

Pearson is right for advising Tim Flannery to limit the concept of Gaia to a matter of personal religious choice, not public policy, but he is probably wrong to ignore the central question of whether all the expensive climate action will actually make any difference to global temperature – and how long it will take. My advice to Pearson would be to encourage his people to get on board the

## OVERCOMING DISADVANTAGE

Carbon Train by wide application of changed burning practices, but be cautious about taking the moral high ground because all the best evidence from the Australian Academy of Science is that it will take over 800 years to significantly reduce temperature even if we reduced emissions to zero tomorrow. This is of the utmost importance and is contained in a 2011 booklet 'The Science of Climate Change' which was sent to all schools.

So, is Pearson a shining example of inspiring leadership, or does he suffer shortcomings like the rest of us? He can easily be criticised for being a loner, not a team-player or co-operative co-worker with other Aboriginal leaders. However, such independence and one-man operation could be both well justified and actually more effective, than the unorganised group-think which comes from culturally-encapsulated Elders in the traditional mould, who suffer a special blindness to their own causality.

Pearson can also be criticised for being blunt, even insensitive, in his dismissal of others' proposals or approaches. His tone of voice and word choice when referring to what he regards as ill-informed policy by politicians, bureaucrats and poorly-advised do-gooders, is sometimes sufficiently scathing as to discontinue further dialogue. Many observers have used the same phrase when referring to Pearson's exaggerated put-downs, saying he 'doesn't suffer fools gladly'. That could be a good thing, especially if he cut out the bad language.

It is likely that Pearson's ideas would gain even wider traction if he were to team up with complimentary visionaries, perhaps like Fred Chaney, chairman of Desert Knowledge Australia, former Minister of Aboriginal Affairs and a director of Reconciliation Australia. Chaney has written incisively about the practicalities of transition from bush camps to town situations, using Alice Springs as the example and advocating Pearson's Cape York sequence of action:

1. Violence control and alcohol management
2. Welfare reform, and finally
3. Education reform

Perhaps, more effectively than any other observer, Chaney has highlighted the need for education and training of Bush people in preparation for moving to urban settings. The disasters following the influx of 1000 unhealthy, uneducated, substance-abusing Bush people to Alice Springs, are used by Chaney to advocate the urgent need for four aspects of policy, closely aligned with Pearson's approach:

- Develop co-operative approaches driven by the people, with government support.
- Ensure that the people are involved in, and claim ownership of the design and implementation of programmes on well-being.
- Make sure that good governance is seen to be applied to all funding allocations and to accountability.
- Obtain a written agreement on at least medium-term government support of programs reliant on both funding and skilled personnel.

Pearson might not take kindly to being paired with another leader, but the price of his loss of independence would be more than compensated for, by teaming up with a nationally well-respected, intelligent and experienced leader with no political axe to grind.

Pearson's directness and overbearing demeanour toward those of opposing views may have benefits in gaining respect for his apparent certainty of judgement. However with a more nuanced response to alternative views, Pearson could gain a whole lot more Indigenous co-operators. While it is easy to say 'evaluate the idea, not the man', the reality is that few people are moved to accept ideas from those who demean them, no matter how good the ideas.

Pearson is perhaps the only person who has a more holistic understanding of Aboriginal issues than anyone in the political parties and in the Indigenous organisations. He was appointed by the Abbott government to advise on 'sustainable communities'.

## Message

Noel Pearson brings a broad and balanced style of leadership to Indigenous futures. While it is acknowledged that leadership ambition drives most political initiative, Indigenous aspiration is currently plagued by unbridled egotism. Unless self-proclaimed spokespersons get the message that the cause is greater than the individual, the present city/country divide will widen and remote disadvantage will persist. Real leaders should know better than to dissipate their energy on self-promotion, instead of uplifting capable individuals from the remote communal cesspit. Value ideas for their intrinsic worth, disengage from the personality cult and recognise that the temporary discomfort caused by visionary advancement is in the best interest of future generations. Pearson has this vision, which he knows will not be painless and which many Aboriginals are not yet receptive to. Timing is everything and Pearson is at least 20 years ahead of his mob.

## THE PEARSON/SARRA SPAT

Ever since Chris Sarra received awards for Indigenous education at Cherbourg in Central Queensland and gained his Doctorate in Education, he and Noel Pearson have been at each other on education theory and practice.

Sarra has done well with the implementation of his Stronger Smarter schooling methods in several, largely Indigenous, schools. Pearson has done well in improving Cape York schooling through a range of inducements and programs at remote schools in dysfunctional communities. Sarra's successes have come in somewhat easier learning situations, largely in urban settings, while Pearson has had to contend with the war-zone situation of violent remote communities.

Why their personal antagonism has got out of hand, is probably because both these strong personalities are committed to helping disadvantaged Indigenous children in different ways. Both have made the mistake of pointedly criticising the other's philosophy and method and despite requests from supportive outsiders to cool it and supplement each other's efforts, their egos appear to require periodically-dispatched barbs at each other, through the press.

This personal spat between two driven leaders would not be important if it didn't reflect a wider malady among Indigenous spokespersons. At the heart of this little conflict, seems to be the matter of the importance or otherwise of traditional Aboriginal identity, in both motivating children to learn and developing an acceptance of identifying with either the Open Society or the traditional culture, as a source of personal grounding and inspiration.

Over a period of several years now, these combatants have been at loggerheads over an American instruction approach called Direct Instruction – a method which has several variants and emphases. At issue is the role and influence of the class teacher and the extent to which the good curriculum package can deliver good outcomes if presented by teachers without the requisite caring, understanding and personalised empathy for disadvantaged pupils from dysfunctional homes. Sarra believes that the DI method of its originator, Siegfried Engelman, falls short of identified local requirements, while Pearson has nailed his colours to the DI mast in conjunction with his 'tough love' arrangements to encourage responsible financial management, using food coupons and welfare withholding, to encourage good diet and school attendance. Sarra uses a co-operative nurturing approach to build student/school/parent co-operation. Initially, both sides failed the integrity test – Sarra, by harping and nit-picking on the theory, and Pearson for less than rigorous assessment of the appropriateness of Engelman's DI. Later, Pearson was able to demonstrate the impressive results on the Cape, of several years of DI implementation. Sarra responded by claiming DI was much too expensive, neglected Aboriginal values and was too Americanised.

At the heart of this conflict is the question of whether Indigenous identity and pride are central (or peripheral) to the learning process and the development of values and social cohesion. Although Pearson has made a persuasive plea for Aboriginal language, he sees Mainstreaming (joining the Open Society) as the solution for those unable to progress in a Homeland situation. Some say the opposite is more realistic. Pearson recognises that over-emphasis of traditional culture can slow the integration process and he wants full mainstream education, but with cultural and language studies as extra-curricular additions.

The danger of over-valuing culture (as Sutton contends) and the resultant separatism which such exaggerated identity can cause, is not always appreciated by the Indigenous culturists. This matter is likely to become central to the Indigenous debate in coming years when integration (with a name-change) will finally be recognised as the only appropriate future for many increasingly enlightened generations of Aborigines. The sooner we stop arguing about trivia and combine our efforts to give Indigenous Australian kids the very best opportunities to join the modern society, the sooner we will move from past guilt and dysfunction, toward a cohesive, productive and contented national population of diverse enriched Australians.

Some years ago, you could walk into any Indigenous counsellor's office at any Australian school or college and you could be guaranteed to be confronted by a booklet called "What Works: The Work Program Improving Outcomes for Indigenous Students". The second edition of this guide was produced in 2005

## OVERCOMING DISADVANTAGE

by David McRae *et al*, funded by the Federal Department of Education, and published by the National Curriculum Services and the Australian Curriculum Studies Association. So it has the imprimatur of the nation's top education authorities.

Why is this booklet important? Because as a workbook for councillors and teachers, it offers some useful tips and, more importantly, it encourages teachers to help students appreciate and emphasise their Indigenous identity. Whether this workbook is aimed at remote or urban settings is not clear, but the reader suspects that teachers from Redfern, Mount Druitt or Fitzroy might have some problems in filling in the personal staff questionnaire which, among other things, asks:

- What's the name of the traditional Indigenous custodians of the land where you are?
- What languages do they speak?
- Where did their lands extend?
- In your area, what are the main historical events associated with the arrival of non-Indigenous people?
- Can you think of the names of six national historically important Aboriginal or Torres Strait Islander people?
- Name ten well-known contemporary Aboriginal or Torres Strait Islander people and what they are known for.
- Who designed the Aboriginal flag and when? (The answer, by the way, is Harold Thomas in 1971.)

Perhaps a demographic survey of the national returns of these questionnaires has already been made. The teacher's responses, with or without the help of local Elders, would offer an insight into whether the relevance of these identity questions for teachers, is as meaningful to the staff as it is to the Department. Stratified by postcode, useful geographical trends could emerge from these data.

Under the workbook heading of 'Cultural respect, recognition and support' the guide tells teachers to remember that, "The vast majority of Indigenous people do not live in remote communities – most live in urban settings in Queensland and New South Wales. They may not have strong traditional links with the area in which they live. They may be deeply urbanised with lifestyles which are very similar to those of non-Indigenous Australians. Educators must be clear about the wishes of *local* communities and clear about soliciting advice and support which will be effective in context: *"Don't make assumptions. Find out."*

The objectives of the guide are clearly to help teachers to give Indigenous students and parents, the feeling of recognition and belonging to the school community. The guide's warning to teachers not to make assumptions on an Indigenous family's position (on cultural intensity and importance of clan country), is significant and hopefully encourages teachers and counsellors to avoid overdoing the purist stance on traditional Indigenous identity.

As a life-long fighter for a fair go for Aborigines, Marcia Langton has recently warned of the dangers of personal isolation within Indigenous Studies Centres of Australian universities. Langton's warning is that these centres can easily become 'isolated comfortable enclaves', implying that Aboriginal students can become uncompetitive as a result of using the centres as culturally comfortable and protective refuges from the reality of the competition in the Open Society and its tolerance of 'The Other'.

Predictably, at least some universities' Indigenous Centres responded immediately and negatively to Langton's criticism, denying that their Centres in any way represent 'escapes' from the competitive reality of the multi-cultural society. Irrespective of the merits of these campus defences, it is high time that an in-depth assessment was made of both Indigenous Centres and Indigenous Studies curricula. At issue here, is the extent to which victimhood, over-intense ethnic identity and separatism, combine to make Indigenous undergraduates less than positively positioned to play their part in the diverse, inclusive and productive multi-culture that is modern Australia.

Indigenous university staff have a problem identifying what level of consensus (if any) exists among Indigenous people and their spokespersons, regarding mainstreaming, land-based traditions, tribal identity, the law, gender roles and spirituality. This does not reflect necessarily on the visionary limitations of individual staff or the worldview of the Indigenous Centre Head, but rather it reflects on the confused state of goal-clarity in the Indigenous population generally. The committed lecturer will ask, "What should we be teaching on autonomy, self-determination, urban migration, the future of remote communities or the future role of Indigenous law and medicine?" The answers should be deeper than ephemeral political rhetoric, but it's difficult to decide whose opinion reflects departmental officialdom.

Teachers of Indigenous Studies subjects, often tend to steer clear of unresolved political issues and policy. Instead they constrain their content within the comfortable boundaries of uncontested history, culture, tradition and spirituality. In this way their students receive another dose of unadulterated Indigenous worldview, ways of learning and valued culture, based on Dreamtime stories, songlines, animal totems and ancestors' sacred places. Should their parents be asking whether this course content prepares them for participation in the coming diverse society and economy? Or whether a de-emphasis of confected intense Aboriginality may well benefit their intended entry into the Open Society? Such de-emphasis can be almost guaranteed to be deemed racist by the purists.

The Australian Bureau of Statistics, in its 2011 report, states that young Aboriginals who speak an Indigenous language are less likely to abuse drugs and alcohol. This is the fourth study in this ABS series. In 2008 almost 50% of youths between 15 and 24 years old in remote areas, spoke an Indigenous language. This proportion of language speakers has declined since then, but Sibille McKeown (ABS, 2011) regards the language/substance abuse link as 'interesting', although she avoids claiming that the connection is causal rather than casual. Latest statistics show that only 12% of Aboriginals currently speak an Indigenous language.

Pearson takes the role of language further, claiming that it contains a 'future goodness that transcends the current ability to understand what it is'. He has used two 'domains' in his Cape York Agenda's education model – the class domain, where English is learned, and the culture domain, where local language is learned. Pearson uses the term 'existential angst' to describe the effect of the on-going fear of losing one's identity through loss of both cultural language and the feeling of belonging, which it engenders in individuals whose traditions are disappearing.

While it is not difficult to appreciate the nub of Pearson's argument, his choice of words doesn't make it easy for his people to grasp the point he's making. Because Pearson is possibly one of very few Indigenous leaders known to have made a personal in-depth linguistic study of his clan language, he tends to get carried away with the 'precious' values he assigns to Indigenous language. This leads him to magnify the significance of language speakers, saying, "Speak your language to your children. This is the noblest and worthiest cause for an Australian patriot." This sentiment, though seemingly overblown to the outside observer, is worthy of the most incisive consideration by educationalists, as it has been in Israel, Afrikaner South Africa and France.

## Message

In motivating young disadvantaged students, we need to be ever-mindful of the dangers of over-emphasising individuals' potential to reach the top. In the process, it is important that young Aboriginals do value self-respect but at the same time are not misled about both actual and personal capacity and the practical value of clan identity.

# WILD RIVERS – A CASE STUDY IN VALUES

Taxpayers need to ask why there is no mention of irrigation in the advertisements defending Wild Rivers land uses. The Wild Rivers legislation of the Queensland Labour Government is dependent almost entirely on the government's need for Green preferences in State elections. As a result, the government has had the Wilderness Society run its public campaign. On 14/5/11 a full page government advertisement in the weekend press quoted half a dozen traditional owners favouring this legislation and emphasising how this will boost jobs through tourism and cultural activities. The advertisement lists all the commercial activities which the Wild Rivers Act allows, including mining and ranching, but excludes irrigated food production.

If there is one thing that the Cape people need to improve their social situation, it is a good diet of fresh fruit and vegetables. The best place to grow these is on the deeper soils of the alluvial riverside flats where water can be economically supplied. All the health and well-being studies show that a reliable local fresh food supply is the key to solving most of their health problems, especially of young Aborigines.

The high-priced low-quality greens available at community stores in the Cape were the subject of a 2010 parliamentary enquiry which did nothing to promote and implement local fresh food production as the obvious answer to local need. To date, no government or Indigenous organisation has come up with a workable comprehensive plan for local irrigated food production. Why is this?

As the epitome of the land use conflict on Native Title land, the Wild Rivers legislation applied to Cape York, stands alone. Over a period of years, two enquiries and the attention of over 200 Members of Parliament had done no more than get the Federal Minister for Environment to withhold a decision until further information was available. Dependence on the Green Vote came at a high price to the unhealthy mob in the Cape.

The press reported (NIT 12/5/11) that Terry Piper of the Balkanu Development Corporation had evidence that the State government failed to consider community submissions when originally approving the first three declared Wild Rivers. No wonder these submissions made no difference to the decision makers. The timing of the approvals and submissions shows clearly that the decisions were made ahead of assessment of crucial Indigenous submissions. What price public consultation?

What the Federal opposition's Draft Bill of 2011 on Wild Rivers aimed to do was to ensure that State government had the consent of traditional owners before declarations were made. This Bill was lost after considerable lobbying of Independents, and left the negotiators in an inequitable morass of conflicting political positions. The whole Wild Rivers saga should be used as an essential study in Indigenous politics, because it encompasses virtually all elements of the continuum of ideologies and values affecting future Aboriginal well-being. Be assured that we haven't heard the last of the Cape's Wild Rivers debate, despite the fact that the Queensland government officially removed the Act from the law books in 2014.

## Message

The education gap is too urgent and widespread to waste effort on egotistic conflict. Councillors should let students find their own cultural comfort zone. Tertiary students must not be ethnically isolated but encouraged to join the diverse Open Society. Encourage community food production projects. Use the Wild Rivers conflict as a prime case of conflicting Indigenous values.

# FUNDING CARBON REDUCTION ON INDIGENOUS LANDS

## BACKGROUND

When climate change became a real issue in 2006, many Indigenous organisations, as very large landholders, lost little time in searching for ways in which they could benefit their people through carbon sequestration. This was a responsible reaction in an era when Aboriginal bush communities were short on wealth-generation and a new source of revenue suddenly appeared on the horizon to supplement mining's boom and bust.

In just two years, with the help of CSIRO scientists, the Northern Land Council was able to stitch-up a deal worth millions of dollars with a large gas company in the Territory. The whole deal revolved around the reduction of $CO_2$ emitted to the atmosphere when controlled bushfires take place in the autumn rather than in the late winter, which had been traditional practice. The methodology and costings developed by the scientists for the Land Council, were apparently rigorous enough to impress both the company and the government – sufficient to culminate in the signing of a Carbon Offset Agreement under which the company will be credited for large tonnages of sequestrated emissions at agreed prices over a period of decades.

To date, this is one of the few large-scale offset agreements which can be seen to benefit a community directly. This successful agreement has led to greater interest by other landholders, in the possibility of payments for carbon sequestration by forest or savanna on freehold land. Even on leasehold land, such as Pastoral Leases, there are many who hold that good management should be rewarded through carbon sequestration payments to the lessees.

While this optimism on carbon payments continued to grow, the carbon tax debate raged in the cities. The debate currently hinges on the answers to two questions – what is the cost of the climate actions proposed, and what difference will they actually make to global temperatures? These questions received different answers from a range of scientists and economists, as to the time-lag between cessation of emissions and meaningful reduction in temperature. The variance in estimates is significant, of the order of tenfold, i.e. lags of a century or a millennium.

It is within this framework of scientific uncertainty that Indigenous organisations must decide on their climate actions. Under these circumstances it could be useful to these organisations, especially those in Northern Australia, to inform themselves of the work of world authorities on the effectiveness of investments in carbon emissions reduction compared to other ways of spending the vast amounts of money concerned, on direct well-being benefits and research.

The 2010 report by ABARE and Geoscience Australia, brings comprehensive evidence to predict that by 2030, fossil fuels will still account for 80% of Australian power generation. Currently that figure is 91%. The prediction was that gas, not wind, will be the main alternative energy source by 2030. By then, gas was predicted to account for 37% of the nation's energy market (including transport). Gas produces about 33% of the emissions of coal-fired stations of equal energy output. Martin Nicholson in his book 'Energy in a Changing Climate', warns that a switch to alternative energy sources could cost Australia up to $4.19 trillion. Nuclear power would be cheaper by several orders of magnitude, but the extent to which the abolition of Australia's carbon tax (2014) slows transition from fossil fuels, is unknown.

# SCEPTICS AND BELIEVERS

It is surprising that, in all the heat of the Australian carbon debate, nobody publicly challenges the final link in the chain from tax to temperature. While most spokespersons say they accept the science, that the science is clear and that action to reduce emissions is now necessary, nobody has persuaded the confused public that the proposed actions actually make a difference.

What the science 'consensus' says, is that it is highly probable that human activities have contributed to warming through $CO_2$ from fossil fuels, and that reversing this trend will be a very slow process. To emphasise this long timeline, it is worth repeating the earlier reference to the Australian Academy of Science (pg.13 of the summary of 'The Science of Climate Change' 2010) which states that if all global emissions ceased, there would be no significant reduction in atmospheric temperature for virtually 1000 years. While the actual length of time stated may be nearer 800 years, the message is that our grand children will not benefit from even very tough and expensive carbon policy implementation.

Why is this millennium time-lag never mentioned by opposing policy proponents? There can only be three alternative reasons: ignorance of the science, denial of the science or unusually long-term perceptive vision which values political benefit 1000 years ahead. The poor public record of political vision, immediately eliminates this last reason and leaves us with ignorance or denial. Since our form of democracy encourages short-term political expediency (give them bread and circuses), the voters must ultimately take the blame for the application of ineffective popularist policies.

However, since democracy can only lead to sustainable societies when the electorate is well informed, we must ask the Australian voters whether they're aware of the fact that they'll be paying for emissions reduction policies which will actually not benefit their grand children – more like a 40 generation wait if a generation is taken as 25 years.

Perhaps it is instructive to reflect on the significance of a millennial delay: a delay akin to what has happened since the Chinese invented gunpowder, or the Incas founded Cuzco, the Muslims desecrated Jerusalem, the Vikings settled Labrador, Vlad ruled Russia, the Arabs gave Europe arithmetic, the Irish expelled the Vikings and the Iron Age came to Zimbabwe.

Perhaps we can easily take the moral high ground and insist that, with our humanitarian altruism, we just know it's the right thing to preserve the habitability of the Earth for future generations. The long history of human evolution, survival and adaptation, shows no evidence of the tool-making primate ever being concerned with anything but present tribal survival. Of course there is an emerging awareness of human dependence on the environment and this has led to burgeoning Futures Studies. Since 1939 when Jacks and Whyte published their 'Rape of the Earth', the need to protect at least the food production capacity of global soils, has been accepted. Yet it would be half a century before the significance of a rise in $CO_2$, as measured at the Hawaiian observatory since the 1950s, entered our future reckoning.

So today, three basic questions need to move to the front and centre of the political debate on carbon:

1. When will we see the benefits of emissions reduction?
2. Do we appreciate the benefits of warming on temperate zone food production?
3. How best can our money be spent to improve human well-being on a warming planet in the short and long-term?

It is the uncertainty about these questions, among others, which causes Australian voters to be less than enthusiastic about paying for carbon action. Poor political judgement based on unfounded assumptions (incorrectly claimed as 'science'), can be almost guaranteed to claim more leaders' scalps in the next two decades, when international trade suffers from boycotts for non-action on (bogus?) carbon commitments.

At the same time, scientists with a vested interest in bringing about carbon reduction, need to be careful not to 'cast the first stone'. There is sufficient evidence to demonstrate that, while quick to damn the sceptics, some scientists have been less than objective in their selection and interpretation of the data and have allowed the hallowed 'peer review' process of publications, to minimise the gravitas of conflicting evidence. Our own CSIRO is not totally free of this embarrassing indictment of climate science. Who's reviewing the peers?

# LOMBORG'S CASE AND ABORIGINAL BURNING

Instead of continuing to pursue the scientific and political arguments, both of which are squeezing the last drop of certainty out of a highly uncertain bio-physical situation, it may be more productive to look carefully at our investment options. One of the best ways of doing this, is to critically evaluate the work of Bjorn Lomborg of the Copenhagen Consensus Centre, a group of global analysts for whom Lomborg produced 'The Sceptical Environmentalist', and more recently 'Cool It'. (A summary of the Copenhagen's major findings is given in the following sections.)

In essence, Lomborg seeks the 'sensible middle ground between global warming rejection and alarmism'. Our politicians will claim that their policies already reflect this 'pragmatic centre'. If so, why then is there much non-acceptance and doubt in the public mind? The simple answer is, that the mixed messages have caused a lack of confidence in the evidence, and especially in the solutions proposed by opposing camps. This is where Lomborg's group can help to test the basic assumptions of both sides. In doing this, the Copenhagen Consensus Group repeatedly return to Al Gore's 'Inconvenient Truth' which does much to heighten awareness of climate change, but misleads the public on both the actual (quantified) trends and causes, as well as how best to invest in remedial action. Many of Gore's 'facts and figures', when critically examined, appeared to be convenient half-truths. Lomborg's group have had a close look at trends in polar bear populations, glacier regressions, the Greenland iceshelf, Antarctic sea ice, sea level rise, causes of human deaths, hurricanes, heat waves, ocean temperatures, flood frequencies and drought. They conclude that many popular perceptions which Gore supports are not backed up by the best quantified information.

Lomborg is probably wrong when he claims that we've done so well in the past because we've been smart about our future. He is right when he claims that sceptics being branded as irresponsible is in itself irresponsible. His public challenge to shallow popular 'group-think' on warming, brought immediate press comment ranging from "highly valuable contribution" to "stealth attack on humanity". These polarised assessments reflect the simplistic divide which allows only two views of the warming phenomenon: unmitigated apocalypse or elaborate hoax. The truth is that both these views are unsupported by the data. In essence, the Copenhagen Consensus builds its approach to carbon action on two facts:

1. Global warming is real and partially man-made;
2. Dramatic (expensive) and fast $CO_2$ reduction is an ineffective and inefficient way of dealing with warming and human well-being.

Lomborg gives several examples of how ineffective many costly emission reduction actions will be. His native Danish example is instructive and demonstrates what the actual benefit of increasing renewable energy to

20% by 2025 would be. For the investment of $4 billion annually, Danes would pay until the end of the century, for the benefit of postponing serious warming by five days. So at a total cost of $300 billion, warming would be delayed from Friday, 1 January 2100 to the next Wednesday. Put another way, this huge investment would bring global benefits worth about $15 million, *i.e. each dollar spent, brought half a cent worth of global good*. Alternately, for $4 billion, Denmark could double its number of hospitals; for $3 billion they could halve global malaria infection and save 850 million lives every year. The remaining $1 billion could increase research into $CO_2$ reduction eightfold. Alternately, $4 billion could give clean drinking water to every person on earth and increase $CO_2$-reduction research tenfold. Lomborg estimates that European emissions reduction could cost $25 billion, but result in a cooling of only 1/20 of 1°C in air temperature. He suggests that *Australia might spend $25B and make only a 1/200 of 1°C reduction in air temperature* (my emphasis).

Lomborg's modelling figures will no doubt be challenged, but he makes two fundamental points:

1. "If we persistently overworry and exaggerate the problems, people eventually tire of the entire discussion and there are ominous signs that this is already (2007) happening."

2. "Our worry makes us focus on the wrong solutions."

The whole "Cool It" book has a clear focus: "We need to remind ourselves that our ultimate goal is not to reduce greenhouse gases or global warming *per se*, but to improve the quality of life and the environment." This 'radical' claim is based on acceptance of the fundamental truth that many other issues affecting human well-being, may in fact be more important than global warming. The basic assertion is that the exaggerated urgency of expensive emission reduction policies, needs to be replaced with both more efficient investments in the human condition and in simpler, cheaper and more effective solutions to warming.

Close examination of the data indicates that radically reducing emissions is probably one of the least helpful ways of serving both humanity and the environment. So why are arguments for alternative and more effective investments in human well-being, not heard in the public debates? Because proponents of emission reductions such as Al Gore, who collected a Nobel

## CONVENIENT HALF-TRUTHS: LOMBORG'S CASE

prize on the way, have already crowded out the awareness platform.

In 2006 George Monbiot published his book 'Heat: How to stop the planet burning' in which every facet of global warming is portrayed as calamitous. Monbiot urges his readers to recognise that this issue is so urgent, that it must override all others, and that the OECD must cut emissions by 96% before 2030(!) if mankind is to have a future. Monbiot ignores costs and alternative priorities, stating that economic options must be seen as 'an amoral means of comparison'.

Mark Lynas, the author of 'High Tide: the truth about our climate crisis' (2004), finds climate denial akin to Holocaust denial. He is supported by David Roberts in his 'Denial Industry' (2006), which calls for a climate 'Nurenberg' – 'war crimes trials for these bastards'. No less than R.K. Pachauri, chairman of IPCC and one of its top scientists asks, "Where is the difference between Lomborg's view on humans and Hitler's?" To these extreme accusations Lomborg simply says: "while I appreciate the moral intent to do good for humanity, the unwavering certainty that $CO_2$ cuts are the best way to help, is problematic." He explains that global warming is the perfect issue for politicians to position themselves as humanitarians and statesmen, taking the lead on the 'grandest issue of the planet's survival'. While the true cost and effectiveness of the 'visionary' policies proposed, are unclear in the view of some sceptics, these Crusaders can even make some taxes look popular – a World First.

So we return to the basic question of how much good can we do and at what cost. This brings us to an evaluation of the 1997 Kyoto Protocol which is still the only agreed (more or less) carbon reduction framework. It was reviewed in 2012 and superseded by the Paris Agreement several years later. This protocol aimed to reduce global $CO_2$ by 20% below the 2000 level. The fact is that even if all countries co-operated to achieve this noble goal, the change in annual temperature rise would have been almost undetectable, i.e. the atmosphere is estimated to be reduced in temperature by 0.1°F by 2050 and by 0.3°F by 2100. This means that the expected worst-case 4.7°F rise, would have been postponed from 2100 to 2105 – five years. Lomborg claims that these estimates are scientifically incontrovertible, which means that Kyoto was no more than a symbolic treaty and serves to emphasise the essential difference between FEEL GOOD and DO GOOD policies. (This difference is crucial to Australian Indigenous projects.)

The cost of implementing the Kyoto cuts was about $180 billion annually – 1.5% of global GDP. Questions now arise as to how best to gain significant results from alternative actions and how best to compare the benefits with non-reduction investments for better living. The economists estimate that a $1/tonne $CO_2$ tax will cost $11 billion and a $30/tonne tax would cost almost $7 trillion. What the tax-payers want to know is quite simply, what do we get for our money? The answer from the combined macro-economic models is, a delay of four years before reaching the dreaded 4.7°F rise.

Richard Tol, the convening author of IPCC's first report on climate change, states that to hold temperature at 2°C above the 2000 level, will require a global emissions reduction of 80% by 2050. The sacrifices made to achieve such a reduction, says Lomborg, will do much more damage to human well-being, than the warming will do.

In 2005, Tol produced the most comprehensive review of the effects of carbon price estimates and concluded that, based on the best assumptions, the real value is unlikely to be above $14/tonne and most likely to be nearer $2/tonne. What this implies is that the damage done by one tonne of $CO_2$ is probably less than $10, so if we tax it high, say at $85 (as one report suggests) we use up $83 worth of social benefit, assuming the actual damage, costs us only $2. This could cause a total global loss of $38 trillion on ineffective tax, which could have been spent on global health and education.

If the tax is set too low it results in excess emissions, if set too high, it impoverishes us for no material benefit. Within the Kyoto framework, Britain put the marginal cost of $CO_2$ damage at $23/tonne, which Lomborg suggests is up to 11 times the actual cost of the effects of the warmer climate. Australia was initially considering a price of $25/tonne. The initial European price was so low that it made no difference to emissions.

The models which the IPCC has used since 1992 include both climate and economic systems. They considered two sets of costs – costs of adapting to warming and costs of not adapting. These cover agriculture, forestry, fisheries, energy, weather damage, sea-level rise, water supplies and infrastructure costs. Within the Kyoto framework, to achieve its aims, the Developed nations would have paid almost $9 trillion by 2012 but the models indicate that each dollar spent would benefit the Developing countries by only sixteen cents.

## CONVENIENT HALF-TRUTHS: LOMBORG'S CASE

Similarly, with investment in alternative energy, Britain would receive back three cents in the dollar on its Kyoto reduction costs, and each dollar would do about one cents worth of good. Lomborg calculates this diminishing return on a cumulative basis, i.e. the more we try to cut carbon the more it costs per tonne and the less good each funding increment achieves. Lomborg is not saying don't act, he's saying pick the low-hanging fruit first. So he picks the most optimistic of IPCC options, i.e. to reduce warming by only 2.7°F, dismissing reduction by 4.7°F as unreal. This latter reduction was the EU's preferred scenario, but it would cost an unbelievable $84/tonne. Lomborg reckons this will only do thirteen cents of good for each dollar spent. This leads the combined advice of all the major modellers to state that, "optimal policy calls for a relatively modest level of control of $CO_2$". They demonstrate that for the first 170 years of modest control, costs will be greater than benefits and they estimate that benefits outweigh costs, only after 2250. The first generation to benefit would be born early in the 24th century.

Reacting to the poor returns on investment in emissions reduction, the Copenhagen Consensus assembled a panel of the world's leading economists in 2004 and asked them to identify where the placing of resources would do the most good first. This think-tank included four Nobel laureates and came up with global lists of the best opportunities to invest in human well-being. Top of the list were disease control, nutrition, clean water, sanitation and trade. Bottom of the list were climate change investments. Their conclusion was to give priority to those pressing needs which are easy and cheap to meet. Their message on climate investment was: focus on cutting costs of emission reduction – such investment is more efficient (bang for the buck), has a better chance of working (actually making a difference) and will really help humanity (global well-being). Our Indigenous landholders need to appreciate this.

Perhaps this summary of Copenhagen's advice should end with an assessment of the effect of warming on food production. The common perception is that higher temperatures mean more drought and lower yields, but the combined results of several global models of food production and trade, share the following four common findings:

1. Despite (and partly because of) warming, the coming century is predicted to witness more than a doubling of agricultural output globally.

2. Isolating the separate effect of climate change from other influences on agriculture, the most *pessimistic* model estimates that climate alone will reduce food production by 1.4% over the century. The most *optimistic* model estimates a 1.7% increase in yield. The warming effect decreases yields from less developed countries but increases yields from developed countries, because the former are generally tropical and the latter mostly temperate. Worst-case scenarios predict a 7% reduction in less developed countries' economies and a 3% increase in developed economies which learn to capitalise on warming.

3. Increased $CO_2$ concentrations act as an aerial fertiliser and increase both crop growth rate and yield. Longer growing-seasons and less frost-days have a major positive effect on yields in the temperate zone. (This could benefit southern Australia significantly.)

4. The world's current 800 million malnourished people are estimated, in the most likely scenario, to increase by 1300 million by AD2080. This is the result of the shorter population doubling times in developing countries. These double every 17-30 years while their food production decreases due to soil degradation. In developed economies, population doubles in 100-300 years while food production in their generally temperate climate increases.

## In Summary

The global modelling suggests that emissions policy should be based on the following findings:

1. Emission reduction won't reduce temperatures for many centuries.
2. Attempts to achieve large and rapid temperature reductions are economically very inefficient and physically impossible.
3. Investment in R & D on climate change, is the best option for social and economic returns on funding.
4. Focus of research should be on adaptation and acceptance of moderate temperature rise as being manageable and globally beneficial.

# BEYOND COPENHAGEN – LET'S GET REAL

Disadvantaged remote Aborigines have been led to believe that they can benefit from carbon agreements, but their situation needs to be viewed within the global carbon framework. It is time however, to move to a new reasoned perspective on climate change and to get away from what the UK Institute for Public Policy Research in 2006 referred to as "alarmism, which might even become secretly thrilling – effectively a form of 'climate porn'." The alarmist repertoire insists that humanity will be killed by this immense and uncontrollable Armageddon, while in fact climate change is but one of humanity's serious issues. Ill-founded alarmism precludes reason, and stagnates action through its quasi-religious doom and death prophecy.

This new language of catastrospeak has even infected some scientific literature, which infers that unless we fix climate, nothing else matters. What is required now, is a mature appreciation of the actual warming effects, rather than the fictitious worst-case scenario, with all its scary debilitating consequences. Equally important is an honest assessment of what we can do about it, because present indications are 'very little'.

While this text was being written, the latest Australian Antarctic expedition was returning with dire warnings that 'things are considerably worse than we thought' on the melting of the polar ice. No word of the expansion of glaciers, the spreading Greenland shelf, cooler temperatures in many countries, widespread drought-breaking rains in many regions and bumper crops in several grain-producing areas.

Amplifying climate risk does nothing to get our financial priorities right, but the media and the conspirators just love it. In the process, the alarmist reports reduce our opportunity for sensible economic dialogue about prioritised investments, which actually make a difference to the human condition. Surely the need for concentrating R&D on adaptation to warming is obvious by this time. How much more evidence do we need to convince ourselves that we can't make anything but a minor difference to warming, and then only over a period of many centuries, and perhaps at great cost if we let the feel-good policy replace the do-good policy.

As referred to earlier, Al Gore captured the global imagination with stunning graphics of highly emotive ecological breakdown– the end is nigh. The chief scientific adviser to the British government, Sir David King, announced in 2004 that if global warming remains unchecked, Antarctica would not only be ice-free, but was likely to be the world's only remaining habitable continent. What message does the public take from this? That warming must be stopped if we are to survive. The assumption is that we know how to do that, and that we have no option but to hugely invest in Greenhouse gas reduction. There is little questioning of this investment's effectiveness and cost, and there is only low-level focussing, not on reduction, but on adaptation. Few argue with the evidence on warming or sea level rise, if present trends continue. However, only Australia and New Zealand have had an increase in maximum land temperatures. Other countries including the US, China and some EU nations have only had fewer frost days. In England which has the longest temperature records (1659) there has been a clear reduction in cold days but no increase in the number of hot days. Lomborg reminds us that in Europe, while about 200,000 people already die of heat stress annually, 1,500,000 die of cold. That's sevenfold cold deaths. In Athens the annual average figures are 1376 heat deaths and 7852 cold deaths. Is it unreasonable to suggest that global warming will lower temperature-induced death rates?

On the local scene, Australian politicians are struggling to juggle scientific 'contradictions' and popular convictions. This is a dangerous time for poll-driven political parties, because frankly, the complexities of the climate debate are beyond the ordinary voters, who may simply seek selected evidence for their preconceived mental comfort zone. The problem is that climatic systems are so intricate physically, that even many of the best scientists are at odds. One of the critical disparities is the time lag in temperature reduction after emission reduction. Is it surprising that the voters' reading of time-lags which vary from a century to a millennium, as claimed by competing reputable scientific bodies, are more than a tad sceptical?

In this circumstance, climate science appears far from settled, while opportunistic politicians have a field-day scaring the voters into opposing Armageddons – one physical, the other economic. The basic assumptions on actual temperature change and actual cost, get lost in a plethora of concocted certainties on the minutiae of cost-sharing and benefits.

In 2011 the Labour government had a set of scary statements for use by all its spokespersons in the public square. These statements told the people that without climate action, Australia will be virtually uninhabitable – drought, fires, coastal flooding etc. What they didn't say was that even with massive government-inspired actions, these catastrophes would probably still happen. But that's the assumption that the mug punter can make, given present information on corrective action.

It is useful to get real about who's emitting what, into the global atmosphere at present: In tonnes of $CO_2$ *per capita*, India is 1.5, China 5.8, Europe 11, US 23 and Australia 27. For the required target of 450 ppm $CO_2$ (2° rise) to be met, the global average emissions will need to approximate India's present 1.5 tonne per capita.

At Cancun in 2010, 89 countries (representing 80% of global emissions), promised large reductions in their $CO_2$ output. Presently the global fatcats are a long way from agreeing with Ross Garnaut, the Labour government's climate advisor, that eventually the only fair agreement would involve everyone abiding by a per capita maximum emission of below 2 tonnes. The 'Tragedy of the Commons' is alive and well, encouraging individuals to benefit at the expense of the common good.

Government then (2011) warned that if we don't act, Australia will be subjected to trade boycotts from nations which are seen to be making a serious carbon reduction effort. One may predict that if there continues to be no global distinction between feeling good and doing good about climate actions, free trade will take a serious but unnecessary battering.

Meanwhile one had to feel sorry for the (then) Minister for Climate Change, Greg Combet, a reasonable man of integrity. While he didn't say so, that serious look on his face during interviews was surely saying 'I wish those scientists would make up their minds – we'd like to say we accept the science, however too many scientists continue to protect their egotistical patch.' Apart from the cold war during the nuclear arms build-up 30 years ago, no government has ever been faced with such a complex global issue in time and space. Only one thing is certain – all simple solutions will be wrong.

Watch this space, we have a very long way to go and many red faces to come, meanwhile scientists and politicians would do well to concentrate on just two questions: what difference will it make and what will it cost? Just do it.

# ALL ABOARD
# THE CARBON (GRAVY) TRAIN

Nobody expects Indigenous leaders to let the Carbon Train pass and not get on board. Like the rest of us, they should take advantage of available government payments – as we all did in 2009 with free school halls, highly subsidised roof insulation and a family cash handout of $900, during the Global Financial Crisis

However, taking advantage of government offerings is different from giving support to the half-truth of the pseudo-science behind the Indigenous payment scheme. It is not Indigenous leaders' responsibility to subscribe to selected interpretations of climate process data. It is not their problem to choose between those scientists who insist that no change in the rate of warming will occur for a millennium after all emissions ceased, and those scientists who state that within a century, global temperature rise can be meaningfully reduced through 'carbon footprint reduction'.

The benefit or otherwise of traditional Aboriginal mosaic burning of country, has been the subject of ecological debate for many decades. (In fact the author convened the Queensland Rural Fire Workshops triennially for 12 years, which included several papers on Aboriginal burning.) In recent times, efforts to involve Indigenous owners in local Landcare programs, has re-ignited some old controversies about the 'naturalness' of Aboriginal fire practices. One example is near Nimmitabel, south of Cooma where Elder Rob Mason was given the opportunity to convince local farmers that there should be more use of fire on their farms. This opportunity arose from farmer Geoff Robertson signing a biodiversity stewardship agreement which included Indigenous knowledge in the management plan.

When assessing the usefulness and effects of Aboriginal burning practices, it soon becomes clear that the *objectives* of when and how to burn, are crucial to the ecological outcomes. Traditionally, burning was originally aimed at attracting game and 'keeping country clean', but the long-term effects of more regular, and out of season, burning on biodiversity and ecosystem structure probably weren't foreseen. It can be assumed that the Australian landscape has been subject to natural fires over many millennia before Man arrived, in fact ever since dry grass and lightning combined in early wet-season thunderstorms. Aboriginals certainly changed both the frequency (and thus intensity) and the season (and thus effect) of natural bushfires.

Most Australians would probably be unaware that NSW already had a two-tier carbon-trading scheme in operation for the decade ending 2012. It was claimed to be the world's first legislated scheme, enacted by the Carr Labour government in 2003. This scheme involved 39 companies in the mandated 'legislated tier' and 11 companies in the voluntary or 'elective tier'. Carbon credits were acquired in three ways: by changing the process by which electricity is generated; by expanding the use of energy-efficient domestic appliances; and by carbon-sequestrating forestry. Andrew Grant, formerly of Ernst and Young's environmental consultancy, has shown that in practice, the cost of properly priced carbon has been significantly lower than the companies had expected, in fact it averaged \$4.50/tonne of $CO_2$. The question remains as to whether this cost would offer any inducement for companies to change from fossil fuels.

As an example of the trading of Land Rights for financial security, the agreement between the Jabir Jabir claimant group and Woodside Energy at James Price Point in the Kimberley, is of special significance. The Kimberley Land Council's Wayne Bergmann negotiated the \$1.5 billion agreement in 2011 (after five years and a court case on tribal claimant rights), to produce a deal which includes employment, education and housing benefits. Bergmann saw this arrangement as a balance between development needs and survival needs. In the final voting, the local people were still split 164 for and 108 against, with five abstentions, reflecting deep-seated inter-tribal differences.

The Premier of WA referred to this agreement as probably the most significant act of self-determination by Aboriginals in Australia's history. The Premier had earlier threatened compulsory land acquisition if the tribal conflict delayed this huge gas project any longer. The gas extraction was planned for a nominal 50 years, after which the land would be returned to the traditional owners. Tax-payers and policy-makers will watch with particular interest the extent to which the funds accruing to the land owners (including \$125 million

## OVERCOMING DISADVANTAGE

from WA government) are allocated to serious well-being programs of lasting benefit to the community. All are hoping that the wasteful disasters of misplaced funds from a number of earlier mining agreements will be avoided.

### Message

Climate change, because of its unprecedented spatial and temporal dimensions, is the most complex issue ever to challenge the world's leaders. Ignore the simplistic wedging of sceptics and believers. Recognise the deficiencies of understanding in the early climate debate. Accept the human tendency toward self-benefit and the predictable diminishing of concern for others further away and later in time. Recognise that tropical disadvantage may be outweighed by temperate advantage in future food production. Appreciate the need to legislate globally to overcome personal and national greed. Agree on human population being the root cause and ultimate solution to global ecological stability. Learn to live with the cosmic unimportance of the fate of the human species.

In summary, those who hotly contest the current wisdom on climate change, would do well to distinguish between sceptics of three different types:

1. Those who are sceptical of the official line on the causes of warming.
2. Those who are sceptical of the effect, if any, of carbon reduction actions.
3. Those who are sceptical of the official line on who should pay for these actions.

The sooner the term 'sceptic' returns to its original positive meaning of challenging the official majority opinion, the better.

# COPENHAGEN CONSENSUS OUTCOMES – DATA FOR ABORIGINAL NEGOTIATORS

The following information, in no particular order, is worth noting when voters and politicians seek clarity on present and historic climatic trends:

1. The break-up of a massive glacier in the Antarctic has received wide media coverage. This area was ice-free only about 400 years ago and

today the Wilkins glacier makes up less than 0.01% of the area of Antarctica.

2. Much media attention was given to the dramatic US 'hurricane years' of 2004 and 2005 but there was no mention of the complete absence of hurricane damage during 2006 and 2007.

3. Al Gore's proposed $140/tonne carbon tax was estimated to cut US emissions by 50%, but would reduce temperature by only 0.2°F by 2100, *at a cost of $160 billion annually for the rest of the century.*

4. Book titles such as "Boiling Point", "Climate Crash" and "Last Generation", do nothing to help voters assess best investments in climate change and adaptation. Apocalyptic religious sentiment has taken over from scientific logic on the factual climatic position.

5. In 2006, a Canadian polar bear biologist summed up the exaggerated claims on the bears' future as follows: "It is just silly to predict the demise of polar bears in 25 years, based on media-assisted hysteria. Canada is home to two thirds of the world's polar bears. Of our 13 bear populations in Canada, 11 are stable or increasing in number. They are not going extinct or even appear to be affected at present. An average of 400 bears are shot each year, largely for human food. Changes in hunting laws will do much more good for the bear populations, than expensive ice-preservation schemes."

6. The Arctic Climate Impact Assessment predicts that the Arctic will experience an overall increase in species richness as temperature rises, and will show increased ecosystem productivity under predicted warming.

7. The warming patterns of the 20th century show that globally, winter temperatures have increased much more than summer temperatures and that night temperatures have increased more than day temperatures. More than three quarters of the winter warming in the Northern hemisphere has been confined to the very cold systems of Siberia and North Western North America, including Alaska.

8. There have been fewer frost days in many countries including Australia, but only Australia and New Zealand have had their maximum temperatures go up. Central England with records since

1659, has had a clear reduction in the number of cold days but no increase in the number of hot days.

9. The first comprehensive global survey of the predicted effect of warming on health was published in 2006. The conclusion is that no massive health disruption or increased death toll is expected. The overall effect by 2050 will in fact, be a significant decrease in fatalities. It is estimated that warming will reduce cardio-vascular deaths by over 1.7 million p.a. and respiratory death by 365,000. This translates to saving 1.4 million people annually. This trend holds for most regions except Africa, where deaths will outweigh lives saved. Overall heat deaths will not outweigh cold deaths for the next 200 years at least.

10. Surveys in various countries show that a majority of respondents prioritise climate change as a vital issue ranked above world hunger, terrorism, HIV/AIDS and 13 other global threats. The reason for this priority seems to be that global warming offers a moral purpose, an opportunity to rise up and join a generational mission which gives new meaning to life – much as environmental campaigning did in the late 1960s, only more desperate, more all-encompassing and more urgent.

11. The centuries 900-1200 A.D. were relatively warm – known as the 'Medieval Warm Period'. Reduced sea-ice allowed colonisation of Greenland and Newfoundland by the Vikings. Alaska was 3-5°F warmer in the 11th century than today and the Rocky Mountains snowline was 900 feet higher than today.

12. In the middle of the last millennium, a marked cooling known as the 'Little Ice Age', affected most countries. It is interesting to note that many events during that Ice Age were reported as negative for human well-being, which was not the case with the Medieval Warming.

13. The most accurately documented overview of glacier movement, shows that glaciers have been retreating continuously since 1800 – half a century before the Industrial Revolution. The ice on Kilimanjaro has been receding since 1880, as recorded in the first published research on the mountain's glaciers.

14. Antarctica's average temperatures are so low (-29°F), that they

prevent virtually all melting or evaporation, resulting in continuous accumulation of snow.

15. If the human capacity to reduce the rate of warming is considered as two control knobs, (one climate, one social) humans have a choice. To make a difference, we could set the knob to avoid less than 10% damage increase, or set it to avoid 500% damage increase. The difference in efficiency of the climate cooling knob and the social benefit knob is 50-fold, giving this size advantage to policies which address social improvement. The faster and greater benefit which can be achieved from social policy action is estimated to be 50 times more than the benefit derived from the same investment in climate control. This is primarily because of the miniscule cooling effect of achievable emission reduction.

16. After the 2002 floods of Dresden and Prague, the German Chancellor used this event as a prime example of why nations should commit to Kyoto. Long records however, showed that centuries of river height measurement on the Oder and Elbe rivers, prove that their summer floods over at least three centuries, have not increased and that their winter floods have actually decreased.

17. The alleged warming effect on the weakening and cessation of the famous oceanic Gulf Stream, which moves warm water from southern latitudes to the North, is one of the allegations most poorly supported by scientific evidence. The Gulf Stream flows from the Gulf of Mexico to Newfoundland. Records show that the Gulf Stream last shut down 8200 years ago during the 'final' glacial melt in North America. Modelling by the IPCC shows that even at triple the predicted warming rate in future, the Gulf Stream would not shutdown. It should be noted that the Gulf Stream shutdown was last foreseen by Wallace Broeker, a geochemist, one week before world leaders met in Japan to agree on the Kyoto Protocol! This was followed in 1998 by William Calvin, in his high profile magazine article, which claimed that, "Europe's climate could become more like Siberia" as a result of the Gulf Stream shutdown. This alarmist prediction claimed that The Hague would be uninhabitable by 2007! Modelling however, demonstrates that the Gulf Stream will continue

while ever the earth rotates on its axis and the global wind systems continue.

18. Sceptics on global warming like to remind the true believers that less than two decades ago there was 'strong scientific backing' for the global cooling theory, which warned the population that the next Ice Age was already on the way, and that governments should initiate cold-adaptation procedures without delay. This stance was rapidly overtaken by the European Heat Wave in mid-2003, in which France suffered 15,000 fatalities, Germany 7000, Spain 8000, Italy 2000 and the United Kingdom, a staggering 35,000 heat-induced deaths.

19. Each year in Europe about 1.5 million people currently die from excess cold – which is at least six times the number dying from heat. During the decade 1997-2007 Europe lost 15 million people to cold, which is more than 400 times the 2003 deaths from heat. The most comprehensive study of temperature and mortality in Europe, concluded that for an increase of 3.6°F, increases in heat mortality would be far outweighed by much larger short-term reductions in cold-related mortalities.

# REFERENCES

## Section One

Ah Mat, R. 2003: The moral case for Aboriginal capitalism. Native Title Conference Proc., Alice Springs, June

Altman, J. 1983: Aborigines and Mining Royalties in the Northern Territory. Australian Institute Aboriginal Studies, Canberra

Altman, J. 2005: Developing options on Aboriginal Land: Sustainable Indigenous hybrid economies in the twenty-first century. In: Taylor *et al* (Eds). The Power of Knowledge, the Resonance of Tradition, Aboriginal Studies Press, Canberra

Altman, J. & Martin, D. (Eds) 2009: Power, Culture, Economy: Indigenous Australians and Mining. ANU Press, Canberra

Altman, J. & Smith, D. 1994: The economic impact of mining money: The Nabarlek case, Western Arnhem Land. CAEPR Discussion Paper 63, ANU, Canberra

Anderson, I. and Bebe, L. 2004: Voices Lost: Indigenous health and human rights in Australia. The Lancet 364:1281

Armstrong, J. 2009: In Search of Civilisation. Allen Lane, London

Atkinson, J. 2002: Trauma Trails, Recreating Song Lines. Spinifex Press, Melbourne

Attwood, B. 2005: Telling the Truth about Aboriginal History. Allen & Unwin, Sydney

Berndt, C. 1977: (Ed) Aborigines and Change, Social Anthropology Series No.11, Australian Institute of Aboriginal Studies, Canberra. Humanities Press. New Jersey

Berndt, C. 1977: (Ed) Aborigines and Change, Out of the frying pan? Or back to square one: In: Berndt 1977 p.402-411. Humanities Press, New Jersey

Berndt, R. 1974: The Relationship of Aboriginals and their land. Kimberley Land Council

Berndt, R. 1992: A profile of good and bad in Aboriginal religion. Aus. & N.Z. Theological Review 17, Auckland

Berndt, R. & C. 1989: The Speaking Land: Myth and story in Aboriginal Australia. Ringwood Press, Melbourne

Bird Rose, D. 1996: Nourishing Terrains. Heritage Commission, Canberra

Boaz, F. 1940: Race, Language and Culture. Macmillan, New York

Bourdieu, P. 1977: Outline of a Theory of Practice. Cambridge University Press. Quoted by Martin 2009

Brennan, F. 1991: Sharing the Country: The Case for an Agreement between Black and White Australians. Penguin, Melbourne

Brock, P. 1993: Outback Ghettos: A History of Aboriginal Institutionalisation and Survival. Cambridge University Press, Melbourne

Canny, N. 1973: The Ideology of English Colonisation. William & Mary Quarterly 30

Capell, A. 1940: The classification of languages in North Western Australia. Oceania 10(3):241

Charlesworth, M., Howard, M., Bell, D and Madlock, K. 1984: (Eds) Religion in Aboriginal Australia. UQ Press, Brisbane

Chase, A. 1981: Empty vessels and loud noises: Views about Aboriginality today. Social Alternatives 2(2):23

Choo, C. 2001: Mission Girls. UWA Press

Cocks, K.D. 1992: Use With Care. UNSW Press Sydney

Collins, R. 1923: Pioneering: The life of the Hon. R.M. Collins. Documented by H. Perry, Watson & Ferguson, Brisbane

Coombs, H., Dexter, B., & Hiatt, L. 1982: The Outstation Movement in Aboriginal Australia: In: Leacock and Lee (Eds) 1982 Politics and history in band societies. Cambridge University Press, Melbourne

# REFERENCES: SECTION ONE

Coombs, H. 1974: Decentralisation trends among Aboriginal communities. Search 5:135

Costello, M. 1930: Life of John Costello. Dymocks, Sydney

Cowlishaw, G. 1978: Infanticide in Aboriginal Australia. Oceania 48(4):262

Cowlishaw, G. 1998: Erasing culture and race: practising "self-determination". Oceania 68:145

Cowlishaw, G. 2003: Euphemism, banality, propaganda: anthropology, public debate and Indigenous comments. Australian Aboriginal Studies 1:2-18

Daly, H. 1973: Towards a Steady State Economy. Freeman Press, San Francisco

Dawson, J. 2004: Washout. Macleay Press, Sydney

De Satge, O. 1901: Pages from the journal of a Queensland Squatter. Hurst & Blackett Ltd., London

Dodson P. 1976: Report on the Third Annual Queensland Conference. Catholic Council, Brisbane

Dodson, M. 1994: The end in the beginning: Re(de)fining Aboriginality. Australian Aboriginal Studies 1:2

Dodson, M. 2003: Violence, dysfunction and Aboriginality. National Press Club, Canberra

Doolan, J. 1977: Walk-off (and later return) of various Aboriginal groups from cattle stations: Victoria River District, N.T. In: Berndt 1977 p.106

Doyle, F. 2004: Whispers of This Wik Woman. UQ Press, Brisbane

Duncan-Kemp, A. 1962: Our Channel Country. Angus & Robertson, Sydney

Duncan-Kemp, A. 1964: Where strange paths go down. Smith & Patterson, Brisbane

Duncan-Kemp, A. 1968: Where Strange Gods Call. Smith & Paterson, Brisbane

Durack, M. 1959: Kings in Grass Castles. New City Press, Sydney.

Durack, M. 1983: Sons in the Saddle. Constable, London

Eckermann, A-K. 1933: Contact. MA Thesis, University of Queensland, Brisbane

Elkin, A. 1964: The Australian Aborigines: How to understand them. Angus & Robertson, Sydney

Essed, P. 1996: Diversity, Gender, Colour and Culture. University of Massachusetts Press

Fitzgerald, B. 1984: Blood on the Saddle: The Forrest River Massacres 1926. Studies in Western Australian History 8:16

Frederickson, G. 1981: White Supremacy. Oxford University Press, New York

Freier, P. 1999: Living with the Munpitch: History of the Mitchell River Mission (Kowanyama) Ph.D. Thesis, JCU Townsville

Gale, F. 1983: (Ed) We Are Bosses Ourselves: The Status of Aboriginal Women Today. AIAS, Canberra

Geertz, C. Distinguished Lecture: Anti anti-relativism. American Anthropologist 86:263

Gerritson, R. 1982: Outstations: differing interpretations and policy implications. In: Loveday 1982

Goldman, H. & Morrissey, J. 1985: The alchemy of mental health policy. American Journal Public Health 75(7):727

Gratton, M. 2000: Essays on Reconciliation. Brookham Press, Melbourne

Gray, G. 2007: A Cautious Silence: The politics of Australian anthropology. Aus. Inst. Abor. & Torres Strait Studies, Canberra

Greer, G. 1971: The Female Eunich. Paladin Press, London

Greer, G. 2008: On Rage. Melbourne University Press

Gunn, A. 1907: We of the Never Never. Hitchenson & Co., London

Gunson, N. 1988: Two hundred years of Christianity. Aboriginal History 12(1):103

Hall, R. 1989: The Black Diggers. Allen & Unwin, Sydney

Hasluck, P. 1942: Black Australians: A survey of native policy in Western Australia 1829-1897. M.U.P. Melbourne

# REFERENCES: SECTION ONE

Hawke, R. 1988: A Time for Reconciliation. In: A Treaty With Aborigines. Institute of Public Affairs, Sydney p.4

Huggins, J. 1994: A contemporary view of Aboriginal women's relationship to the White women's movement. In: Grieve and Burns (Eds). Australian Women. Oxford University Press

Hirst, J.B. 1992: The Pioneer Legend. In: Images of Australia: (Eds) Whitlock, G. and Carter, D. UQ Press, Brisbane

Hobsbaum, E. & Ranger, T. 1983: The Invention or Tradition. Cambridge University Press

Howard, J. 1988: Treaty is a Recipe for Separation. In: Hawke 1988

Howson, P. 2000: Reality and fantasy: the abject failure of Aboriginal policy. Quadrant, April:20

Hughes, H. 2007: Lands of Shame: Homelands in Transition. Centre for Independent Studies, St. Leonards, Sydney

Hughes, R. 1988: The Fatal Shore. Pan Books, London

Jarret, S. 2009: Higher Education Supplement. The Australian 10/9/2009

Johns. G. 2008: The Northern Territory Intervention in Aboriginal Affairs; Wicked Problem or Wicked Policy? Agenda 15(2):165

Kidd, R. 1997: The Way We Civilise. UQ Press, Brisbane

Kolig, E. 1977: From Tribesman to Citizen. In: Berndt 1977, p.33

Kowal, E. and Paradies, Y. 2005: Ambivalent helpers and unhealthy choices. Social Science & Medicine 60:1347

Kriewaldt, M. 1960: The application of the criminal law to the Aborigines of the Northern Territory of Australia. West Australian Law Review 5:1

Kunitz, S. 1994: Disease and Social Diversity: The European Impact on the Health of Non-Europeans. Oxford University Press, New York

Langton, M. 1981: Urbanising Aborigines: the social scientists great deception. Social Alternatives 2(2):16

Langton, M. 1988: The Getting of Power. Australian Feminist Studies 6:1

Langton, M. 2007: Trapped in the Aboriginal Reality Show. Griffith Review 19:143

Langton, M. 2008: End of the 'big men' politics. Griffith Review 22:11

Lea, J. & Zehner, R. 1986: Yellow Cake and Crocodiles. Allen & Unwin, Sydney

Lickiss. J. 1971: Aboriginal Children in Sydney. Oceania 41(3):201

Loos, N. 1982: Invasion and Resistance: Aboriginal-European relations of the North Queensland Frontier 1861-1897. ANU Press, Canberra

Loos, N. 2007: White Christ Black Cross. Aboriginal Studies Press, Canberra

Loveday, P. 1982: Service Delivery to Remote Communities. North Australia Research Unit, Darwin

Macintyre, S. 2003: The History Wars. Melbourne University Press

Macklin, J. 2008: Beyond Mabo: Native Title and Closing the Gap. Mabo Lecture, JCU, Townsville 21/5/08

Maddock, K. 2001: Sceptical thoughts on customary law. In: G. Johns (Ed) Waking of The Dreamtime. Media Masters, Singapore

Makin, C. 1970: A socio-economic anthropological survey of people of Aboriginal descent in the metropolitan region of Perth. Ph.D. Thesis, Anthropology. UWA, Perth

Malinowski, B. 1913: The Family among the Australian Aborigines: A Sociological Study. Schocken Books, New York (Reprinted 1963)

Manne, R. 1996: Forget the guilt, remember the shame. The Australian 08/07/1996

Manne, R. 2002: Mabo: a moral crisis festers. The Age, 27/05/2002

Manne, R. 2003: Whitewash. Black Inc., Melbourne

Martin, D. 1993: Autonomy and Relatedness. Ph.D. Thesis, ANU Canberra

Martin, D. 2001: Is welfare dependency welfare poison? Assessment of Noel Pearson's proposals. Discussion Paper No. 213, Centre for Aboriginal Economic Research, ANU, Canberra

## REFERENCES: SECTION ONE

Martin, D. 2003: Rethinking the design of Aboriginal organisations. CAEPR Discussion Paper 248. ANU, Canberra

Martin, D. 2008: Aboriginal sorcery and healing and the alchemy of Aboriginal policy making. J. Anthropological Society, South Australia 33:75

Martin, D. 2008a Domestic Violence: homicide amongst remote-dwelling Australian Aboriginal people. International Conference on Homicide, Surfers Paradise, 3/12/2008

Martin, D. 2009: The governance agreements between Aboriginal people and resource developers: Principles for sustainability. In Altman and Martin. 2009

McConnel, U. 1931: A Moon Legend from the Bloomfield River, N. Qld. Oceania 2(1):9

McGrath, A. 1987: Born in the Cattle: Aborigines in Cattle Country. Allen & Unwin, Sydney

McKeich, K. 1971: Problems of part-Aboriginal Education, Ph.D. Thesis. UWA Perth

McKnight, D. 2002: From Hunting to Drinking. Routledge, London

Melleuish, G. 2009: Leave history alone. The Australian 1/8/09:12

Mulveny, D. 1993: Australian Anthropology: Foundations and Funding. Aboriginal History 17(2):105

Neill, R. 2002: White Out: How Politics is Killing Black Australia. Allen & Unwin, Sydney

Nowra, T. 2007: Bad Dreaming: Aboriginal Men's Violence against Women and Children. Pluto Press, North Melbourne

O'Fairheallaigh. 2000: Negotiating major project agreements: The Cape York model. Discussion Paper 11, AIATSIS, Canberra

Pearson, C. 2009: The Politics of Suffering by Peter Sutton. Review by Christopher Pearson, Weekend Australian 13/06/2009

Pearson, N. 1968: Colour and the police. The Criminologist 3(10)

Pearson, N. 2000: Our Right to Take Responsibility. Noel Pearson and Associates, Cairns

Pearson, N. 2009: Up from the Mission. Black Inc., Melbourne

Perez, E. 1958: Kalumburu, formerly Drysdale River Benedictine Mission. Abbey Press, New Norcia

Peterson, N. 1993: Demand sharing. American Anthropologist 95(4):860

Piddington, M & R. 1932: Report on fieldwork in north-western Australia. Oceania 2(3):342

Pilkington, D. 1996: Follow the Rabbit-Proof Fence. UQ Press Brisbane

Reynolds, H. 1987: Frontier. Allen & Unwin, Sydney

Reynolds, H. 1995: Fate of a Free People. Penguin, Sydney

Reynolds, H. 1996: Aboriginal Sovereignty. Allen & Unwin, Sydney

Reynolds, H. 1999: Why weren't we told. Penguin, Sydney

Roberts, B. 1998: What Constitutes a Fair Go for Aborigines? Discussion Paper. USQ Toowoomba

Roberts, B. 1998: The concept of Indigenocentrism in Ecojustice. Ecojustice Conference, Combined Churches, Adelaide

Roberts, B. 2008: Son of the Veld. Autobiography. Cairns

Roberts B. 2009: Where Angels Fear to Tread. Unpublished review. JCU Cairns

Roberts, J.P. 1975: The Mapoon Story by the Mapoon People. International Development Action, Fitzroy, Melbourne

Roth, W. 1897: Ethnological studies among the north-west-central Queensland Aborigines. Government Printer, Brisbane

Rowley, C. 1966: Some questions of causation in relation to Aboriginal affairs. In: Sharp & Tatz (Eds) Aboriginals in the Economy. Jacaranda Press, Brisbane

Rowley, C. 1970: The destruction of Aboriginal society. ANU Press, Canberra

Rowse, T. 2000: Obliged to be Difficult: Nugget Coombes, Legacy in Indigenous Affairs. Cambridge University Press.

Rubuntja, R. 1988: Land Rights News 2(9):24

Satour, T. 2001: Lessons from History and Abroad: Black Innocence, White Guilt and the New Authoritarian Separation. Unpublished paper, Cairns

Scambary, B. 2007: My Country, Mine Country. PhD Thesis, ANU, Canberra.

Searcy, A. 1909: In Australian Tropics. George Robertson & Co., Adelaide

Sen, A. 1999: Development as Freedom. Oxford University Press, London.

Sen, A. 2009: The Idea of Justice. Alan Lane, London

Silberbauer, G. 1973: Sociology of the G/wi Bushman. Ph.D. thesis, Monash University, Australia

Smith, D. 2002: Jurisdictional devolution: Towards an effective model for Indigenous community self-determination. Discussion paper 233, CAEPR, ANU, Canberra

Stanner, W.E.H. 1968: After the Dreaming. Boyer Lectures, ABC, Sydney

Stanner, W.E.H. 1979: White Man Got No Dreaming: Essays 1938-1973. ANU Press, Canberra

Stone, S. 1974: (Ed) Aborigines in White Australia: A Documentary History of the Attitudes affecting Official Policy and the Aborigine 1967-1973. Heineman Educational, Melbourne

Strehlow, T. 1956: The Sustaining Ideals of Australian Aboriginal Societies. Aboriginal Advancement League of South Australia, Adelaide

Strehlow, T. 1969: Journey to Horseshoe Bend. Angus and Robertson, Sydney

Sutton, P. 1988: Myth as history, history as myth. In: Keen (Ed) Being Black. Australian Institute of Aboriginal Studies Canberra: 88

Sutton, P. 2001: The Politics of Suffering: Indigenous policy in Australia since the 1970's. Anthropological Forum 11:125

Sutton, P. 2009: The Politics of Suffering. Indigenous Australia and the end of the liberal consensus. Melbourne University Press

Tatz, C. 1962: Shadow and substance in South Africa. Natal University Press, Durban

Tatz, C. 1990: Aboriginal violence: a return to pessimism. Australian Journal of Social Issues 25:245

Tatz, C. 2001: Aboriginal Suicide is Different. Aboriginal Studies Press, Canberra

Taylor, J. 1973: Anthropologists Report. Queensland Institute of Medical Research. 27th Annual Report: 26

Taylor, J. 1977: Diet, health and economy. In: Berndt (Ed) 1977:147

Taylor, J. 1989: Migration and population change in the Northern Territory. Australian Geographical Studies 27(2):182

Taylor, J. 2001: Anangu Population Dynamics and Future Growth in Uluru Kata-Tjuta National Park. ANU, Canberra

Thompson, L. 1993: From Somewhere Else. Simon & Schuster, Sydney

Tindale, N.B. 1974: Aboriginal Tribes of Australia. ANU Press, Canberra

Tonkinson, R. 1977: Aboriginal self-regulation and the new regime. In: Aborigines and Change (Ed) R. Berndt. Humanities Press, New York

Tonkinson, R. & Howard, M. 1991: (Eds) Going it alone? Prospects for Aboriginal autonomy.

Trigger, D. 1992: Whitefella Comin,?: Aboriginal Response to Colonisation in Northern Australia. Cambridge University Press, Melbourne

Trudgen, R. 2000: Why Warriors Lie Down and Die. Aboriginal Resource and Development Centre, Darwin

Tugby, D. 1973: (Ed) Aboriginal Identity in Contemporary Australia. Jacaranda Press, Brisbane

Von Sturmer, J. 1973: Changing Aboriginal identity in Cape York. In: Tugby 1973

# REFERENCES: SECTION ONE

Watson, Lukin P, 1983: This precious foliage: A Study of the Aboriginal psychoactive drug pituri. Oceanic Publications, University of Sydney Press, Sydney

Watson, Lukin P. 1998: Frontier Lands and Pioneer Legends. Allen & Unwin, Sydney

Wharton, H. 1995: Yumba Days at Warrego Camp. UQ Press, Brisbane

White, I. 1985: (Ed) The Native Tribes of Western Australia. National Library of Australia, Canberra

Williams, N.M. 1984: Yonglu concepts of land ownership. In: Peterson & Langtree (Eds). Aboriginal Land and Land Rights, Canberra

Willkis, B. 1992: From Indispensability to Redundancy: Afghans in Western Australia 1887-1911. Papers in Labour History 9, June

Windschuttle, K. 2000: The myth of frontier massacres in Australian history. Quadrant 44(10)

Windshuttle, K. 2002: The Fabrication of Aboriginal History. Macleay Press, Sydney

Woodward, A. 1974: Aboriginal Land Rights Second Report (Woodward Report). AGPS, Canberra

Woolmington, J. 1986: The Civilisation/Christianisation Debate and the Aborigines. Aboriginal History 10(2):90

Wright, J. 1985: We Call for a Treaty. Collins/Fontana Publishers, Sydney

Young, E. 1984: Outback Stores: Retail Services in North Australia Aboriginal Communities. North Australian Research Unit, Darwin

Young, E. 1988: Land Use and Resources: a black and white dichotomy. In: Heathcote & Mabbutt (Eds) Land, Water and People. Allen & Unwin, Sydney

## Section 3

Australian Academy of Science 2010: The Science of Climate Change. AAS, Canberra.

Birch, C. 1990: On Purpose UNSW Press, Sydney.

Collins, P. 1990: In Search of the Church: Catholics at the Crossroads. National Outlook 12(5): 6-11

Dodson, P. 1988: The Land Our Mother, the Church Our Mother. Compass Theology Review 22(1); 1-3

Gore, A. 2006: An Inconvenient Truth. Paramount DVD, N.Y.

Hulme, M. 2006: Chaotic World of Climate Truth. BBC 4/11/06 bbc.co.uk

IPCC. 2001: Climate Change 2001 The Scientific Basis. Cambridge University Press

John Paul II 1986: The Pope in Australia. St Paul Publications, Homebush NSW

King, D. 2004: Environment – Climate Change Science: Adapt, Mitigate or Ignore. Science 303: 176-7

Kneebone, E. 1991: An Aboriginal Response. In: Creation, Spirituality and The Dreamtime, C Hammond (Ed.). Millennium Books, Sydney.

Lomborg, B. 2001: The Sceptical Environmentalist. Cambridge University Press

Lomborg, B. 2008: Cool It. Vintage Books, N.Y.

Lovelock, J. 1979: Gaia: A New Look at Life on Earth. Oxford University Press

Lynas, M 2004: High Tide: The truth about our climate crisis. Picador, N.Y.

Monbiot, G. 2006: Heat: How to stop the Planet burning. Allen Lane, London

Pachauri, R.K. 2006: In Lomborg 2008.

Roberts, B.R. 1973: Ecological Education – A Challenge to Extension. South African Journal of Agricultural Extension 2:5-7

Roberts, B.R. 2009: Where Angels Fear to Tread: A Seekers Journey toward faith, reason and environmental ethics: Discussion Paper, JCU, Cairns

# REFERENCES: SECTION THREE

Roberts, D. 2006: The Denial Industry. At gristmill.grist.org

Rose, .D. 1992: Dingo Makes Us Human: Life and Land in an Australian Aboriginal Culture. Cambridge University Press

Stanner, W.E.H. 1979: White Man Got No Dreaming. ANU Press, Canberra

Stockton, E. 1990: Landmarks: A Spiritual Search in a Southern Land. Parish Ministry Publications, Eastwood, Sydney.

Stockton, E. 1995: The Aboriginal Gift: Spirituality for a Nation. Millennium Books, Sydney

Tol, R.S. & Yohe, G.W. 2006: A Review of the Stern Review. World Economics 7(4) 233-256

# APPENDIX I

## CUSTOMS OFFICER SEARCY – EMPIRE PERSONIFIED IN BLACKFELLA COUNTRY

One could hold up any one of a dozen administrators or squatters of the late 1800's as a case study in the mindset and values of the settler society, but Alfred Searcy, Collector of Customs for fourteen years in Darwin from 1882, strikes the author as the epitome of 'Empire men'; including his use of the colloquial term for Indigenes, which to meet modern usage, is written here as 'native'.

In his memoirs "In Australia's Tropics" (1909) Searcy reflects so tellingly his generation's worldview and opinion of tribal people that he is used here as a typical European observer of Australia's northern frontier. His preface by Ernest Whittington, as published in the South Australian Register, lays great credence in his writings, stating "Anything which Mr. Searcy has set down………. is at least an absolute fact which can be verified". While the present author has reason to doubt such veracity, Searcy is a useful case study of his times.

Rather than scour Searcy's 400 page tome for references to classified topics, at the risk of fragmentation, it is sufficient to simply *quote his statements* in the order in which he relates them to gain a picture of the life on the frontier and values of his day:

"If the settlement (of Northern Australia) had been made by any other nation, I expect it would only have supplied another evidence of the fact that the Anglo-Saxons are the only people who can colonise successfully.

It is well-known that for centuries the Malays paid annual visits to the

## APPENDIX 1: CUSTOMS OFFICER SEARCY

northern coast of this continent and carried the spoils to Macassar (today's Ujung Pandang in Sulawesi). They had removed millions of pounds worth of trepang (sea-cucumber or *beche-de-mer*), pearls, pearlshell, tortoise shell and timber.

There were some 60 praos (wooden fishing boats) upon the coast. These people were Mahometans (*sic.*) and expressed great horror to see hogs. The praos (first noted by Flinders in 1803) seemed to be about 25 tons and to have 20-25 men in each. About 125 years ago one of the praos was driven by the NW monsoon to the coast of New Holland and finding trepang to be abundant there, they have fished there ever since. The praos had hulls of wood with deck and yards of bamboo, sails of matting and ropes of plaited cane. They were steered by two rudders at the stern and most had stone anchors lashed to wood.

The natives collected pearls during the absence of the Malays (Indonesians) for whom they saved them and received in return grog and tobacco. The Malays took away immense quantities of tortoise-shell (hawkbill), which was also collected by the natives.

The liquor the Malays carried was awful stuff. From my experience natives can carry a fair amount of good liquor but this stuff seemed to drive them mad. I invariably gave my boys a nip or two a day when hunting although, of course, it was against the law. The love of drink is strongly planted in the natives and they will obtain it how and when they can. The Aborigines of the north coast are far and away superior, both in physique and intelligence to the natives down south (Adelaide). The food supply in the north was unlimited. All the rivers and swamps were teeming with game and fish. Edible roots are always obtainable in the jungles while on the coast shellfish, dugong and turtle abound.

Smallpox, which was introduced by the Malays, at times, swept right across the continent. Buffalo, which were the offspring of those left by the soldiers in 1826 (at Fort Dundas) became a regular industry. Fifty thousand hides passed through the Customs House in little over ten years.

The Malays never succeeded in making friends with the natives on Melville Island. The reason why the Blacks were so suspicious was that Malay slavers had previously carried some Aboriginals as slaves. The island is called Amba, the Malay word for slave.

## OVERCOMING DISADVANTAGE

Being the end of the dry season, of course, nearby all the grass was down and in most places burnt (by the natives). In the dry season the vegetation is generally fired by the natives for hunting purposes. I have seen some forty miles of country in a blaze at once. The natives considered the flying fox a great delicacy and only old men are allowed to eat it.

Mr. Stretton has been over thirty years in the Northern Territory and is an extremely valuable officer. He is a great authority on the Aborigines. He showed conclusively that there is a mixture of Malay blood with the natives of the north coast. That intercourse with some foreign people existed more than a century ago is proved by the records of Matthew Flinders.

There were many murders by natives that the police had to look into...... There can be no doubt that many of the murders were caused by the White men taking away the Black women from their tribes. Nearly all the drovers, cattlemen and station hands had their 'Black boys' (gins). No objection was raised by the Black men to interference with their women so long as they were not abducted. The Black women are, as a rule, well treated by those who take them. In the great out-beyond *half-caste children never live* (my emphasis).

There can be no doubt that at times many of the Blacks have been put away by the same (White) brutes just for the fun of killing, by others for revenge, but mostly the natives brought the trouble on themselves by interfering with the cattle. Some years ago I got a letter from a man who was attacked by natives in the Gulf country and received some eleven spear wounds. He recovered. In his letter he said, "I now shoot on sight; killed to date thirty-seven."

Donegan noticed a peculiar custom amongst the Black tribes inhabiting the Gulf country between the Roper and Normanton (rivers) in Queensland. It seemed that they were in the habit of exchanging children with each other for the purpose of learning each other's languages and customs. There were very few fights between the respective tribes. It seemed as if in that system of education they were ahead of us with all our boasted civilisation.

Mr. F. Bradshaw, a Victoria River squatter was killed on his launch and the launch looted. Mr. Bradshaw was well known for the kindness with which he had always treated the Blacks on his station and the great trust he had always placed in them. It had been predicted that his kindness would someday be repaid with treachery. The native, even the half-civilised one, is an uncertain animal, and always possesses the brute desire to kill.

## APPENDIX 1: CUSTOMS OFFICER SEARCY

The features of the Port Keats (present Wadeye) Blacks bear a remarkably eastern, almost Jewish cast. They are inclined to be copper-coloured, with rather an aquiline nose. The hair, instead of being woolly, is long and straight. I have never seen, or even heard of, natives of a similar type being found on the north coast. There is a foreign strain in these people somewhere.

Dr. A.F. Lynch (who visited Searcy) states: "Nearly every Fitzmaurice River tribe lubra has four or five children at her feet. I don't think there is any doubt about the Fitzmaurice natives being cannibals. I secured a couple of dilly-bags, and in one I found the remains of a human hand, that of a child, which had been cooked. Their spears are often dipped into the poison of decayed human flesh.

On Wandy Wandy's liberation (from prison on a manslaughter charge) he was taken in hand by the Jesuit Fathers who had a mission station close to town (Darwin); but the outlaws end proved how futile their labours were. I knew the Fathers well. A finer lot of dear, earnest, hard-working men it would be impossible to find anywhere. All their endeavours, however, to civilise the Blacks came to naught and the mission stations were given up.

[Referring to the failure of Fort Dundas in about 1835] Searcy writes: The Blacks were hostile then, as they are now. They have had a long immunity from trouble, and that, no doubt, added to the traditions of how they drove the White men away from the fort, and the Malays from the coast, was calculated to make them worse. Their word "boom" refers to the rifle, apparently a familiar sound to the natives which did not recall pleasant memories.

The hunters had a number of mainland boys with them, who were in mortal dread of the island Blacks. Weapons such as boomerangs were not known on Melville Island although the Malays had bows and arrows. The woomera was not used on the island and these islanders were far and away behind their brethren of the mainland in the manufacture of spears.

During the previous four and a half months to when I visited the island (Melville) the White hunters had shot two thousand buffaloes. It was considered that the natives would run down the calves and kill them thus keeping the increase in check. Experience showed, however, that such was not the case……It was found that the natives had no idea that young buffalo was good tucker. The buffalo hunters found that by burning the grass judiciously, they can get green feed all through the dry season.

## OVERCOMING DISADVANTAGE

The spring tide at Daly River is twenty-one feet; the river is navigable for sixty miles, the last part being fresh water. Big crocodiles abound but the natives do not fear them, poking a stick in their jaws if they attack. [Searcy seemed unaware that many tribes revered the crocodile, believing they carried the clans' ancestral spirits, making the crocodile a family totem.]

At Copper Landing (on the Daly) the natives, from that brute desire to kill and destroy, suddenly attacked the miners, all White men, while at work, and killed three outright, a fourth being left for dead.......The victims were real good men, who had always treated the natives with the utmost kindness and consideration. To my idea, they erred on the wrong side.......There can be no doubt that terrible reprisals took place, but not to the outrageous extent reported (in the press) at the time. I am afraid, however, that during the excitement some innocent natives went under.

Not far from Copper Landing was the Jesuit Mission Station. It was in full swing then.......From my experience with the natives, it always seemed to me that they were perfectly willing to listen to the 'Word' as long as they had free tucker and plenty of tobacco. As an excuse I have heard them say "Too much J.C. all day long; no more tobacco".

My friend Dr. Lynch made a study of the Daly River and Fitzmaurice tribes. He said 'I became, like most other people do, little concerned about danger. I went among the Blacks with perfect confidence. Still I am of the opinion that you should never trust a Black fellow. It is like the tamed tiger tasting blood, there will come a time some day when the Black man will turn on you. His savage instincts are easily aroused. The native has an innate desire to kill. It is part and parcel of his being. He thinks the White man is in his country to do something criminal to his best interests and to exercise a malign influence. He kills the White man on the same principle that the White man kills a black snake. I had a friendly game of cards with the station manager one night. We parted and went different ways on the morrow. In a few hours my friend had a tomahawk in his head, spears in his body, and his hands and feet chopped off" (wrote Dr. Lynch).

Among other things Dr. Lynch told me that the Blacks up in this country are born deceivers.......All the corroborees, chants and ceremonials deal with phallic worship. The songs and dances are of a most bestial type. A young buck who kills a Black fellow is looked upon as a hero, but he who kills a

# APPENDIX 1: CUSTOMS OFFICER SEARCY

White man is regarded as a god. The murder of the Whites is usually planned by the old gins, who carry on the traditions of the race and exercise a sort of witches' spell, Up in these parts the natives indulge in the practice of singing a man dead…….The poor victim of the singing goes away into the bush and literally lies down and dies.

I had a friend named "Footsack"…….who had been in Zululand and was even using the word (to dogs) which I understood meant 'clear out'. One night when up-country camping out, his mates yelled "look out Footsack, natives"……When camping in bad native country the usual custom is to sling the (mosquito) nets, light the fire….then sneak off (to sleep) some distance from the camp. Over and over again fellows have found spears through their nets when they returned in the morning.

Turtle, both greenback and hawkbill are plentiful in the waters around Port Darwin (named by Captain Stokes of the Beagle in 1839, after his friend, the naturalist Charles Darwin). Mr. Christie, in writing to me about the turtles says the hawkbill lays from 110 to 137 eggs. The greenback doesn't lay here (at Darwin). The principal egg-layers here are the turtle Dernochelys. Their average would be about 30 (eggs), the highest 78 in one nest. One turtle will lay five to six times a fortnight…….One canoe will bring in a thousand eggs in one trip from Quail Island. Christie got lovely turtle shell from the natives…….which realised forty-nine shillings per pound in London. Mr. Christie wrote that the prawns we get here in the billabongs (open to the sea) go up to one foot, tail to head, not counting the feelers. The natives reckon the prawns at Lesser Peron Island are much bigger than the ones here.

(When pearlshell was discovered in Darwin harbour in 1884) "there was a great rush of boats, upwards of one hundred boats (from Thursday Island), reporting at Port Darwin. Something like forty tons of shell was secured in the harbour…….For pearling the White men are not in it with the Japanese and Manillamen. The White men were not amenable to discipline and could not be depended on…….At times the White divers behaved outrageously. There was such a mixture of nationalities in the crews of the pearling boats.

As the natives take most kindly to all the White man's vices, naturally they are great smokers and commence very young. I have seen a youngster drop the (mother's) breast, take a lighted pipe from the mother's mouth, and proceed to blow a cloud on its own account.

## OVERCOMING DISADVANTAGE

I have already mentioned how the Blacks gorge when a good opportunity arises…….so do little natives. In Port Darwin a merchant known as George who at stated intervals would supply the young natives (who worked for him) as much tucker as it was possible to take in during one session. It was a revelation the quantity the little Black cusses could put away. Their 'capacities' would gradually distend until they had the appearance of proverbial pup…… the little natives were happy and tight…….

I do not suggest that White men should actively engage in the cultivation of tropical crops, for I am of the opinion that that can only be carried out by coloured labour."

Note: It will be observed that Searcy refers only to negative attributes of the Aboriginals, as seen by Victorian Europeans but made no effort during his long stay in the Territory, to understand the Indigenous culture and the meaning of its beliefs and practices as one of the oldest living cultures on earth.

# APPENDIX 2

## WHAT CONSTITUES A FAIR GO FOR ABORIGINES?

Brian Roberts
Land Use Study Centre, USQ
3 September 1998

## 1. BACKGROUND

During the past decade this Centre has been involved in various aspects of land use planning and management. These include water rights, fisheries, dam proposals, wildlife preservation, tree clearing and rezoning. In recent years non-Indigenous landholders have tended to perceive the problems of flood, drought, fire and pests as having been compounded by the emergence of Native Title as a new factor in land use planning and management. The term 'fair go' used in the title of this paper is well understood by non-Indigenous Australians but has seldom included Aborigines. In the same way, the reference to Aborigines as stakeholders rather than owners in the land debate devalues the original owners' view of their stake in the resources under question. However, it should be understood that Aborigines do not claim to 'own' the land in the European sense, but rather to have inherited usufruct or 'use rights' from their ancestors. In fact they believe that the land owns them.

It is recognised that while many of the statements on Aborigines which are contained in this paper are largely true, they may be best stated by Aborigines rather than by outsiders. However, readers will look in vain for clarity on 'whose side is the writer on?', because this overview does not select evidence to support a preconceived outcome, but rather it seeks to weigh the strengths and weaknesses on both sides of the current land debate. It makes no apology for limiting its source materials largely to the popular press, for it is here that the most stark opposing views are writ large. This paper aims to clarify thinking on a complex and divisive issue. At the same time it may contribute toward elevating the land debate to a higher plane where human rights and equality take precedence over political expediency and situation ethics.

The Land Use Study Centre was intimately involved (Roberts 1995) in the Cape York Peninsula Land Use Strategy (CYPLUS). In this project it became clear that the Aboriginal land issue cannot be considered rationally in isolation from associated issues. This paper aims to examine some of those issues, most of which are basic philosophical issues on which future policy will have to be built if a 'fair go', equitable to all, is to be achieved.

## 2. HUMAN RIGHTS

The human rights concept had been around long before the United Nations or Amnesty International clarified their intent for global application to the human condition. Such rights have come to focus attention on the inequalities between groups, tribes, sexes, nations, religions and ages. Little has been written (with the exception of Nash 1991) on non-human rights, although in the environmental (biodiversity) sphere this becomes the subject for serious comparative studies. The extension of ethics to fellow organisms other than *Homo sapiens* requires attention when original occupation becomes a bargaining chip in the land claim game. This will be referred to later in the context of the Eurocentric vs. Ecocentric debate. If animals do turn out to have souls, many of us carnivores will be in big trouble. This question has been around since St Francis of Assisi (patron saint of ecology) who worked on the premise that gentleness toward animals might prove a guarantee of sensitivity towards human beings as well. This 'brother bird and sister flower' idea was dumped by Christianity, but to this day Buddhists and Hindus maintain this reverence for all life. So what? So Aborigines in their viewing of mammals, reptiles and birds as sources of food, as custom and totem provided by the creation for their use, might care to re-examine the spiritual benefits of vegetarianism, as have many non-Indigenous Australians. Human rights are seen as having not only justice components, but biophysical, psychological and environmental dimensions. Thus the classical revolutionary cry for liberty (freedom), democracy and equality, are expanded to include needs from physiological to sociological.

# APPENDIX 2: WHAT CONSTITUTES A FAIR GO FOR ABORIGINES

Although it took until 27 May 1967 for Aborigines to gain the vote, it should not be overlooked that over 90% of Australians supported that referendum – the largest 'yes vote' ever in a national referendum. It might be useful to debate what motivated those voters and how such motives might contribute to the current attempts at establishment of a conciliatory relationship between Indigenous and non-Indigenous Australians.

Presently the human rights protagonists in Australia concentrate on Land Rights for Indigenous people. This perceived right is based on the special relationship between these people and their land, both spiritual and material (food). This bond with country by rural Aborigines isn't challenged; what is challenged, at least by a portion of Australian society, is whether such bonds (leading to rights) pertain to long-urbanised communities, and by what mechanisms such Land Rights should reasonably be fulfilled.

Increasingly, a new concept is creeping into the establishment of Land Rights as a subset of human rights. That is the concept of 'deserving' or 'warranting' or 'earning' such rights – rights now seen by many as not being automatic ('as of right') but rather as being justified only when deserved. This concept finds a parallel in so-called cross-compliance policies in which benefits are conferred only when conditions are met. Being first may no longer be enough.

The claim that, because one's ancestors once occupied certain country, one's present family has inalienable rights to repossess such land, has real difficulties, especially for those who represent the present 'power culture' and are steeped in a history written by the victors. The first difficulty is that of accepting the facts about the history of conquest. All human history is some sequence of invasion and dominance of physical power – Europe, America, Asia and Australia. In all these countries there are groups who no longer own the land of their forefathers. This is fact, not a defence of military or civil power as the means of gaining historic *de facto* ownership as distinct from *de jure* ownership. It should be asked at what organisational level or group identity should Sovereign rights (ownership) be given? The nation, the tribe, the clan, the family or the individual? It should be pointed out that past civilisations were never judged on how they treated their oppressed (or their environment) and perhaps it is time to rethink our measures of progress.

There is a need to consider human rights within a framework of a Bill of Rights for all citizens, as in the U.S. Constitution. Such a Bill could include freedom of movement including entry to and exit from Australia; freedom from discrimination on the basis of race, origin, gender, ethnicity, religion or marital status. Presently, there is a perceived reverse discrimination which is seen to offer Indigenous peoples advantages because of their historic disadvantage based on race. This perception is shared by both right-wingers and battlers of various political persuasions.

The punishment of Aboriginal children for speaking their language at mission schools, finds parallels in the Anglicanisation of Boer children in South Africa after 1910; in the unsuccessful imposition of the Afrikaans language on black scholars in South Africa after 1948, and in the English attempts to eliminate Cymru culture in Welsh schools of the 1800s. The historic message is that, because these small group languages have great value in their cultural richness, they should be accepted and nurtured as such. Those who cherish these languages should not expect others to want to learn their languages for anything but insight into the contribution of those tongues to knowledge and understanding – in this case, of the bonds between humans and mother earth, plus the dietary and health knowledge held only by Indigenous peoples. The usefulness and thus perceived significance of the Dreaming stories to other peoples are probably less important. At the same time it is recognised that local languages are highly revered by their users and are, in many cases, the only languages which adequately encapsulate and express local culture. This endemism is vital not only in validating clans' country but also in maintaining cultural connectedness. Aborigines have no monopoly on these bonds; they are equally well developed in both the Old and the New Worlds.

## 2.1  History, Guilt and Victims

The global movement of settlers, cultures and religions is a very old phenomenon. The Egyptians, Phoenicians, Greeks and Romans established 'new colonies' all over the Old World. The Chinese sailed to Africa and the Middle East. The Hindus and Muslims from various Asian countries spread their religions to new lands throughout the East. Later, the Portuguese, Spanish and Dutch preceded the English as the last of the colonising powers, with relatively minor excursions by others such as the French and the Germans. So, when some 800 convicts arrived at Sydney Cove on 26 January 1788, they

## APPENDIX 2: WHAT CONSTITUTES A FAIR GO FOR ABORIGINES

were late-comers not only to the Great South Land, but also to the global human movement phenomenon. When the fate of the original occupiers of those other invaded/settled countries is examined today, we find some form of assimilation with the new-comers in virtually all cases. So why is assimilation (which can also maintain culture) so unacceptable to the separatists in the Australian case? Two reasons may be, (a) the indispensable links between original hunter-gatherers and their landscapes and (b), the acceptance by most Australians of the idea of a 'fair go' – unlike many other countries where elimination of special, different, separate and widespread Land Rights has been the norm.

When on the 3rd of June 1992, the High Court, in a majority decision (of six to one) judged that the Mabo case proved that Australia was not *terra nullius* (unoccupied, unused), Land Rights changed forever in this country. This decision, according to Brennan (1993), belatedly acknowledges the unwritten Law of the Land. (See Section 1 – Appendix III for Dennis's (1930) 'Spoilers'.)

The inheritance of generational guilt has only recently become a factor in the Indigenous debate in Australia – ever since conservative politicians referred to the perceived negative effects of what they termed the 'guilt industry'. Even more recently, this concept has been strengthened, perhaps unintentionally, by Reynolds and Langton's Frontiers series on ABC-TV in early 1997. Violent history has two effects which are of concern to the present Indigenous debate – shame on the oppressors, dispossession and placelessness on the vanquished. When many of the latter are, at most, only a few generations removed from an original hunter/gatherer culture, the problems of competing in a modern technological economy are magnified.

The on-going argument on whether Australia was settled or invaded was ignited by Reynolds (1995), who believes that this question is more than academic. Thus, while Brennan believes the Indigenous people were never conquered, Reynolds uses the Tasmanian wars, in which some 5,000 Aborigines were killed, to demonstrate otherwise. The importance of the argument is that it turns rebels into patriots, guerrillas into defenders and the lawless into brave and righteous clansmen. As such, they should have pride of place as national heroes appearing on war memorials. Should not all Australians mourn those who died defending their Homeland – perhaps on Anzac Day.

## OVERCOMING DISADVANTAGE

Blainey's (1993) two contrasting views of history, i.e. the Three Cheers View and Black Armband View, have been brought into sharp focus in recent years. This comparison forces Australians to confront the questions of what was good, what we should be proud of, what we should be ashamed of and by what criteria we should judge our success/progress. Blainey suggests that 50 years ago, fewer than 50,000 Australians would have seen white treatment of Aborigines as a 'blot on our history'. Today several million see it as the major blot on our national record, and perhaps half our population sees this part of our history as 'highly regrettable'. In denouncing earlier generations as being brutal and discriminatory, Blainey believes we do ourselves a national disservice when we allow this to discount, almost ignore, their hard-won successes in many other fields.

This pride/shame dichotomy probably applies to both blacks and whites in Australia. Presently it's the whites' turn to take the raps for what seemed to be 'OK then, but not OK now'. But the flip-side to this sensitivity is the way in which political correctness is causing journalists, academics, feminists, politicians and sociologists, to ignore or at least remain silent on, less acceptable (to Europeans) aspects of Aboriginal customs and behaviour, for fear of being accused of racism or redneck-ism. Criticism for stating what is not politically palatable has led to moral cowardice, which hampers social progress. The fear of patronising Aborigines has caused helpers to withhold their otherwise useful contributions toward upliftment of the Aborigines – even the word 'uplifting' is liable to be interpreted as an insult. Dismissing some Aboriginal behaviour as either 'just the Aboriginal Way' or 'too hot to handle' as Rosemary Neill puts it, is a cop-out, a form of dishonesty and ultimately a moral failure. Take the issue of domestic violence where Aboriginal women are reported to be 33 times more likely to be killed than other Australian women. When will we hear the feminists' voice on this tragic issue? Rather than using such statistics to denounce a disadvantaged group, they could be used to bring home a cry for help, a symptom of a people in need of urgent support.

Presently those who want to accept history (with all its appalling human tragedies) and get on with looking ahead at problem-solving, are accused of insensitivity and of denying history's implications. Demands for integration of factual Indigenous history into Australian schools are based on the idea that, if coming generations are fully aware of the past, they will be more understanding

## APPENDIX 2: WHAT CONSTITUTES A FAIR GO FOR ABORIGINES

and even-handed in future inter-racial dealings. Whether this will be the outcome remains to be seen. It may well lead to an attitude of 'you owe us' on the part of the vanquished – and with some justification. But is this the way to meet the future, or does it simply feed discontent and lead to an attitude in which past persecution leads to a lack of willingness to look inwards and become self sufficient? Blaming others for one's lack of progress must be matched by the will to succeed, although success may be very differently defined within Indigenous cultures. Without their land being given back to them, most remote Aborigines apparently cannot even make a start on the road to progress in their terms – 'our country is part of us; without it we can't exist'.

The other side of these historic effects is the very real social and personal damage done by past happenings to present survivors of recent history. It is the living trauma suffered by such persons which affects their ability to be positive, productive and interactive members of the new society they find themselves in. There will be no early outcome from the behaviour/ environment debate in which child removal, institutionalisation and abuse form the background for present drunkenness, violence, vandalism and incarceration. We shall return to this issue.

When Paul Keating very publicly admitted, and apologised for, past mistreatment of Aborigines in 1992, the audience at Redfern Park were probably mostly people with tenuous personal links to the land outside metropolitan Sydney. Their cultural activities would be through art, music, drama and dance. Their countrymen at Aurukun, Kakadu or Uluru would no doubt wish to express their culture more directly on their land, in the landscape, together with the animals, birds and plants of their land. Reynolds (1995a) in his revisionist history of internal race relations in Australia, recognises that the new Aboriginal nationalism, is in fact riding on the back of the cultural revival of Indigenous art – in all its forms. Rothwell (1996) makes the point that the surprising element of the rise of the 'Aboriginal presence' is the rate at which it has occurred – three decades from being 'disenfranchised outcasts to favoured icons' with sophisticated spirituality and ecological sensitivity. As referred to elsewhere in this paper, the real value of the practice of these attributes in modern Australia warrants critical examination, especially when the use of modern hunting technology becomes the vehicle for implementation of otherwise worthy ideals.

## 2.2 Present Standard of Living and Quality of Life

The basic question of 'separateness' as a goal for future Aboriginal communities needs urgent attention. Partington (1996) was given short shrift by the separatists when his book *Hasluck versus Coombs* called for a more understanding consideration of the merits of assimilation. Pointing out that the investment of over $10 billion over the past two decades had in fact left the Aborigines worse off in terms of health and living conditions, Partington challenges Australians to be honest about the failure of the separatist policy based on Land Rights. Tatz (1994) who visited 77 Aboriginal communities in five States in 1971 and again 20 years later, reported on the comprehensive evidence that, by a range of social, health and quality of life measures, Indigenous people had gone backwards. Howson (1996) calls for brutal honesty on the outcomes of land grants such as those in the Pilbara and at Wave Hill, which he terms 'poverty' traps'. These places, he says, are 'vehicles that simply guarantee Third World living conditions indefinitely'. Land rights may not necessarily provide employment, but appropriate funding for multiple use of land, could go a long way to encourage self-sufficiency. Nor do Land Rights guarantee cultural vitality. 'Providing opportunities for employment will do much more to establish a sense of pride and self-determination than will Land Rights' (Howson 1996).

Most commentators on Indigenous living standards generally give attention to only one of the three groups, namely rural, town or city. Such partitioning by researchers is understandable since the situations, land-links and lifestyle of these groups are different. However, there are similarities, in as much as poor health, low literacy, alcoholism and violence are characteristic of too many Indigenous communities across this spectrum.

In evaluating living standards, the definition of high standards becomes important. As a subset of the Australian nation, Indigenous peoples may, to varying degrees, use materialistic European measures of social attainment – house, car, income and consumer goods. The extent to which this replaces Indigenous values is probably proportional to their extent of exposure to Western lifestyles and the opportunities they have had to become acquirers of materialism.

Importantly, Aboriginal society in its pre-European form did not include the Western concepts of competition, acquisition or aggression for personal gain. In hunter-gatherer societies, nothing more than survival may have been

## APPENDIX 2: WHAT CONSTITUTES A FAIR GO FOR ABORIGINES

the measure of success. But in today's society, unless individuals 'compete' at least in the sense of earning their keep, they can easily be perceived as being dependent on the efforts of others. Thus while there is general agreement that the majority of today's Indigenous people do not enjoy the living standard of other Australians (including Asian and African Migrants), there are serious differences of opinion on the causes of such discrepancies. Aboriginal spokespersons suggest that the first requirement is to return to their land, then to develop management plans and finally they hope that jobs might follow.

The universal Poverty Cycle links unemployment to malnutrition and inability to learn and work, then links poor health to lower longevity and further susceptibility to disease. The availability of both clean water and educational opportunities to rural Aborigines, for instance, are still at unacceptable levels in many cases. However, the economic rationalists will continue to ask why it is necessary to carry the very high costs of the required services to very small economically unsustainable communities in remote areas, for both black and white bush dwellers.

For many decades it has been recognised that until alcoholism has been reduced, raising general living standards will remain difficult. While the argument that alcohol, as a form of escapism from the traumas brought on by historic disadvantage in many forms, carries weight, it does nothing to ease the burden of families affected.

A group desiring to justify its existence as a viable contributing population group in this era of increasing resource scarcity, will have to do better than the simple 'we were here first' or 'we have been wronged' claim. The leading Aboriginal view is that they are not looking for charity, only for justice. They will need to represent communal values which are regarded by competing groups (clans, ethnic identities, cultures) as worthy, respected and appropriate to the coming century. Being proud of our past and taking pride in our cultural achievements are laudable, but we should admit to the unacceptable elements of our culture. Last year Lefkowitz (1996) was accused of 'white racism' for her book *Not Out of Africa: How Afrocentrism Became an Excuse to Teach Myth as History*. What she was examining was the lack of worthy values and customs in the African communities which black Americans called their roots – the pride in being African-Americans. That book was followed by another, *Out of America: A Black Man Confronts Africa* in which the author

(Richburg 1996) is appalled by the present barbarism of his forebears. He says, 'Most hypocritical is that many black Americans who were most vocal about Apartheid in South Africa are silent about the lack of democracy and human rights in black Africa. They offer tortured explanations as to why America shouldn't criticise Africa and why America shouldn't impose its standards… It's as if repression comes only in white.'

How do these dangers of 'over-glorification' (Richburg 1996) of a community's roots, relate to Indigenous Australians? They should help Aborigines to take only the best from their past and build on it. They should help to identify those negative elements which are best left in the past. They should help Aborigines to recognise the beneficial, cultural and behavioural changes required for future prosperity.

Rijavec's film *Exile and the Kingdom*, as first screened on ABC-TV in the early 1990s, portrays the tragic sequence of loss of land → despair → drinking → violence → social breakdown. It is this placeless, hopeless and jobless community that Adams (1993) refers to when he says. 'The voice of the redneck is loud in the land. People whose culture is little more than country and western music and a few Eastwood movies rented from the video store, can be heard laughing at any suggestion that our Aborigines might have a culture. And the words of bigots with a grammar school education, make much the same point in their pompous patronising letters to the editor' (Adams 1993). Such inflammatory remarks do little to fix the reconciliation problem, and this type of stereotyping of group cultures and beliefs, simply adds to the conflict. What is required now is genuine tolerance and generosity of spirit. These are the basic ingredients of settling the Native Title issue. Without them no '10 (or 20) point plan' has a future.

## 3. LIFESTYLE

## 3.1 Services

As in standard of living, the rural, town and city communities enjoy different levels of services, not just essential services. The same applies to non-Indigenous communities in these localities, but Aborigines appear to have additional problems in accessing the available resources. This is caused by financial stress, poor communication, poor motivation and in some cases subtle and

## APPENDIX 2: WHAT CONSTITUTES A FAIR GO FOR ABORIGINES

not-so-subtle discriminatory practices by those offering or publicising the services.

Again, both health and education are cases in point, but generalisations about Indigenous people would be as inappropriate as about any other population group. So Redfern and Palm Island must each be analysed on the basis of what services are available, to what extent are they used, and if not fully used, for what reasons people are not taking advantage of available health, education, information and social services. The 'reasons behind the reasons' then need to be sought and corrective action taken, by way of ongoing long-term programs. These should be developed by and run by Indigenous people, as a means of educating their own people into ways of helping themselves.

## 3.2 Training

Education has been mentioned in the context of basic abilities required to break out of the poverty cycle. Training on the other hand, is fitting individuals for making a particular contribution to the wealth-generating economy. There are of course several Aboriginal Training Programs in place, some of which have successfully built on the talents for which this race have become known: bushcraft, bushtucker collection, stockmen, tour guides and other careers aligned to the land-based interests of rural Aborigines. There are many other skills for which they are not (yet) known. These could be developed and used, starting with social service, music, arts and community health. Meanwhile the growing numbers of professional Aborigines is very heartening.

The Indigenous Land Corporation started operating in June 1995. Its objective was to assist Indigenous people to acquire and manage land 'to derive economic, environmental, social or cultural benefits' (ILC 1996). In recent years attention has been given to the (long-overdue) 'Caring for Country: National Curriculum Development Program'. Here, perhaps for the first time, Australia has an appropriate framework for reaping the benefits of combining Western Ecology with Traditional Ecological Knowledge (TEK). Good examples of documented TEK (Williams' and Baines 1993) are the Aboriginal Plant Classification of Arnhem land, and the Food Calendars of Borroloola in the Gulf. Roberts (1996) has described how such knowledge can enrich ecotourism on Aboriginal land. In the CYPLUS study (Roberts

1995) it was recommended that special training for Aboriginal landholders and rural workers could be introduced to increase their effectiveness in the cattle industry. The concept of TEK is now included in USQ's external Environmental Studies unit written by this Centre. In the same way, all teacher trainees at USQ take Australian Indigenous Studies as a compulsory subject.

Training which integrates Natural and Cultural Heritage would be of special advantage for communities involved in rural production or tourism. Such knowledge could combine the requirements for sustainable land use (marketable products) with the spiritual and cultural values which increasingly are being recognised as a new additional basis for land valuation. While such values are referred to as non-productive values (like aesthetic and bequest values) they are becoming more important in impact statements which must evaluate all values affected by proposed developments.

In the city environment, everything should be done to encourage Aboriginals to make full use of tertiary education opportunities in all spheres that could be of benefit to their communities. These spheres should go far beyond those disciplines traditionally allied to their culture – song, dance, art, story-telling and Indigenous customs. A rapidly expanding core of well qualified Aboriginal teachers will be the single most important element in the development of a vigorous and vital community.

While many observers of the Aboriginal education debate see the main issue as the inclusion of Aboriginal Studies either in all schools or in Aboriginal schools, the rest of Australia still grapples with the problem of reaching consensus on which values should be taught in all schools. In a survey of six States, Clarnette (1989) found the following values most frequently listed (in order) by Education Departments' policies:

- Self-esteem
- Respect for others
- Cooperation
- Social Justice
- Honesty
- Respect for Environment
- Respect for Truth
- Kindness

APPENDIX 2: WHAT CONSTITUTES A FAIR GO FOR ABORIGINES

- Tolerance
- (and eight other values).

Interestingly, the following values are not listed by any of the States: Patriotism, Self-reliance, Courtesy, Respect for Authority or Competitiveness, although a survey of the mottoes of Australia's leading schools include the following virtuous concepts: Truth, Bravery, Faith, God, Duty, Courage, Achievement, Knowledge, Toil, Power, Perseverance and Endurance.

These apparent virtues could be taken as a list of what non-Indigenous Australians believe (or used to believe) to be worth striving for. What might the Indigenous list include? Perhaps it would be a very similar list, but using different words. Perhaps it would differ markedly from this Eurocentric listing. The differences need to be stated, recognised and respected.

## 4. JUSTICE AND AN APPROPRIATE LEGAL FRAMEWORK

## 4.1 The Need for Agreed Targets for Aboriginal Prosperity

One of the major causes of present conflict on the 'Aboriginal Question', is the lack of clarity and consensus on where we want to end up with the present deliberations on Aboriginal justice, Land Rights and autonomy. Aboriginals may have a very clear image of their aspirations, but they will need to persuade other Australians that such goals are realistic and equitable for taxpayers, government and the working class. One starting point is to consider first the environmental, production and social goals for the Australian nation as a whole. Cocks (1992) states these as follows:

**National Planning Goals**

Group A: Conservation Goals

- Maintenance of national soil productivity.
- Maintenance of national water supply and air quality.
- Maintenance of biodiversity.
- Protection of historic and cultural sites.
- Development of a high-quality national park network.

Group B: Production Goals

- Continued availability of primary production resources.

- Socially beneficial resource development
- Maintenance of infrastructure to continue resource-based industries.

Group C: Social Goals

- Development of an effective national communication and transport network.
- Development of an effective network for the supply of water and energy.
- Improvement of urban infrastructure and services.
- Protection against natural and induced hazards.
- Development of an effective network of recreation areas.
- *Meeting the legitimate land needs of Aborigines.* (My emphasis.)
- Properly evaluate land use options where conflict occurs.

The argument is not only about whether the nation requires clear and agreed objectives, but also the priority and thus the financial resources which should be allocated toward achieving each of these (worthy) goals. From the Indigenous community's viewpoint, the problem clearly lies with the definition of 'legitimate' in as much as it refers to their claims, rights and legal position.

Before concentrating on the extent to which achievement of Aboriginal aspirations falls short, it should be remembered that several of the other listed national goals currently fall seriously short of satisfactory achievement. The reasons for this are a combination of a lack of motivation, ignorance of the significance of not applying corrective action (e.g. on land degradation), shortage of funds, a lack of economic technical solutions and the dominance of short-term political expediency at the expense of vision and statesmanship.

Brennan (1994) describes the goals of Indigenous people as follows: 'Ultimately Indigenous Australians need to be convinced that they have a real choice within acceptable political and economic limits, to live as Aboriginal Australians and respected as members of a distinct people within the Australian nation…'. Real choices are only possible when they represent genuine practical options, and these need to meet the equity criterion.

What are the differences between self empowerment, self determination, self sufficiency and self government? These concepts are similar but have vastly

## APPENDIX 2: WHAT CONSTITUTES A FAIR GO FOR ABORIGINES

different implications for both Aborigines and for Australia. O'Donoghue (1996) may be incorrect when she accuses government of appearing 'ill-informed and unwilling to accept both the reality of Australia's colonial history, and the consequent disadvantage suffered by my people'. The question arises as to what actions from government are appropriate to being seen to accept history and suffering. The best thing government can do to counteract past disadvantages is to offer the opportunity to the present generation of Aborigines to join the wider economic community which offers their children the best future. 'Best' in terms of income, health and quality of life, need not reflect the materialistic consumerism of present urban Australia, but needs to be self-sufficient in wealth-generation terms. You can't live on culture. In the same way you can't live on religion, but without adherence to a spirituality which gives meaning to life and relevance to one's efforts, life may lose much of its richness and significance, even if materialistic standards rise. Australian governments have yet to recognise the 'spirituality of land' for Aborigines in the context of freedom of religion being one of the cornerstones of the Australian constitution. The vision for successful Indigenous futures now require urgent attention. For evaluating each Aboriginal Program, we might use criteria such as the following which combine to reflect national policy:

- Is it equitable?'
- Is it economically efficient?
- Does it maintain natural resource capital?
- Does it lead to net social benefit?

No doubt some observers would argue that to be politically appropriate, Indigenous policy does not need to be either economically efficient or socially beneficial to the nation overall. So the first debate should be on the criteria or measures of success. Australia has yet to have this debate – the debate we had to have! Using such agreed criteria, the objectives or goals could be considered, and from the objectives, the targets and milestones (datelines) could be derived – for triennial reviews.

When considering the values of a future Australian society of which Indigenous people are an integral part, a set of values which are shared by all citizens, could engender racial harmony within a heterogeneous society. Is it possible to establish a consensus on beliefs about what is good for both individuals and for society? For instance, Wiltshire (1994) proposed that a State education system might be based on four core values. Converting these to a National Charter of Values we might aim at the following moral high-ground:

**Draft National Charter of Values**

1. *Affirming a belief that each person is uniquely valuable, Australia will value a commitment to*:
    - individual self-respect and pride in identity
    - honesty and personal integrity
    - acceptance of, respect for, and care of others
    - open-mindedness to the views and experiences of others
    - social justice
    - each person realising his or her own potential as a human being
    - initiative and enterprise

2. *Affirming a belief that we all share a responsibility to contribute to the welfare of our society, Australia will value a commitment to*:
    - cooperation, democratic processes, and active and informed citizenship
    - ethical behaviour that is socially responsible
    - recognition of and respect for, the variety and uniqueness of what different groups bring to society
    - partnership between school, home and community
    - accountability for the use of social resources.

3. *Affirming a belief that all people interdependently share stewardship of the earth and its riches, Australia will value a commitment to*:
    - ecological sustainability
    - economic and social development for the benefit of all
    - international understanding and cooperation
    - processes to shape a better future

4. *Affirming a belief that all people share a need for knowledge and meaning,*

# APPENDIX 2: WHAT CONSTITUTES A FAIR GO FOR ABORIGINES

*Australia will value a commitment to*:
- curiosity and questioning insight
- logical, critical and reflective thinking
- intuition and creativity
- the search for truth
- a variety of ways of knowing and of learning
- the importance of lifelong learning

How might an Aboriginal Draft Charter of Values read? Are the above values sufficiently global and basic so as to transcend cultural boundaries? I think so.

When evaluating policy, the juxtaposition of equity and efficiency is commonly used to infer that these two basic measures are mutually exclusive. They are not. The opposing views of 'social engineers and bean-counters' leads, in a democracy such as Australia, to political manoeuvring to capture the votes of both the idealists (socially conscious) and the realists (economic rationalists) depending on media preferences at election time and learned historic hang-ups.

From the Aboriginal point of view, a pragmatic approach may be required to the question of what can be expected by way of special favours in tough economic times. Presently they ask no more than equality of treatment. Thus while programs which imply that exceptional treatment is warranted in view of past disadvantage, may gain some overall acceptance, full recompense for historical wrongs is unrealistic when everyone is doing it tough. Nor does it guarantee reconciliation or forgiveness.

If bridges are to be built between Indigenous and non-Indigenous Australians, then one group can't be seen to be winning all. There is, for instance, widespread discontent with the way in which Aborigines were permitted to take protected fauna and flora. This is aggravated by the way in which traditional rights are implemented using modem technology – Toyotas, high powered rifles and chainsaws. In the same way, the simultaneous receipt of both their land back (free of monetary charge but at immeasurable social cost) and social security payments, understandably angers hard-pressed pastoralists and others who are eligible for neither.

These perceived inequities cause both sides of the debate to take the moral high-ground, by starting with their preferred answer, then seeking selective evidence to support their preconceived position of self-righteousness. These strongly-held opposing views are quite understandable when the value systems of the proponents are contrasted. This matter of inappropriate Eurocentric values is usually considered in environmental terms in juxtaposition to Ecocentrism. Now these two positions need to also be compared to Indigenocentrism, preferably in the form of a flexible triangle.

One of the issues relating to the equity/efficiency nexus, is the capacity of landscapes to permanently support larger numbers of Indigenous people than was the case historically. Many harvesting systems work well at low intensity but with increasing populations, both hunting and fishing can exceed natural production capacities, When this occurs with populations of threatened species, a re-think of cultural rights is indicated.

## 4.2 Reconciliation – what, why, who, how?

The concept of reconciliation usually assumes that there was previously a conciliatory relationship between the parties. This was hardly ever the case in Australia and a more appropriate term is required if this process is to progress. In essence, the reconciliation process aims to gain greater acceptance, respect and cooperation between Aborigines and other Australians. Does this apply to all non-Indigenous Australians, and if so, is there an assumption that other ethnic groups' relationships with Aboriginals require upgrading? Should there be a reconciliation with Asian Migrants post-Hanson?

So what needs attention for reconciliation to be achieved? One way of answering this is to get each group to produce an agreed list on how the other should change to meet perceived behaviour requirements. However, it is unlikely that either such a process or the present fraught process, will achieve any significant 'meeting of the minds'. How could the objectives of the formal Reconciliation process be achieved? Probably not by formalising the process, but rather by relying on community networks and small groups of volunteers acting individually and driven by personal commitment to better race relations. Whether the extracting of formal apologies really assists the process is doubtful.

Brunton (1993) argues that Aboriginal policy is a tragic failure essentially because it is fundamentally misdirected through being based increasingly on cultural relativism. How would the worsening position of Indigenous people

## APPENDIX 2: WHAT CONSTITUTES A FAIR GO FOR ABORIGINES

be explained after such significant expenditure on this group in the past two decades? Hyde (1994) states that survey results show Australians to be generally more tolerant toward Aborigines than toward Indians, Vietnamese and other Asian Migrant groups. He suggests that the question of whether people can really take control of their lives in the modern world while maintaining a traditional orientation, will now have to be confronted by policy-makers and Indigenous people alike. On this matter, Brunton (1993) asks 'Can people achieve their aspirations for individual and social efficacy, without some personal responsibility and self control?'

Some anthropologists have apparently identified Aboriginal aspirations as an 'oppositional culture'. So we must ask whether those who subscribe to such a culture, exceed their 'capacity to trust and cooperate productively with non-kin and strangers'. Is there then a case to change both European and (past) Aboriginal cultural values to meet a changing world? Among non-Indigenous people the old values relating to sexism, gay marriage, smoking, equal opportunity, conservation, birth control, euthanasia, career planning, littering, recycling, water use, drink driving, macho behaviour, racism and immigration, have all changed for the better in the past decade or two. If they are to survive, should not all cultures be sufficiently dynamic to change and adapt to the changing world in which they find themselves? If so, they should not be asked to accept principles or values that they don't believe and can't be committed to, but such non-acceptance will have to be rational and realistic in terms of future implementation. Of course non-Indigenous people can learn some useful values from Aboriginals. The opposite is also true, but the accusations of being racist or assimilationist are nullifying the potential usefulness of the alternative values and assistance offered.

O'Donoghue (1995) believes that this nation still needs to right some of the wrongs of the past and she makes proposals for achieving this in her seminal report 'Recognition, Rights and Reform'. Some proposals are symbolic and important to Indigenous people, e.g. recognition of their flag, recognition of the First Australians in the Constitution, and achieving 'real self-determination'. O'Donoghue suggests that the best reasons for accepting these proposals have to do with our humanness, our sharing of the continent and what it means to be Australian in the eyes of the future global community. She believes Aborigines are now 'willingly accepted as equals' by many Australians.

A problem arises when 'being equal' under the law, is defined. Does this equality include special dispensation for past wrongs and discrimination? If so, what's a fair thing? How do we value such wrongs (in terms of compensation by another name) and for what period should such recognition of recompense apply? A second problem concerns the acceptance of help, advice, support and cooperation, in achieving real self-determination without accusing empathetic non-indigenes of being patronising. Such rejection is particularly hurtful to genuine supporters. The stance which tells others to' 'keep out of our business' is immature, unhelpful and inefficient; constructive suggestions should be accepted with a cooperative show of trust, no matter how undeserved in historic terms.

Cohen (1996) calls a spade a spade when he states, 'No one has the courage to say publicly that hunting kangaroos, eating bush tucker and painting bark pictures, will not prepare Aborigines to compete in a 21st century that will require sophisticated technological education just to keep pace'. It could however, bring health, happiness and contentment from connectedness with their country, while empowering them to take the next steps into modem society. Cohen believes that it is the use of 'self-determination' as a political slogan which has done most to cause confusion. He is of the view that true self-determination must embrace economic self-sufficiency. As with other Australians, this means joining the workforce. In turn, this means 'an end to the dole as an unqualified right' (Cohen 1996). So the question now facing us is: 'Has separatism under the guise of self-determination shifted Aborigines backwards instead of forwards'?. Yes or no. If yes, why, and what's the alternative?

It is high time Australia took a long and reasoned look at resurgent modern assimilationism as a means of ensuring an improved quality of life for Aborigines. Not to discard their culture, not to denigrate their traditions, not to challenge their beliefs, but to offer those concerned about their offspring's long-term future, a means of competitive survival and improvement.

## 4.3 The Law and Indigenous Justice

Since the 1800's, State laws dealt with Aboriginals by enacting separate legislation. Earlier legislation often used the term 'Protection', ostensibly to protect Indigenous people from the perceived disbenefits of remaining in their tribal situation. Land ownership by Aboriginals was a non-event in an era

## APPENDIX 2: WHAT CONSTITUTES A FAIR GO FOR ABORIGINES

when the Crown was concerned only with leasehold and freehold tenure for non-Indigenous Australians. So when the Wik decision of 1996 was made in favour of Aborigines by four judges to three on the High Court bench, it was evident that interpretation of the law on Native Title, split even the best legal brains in the country. This has led many in the mainstream to adopt irrational defensive positioning, based mainly on fear, uncertainty and incomplete facts concerning the earlier Mabo decision and the Native Title Act of the Labor government.

The attainment of what might be called a new Indigenous Social Justice, will be complex indeed, especially if it is to encapsulate the tenets of Tribal Law within the Australian legal system. There are numerous ethnic groups in this country who follow some code of conduct related to their religion, history, nationality or culture. While these codes do not include the ancient values associated with ownership of 'country', they require congruence with Federal and State laws. In the same way, the rights of Islamic women or Buddhist men are required to meet the requirements of the Australian constitution and its legal underpinning, irrespective of the cultural mores of the ethic group concerned. Aborigines would claim to be different, based on original ownership of this land.

What has to be decided, is the extent to which European law and the Westminster system require to be supplemented by Aboriginal law and whether such law applies nation-wide or only to specific regions. Whether it is desirable or indeed practical to apply geographic tribal variations to Indigenous law, also requires determination.

The idea of swift and direct tribal law determination of punishments for transgression of socio/cultural standards of behaviour, has wide appeal in remote areas and may well effectively supplant European judgement and sentencing in future Aboriginal areas. It would certainly reduce the present unacceptably high incarceration rates.

When considering the alternatives open to Aboriginals, Brennan (1994) recognises that public policy must be evaluated on the basis of both Aboriginal aspirations and the public interest. He asks whether it is not reasonable for Indigenous people to not only seek restitution of their rights, but also to seek compensation for dispossession. In addition, some Indigenous leaders go so far as to maintain that the State itself in fact has no legitimacy. This stance is based on the fact that, in the claim of Sovereignty, the Indigenous peoples were not conquered in war, were not formally consulted on ownership and their consent was never given when the Crown asserted its Sovereignty over Indigenous land. Thus in the Mabo judgement the High Court was recognising, for the first time, the lawful authority of Aboriginals over their land and in that sense, their form of domestic Sovereignty, similar to that held by Amerindians in the US.

An additional dimension of the Rights debate, concerns accusations that the demands of Greens and Animal Liberationists, have overshadowed the insistence of Indigenous people wishing to continue their traditional hunting activities. When such activities are regarded as customs, traditions and even religion, their rejection can justifiably be regarded as a violation in human rights. The claim of the Foundation for Aboriginal and Islander Research Action (FAIRA) (Weatherall 1992) that the hunting of protected fauna is an Indigenous Right, is currently in conflict with the basic requirements for threatened biodiversity preservation. These requirements have not been laid down by non-Indigenous Australians, but are demanded by the Laws of Nature if biodiversity is to be saved.

## 5. ECONOMIC VIABILITY AND FUNDING OF ABORIGINAL SERVICES AND ENTERPRISES

One way and another, the increased funding of services to Indigenous communities appears to have had little effect on the actual standard of health, education, housing, water supply, diet and longevity of many remote communities of Aborigines. Analysis of the level of accountability of the financial allocations made in these (and other government-funded) spheres, is complicated by the difficulty of gaining reliable data on both partitioned expenditure and physical outcomes which can be used as a measure of achievement of objectives.

Unsubstantiated accusations of waste and lack of accountability, shed no light on the actuality of the situation on the ground. Equally, defensive responses which emphasise the difficulties and constraints which faced ATSIC or its successors in endeavouring to discharge their responsibilities, are similarly unhelpful in identifying the efficiency barriers. Clearly, allowance must be made for the managerial shortcomings of community councils or

## APPENDIX 2: WHAT CONSTITUTES A FAIR GO FOR ABORIGINES

other Indigenous organisations who are yet to acquire the financial skills and meet accountability requirements for responsible handling of public monies in the hierarchy of government set up to 'protect' individual citizens against maladministration.

It is unfortunate that opinions on financial accountability often suffer from unjustified generalisation. Similarly, those who would defend the general level of accountability achieved, require honesty and a commitment to review and improve spheres of inappropriate use of funds. Indeed, there is a call, with considerable justification, for justice to be seen to be done, in bringing fiscal misconduct into the open. There has been a reluctance to examine, evaluate and prosecute where necessary, those who would misuse public funds, be it from ignorance or intent. There has been even more reluctance on the part of government to admit that it is the top-heavy bureaucracy which is one cause of the poor performance of ATSIC and some Land Councils.

The rorting in government programs is of course in no way limited to Indigenous organisations and individuals. On the contrary; the lack of checks and balances in the Australian public sector has allowed on-going rorting of the system. This is apparently occurring on a considerable scale in various Social Security subprograms where effective monitoring of malpractices is difficult and expensive.

Cohen quotes Tatz (1996) as asking 'Where are the academics, journalists and professional men and women who once offered advice, comment, constructive criticism and ideas? They have been subjected to psychological thuggery and bullied into silence for fear of being called racist'. During the past 30 years Australians have increasingly been asking why the programs of governments of both persuasions have produced so little benefit for Aborigines, given the billions of dollars spent. Cohen (1996), a former minister, has some harsh words when he says that the 'waning sympathy' for Aborigines could be stemmed if they would (a) stop acting as the permanent victims and (b) do more to help themselves. But he also points to the thousands of Aborigines who are success stories in their own right, having succeeded against overwhelming odds in becoming respected citizens. The potential motivating influence of such social achievements is too often overlooked by the print and electronic media, who seem to prefer to portray Aborigines as permanent victims, shown in the worst possible situations and thus encouraging the view that critics of the pro-Indigenous stance are racist. But O'Donoghue (1996) makes the point that, rather than infer that in some cases major funds have somehow gone missing, it should be recognised that Indigenous people are 'cheated by the system'. She makes the interesting comparison with the Diesel Fuel Rebate Scheme which not only cost more than ATSIC cost in 1995, but received the damning report by the National Audit Office on the $12 billion dollar fuel scheme, which caused none of the indignation which such Aboriginal rorts (in this case $32 million a year) justifiably cause. O'Donoghue claims that the accusation of lack of accountability on ATSIC's part is 'disproportionate, hypocritical and punitive' because the people rather than the system are being blamed.

The fundamental decision is however not on accountability in the first place, but rather on the quantum of federal funds which should rightly be allocated to what has been termed 'Aboriginal Reconstruction'. This is probably not an appropriate term because it may infer a return to past social structures which could in fact be counter-productive. But, if a clearly-defined Aboriginal nationhood is an agreed goal within Australia's national unitary objectives, then development of an innovative framework of structures and procedures is required. Geographically it is probably not be possible for the dispossessed to repossess all their former territories. The tribal and clan country map of yesteryear may have to be relegated to history – as it has been in other countries. This is not to say that a comprehensive series of tribal areas should not be negotiated, but rather that what will be, cannot closely match what was.

The original requirement of the Native Title Act for claimants to be able to demonstrate continuous occupation or connection to claimed land, is historically unreasonable, given the systematic destruction or removal of communities from their country. Added to this, the total disregard by the authors of this legislation, for the way in which different tribes were herded together on alien reserves and islands makes a mockery of such 'continuous connection'.

## 6. OVERSEAS LESSONS

In their search for international support for Land Rights; ATSIC (1994) made a special study of overseas cases of Indigenous peoples' rights. They chose

Canada as their most useful comparison, mainly because of the number of successful legal challenges to land ownership in that country. Neither the American Indian nor the New Zealand Maori cases provided sufficiently suitable Land Rights comparisons, to be of particular use as precedents to ATSIC. Meanwhile, the Sami people of Sweden provide an interestingly different situation, where the Indigenous reindeer herders of the Arctic Circle actually live and work in five different Scandinavian countries. They are claiming the rights to both their land and a parliament of their own.

In all the above countries, governments have the legal right to extinguish Native Title by purchase or by legislation. But in all cases, except the US, compensation is payable (ATSIC 1994). It is interesting to note that Canada uses the term 'Aboriginal' as synonymous with Native or Indian and meaning First People. The political strength of the Canadian Indians (Inuit) lies in their pan-Canadian (nation-wide) organisations which represent united claimants from different clans. However, their Land Rights are not ownership rights under common law; rather they are *sui generis*, interests (self generated) in the land itself. In 1992 a two million square kilometre Indian territory (the Nunaveet) was created, then $1.5 billion paid in compensation and a government structure formed.

## 7. NATURAL RESOURCE MANAGEMENT
## 7.1 Multiple Use

Mention has been made earlier in this paper, of the need to heed not only tribal and government laws, but also the laws of nature, when dealing with resource management. These apply to activities such as fire, clearing, weed control, wildlife protection, rare plant conservation, fishing, fish stocking, animal disease control and feral animal control. In addition, the carrying capacity of each landscape needs to be estimated for single land uses and for multiple land use, as recommended in the Cape York example (Roberts 1995).

*Clearly, there are very few landscapes or ecosystems which can be most beneficially used if employed for a single use only.* It is for this reason that the pastoral industry options study of Cape York called for major stakeholders (pastoralists, Aborigines and National Parks) to consider all combinations of multiple use of each of their presently designated single use lands.

## 7.2 Ownership and Access

All leasehold land is presently the property of the Crown under Federal and State law. Even freehold land can be reclaimed or resumed by the Crown under Compulsory Acquisition, when this is deemed to be in the public interest, although compensation would normally be payable. What has happened since about 1910 in Queensland, is that pastoral leaseholders have increasingly tended to regard such land as their own, and have become a law unto themselves as far as Aboriginal access is concerned. The historical evidence brought by Reynolds (1995) and others, shows clearly that the original grazing leases had 'Aboriginal reserve' clauses (traditional use) included in the understanding of lessees' rights. The land was Crown Land on which graziers were given only grazing rights, with no intent of limiting any traditional uses of such leases by Aborigines. Early this century these 'reserve' clauses were discontinued on Queensland leases, although they remain on Western Australian and Northern Territory leases. Clearly, the ownership of these leases do remains with the Crown and the use rights of lessees are limited to grazing and the activities and structures associated with animal production. The Wik decision (a 4:3 majority judgement) gave land title rights to those Aborigines who could show original and continuous occupation of the Wik lands now under pastoral leases.

Despite the demonstration of the practicality and mutual acceptability of regional agreements such as the proposed Cape York Heads of Agreement in 1995 and several arrangements negotiated by mining companies, sections of the pastoral industry and the National Farmers' Federation found anything other than total extinguishment of Native Title on pastoral leases unacceptable. Their argument was based on lessees' alleged inability to undertake their business, and to access loan funds, under the perceived uncertainty created by Native Title which could be claimed over their leases.

The problem of title holding arises partly from the use of the term 'Native Title' which infers (at least in the public mind) full right of occupation and use. It would facilitate the debate considerably if the term 'Native Access' were used, so making the rights of Leasehold Tenure for graziers clear. The Wik decision made it clear that graziers' pastoral rights would not only be guaranteed, but also that, if there was conflict of interest between pastoral and Aboriginal land use, the former would prevail. These rights did not include sole occupancy –

and never did. There remains a fundamental legal problem with the holding of title to the same piece of land by more than one party, thus the need to re-name Native Title.

The assumption that the legally-enacted extinguishment of Native Title is the only way to gain certainty for lessees, is incorrect. There is no reason why negotiated regional agreements cannot become binding as legal contracts under Common Law, as has apparently occurred in a number of mining agreements; the Anaconda Nickel agreement in Western Australia is a case in point. The fact that the preamble to the Mabo decision refers to extinguishment of Native Title on pastoral leases, should not be seen as the only way of gaining certainty of tenure and land use in a situation where clearly neither the pastoralists' normal activities nor their monetary borrowing capacity would be affected by a regionally-negotiated legal agreement. Such agreements could include land, vegetation and water.

These leases are Crown land. As such they belong to the people of Australia. What rationale could be used to dispossess the original owners of the use of such land resources? The uncertainty factor can easily be overcome, and with a modicum of 'doing unto others' on which the Christian society is built, cooperative multiple-use should be easy to achieve. Without goodwill and a generosity of spirit, no changes to the law are likely to bring a lasting peace between the competing land users.

## 7.3 Productive Land Use

The Eurocentric view of 'productive use' assumes the production of saleable goods – in this case, commercial rural products such as beef.

In the Aboriginal culture, productive use has different connotations and may not involve the market economy. Land as habitat and source of food and spiritual sustenance, is uppermost in the drive for repossession of Indigenous lands. Such non-commercial land values may require urgent incorporation into the Australian concept of the full worth of real estate. Some may say that rationale should not be confused with wisdom and it may be wise to develop the concept of shared usufruct in land care.

Surely the cultural and religious ties to land can be maintained and nurtured, while Indigenous and non-Indigenous people organise sufficient income-generation and spiritual sustenance to become self-sufficient. The problem arises when Indigenous people expect both free land and social security payments as some kind of right, based on recompense for past wrongs. If Aborigines can enter the beef industry, if graziers can be rewarded as custodians of sacred or high conservation value sites, if Aborigines can have responsible access to sites on pastoral leases, and if selected sections of National Parks can be opened to grazing, much could be achieved to attain both a sustainable society and a sustainable landscape.

## References

Adams, P. 1993: The Black Man's Burden. Weekend Australian Review, 10 July, p2.

ATSIC, 1994: Current Issues, Native Title. International Responses. ATSIC, Canberra, February, p2.

Blainey, G. 1993: Goodbye to All That. Latham Memorial Lecture. Weekend Australian Focus, May, p16.

Brennan, F. 1993: In the Name of Justice. Graduation Address, Faculty of Law, UNSW, Sydney. Sunday Mail; Brisbane, 10 May, p2.

Brennan, F. 1994: Future Directions Conference, Centre for Comparative Constitutional Studies. Published as Indigenous Australians: The Choices. Weekend Australian Focus, 16 July, P25.

Brunton, R. 1993: Black Suffering, White Guilt. Institute of Public Affairs, Canberra.

Clarnette, W. 1989: Education Without Honour; Weekend Australian, 7 April. p17.

Cocks, D. 1992: Use With Care: Managing Australia's Natural Resources in the Twenty-First Century. UNSW Press, Sydney.

Cohen, B. 1996: The Gulf Between Black and White. Weekend Australian, 11 May, p26.

Dawe, B. 1989: When First the Land Was Ours. In: Land Care Manual, UNSW Press, Sydney, p2.

# REFERENCES

Dennis, H. 1952: Random Verse: A Selection of C.J. Dennis' verse. From The Herald, Hallcroft Publishers, Melbourne.

Howson, P. 1996: Separatism a Shortcut to Aboriginal Tragedy. Weekend Australian, 29 June, p6

Hyde, J. 1994: Don't Blame Racism for Blacks' Plight. Weekend Australian Focus, p22.

ILC 1996: Indigenous Land Corporation, Adelaide, S.A. The Courier Mail, 23 November, p27.

Lefkowitz, M. 1996: Not Out of Africa: How Afrocentrism Became an Excuse to Teach Myth as History. Quoted by C. Stewart in Poisoned Roots in Weekend Australian Focus, 12 April. p25.

Nash, R. 1991: The Rights of Nature. Primavera Press, Leichhardt, NSW.

O'Donoghue, L. 1995: Recognition of Indigenous People will help define national identity. In: The Changing Face of Australia. Weekend Australian, 8 April, p32.

O'Donoghue, L. 1996: Who's Accountable to Whom? Weekend Australian, 15 June, p26.

Partington, G. 1996: Hasluck vs. Coombs: White Politics and Australia's Aborigines. Quoted by Howson, Weekend Australian, 29 June, p6.

Reynolds, H. 1995: A War to Remember. Weekend Australian Review, 1 April, P3.

Reynolds, H. 1995a: Fate of a Free People. Penguin, Sydney.

Richburg, K. 1996: Out of America: A Black Man Confronts Africa. Quoted by C. Stewart in Poisoned Roots, Weekend Australian Focus, 12 April, p25.

Roberts, B. 1995: Pastoral Industry Study Report. Cape York Peninsula Land Use Strategy, Landcare Management Services, Toowoomba: 138-151.

Roberts, C. 1996: The Injinoo Community and Pajinka Lodge. In: National Parks: Private Sector's Role. (Eds. T. Charters *et al*) USQ Press, Toowoomba, p147

Rothwell, N. 1996: Whose Culture is it Anyway? Weekend Australian Review,

30 March, p1.

Tatz, C. 1996: Centre for Comparative Genocide Studies, Macquarie University. Sydney Morning Herald, 18 April.

Weatherall, W. 1992: Aborigines May Clash With Greens Over Hunting. The Nation, Toowoomba Chronicle, 29 December, p7.

Williams, N. and Baines, G. 1993: Traditional Ecological Knowledge. C.R.E.S., ANU, Canberra, p129.

Wiltshire, K. 1994: Draft Charter of Values. Shaping the Future: Report of the Review of the Queensland School Curriculum. University of Queensland, Brisbane.

# APPENDIX 3

'SPOILERS'

Ye are the Great White People, masters and lords of the earth,
Spreading your stern dominion over the world's wide girth.
Here, where my fathers hunted since 'rune's primordial morn,
To our land's sweet, fecund places, you came with your kine and corn.
Mouthing your creed of Culture to cover a baser creed,
Your talk was of White Man's magic but your secret god was Greed.
And now that your generations to the second, the third have run.
White Man, what of my country? Answer, what have you done?
Now the God of my Simple People was a simple, kindly God,
Meting his treasures wisely that sprung from this generous sod,
With never a beast too many and never a beast too few,
Thro' the lean years and the fruitful, he held the balance true.
Then the White Lords came in their glory; and their cry was: "More! Yet more!"
And to make' them rich for a season they filched Earth's age-old store,
And they hunted my Simple People – hunters of yester-year
And they drove us into the desert – while they wrought fresh deserts here.

*C.J.Dennis*
*Circa 1930.*

# Index

## A

Abbott government 323
Aboriginal
  Act 1906 13
  as synonym 395
  creation story 269
  culture 15, 20, 22, 45, 55, 56, 58, 63, 69, 72, 102, 111, 127, 130, 144, 149, 153, 241, 295, 310, 314, 397
  custom 108
  descent 55, 112, 138, 265, 356
  Draft Charter of Values 387
  duty 157
  flag 243, 326
  Freedoms, Four 77
  future, Indigenous and Australian 58
  futures 24, 26, 29, 54, 73, 74, 86, 133
  Industry 312
  integration 135
  Land Rights Movement 315
  Medical Service 96, 316
  medicine men 119
  nation 76, 86
  press 312
  Provisional Government 78
  religion 129, 160, 161, 273, 352
  rights clause 50
  Treaty Committee 80
  women fenced in 46
Aboriginality 12, 17, 54-60, 68, 69, 157, 168, 170-176, 235, 268, 279, 306, 309, 328, 352, 353
Aboriginals and Change (Publication) 53
Aboriginals' rights 49
Aborigines, Protector of 35, 46, 50, 177, 302
Aborigines, Treaty with 76
Aborigines, urban 59, 79, 136, 240, 264, 308
acceptance, by others, and of policy 7, 12, 17, 33, 35, 39, 42, 58, 66, 69, 83, 95, 99, 120, 129, 130, 136, 141, 155, 164, 165, 170, 178, 181, 182, 193-199, 201-205, 209, 215-219, 237, 242-247, 250, 254-258, 272, 305, 324, 335, 336, 340, 375, 386-390
accountability 84, 96, 110, 323, 386, 392-394
Adams, P 380
Adelaide 19, 47, 358, 359, 365, 399
Affluenza 133
African-American 177
Afrikaners 182, 201, 329
afterlife 232, 255, 257, 278
After the Dreaming (Publication) 48, 271, 359
Agreements 74, 142, 185, 213, 218, 331, 337, 352, 396
agreements, carbon offset 331
Ah Mat, R 127, 351
Ainslie, G 320
alarmism, on climate change 335, 341
alcohol 7, 34, 60, 63, 72, 91, 92, 98, 99, 105, 107, 112, 116, 162, 172, 219, 235, 282, 285, 303, 322, 328, 379
alcohol, avoidance of 162
alcohol roadblocks 112
Alice Springs 78, 100, 107, 227, 254, 293, 301, 319, 322, 351
Allah 16, 114, 156, 161, 238, 246, 254
Altman, J 138, 357
Amata Substance Misuse Centre 293
Amazon river basin 232
Amba Island 365
American Indian tribes 76
Amnesty International 303, 372
Anaconda Nickel agreement 397
ancestors 9, 11, 24, 43, 72, 124, 182, 190, 215, 232, 233, 242, 244, 260, 269, 270, 273, 288, 297, 305, 313, 328, 371, 373
Ancestral Country 261
ancestral spirits 71, 216, 269, 368
ancestry 71, 100, 123, 137, 170, 177, 241, 255, 277, 313

# INDEX

Anderson, A 296
Anderson, I 115
Anderson, P 318
Andrew Forrest 310
Angel Gabriel 246
Anglicanisation 374
Anglo-Saxon 61, 68, 134, 135, 198, 276
animal/human spirituality 234
Animal Liberationists 392
An Inconvenient Truth (Publication) 335, 362
ANRC (Australian National Research Council) 30
Antarctic sea ice 335
anthropologists 5, 11, 18, 26, 27, 28, 29, 30, 31, 42-47, 54-57, 71, 97, 98, 101-107, 120, 142, 145, 175, 216, 232, 389
Anti-Semitic Nuremberg laws 279
ants 262
Anzac Day 375
Apartheid 2, 34, 35, 36, 57, 58, 110, 121, 157, 158, 162-67, 189, 194, 199, 229, 285, 301, 380
apathy 20, 63, 131, 132, 308, 315
Apostolic Mission at Jigalong 55
APY land 293
Arabic lingua franca 241
Arabs 246, 333
Aramaic 246
Aranda people 242, 269
Aranda people. See also Arrerta, Arrernte 242, 269
Arberry, A 250
Archbishop of Canterbury 253
Archer River Mission 71
Arctic Circle 395
Arctic Climate 347
Ardoch station 46
A Review of the Stern Review (Publication) 363
Argyle Diamond Mine 271
Argyle Participation Agreement 142
Aristotle 232, 320
Armstrong, J 133, 134, 351
Army Reserve 125
Arnhem Land 27, 57, 113, 351

Arnhemlanders 57, 294
Arrernte / Aranda people of Central Australia 242
Arthur, Julie 286
aspirations 56, 60, 134, 138, 144, 167, 171, 175, 191, 264, 268, 301, 383, 384, 389, 391
assimilation 13, 15, 20-22, 36, 77, 78, 86, 110-113, 296, 310, 375, 378
assimilationist 83, 274, 302, 389
ATSIC 75, 79, 84, 85, 97, 106, 122, 143, 279, 304, 393-398
Attwood, B 22, 351
Aurukun 28, 29, 30, 70, 72, 97-99, 105, 107, 114, 115, 124, 125, 214, 377
  Mission 72, 115
  Mission Diaries 115
Australia Institute 173
Australian
  Academy of Science 322, 333, 362
  Anthropology 26, 31, 354
  Board of Missions 20
  Book of Atheism (Publication) 257
  Bureau of Agricultural Research Economics (ABARE) 332
  Bureau of Statistics 311, 328
  Curriculum Studies Association 326
  Employment Covenant 310
  Institute of Aboriginal Studies 53, 351, 359
  Islam 240
  Rules 135
Australians
  Origins to Eureka (Publication 52
  Australia's history wars 52
  Australia's Tropics (Publication) 364
  Autonomous Regions 264
  Autonomy 73, 356
Ayatollah Khomeini 242
Aztec 42
Aztecs 115

## B

baboons 261
Balkanu Development Corporation

403

330
Bamaga 21
Bandicootcha 71
Bantustan 158
barbarians 235, 236
Barcoo River 41
bark pictures 390
Barunga Statement 75, 79
Basics Card 303
bauxite mine 72
Beagle Bay 16, 17, 18
bean-counters 387
beatings and chaining 21
Beattie, P 314
Beckett, J 31
beef production 94, 140
behavioural change 119, 183
Behrendt, L 300, 301
Beirut 98, 108
Benedictine Fathers 25
Benedictines at Kalumburu 40
Benefits of Mainstreaming 214
benign co-inhabitor 180
Bennelong Society 106, 126
Bergmann, W 345
Berndt, C 27, 56, 57
Berndt, R and C 11, 27, 53-57, 351-355, 360
Best, Reverend 40
Betoota 42
Bible Society 69
Bicentennial celebrations 81
Bicentennial Year 81, 82
Big Mick 'the lawyer' 51
Bill Gray (CEO of ATSIC) 85
Bill of Rights 373
Birch, C 362
Birdsville 41
birth control 218, 255, 389
birth rate 214, 317
Black anger 146
Black Chicks Talking (TV Series) 155, 158
Black Death 119
Black Diggers (Publication) 40, 354
Black Justice 91
Blacks, dispersal of by shooting 32, 42

Black/White relations 74, 87, 236
Black/White struggle 43
Black women as drawcard 46
Blainey, G 22, 133, 376, 398
blame game 108, 145, 292
blaming 100, 104, 108, 118, 130
blanket of silence 100
Bleakley, J, Chief Protector 29, 31
blood, drinking 28
bloodless struggle 44
boarding school 20, 47, 87, 90, 123, 219, 243, 284, 314, 315
Boas, F 120
boat people 159, 242, 297
Boer children 374
Bogan 253, 259
Boiling Point 347
Bolt, U 177
Bonett, W 257
boomerangs 367
Border region 43
Borneo 240
Bourdieu, P 140, 352
Boyer Lectures 271, 359
Bradshaw, F 366
Brain and Culture (Plublication) 290
Brennan, F 73-76, 80-85, 185, 352, 375, 384, 391, 398
Brides of Christ 17
Bringing Them Home (Publication) 23, 24
Brisbane 43, 90, 131, 182, 279, 352-361, 398, 400
Brisbane floods 279
British colonial government 49
British Empire 24, 30
British Muslim Council 253
Britons 115
Broeker, W 349
broken society 101
Brook, P 109
Brough, M Minister for Indigenous Affairs 101, 299
Broun, J 305
Brown, E Reverend 71, 309
Brown, 'Nigger' 309
Brunton, R 389, 398

# INDEX

buffalo 367
bullied into silence 393
bureaucratic complacency 131
bureaucrats 5, 7, 14, 71, 91, 97, 98, 103, 114, 199, 322
burka 281
Bush Buddhism 181
bush food 216
Buthelezi's Zulus 157

## C

Calma report (Publication) 143
Calma, T 85, 143
Calvin, W 349
Campaign Aboriginals 306
Canada 80, 200, 281, 347, 395
Cancun 343
Canning Stock Route 24
Canny, N 39, 352
capacity-building 14, 176, 215
Cape Flattery 94, 139
Capell, A 20, 352
Cape York
 Heads of Agreement 396
 Institute for Policy and Leadership 96
 Land Council 95, 105, 314
 Pastoral Industry Study 28
 Peninsula Agenda 89, 315, 316, 328
 Peninsula Land Use Strategy (CY-PLUS) 372, 381
capitalism 140, 141, 310, 351
Captain Stokes of the Beagle 369
carbon credits 345
Carbon (Gravy) Train 344
carbon payments 331
carbon tax 159, 331, 332, 347
Caring for Country, National Curriculum Development Program 381
Carr Labour government 345
Carr, R Constable 40
caste barrier 108
catalogue of issues 106
catastrospeak 341
Catholic 16, 19, 25, 62, 74, 174, 196, 255, 273, 353

Catholic Bishops 74
causation theory 108
causes, of poverty, discrimination and progress 32, 37, 55, 71, 87, 91-95, 100, 104-108, 116-119, 136, 147, 158, 164, 190, 242, 286, 295, 298, 307, 334, 335, 346, 379, 383
Cautious Silence, (Publication) 26, 354
cave painting 289
Caxton's Press 69
Celtic Irish 39
Celts 10
Central Australia 105, 113, 115, 118
Central Land Council 303
Centre for Independent Studies 126
Centrelink 176, 199, 304
Century Zinc Limited (CZL) 139
ceremony 46, 125, 145, 200, 248, 270
Chaney, F 78, 322
Channel Country 41-47, 353
Chaotic World of Climate Truth (Publication) 362
Chapman, H, treasurer 30
Charcoal 'the manager' 51
Charleville 41
Charter of National Values 275
Cherbourg 31, 194, 242, 324
child abuse 100, 101, 123, 163, 217, 282
Chimpanzee 262, 289
Chinese 13, 33, 223, 333, 374
Chinnery, E 27
Choo, C 12, 13, 14, 16, 17, 25, 36, 40, 352
Christian children 238
Christian Confirmation 125
Christianity 15-28, 39, 45, 91, 159-162, 174, 194, 214, 235, 236, 240, 244-248, 252-258, 270-277, 354, 372
Christianity and Civilisation 39
Christian Science 119
Citibank 173
civilisation 11, 24, 39, 43, 68, 172, 180,

405

209, 227, 241, 258, 260, 290, 366
clan language  66, 328
Clarke, D  158
Clarke, G  84, 85
Clarnette, W  266, 382, 398
climate records since 1660  348
climatic change  164
Closing the Gap  163, 213, 220, 294, 356
CO3  331, 332, 333, 335, 336, 337, 338, 339, 340, 343, 345
COAG (Council Of Australian Governments)  163, 213, 220, 264, 307
Coaldrake, F  Archdeacon  21
Coalition government  78
Cocks, D  64, 352, 383, 398
Coe, P  76
Cohen, B  390, 393, 398
cohesion  59, 72, 83, 120, 121, 122, 133, 148, 155, 166, 181, 189, 198, 201, 206, 235, 243, 244, 246, 247, 249, 259, 260, 263, 272, 286, 325
cold deaths  342, 348
Collector of Customs  33, 364
Collins, P  255
Collins, R  41, 44
colonial government  39, 49
Colonial Office  46, 49, 50
colonisation  12, 38, 39, 85, 100, 115, 121, 130, 209, 236, 258, 348
Colosseum  244
coloured labour  370
colour, pride in  60
Combet, G  343
commandments  162, 275
Common Dish  277
Common Good  129
communalism  128
community canteen  92
Community Development Employment Program  94, 303
Community Food Production  223
community gardens  132, 223
community rescue  168
community submissions on Wild Rivers Legislation  330
compact  82
Compass Theology Review (Publication)  273, 362
compensation  75, 76, 79, 83, 103, 190, 191, 207, 211, 263, 390, 392, 395, 396
compulsory land acquisition  345
Confucian wisdom  273
Conrad, P  170, 171
conscience  19, 31, 48, 91, 116, 122, 232
Constitution  83, 192, 206, 217, 374, 389
constructive criticism  393
consumerism  23, 164, 178, 278, 385
contentment  133, 162, 390
continuous possession  51
convict era  43
Cook, J, Captain  18, 33, 105
Cool It (Publication)  335, 336, 362
Coombs, H (Nugget)  77, 78, 294, 352, 353, 378, 399
Coombsian hangover  163
co-operation  82, 84, 96, 120, 156, 183, 189, 196, 197, 268, 325
Co-operative Research Centre  318
Cooper Creek  41, 43, 48
Copenhagen Consensus Centre  334
corrective action  94, 102, 107, 116, 212, 343, 381, 384
corroboree  9, 180
cosmology  125
cost-effective policies and actions  137, 145, 147, 149, 150, 166, 215
Costello, J  41, 43, 44, 353
cost of climate actions  331
Council of Bishops  255
country, links to  60, 86, 142, 275, 296, 319
Courier Mail  106, 399
Craig, T  23
Cranswick, R  Reverend  21
crocodiles  368
cross-cultural understanding  47
Crusades  61, 236, 238, 240, 253
CSIRO  64, 331, 334
Culotta, Nino  243

INDEX

cult of forgetfulness 48
Cultural
 adaptation 134, 227
 appropriateness 75, 144, 156
 humbug 102
 intensity 54, 137, 314, 327
 pathology of grog 92
 purists 129, 202, 265, 296
 relativism 69, 102, 103, 126, 389
 support 222
 tolerance 182, 278
 warriors 121
cultural images, habits and icons 58
culturally appropriate 109, 110, 117, 127, 140, 149, 156, 187, 262, 263, 283
culturally-appropriate activities 20, 307
Culture - Indigenous, Western, Australian, Usefulness of 1-29, 35, 45, 47, 52-77, 87-91, 94, 98, 101-104, 109-118, 124-127, 130-145, 149, 153-166, 172-174, 179, 180, 182, 186, 189, 190, 195-197, 201, 202, 206, 209-217, 220, 222, 229, 232, 233, 237, 239, 240-244, 253, 254, 260, 262, 268-273, 277, 280, 288- 291, 294-299, 303-305, 310, 311, 314, 324-328, 353, 370-397
culture's exaggerated credit rating 111
culture wars 5, 52, 55, 61, 89
Curry, T 285
custodial protection 318
Customary Law 149, 150
customs 17, 21, 24-29, 35, 36, 45, 47, 57-61, 64, 86, 100, 104, 110, 116, 120, 141, 160, 233, 242, 280, 288, 306, 366, 376, 379, 382, 392

**D**

Dadirri 273, 277
Daly, H 68
Danish cartoons 281

Dark Ages 255
Darling Downs 44
Darwin, C 369
Darwinian and Christian beliefs 29
David 240
Dawkins, R 238, 256
Dawson River 22, 44, 353
Deadly Funny (TV) 160
Debil Debil 270
Declaration of Responsibilities 185, 187, 204
Declaration of the Granting of Independence to Colonial Countries and Peoples 78
Declaration on the Rights of Indigenous Peoples 2007 (UN) 185, 200
Deed of Grant in Trust (DOGIT) 163
Defamation Act 280
degradation 35, 36, 48, 77, 92, 100, 340, 384
deity-free faith 194, 238, 275, 276
democratic system 169
Denial Industry 337, 363
Denmark 336
Dennis, C J 375, 399, 401
Department of Drug and Alcohol Services 293
Department of Health 317
de Satge, O 41, 44, 48
Desert Knowledge Australia 322
desire to kill 366, 368
de-tribalisation 136
Development - Intellectual and Material 1, 6, 10-14, 21, 34, 36, 51, 55, 72, 77, 78, 84, 139, 143, 149, 153, 163, 165, 174, 178, 180, 187, 188, 198, 202, 203, 206, 211-213, 223, 231, 241, 255, 263, 264, 268, 278, 294, 295, 299, 317, 321, 325, 345, 382, 384, 386, 394
Diamantina River 41
Diamond, J 230, 271
Diesel Fuel Rebate Scheme 394
diet 9, 68, 103, 110, 116, 127, 132, 148, 218, 219, 224, 234, 237, 325,

407

329, 392
dignity 98, 111, 185, 187, 201, 202, 210, 211, 245
dilly-bags 367
Direct Instruction 324
disadvantage 6, 22, 52, 62, 75, 80, 81, 86, 95, 100, 108, 113, 117, 123, 132, 133, 142, 147, 166, 167, 170, 175-177, 187, 190, 195, 211, 222, 230, 259, 293, 298, 315, 318, 323, 346, 374, 379, 385, 387
discrimination 12, 39, 60, 94, 108, 110, 134, 155, 156, 163, 166, 188, 190, 191, 197, 200, 201, 202, 210, 211, 374, 390
dispossession 22, 74, 79, 94, 110, 114, 197, 222, 263, 375, 392, 394
distrust 60
diversity 48, 111, 125, 128, 149, 158, 170, 189, 195, 206, 237, 240, 245, 254, 272
DNA 62, 157, 174-177, 230, 289, 313
DNA tests 313
Dobson, V 173
Dodson, M 11, 12, 56, 243, 296, 314, 353, 362
Dodson, P 11, 296
do-gooders 103, 121, 131, 278, 295, 322
Doidge, N 288, 290
Doing unto others (Biblical quote) 254
Domesday Book 69
domestic nations 76
domestic violence 36, 63, 92, 123, 130, 172, 196, 206, 212, 217, 376
dominance 54, 102, 136, 143, 233, 234, 258, 373, 384
dominion over the earth (Genesis quote) 19
Doolan, J 51, 52, 353
Doran, C 34
Downunder Doctrine 274
doxa 140
Doyle, F (Oochunyung) 70, 71, 72, 353
drawcard 32, 46

Dreamtime 10, 70, 112, 180, 244, 254, 255, 269, 271, 274, 328, 356, 362
Dreamtime Stories 254, 269
Dresden floods 349
drug misuse 110
Druid creation stories 260
drunkenness 92, 130, 377
Drysdale Mission 40
Dublin 39
dugongs 365
Duncan-Kemp, A 41, 45, 47, 48, 353
Duncan, W 41, 44, 45, 46, 47, 48, 353
Dunn, K 281
duplication of services 110
Durack, M 41, 45, 46, 353
dysfunction 67, 99, 106-109, 113, 116, 117, 124, 128, 133-138, 150, 163-167, 172, 212, 213, 220, 242, 282, 286, 299, 308, 316, 325, 353
Dystopia 138, 172, 300

E

Earl Grey 46, 49
Earth 65, 68, 178, 179, 234, 255, 267, 270, 333, 362, 401
Eckermann, A-K 60, 354
Ecojustice Conference (Publication) 19, 358
Ecological Education - A Challenge to Extension (Publication) 362
ecology 372
economic independence 37, 89, 93, 97, 156, 165, 187, 205, 221, 264
ecosystems 64, 65, 66, 395
education of children 318
Edward River Mission 21
efficiency of policy 387
egalitarianism 43, 176
Elbe river 349
Elders 20, 34, 45, 46, 55, 57, 67, 71, 72, 98, 105, 116, 118, 124, 136, 139, 141, 148, 169, 174, 181, 190, 203, 216, 218, 239, 243, 247, 269, 276, 299, 311, 314, 322, 326
Elder system 169, 170, 218

elephant 293
Elkin, A Dr 20, 27, 31, 45, 270, 354
Ella, M 62
Embley River 71
emissions reduction 332, 333, 334, 336, 338, 339
emotional capital 168
employment 6, 57, 75, 94, 124, 126, 131, 132, 139, 144, 145, 149, 150, 164, 188, 205, 219, 222, 263, 292, 300, 307, 308, 316, 319, 345, 378
Energy in a Changing Climate 332
enforced assimilation 110
England's First People 260
English Herbals 70
enlightenment 137, 180
Ernst and Young, financial analysts 345
escapism 166, 379
ESD (Ecologically Sustainable Development) 178, 193, 278, 321
Essed 12, 354
Essence of Issues affecting Aboriginals 212
ethnic groups 12, 111, 113, 134, 135, 136, 137, 147, 149, 194, 209, 222, 388, 391
Euphorbia 261
Eurocentric 19, 122, 372, 383, 388, 397
Eurocentric vs. Ecocentric 372
European, values, history, and lifestyle 9, 10, 12, 13, 14, 16, 19, 20, 23, 24, 39, 42, 44, 50, 54, 67, 71, 73, 81, 102, 110, 125, 135, 137, 175, 177, 180, 198, 245, 262, 271, 336, 338, 350, 355, 356, 364, 371, 378, 389, 391
Europhiles 69
evolutionary ladder 234
evolutionary succession 233
exceptional eyesight 176
exclusion 48, 49
Exile and the Kingdom (Film) 380
existence, aimless 20
existential angst 328
express the meaning of Aboriginality
in its original authentic form 174
extended family 310
Eyre, E 129

**F**

Fair Go, What Constitutes a Fair Go for Aborigines (Publication) 1, 10, 15, 53, 54, 61, 69, 81, 94, 96, 100, 259, 358
family benefit 129, 145
family loyalties 114, 169
Farrar's Creek 42
Federal Department of Education 326
FEEL GOOD and DO GOOD policies 337
feel-goodism 121
Female Eunuch (Publication) 37
fertility rate 318
Filipinos 33
fire 9, 42, 64, 65, 67, 68, 142, 233, 270, 344, 369, 371, 395
  Queensland Rural 344
fire management 64, 68
fire, misuse of 142
Firkel, M 231
First Australians 389
First Nation 36, 54, 82
Fischer, T 22, 81
Fisher, H shearing contractor 46
Fitzmaurice River 367
flawed justice 102
flightless birds 65
Flinders, M 365
flogging and chaining of Aboriginals 30
fly-in fly-out 127
flying foxes 366
foetal alcohol syndrome 112
football 136, 177
Footsack 369
Forced Integration VII
Forced Separation VII
Forrest River Mission Board 20, 40
Fort Dundas 365, 367
Fortescue Metals 310, 311

Forty generations cooling rate  333
Foucault, M  6
Foundations for the Future (Publication)  82
Fourth World  115, 145
Franklin, L  176
fraud  44
Fredrickson, G  38
free choice  86, 321
freedom of choice  173, 305
Freeman, C  62, 284, 353
Fremantle, C  Captain  24
French  16, 140, 374
fresh fruit and vegetables  223, 329
Freud, S  290
Friedman, M  173
Frodsham, Bishop  36
Frontier Lands and Pioneer Legends (Publication)  41, 361
Frontiers, series ABC-TV  375
full-blood  175
fundamentalism  111
funding  31, 52, 68, 107, 110, 117, 118, 123, 140, 149, 169, 183, 306, 309, 323, 339, 340, 378, 392
fungibility  141, 190, 218
Future - Australian, Indigenous and Global  1-6, 25-29, 33, 36, 42, 48, 52-59, 64-70, 75, 79, 82-87, 91-97, 101, 106-112, 120, 122-133, 139-143, 149, 153-158, 162, 164, 169, 172, 182, 187, 190, 194-198, 204-217, 227, 232-235, 239, 245, 249, 250, 256-268, 271, 276-278, 281, 283, 288, 292, 295, 297, 302-308, 312, 314, 317, 319, 320, 324-330, 333-337, 346-349, 372, 377, 378, 380, 385-391

## G

Gadaffi, M  General  84
Gaia  235, 270, 321, 362
Gallipoli  259
gambling  172, 282, 283
Garnaut, R  343

gay marriage  389
generational change  114, 146, 219
Generation One  310
genes  57, 175, 277, 313
Genesis stories  181
genital mutilation  120, 149, 242
Gen Y  259
Georgatos, J  311
George, J (Awunpun)  70, 71
George, R  71
Georgina River  41
Geoscience Australia  332
German  16, 39, 99, 349
  Germans  40, 374
  Moravian Mission  99
Get over it, get on with it.  55, 95, 197, 199, 308
Gibbs, H  Justice  76
Gibson, P  303
Giese, H  301, 302
Gift
  Aboriginal  363
Gillen, F  269
Gillespie, N  315
gins  369
  second class of  46
Gislen, A  288
Global Financial Crisis  344
Gnibi College  318
God  14-19, 36, 66, 95, 114, 161, 181, 194, 232, 236-257, 266, 275, 278, 292, 306, 383, 401
Golden Rule  66, 161, 181, 196, 245, 276, 283
Goldman, H  126, 354
Gondwanaland  231
Gooda, M  307
Good Samaritans  17
Gordimer, N  59
Gore, Al  335, 336, 342, 347
Gospel, enlightening  32
Gospel of Jesus  246
Goss, W  105, 314
Gove Peninsula  57
governance  124, 139, 143, 162, 169, 170, 192, 220, 229, 258, 308, 323, 357

Government Gazette  50
grandchildren  1, 112, 136, 153, 183, 194, 293, 297, 298
Grant, A  345
Grant, S  313
gravestones  34
Gray, G  26
Great Southland  10, 73, 181, 244, 277
Great White People  401
greed  162, 256, 320, 346
Greek communities  113, 134, 174, 179, 241, 247
Greeks  243, 374
greenhouse emissions  142
Greenland iceshelf  335
Green preferences  321, 329
Greens  392, 400
Greer, G  36, 37, 38, 354
Greeves, V Dr  299, 300
Gribble, E  20, 22
group-think  165, 322, 335
guideposts  96, 156, 162
guiding principles  145
Guilt Industry  22, 83, 375
Gulf  33, 139, 287, 298, 349, 350, 366, 381, 398
Gulf Stream shutdown  349
Gunson, N  14, 354
Gurindji people  51
Guyana  121

# H

Hadza  230, 231, 232
Hagan, S  309
half caste  17, 23, 24, 25, 366
half-caste children  17, 25, 366
Hall, R  40, 74, 354
Hand, G  79, 81, 82
Hansonism  169, 171, 179
Happy Clappers  160
Hasluck versus Coombs  378
Hawaiian observatory  334
Hawke, R Prime Minister  76, 79, 80, 82, 83, 84, 355
Hayek, F  173
Health - Indigenous and Other  6, 7, 14, 54, 56, 63, 86, 87, 90, 92, 99-110, 115-122, 129, 131, 137, 147-149, 159, 163, 165, 181-192, 202, 206, 207, 209, 212-219, 224, 232, 298, 299, 306, 307, 315-318, 329, 338, 348, 351, 354, 360, 374, 378-381, 385, 390, 392
heat deaths  342, 348
Hebrew  246, 253
Hegel's social man  54
heroic frontier myth  47
heterodoxy  140
Hey, N  20, 71
hierarchical structure  122
hieroglyphics  289
High Court  49, 50, 72, 76, 236, 310, 375, 391, 392
Hillsong Church  160
Hindus  372, 374
Hirst, J  42, 43, 44, 355
historians  49, 130
Holding, C  81
Hollows, Fred  177
Holocaust  280, 337
Homeland development  153, 264
Homeland viability  296
home ownership  117, 126, 145, 148
homicide  48, 114, 115, 120, 357
Homo sapiens  66, 262, 372
Hope Vale  19, 20, 88, 90, 91, 98, 130
Hope Vale Lost (Publication)  91
hostility  60
House of Lords  170
housing  6, 51, 56, 63, 87, 92, 99, 110, 116, 117, 122, 131, 133, 147, 148, 163, 202, 212, 214, 215, 218, 220, 291, 303, 306, 345, 392
Howard, J Prime Minister  22, 56, 73, 76, 78, 83, 84, 89-92, 100, 101, 109, 143, 171, 200, 315, 352, 355, 360
Howson, P  378
How to stop the planet burning (Publication)  337
Huggins, J  12, 355

Hughes, H  126, 127, 128, 355
human/animal connection  234
human carrying capacity  94, 165
humanitarian values  142
humiliation, public  21, 105
Hunter, E  312-317
hybrid economies  144, 351
hybrid vigour  175, 313
Hyde, J  389, 399

I

Ice Age  348, 350
ideal person  60
identity, pride in  142, 267, 386
illiteracy  69, 298
Images of Australia (Publication)  42, 355
Imam's Council  245
Immigration Nation  245
immunity to disease  65
Impact Assessment  347
incarceration  218, 315, 316, 377, 391
incentives  103, 192
incompatibility  111, 133
Indians  13, 33, 39, 67, 76, 389, 395
Indigenocentric  19
Indigenous
  art  107, 110, 377
  cultures  13, 178, 179, 377
  descent  265
  Forgiveness Movement  121
  Freehold  141, 190
  Indigenous Newslines (Publication)  185
  law  120, 192, 193, 194, 207, 213, 327, 391
  population  38, 48, 113, 128, 142, 163, 193, 213, 327
  rights  38, 48, 86, 265
  Studies  327, 328, 382
  well-being  1, 87, 89, 127, 153, 200, 202, 214, 227, 263, 264, 291, 309
Indigenous Futures, Recommendations on  212
individual's responsibility  118

infantilisation  15
infrastructure  62, 63, 73, 79, 94, 105, 106, 128, 131, 137, 139, 145-150, 190-192, 195, 207, 213, 221, 223, 250, 263, 278, 291-296, 303, 338, 384
Infrastructure Investment  X
inspiration  285, 324
Institute of Public Affairs  398
integration  34, 36, 78, 89, 135, 232, 237, 241, 245, 294, 295, 325, 376
intellectual capacity  177
Intelligent Designer  275
intense localism  143
inter-marriage  86, 208
International
  Conference on Social Norms  96
  human rights representatives  81
  Working Group on Indigenous Populations in the mid 1980's  81
International Panel on Climate Change (IPCC)  337, 338, 339, 349, 362
inter-racial marriage  137
Intervention  92, 101, 212, 282, 294, 301-307, 318, 355
intolerance, of racial groups  24, 61, 121, 243, 250, 260, 281
Inuit  82, 178, 233, 395
invasion  16, 25, 40, 234, 261, 373
Iran  242
Iraq  241
Irish  37, 39, 177, 227, 235, 236, 237, 273, 313, 333
Irish Catholics  236, 237
Iron Range  21, 34
irrigated food production  329, 330
Islamic
  civilisation  241
  community  159, 240
  Empire  240
  schools (Australia)  238
Islam in Australia (Publication)  241, 273
Italian communities  113, 273
Iwenhe Tyerrtye (Publication)  173

# INDEX

## J

Jabir Jabir claimant group  345
Jacks, G  333
Jackson's Track  284
Jacky-Jacky  62
James Cook University  18, 105
James Price Point  345
Japanese  13, 33, 34, 40, 285, 369
Jarrett, S  129, 130
Java  10, 240
Jesuit Fathers  367
Jesuit Mission Station  368
Jesus and the Dingo (Publication)  271
Jesus story  19, 251
J Factor (Julie Arthur)  286
Jo'burg Japie (South African slang)  298
Johansen, L  95
Johns, G  119, 126, 127, 227, 293, 294, 295, 296, 297, 310, 311, 312, 316, 317, 355, 356
Johnson, P  177
Jonah  240
Joshua  261
Judeo-Christian tradition  122
justice  24, 33, 41, 50, 73, 74, 81, 86, 92, 102, 103, 114, 122, 172, 193, 213, 218, 244, 245, 256, 263, 315, 316, 372, 379, 383, 386, 393
Justice for Aboriginals, (Publication)  30
Justice of the Peace  72

## K

Kaberry, P  28
Kalumburu Mission  40
Kanakas  13
Kant's moral man  54
Karumba  139
Karuwali  41, 42, 44, 45, 46, 47
Kelly, C T  31, 318
Kelly, L  Dr  318
Keneally, T  52, 237
Kidd, R  30
Kidd, S  41
Kilimanjaro  348

Kimberley  12, 16, 23, 25, 33, 40, 142, 298, 310, 315, 316, 345, 352
Kimberley Land Council  345, 352
King, D Sir  342
King James Bible  68
Kings in Grass Castles (Publication)  41, 46, 353
Kipling, R  90
Kneebone, E  271, 362
Knowledge, Teaching of  215
Koch, T  106
Koepangers  33
Kolig, E  53, 54, 55, 355
Koori Mail  309
Kowal, E  118, 355
KPMG, accountants  278
Kriewaldt, M  Justice  120, 355
Kruger Park  261
Kunitz, S  117, 355
Kunmunya (Forrest River) Mission  40
Kyoto Protocol  337, 349

## L

Labour government  307, 343, 345
labour system  45
Lake Grace  23
Landcare programs  344
Landmarks, A Spiritual search in a Southern Land (Publication)  255
Lands Department  50
land theft  48
Lane, M  300, 301, 305, 351, 359, 362
Langton, M  37, 56, 81, 86, 97, 98, 114, 314, 327, 355, 356, 375
language groups  42, 157
Last Generation  347
laws  48, 63, 75, 83, 86, 120, 162, 163, 172, 186, 190-193, 207, 217, 231, 248, 269, 279, 320, 347, 390, 391, 395
Lawson, Henry  43
Lawyers' Picnic  33, 51
League of Nations  241
Lebanon  240, 241
Left and Right  89

Legal Service  96
Lesser Peron Island  369
Liberal consensus  99, 104, 360
Liberal progressive policies  106
liberation politics  111
licenses, renewal of  44
Lickiss, J  60, 356
lifestyle  16, 17, 22, 33, 55, 56, 72, 83, 119, 136, 145, 147, 157, 218, 231, 232, 233, 234, 242, 263, 266, 283, 289, 299, 311, 313, 318, 378
Light on the Hill  164
Lingiari, V  51, 301, 304
linguistic study  328
literature  5, 11, 13, 25, 31, 40, 60, 68, 69, 73, 125, 127, 132, 142, 164, 197, 201, 238, 239, 341
living off the land  48
Lockhart River  21, 94
Loff, B  115
logging  79
Lomborg, B  334, 335, 336, 337, 338, 339, 342, 362
longevity  47, 87, 106, 118, 214, 379, 392
Loos, N  18, 19, 20, 21, 23, 356
loss of language  72
loss of national memory  48
Lot 22  (Publication)  71
Lourdes  244
Lovelock's Gaia  270
Lowitja Institute  318
low literacy  378
Luddites  61
Lunn, H  170, 171
Lutheran  19, 48, 90, 314
Lutheran Mission Cooper Creek  48
Lynas, M  337
Lynch, A  Dr  367

# M

Mabo, E  18, 32, 48, 56, 76, 356, 375, 391, 392, 397
Macassans  33
Macklin, J  Minister for Aboriginal Affairs  139, 141, 314, 356
Madagascar  261
Maddock, K  120, 356
Madrassa schools  250
Maggie, (Moses wife)  47
Magna Carta  69, 73
Mainstream - Values, Lifestyle and Norms  14, 60, 62, 77, 91, 93, 94, 102, 113, 124, 127, 130, 132-135, 145 -150, 157, 166, 172, 176, 179, 182, 193-221, 230, 236, 241, 242, 245, 259, 264, 267, 268, 272, 273, 277, 281-283, 294, 296, 300, 309, 312, 325, 391
Major, T  310
Makin, C  59, 356
Malays  13, 33, 364, 365, 367
male Aboriginal frustration  125
male rage  36, 37, 38
male roles  110
Malinowski, B  116, 356
Man and Nature  256, 269, 270
Manaus (Amazon Basin)  232
Mandala  276
Mandela, N  59, 157, 198
Mansell, M  56, 75, 78, 84, 86
Marn Grook  177
Martin, D  91, 107, 120, 124-128, 138-144, 319, 332, 351, 352, 356, 357
Martin Luther King's Story, I Have a Dream  (Publication)  91, 319
Mary, (Virgin Mary)  252
Mashco-Piro tribal women  232
Mason, R  344
materialism  378
Mayo, Dr, Yale anthropoligist  30
McAllister, P  176
McConnel, U  28, 30, 31, 357
McEwen, J  27
McKeich, R  60, 357
McKenzie family  72
McKeown, S  328
McKillop, M  17
McKnight, D  26, 37, 107, 357
McLean, G  91
McMahon, W  Prime Minister  77

## INDEX

McRae, D  326
Mecca  194, 240, 244, 246
Medieval Warm Period  348
Mediterranean countries  134
Melbourne  30, 43, 105, 318, 351, 352, 354, 356, 357, 358, 359, 360, 399
Melbourne Herald  30
Melleuish, G  Historian  52, 357
Melville Island  365, 367
Meninga, M  62
Merritt, C  280
Messages for Policy Makers  IX
Messiah  252, 255
Meston, A  35, 36, 46
Methodist  249
Middle East  219, 241, 247, 248, 249, 281, 290, 374
migrants  234
Miles, C  Shadow Minister for Aboriginal Affairs  83
Mining  77, 310, 351
mining companies  21, 139, 291, 396
Missionaries  14, 28, 29, 55, 63, 128, 160, 161, 223, 238, 239
mission as refuge  55
Mission Girls (Publication)  12, 352
Missions  14, 18, 20, 21, 25, 29, 30, 31, 63, 72, 100, 115, 160, 161
Mitchell River  21, 30, 354
Mitchell River Mission  21
Mithen, S  289
mobility  103, 157, 164, 166, 194, 209, 214, 219, 316, 318
modernisation  111, 112, 127, 133, 154, 157, 178, 201, 210, 216, 262, 272, 308, 314
modernity  98, 133, 143, 171, 178, 240, 276, 294
modern reality  182
Mokan, J  Dr  9
Monbiot, G  337
Montaigne, M  39
Moon Legend from Bloomfield River (Publication)  28
Mooraberrie Station  45
Moore River Mission  23
moral guidelines  256

moral high ground  118, 178, 249, 322, 333
Moreton Bay  43
Mornington Island  37, 107, 130
Morrish, R  41
mosques  241, 243
Mother Earth  36, 67, 68, 374
motivation  14, 60, 103, 121, 138, 166, 175, 183, 191, 199, 202, 208, 211, 230, 302, 316, 380, 384
Mount Hira  246
Mt Druitt  22
Muhammed  161, 238-252, 281
Muhammed Ali  159
Mullahs  244, 276
Mulligan River  41
multicultural  64, 75, 120, 121, 128, 195, 210, 283, 291
Mundine, A  159, 162
Mundine, W  56, 305, 310
Murray-Darling orchards  110
Murray Islanders  76
Murray, L  277
Muslims  156, 193, 238, 241, 242, 243, 244, 245, 246, 250, 273, 333, 374
mutual use  49
Myalls  34, 68
Myths of the Munkun, (Publication)  30

## N

Nash, R  234, 372, 399
National
  Aboriginal Board  265
  Aboriginal Consultative Committee  73
  Audit Office  394
  Curriculum Services  326
  Emergency Response (the Intervention)  100
  Geographic (Publication)  231
  Indigenous Times  309, 311
  Indigenous Women's Alliance  306
mediocrity  171
Parks  396, 398, 399
Planning Goals  383

Press Club  82, 353
Sorry Day  121
unity  78
Native
  Access  396
  Administration Act 1905-1937  13
  Police  32, 63
  Title  18, 32, 33, 48, 50, 51, 56, 70, 72, 73, 76, 77, 79, 88, 94, 97, 101, 104, 139, 140, 141, 158, 162, 163, 164, 167, 190, 203, 212, 213, 217, 220, 260, 261, 264, 292, 307, 311, 319, 330, 351, 356, 371, 380, 391, 394-398
natives  18, 28, 31, 32, 40, 49, 365-370
NATSIWA (National Aboriginal and Torres Strait Islander Women's Alliance)  306
Nature  19, 65, 67, 174, 179, 234, 255, 256, 269, 270-276, 392, 399
Nature, separation from  19
Neanderthals  180
Need for a Treaty  217
needs basis, for support policy  147
negotiating table  85, 142, 307
Neill, R  38, 106, 357, 376
nepotism  129
neuroplastic research  288, 290
New Commandments  256
New Holland  365
New Norcia  25, 358
New Scientist journal  257
New South Wales Land Rights Act 1983  79
New Zealand  65, 117, 200, 286, 342, 347, 395
Nicholls, J  293
Nicholson, M  332
Nimmitabel  344
Noah  240
Nobel laureates  339
Noff, F  160
non-Aboriginal  113, 130, 279
Norforce  101
Normans  260
Normanton River  366
norms  15, 39, 61, 62, 88, 90, 93, 96, 100, 101, 112, 116, 129, 130, 133, 136, 138, 141, 146, 166, 168, 171, 172, 175, 178, 206, 210, 217, 220, 229, 253, 258, 259, 262-269, 294, 300, 304, 316, 320
Northern Land Council  331
Northern Territory  44, 75, 79, 84, 93, 101, 121, 295, 296, 304, 351, 355, 360, 366, 396
Northern Territory Minister for Indigenous Policy  296
Not in Our Name (Publication)  121
Nowhere People, (Publication)  34
Noyce, P  23
Nuclear power  332

## O

objective (s)  5, 6, 56, 64, 90, 101, 112, 126, 147-150, 154, 182, 313, 334, 381
Ockers  136
O'Dea, K Professor  234
Oder river  349
O'Donoghue, L  37, 84, 304, 314, 385, 389, 394, 399
O'Farrell, P  237
Of Cannibals (Publication)  39
of children  60, 101, 116, 137, 161, 273, 318
Old World  374
On Purpose (Publication)  362
On Rage, (Publication)  36, 354
Open Society  1, 230, 265, 298, 303-306, 324-330
opportunities  61, 83, 133, 134, 139, 149, 153, 176, 211, 214, 219, 222, 299, 304, 308, 325, 339, 378, 379, 382
oral tradition  14, 69, 112
orbiting (to Homelands)  107, 109, 140, 316, 317, 319
O'Shane, D  285
Ottoman Empire  261
Our Channel Country (Publication)  46, 353

INDEX

outback ghetto 109
outback resident 292
out-marriage 137, 216
outstations 51, 97, 98, 105, 147, 215, 299, 300
Overcoming Indigenous Disadvantage (Publication) 87
overcrowding 133
over-sensitivity 114, 229
Oxford University Press 250, 276, 354, 355, 359, 362

# P

Pachauri, R 337
Pacific Islanders 110
paedophilia 92
pagan 160, 255, 270, 272
Pallottines 17
Palm Island 30, 98, 99, 242, 381
Paradies, Y 118, 355
Paradise Lost 108
Parliamentary Debates 50
part-Aboriginals 60
Parthenon 244
Pascoe River 34
passive welfare 77, 88, 90, 92, 93, 96, 107, 109, 126, 127, 222
pastoralists 18, 25, 32, 35, 41, 42, 43, 44, 47, 49, 50, 51, 63, 388, 396, 397
pastoralists acting illegally 51
pastoral leases 32, 43, 46, 48, 49, 99, 396, 397, 398
paternalism 60, 94, 319
Paton, A 59
patriarchy 13, 117, 121, 208
patronising attitude 14, 73, 78, 100, 103, 131, 237, 376, 380, 390
Patterson, Banjo 43
payback wounding 120, 149
pearling 29, 34, 369
Pearson, Noel, policies and contributions 37, 56, 77, 81-112, 122, 126, 127, 130, 140, 147, 156-158, 201-204, 222, 227, 253, 259, 300, 301, 305, 314-328, 356-358
peasant's revolt 170
Perez, K 25, 358
Perkins, Charlie 75, 81, 82, 175, 314
Perron, M 79
Persian 241
personal capacity 62, 147, 183, 222, 321, 329
personality cult 323
Pertjert, B Deacon 254
Peterson, N 126, 358, 361
Pew International 281
Phillips, T 121
Philosopher's Stone 126
philosophy 48, 56, 58, 104, 232, 257, 294, 296, 309, 317, 324
Phoenicians 374
Piaget, J 290
Piddington, R 28, 358
Pilbara 140, 378
Pilkington, D 23, 24, 358
Piper, T 330
Plato 258
Pleistocene age 289
plural monoculturism 254
polar bears - Canadian 347
police 7, 26, 30, 46, 63, 72, 112, 121, 136, 161, 291, 292, 357, 366
policy
  framework 229, 317
Policy, failure of Aboriginal 99, 355
Policy - Indigenous and Other 1-37, 51, 52, 56-65, 75-89, 97-111, 116, 119, 123-130, 138, 146-153, 163-170, 174-176, 187, 191, 200-206, 211-215, 224, 227-230, 239, 245, 256, 257, 259, 263, 264, 291-322, 328, 333, 339, 340-349, 354, 355, 357, 359, 372, 378, 385-389, 391
political correctness 28, 95, 102, 118, 376
politics 26, 31, 76, 81, 82, 89, 98, 103, 104, 111, 117, 128, 143, 182, 197, 257, 285, 304, 305, 308, 319, 330, 354, 356
polygamy 27, 61, 242

poor Whites  60
Pope John Paul II  254
population pressure  64, 65, 178, 231
Pormpuraaw  114
Port Darwin  33, 369, 370
Port Keats  254, 367
poverty cycle  109, 146, 220, 299, 318, 319, 381
Poverty Cycle, Sequential  218
powerful families  169
pragmatic centre, of climate action  335
Prague floods  349
praos  365
pre-colonial tribal differences  114
Presbyterian  21, 29, 30, 71
pretence  2, 37, 111, 126, 159, 168, 229, 235
Price, Bess  301, 316
Price, D  303
primitive peoples and lifestyles  13, 14, 23, 27, 30, 39, 65, 69, 114, 116, 120, 129, 173, 179, 180, 231, 232, 235, 258, 270, 289
Prior, M Deacon  19
prison population  315
Professional Aboriginals  312
Protection  31, 81, 383, 384, 391
Protector of Aborigines  30
Protestants  237
Psalms of David  246
psychological escape  182
psychological thuggery  393
Public Prosecutor  93
Pullen, N  280, 281
pull factors  155, 171, 297, 298
push factors  155, 159

## Q

Q&A (TV Program)  302
Quail Island  369
Queensland
  archives  50
  Coast Islands Declaratory Act  76
  government  30, 46, 330
  Legislative Assembly  44
  National Bank  46
  University  28, 74, 354, 400
  UQ (University of Queensland)  182, 352, 353, 355, 358, 361
  Western  11, 41, 45
Queensland Country Life (Publication)  32
Quran, (Koran)  241, 246

## R

racial discrimination  94, 190, 191, 200, 210
Racial Discrimination Act  108, 279, 280
Racial Discrimination, Convention on the Elimination of  186, 200
racial intelligence  60
racial sensitivity  114, 227
racism  5, 12, 13, 94, 95, 121, 150, 155, 156, 169, 180, 200, 201, 210, 220, 227, 235, 236, 281, 297, 312, 315, 376, 379, 389
racists  12, 38, 95, 99, 118, 121, 153, 177, 191, 209, 210, 229, 235, 280, 281, 282, 295, 328, 389, 393, 394
racist stereotypes  38
rage  36, 37, 38, 104, 125
rage, terminal  38
Rainbow Serpent  10, 16, 70, 124
Ravenshoe  79
real communities  167
real economy  93, 94, 134, 139, 145
realism  66, 109, 164, 168, 183, 184, 215, 221, 255
real jobs  132, 302
recompense  387, 390, 398
reconciliation  46, 52, 73, 74, 75, 83, 89, 99, 103, 104, 121, 122, 123, 124, 380, 387, 388
Reconciliation Australia  322
Reconciliation Bridge Walk  121
reconciliation process  388
Redfern  22, 59, 135, 326, 377, 381
Redfern Mob  59
rednecks  159
Reformation  39

# INDEX

refugees 74, 120, 135, 136, 181, 287
regionally-negotiated agreements 397
Religious
  Beliefs relating to Country 217
  bigotry 136, 201, 235
  conversion 160
  Studies 276
remote communities 92, 128
remote communities, conditions and challenges 7, 59, 78, 91, 93, 102, 106, 109, 132-138, 142-147, 160, 167, 170, 172, 183, 188, 192-199, 213-215, 219, 264, 292, 294, 303, 308, 317, 324, 326, 327, 392
Remote Futures 215
Renaissance 39
Reserves 57, 63
reverse racism 95, 210
Reynolds, H 18, 22, 32, 34, 48, 49, 50, 358, 375, 377, 396, 399
rhinoceros 261
Richardson, G Senator 79
Rift Valley 230, 233
Rights of the Child (Publication) 204, 212, 318
Right to take Responsibility 90, 95, 203
Rijavec, F 380
Rio Tinto Mining Company 302, 310
Roberts, B 2, 12, 19, 28, 58, 255, 270, 271, 313, 337, 358, 362, 363, 371, 372, 381, 395, 399
Roberts, Black Jack 313
Roberts, D 337
Robertson, G 344
Roberts, S 271
Robinson, G 119, 314
Rocky Mountains 348
Roebourne 310
Rogers, N 100, 107
role models 62, 124, 137, 219, 283, 285, 288
Romans 10, 179, 374
roots and wings 57, 154, 284
Roper River 44, 366
rorting 393

Rose, D B 11, 269, 352
Rose, L 285
Roth, W 18, 50, 358
Rothwell, N 316, 377
Rowley, C 59, 73, 108, 358
Rowse, T 110, 359
Royal Commissions 18, 22, 113, 315
Rubuntja, W 75, 359
Rudd/Gillard government 308
Rudd, K Prime Minister 33, 52, 84, 101, 105, 121, 143, 192, 308, 310, 314
Rudd's national apology 84
Rugby school 44
Russert, T 283, 284
Ryan, M 304

## S

sacred sites 64, 67, 77, 160, 161, 208, 271
Saeed, A 241, 242, 273
Saibai Island 31
Salman Rushdie 242
Salt, B 278, 279
Samaritanism 279
Sami 395
Sanson Institute 234
Sapolski, R 289
Sarra, C 324, 325
Satanic Verses (Publication) 242
Satour, T 110, 111, 359
savage instincts 368
savages 24, 39, 66, 69, 177
Scandinavia 178
Sceptics and Believers - carbon debate X
school curricula 68
Schwartz, G Pastor 20
Science of Climate Change (Publication) 322, 333, 362
scientists 25, 26, 27, 28, 31, 66, 126, 216, 261, 331, 332, 334, 337, 342, 343, 344, 355
Scottish stock 313
Sea Changers 264
sea level rise 335, 342

419

Searcy, A  33, 364
Seattle, Chief (US)  67, 179, 271
Self-determination  73, 186, 187, 306
Self-Determination Structure for COAG Investment  220
self-discipline  162, 285, 294
self-perception  15, 109, 201
self-regulation  136, 360
self-respect  21, 99, 108, 132, 221, 264, 267, 300, 315, 329, 386
self-sufficiency  75, 78, 79, 83, 138, 153, 187, 190, 195, 199, 205, 209, 287, 378, 390
Sen, A  253, 317, 321, 359
sense of belonging  67, 142, 148, 155, 158, 170, 222, 277, 286
separate services  149
separatism  1, 76, 83, 120, 121, 138, 162, 166, 229, 241, 282, 294, 296, 325, 327, 390
Separatism in Townsville, (Publication)  34
separatist, policies and attitudes  6, 110, 117, 123, 149, 167, 236, 296, 304, 378
Sermon on the Mount  54, 70
sex-slave activity  46
sexual relations  25, 45
Shakespeare  68, 174, 180, 258
Sharia law  193, 253, 254
Sharing the Country (Publication)  73, 185, 352
Sharp, L  30, 31, 358
shellfish  365
Shi'is  241
Siberia  347, 349
singing a man dead  369
single use of land  395, 396
Sisters of St. John of God  17
sit-down money  90, 109
slavery  18, 38, 45, 232
smokers, picanni  369
smoking  282, 283, 320, 389
smoothing the pillow of a dying race  36
social breakdown  219, 259, 286, 292, 380

Social Darwinism  119
social engineering  27, 137, 163
Social Justice  200, 266, 267, 307, 308, 382, 391
Social Justice Commission  307, 308
societal issues  214
sociologists  14, 54, 59, 68, 96, 216, 301, 376
Solomon  240
Some questions of causation in relation to Aboriginal affairs (Publication)  108, 358
Sons in the Saddle (Publication)  45, 353
sorcery  27, 114, 117, 119, 124-126, 136, 188, 216, 302, 357
South Africa  24, 26, 34, 38, 43, 156, 158, 163, 201, 249, 261, 285, 301, 329, 360, 374, 380
South African Truth Commission  121
Southern Cross University  318
South Sulawesi  273
Soutphommasane, T  253
Sovereign rights  373
sovereignty  76, 80
Spanish Conquistadores  232
spears  230, 233, 367, 368, 369
Spencer, W  269
spiritual home  160, 161, 162, 247
spirituality  18, 21, 161, 234, 235, 238, 239, 254, 270-272, 327, 328, 377, 385
Spirituality for a Nation  276, 363
Spoilers (Poem)  375, 401
sporting capacity  62
squatters  32, 36, 43, 46, 161, 364
squattocracy  33, 43, 47
standard of living  156, 172, 380
Stanner, W  48, 74, 77, 112, 115, 116, 271, 272, 359, 363
static cultures  291
statistics  87, 113, 130, 159, 213, 214, 242, 282, 328, 376
stayers and movers  298, 301
Steady State Economy (Publication)  68, 353
stewardship of the Earth  267

# INDEX

St Francis of Assisi  275, 372
stockmen  43, 47, 93, 381
Stockton, E  255, 256, 270-277, 363
Stolen Generation  18, 23, 37, 108, 121, 296
Stolen Generation Apology  121
Stolen Wages Compensation  121
Stonehenge  9, 161, 244, 260
stories, Indigenous and other  10, 18, 19, 43-45, 70, 86, 107, 111, 112, 113, 157, 161, 174, 180-182, 232, 239, 244, 257, 260, 270, 271, 275, 295, 311, 328, 374, 393
St Patrick's Day  235, 237
Strehlow, C  115, 118, 269, 359
Stretton, W  366
Stronger Smarter schooling  324
strong men  84, 101, 102, 112
stud gins  46
Sturmer, J  54, 55, 105, 360
substance abuse  87, 94, 126, 167, 206, 212, 214, 215, 282, 328
suicide bombing  173, 309
Sulawesi  273, 365
Sulu  288
Sumarian civilisation  67
Sunni  241, 242
Sunset Markets  34
superstition  114, 136, 274, 321
suras, (Koran chapters)  246
survival  12, 14, 15, 24, 26, 40, 59, 64-72, 92, 102, 116, 127, 140, 141, 164, 172, 175, 185, 187, 194, 195, 201, 202, 210, 216, 230, 231, 236, 239, 254, 273, 289, 307, 333, 337, 345, 378, 390
sustainability  139, 141, 164, 231, 268, 357, 386
sustainable societies and communities  I, 55, 61, 65, 108, 141, 142, 148, 149, 154, 162-167, 172, 178, 180, 212, 221, 223, 233, 235, 239, 255, 256, 263, 270, 271, 277, 278, 292, 295, 298, 319, 321, 323, 333, 382, 398
sustaining fiction  100
Sutton, P  88, 97-129, 136, 137, 145, 146, 297, 314, 325, 357, 359, 360
Swan River  24
Sweden  395
Sydney  20, 22, 43, 49, 60, 90, 121, 126, 134, 135, 137, 214, 250, 253, 280, 281, 314, 351-363, 374, 377, 398-400
Sydney Cove  374
Sydney University  20, 90, 281, 314
symbiosis  270

# T

Taking Action to Tackle Suicide (Publication)  316
Tanzania  230, 262
Targets for Aboriginal Prosperity  383
Tasmania  176
Tasmanian wars  375
Tatz, C  38, 58, 59, 109, 115, 358, 360, 378, 393, 400
tax-payer  195
Taylor, J  38, 113, 351, 360
Teachers of Indigenous Studies  328
technology  10, 64, 65, 133, 377, 387
teenagers  134
temperate advantage, of climate change  346
Ten Commandments  53
Ten Point Plan  73
territorial integrity  78
terrorism  241, 243, 348
Thailand  288
Thames Valley  9
Thatcher, M  145
The Brain that Changes Itself (Publication)  288
The Cry for the Dead (Publication)  44
The Good Book, A Secular Bible (Publication)  257
The Great Australian Silence  48
The Hadith  246
The Hague  349
Theism, mono, poly, pan  276
The Knowledge  64, 65, 66, 67, 68, 69, 125, 213, 215
The Pale  39

421

The Politics of Suffering (Publication) 88, 97, 314, 357, 359, 360
The Rights of Nature (Publication) 234, 399
The Sceptical Environmentalist (Publication) 334, 362
The Trouble with Tradition (Publication) 51
They're a Weird Mob (Publication) 243
Third World challenges 227, 378
Thomas, H 326
Thomas, W 177
Thompson, L 134
Three Cheers view and the Black Armband view 52, 376
Thursday Island 369
Thylungra Station 41
Tickner, R 81
Timorese 13
Tindale, N 11, 42, 360
Tiwi Islanders 294
tolerance 95, 111, 113, 116, 120, 136, 153, 156, 162, 174, 182, 183, 189, 196, 201, 237, 245, 247, 249, 250, 253, 260, 272, 276, 278, 327, 380
tolerant, fellow citizens 39, 64, 130, 135, 136, 229, 237, 245, 259, 274, 281, 282, 389
Tol, R 338
Tonkinson, R 55, 360
Too Much Sorry Business (Publication) 114
Toowoomba 255, 309, 358, 399, 400
Torah of Moses 246
Torres Strait islands 76
tortoise-shell 365
Totemic System 31
tour guides 381
Town Camp (Alice Springs) 302
Townsville 34, 314, 354, 356
traditional
  beliefs 61, 130
  healing 120
  owners 44, 142, 329, 330, 345
traditionalism 111, 141, 240, 296, 307

Tragedy of the Commons (Publication) 65, 221, 343
training programs 139
transcendentalism 271, 272
transcultural shift 274, 275
transition, to modernity 16, 17, 62, 142-144, 157, 168, 175, 187, 194, 201, 222, 233, 259, 322, 332
transparency (funding and spending) 308
trauma, youthful trauma on affected adults 14, 70, 94, 95, 135, 197, 199, 235, 259, 308, 377
Treaty 73, 76, 80, 82, 192, 213, 217, 220, 355, 361
Treaty of Commitment 80
Tree Changers 264
trepang 33, 365
triage 183, 184
tribal people 45, 47, 182, 364
tribal spokesperson 47
triennial reviews 385
Trigg, R 276
triple-bottom-line 256
tropical crops 370
tropical disadvantage 346
Trudgen, R 113, 360
trust 191, 209, 366, 368, 389, 390
Tully 41
Turner, M 173, 174
turtle 365, 369
turtle greenback 369
Tutu, D Bishop 121
twilight zone 171
two-tier carbon-trading scheme 345
Tybingoompa, Aunty Gladys 72

## U

Ubermensch 39
Ujung Pandang 365
UK Institute for Public Policy Research 341
UK's Commission for Racial Equity 120
unbeing 61, 62
Unconditional Love 287

# INDEX

unfaith, statement of 23
Ungunmerr, M 273
United Nations 78, 144, 185, 191, 235, 309, 372
United States 23, 126
Uniting Care organisation 293
Uniting Church 72
University Indigenous Centres 327
University of California 261
University of London 28
University of Western Sydney 281
unplanned outcomes 6, 101, 133, 164, 167
Untermensch 39
Updating Culture and Tradition 216
Up from the Mission (Publication) 88, 91, 358
Urban Equality 221
urbanisation 137, 176, 264
U.S. Constitution 374
Use With Care (Publication) 64, 352, 398
Ute people 297
Utopia 138, 167, 172, 182, 299, 300
Utopia Outstations 299

## V

value-adding 144, 164, 168
Values - Indigenous, Mainstream Australians and Other 1, 2, 5, 11-19, 24, 26, 27, 42-47, 53-64, 74, 86-91, 94, 96, 97, 98, 102, 105, 112, 116, 126-128, 133, 134, 138, 141-146, 154, 156, 161, 164, 166, 171, 173, 181-189, 196, 202, 205, 206, 209-222, 230-245, 250, 259, 262, 263, 266-269, 273-277, 286, 291, 294, 297, 306, 312-318, 320, 325, 328, 330, 333, 364, 378, 379, 382-391, 397
vegetable gardens 108, 148, 181
vegetables 71, 132, 161, 223, 329
Vestey's Stations 51
Victim Blaming 114, 117, 312
victimhood 62, 103, 108, 123, 134, 135, 153, 182, 203, 259, 301, 314, 327
Victoria and Humbert Rivers 51
Victoria River 51, 304, 353, 366
Victoria River District 51, 353
Victoria, State of 284
Vietnamese 245, 389
Violence - Historic and Domestic 6, 12, 22, 36-38, 42, 61, 63, 91, 92, 100, 104, 105, 112-116, 121, 123, 129, 130, 133-137, 142, 158, 167, 172, 173, 196, 206, 212, 217, 219, 235, 242, 245, 250, 253, 258, 282, 287, 297, 298, 302, 307, 360, 376-380
Virtues, Compassion, Patience, Gentleness, Simplicity 255
vitamin C 9
von Sturmer, J 105
Voortrekker Monument 244
voters 81, 83, 121, 131, 132, 282, 304, 306, 320, 333, 334, 342, 346, 347, 373

## W

Waanji Native Title Group 140
Wadeye 367
Walter, Father 17, 18, 50
water supplies 223, 291, 383, 392
Watson, P 41
Watson, S 182
Wattie Creek 51
Wayside Chapel 160
Ways of Knowing 268, 387
wealth-generation 54, 93, 97, 124, 127, 138, 139, 140, 144, 148, 164, 207, 262, 299, 331, 385
weapons 65, 119, 233
Weatherall, W 78, 392, 400
Webb, S 177
Weipa 20, 21, 28, 70-72, 77, 94, 139
welfare dependence 143
welfare payments 86, 88, 93, 107
Well-being, indicators 92, 142
Welsh Cymru culture 374
Wesley, J 293

423

Western Australia  16, 17, 49, 55, 139, 140, 310, 319, 345, 346, 352, 354, 361, 397
Western Sydney  250, 253, 281
West Timor  33
Wet Tropics Rainforest  79
Wexler, B  290
whalers  177
What Works, The Work Program Improving Outcomes for Indigenous Students (Publication)  325
Where Angels Fear to Tread (Publication)  15, 28, 255, 358, 362
Where Strange Gods Call (Publication)  46, 353
Where Strange Paths Go Down (Publication)  41, 46
Whispers of this Wik Woman (Publication)  70
White Australia  13, 245, 359
White Australians  43, 96, 120, 170
White culture  15, 155
Whitefella's identity  170
White guilt  146, 229
White incursion  56
White interference  57
White Lords  401
White Man Got No Dreaming (Publication)  74, 359, 363
White man's vices  369
White Out, How Politics is Killing Black Australia (Publication)  106, 357
White Supremacy (Publication)  38, 354
White Trash of Asia  259
whitewash  114
Whitlam, G  56, 79
Whyte, R  333
Why Warriors Lie Down and Die (Publication)  113, 360
Why Weren't We Told (Publication)  49
Wik case  32, 48, 77
Wik decision  391, 396
Wik Mungkan  124

Wik-Mungkan language  99
Wik Native Title  48, 56, 70, 77
Wild River catchments  321
Wild Rivers legislation  329, 330
Wilkins glacier  347
Williams, R  11, 257, 361, 381, 400
Wiltshire, K  267, 276, 386, 400
Windorah  41
Windshuttle, K  22, 361
Winterbottom, Dr  45
wisdom  35, 66, 67, 104, 153, 162, 188, 281, 346, 397
wishful thinking  111, 165, 167
Wogboy  134
Wollongong University  52
Woodward Commission  59
woomera  367
word games  85
Words Fail Me (Publication)  170
work ethic  90, 112, 136, 156, 158, 188, 199, 221, 286, 295, 298, 300, 301, 314
Working Futures - Remote Service Delivery (Publication)  296
worldview  47, 60, 62, 69, 88, 140, 141, 263, 273, 291, 327, 328, 364
World War II  40
Wright, J  44, 361
written language  9, 69, 236
wrong solutions $CO_2$  336

# Y

Yale University  30, 290
Yarrabah  20, 22, 79, 113
Year of the Blackfellow  77
Yindjibarndi  310
Yolngu People  296
young girls to older men  25
Young, S  51, 280, 310, 345, 361
Yunupingu, G  84, 295, 301, 302, 314

# Z

Zinifex  140, 141
Zoopharmacognosy  262
Zulu  42
Zumbo, F  280

# INDEX

www.ingramcontent.com/pod-product-compliance
Lightning Source LLC
Chambersburg PA
CBHW020238030426
42336CB00010B/525